THE ANNALS

of The American Academy *of* Political
and Social Science

VOLUME 353

MAY 1964

THE ANNALS

of The American Academy *of* Political *and* Social Science

THORSTEN SELLIN, *Editor*

MARVIN E. WOLFGANG, *Acting Assistant Editor*

CITY BOSSES AND POLITICAL MACHINES

Special Editor of this Volume

LEE S. GREENE
Professor of Political Science
University of Tennessee
Knoxville, Tennessee

Essay Index Reprint Series

BOOKS FOR LIBRARIES PRESS
PLAINVIEW, NEW YORK

Library of Congress Cataloging in Publication Data

American Academy of Political and Social Science,
   Philadelphia.
   City bosses and political machines.

   (Essay index reprint series)
   Original ed. issued as v. 353 of the Annals of the
American Academy of Political and Social Science.
   1. Municipal government--United States--Address ,
essays, lectures. 2. Politics, Practical--Addresses,
essays, lectures. I. Greene, Lee Seifert, 1905-
ed. II. Title. III. Series: American Academy of
Political and Social Science, Philadelphia. Annals,
v. 353.

[JS331.A59 1973]   352'.008'0973   72-14147
ISBN 0-518-10000-6

CONTENTS

BOOK DEPARTMENT

POLITICAL SCIENCE AND GOVERNMENT

WAR AND FOREIGN POLICY

BIOGRAPHY AND HISTORY

The articles appearing in THE ANNALS are indexed in the *Reader's Guide to Periodical Literature* and the *Public Affairs Information Service Bulletin.*

FOREWORD

There was a period in municipal history when the "boss" was dramatized as the major element in municipal and state politics. Now, it is widely assumed, and often shown, that the boss has disappeared. The circumstances which gave rise to his power—the influx of immigrants unfamiliar with American ways, a set of democratic electoral devices ready for manipulation, unrestrained economic individualism, and a dearth of social services—have altered. The flow of immigrants has been cut to a trickle—if we except the modern counterpart, the Negro and Puerto Rican moving north, as our authors note; Franklin Roosevelt and his reforms ruined the boss as a purveyor of social benefits; the country grew, partly at least, out of its jungle-like economic warfare. Consequently, it is not so easy now to locate the municipal boss.

The search for the nature of municipal political leadership continues. Urban leadership now functions under nonpartisanship in some cities and in others under reform movements inside the Democratic party. Belief in the existence of political elites dies hard; the cases examined in these essays, however, indicate that many different varieties of political patterns exist in the United States, in situations which are often highly fluid, with political power widely shared.

The business group, often credited in the popular mind with secretly held power, seems limited, as in Los Angeles. Labor, although politically ambitious, has not achieved great and certain power, even in cities which may seem labor strongholds. Party lines at the municipal level are weak; candidates do not hesitate to desert party colleagues. Municipal political life is often characterized by shifting factions, highly personalized and not always clearly visible.

The city-manager form, often thought—erroneously, I believe—to be designed with the idea that politics could be banished from administration, has flourished in some cases under certain types of machine rule. Thus, in Kansas City, the machine survived the introduction of the manager plan, which it absorbed. Eventually, the machine was overthrown and the manager plan continued. It has survived recent political squabbles. In Florida manager cities, variety characterizes political life, with managers overshadowed by more powerful figures, except in cases where the manager builds his own machine.

The city boss has generally been required to take account of the state, if for no other reason than the legal structure which put the city at the state's mercy. But bosses could not always control the state; political styles of state and city were often at variance. Such appears to be the case in Louisiana, where the major city follows a style still differentiated from that of the state. Success in New Orleans is still no guarantee of success in the state.

Particular interest attaches to the role of the leader in the reformation of local governmental structure. Dade County, Florida has undergone a significant local readjustment—since under constant harassment—and Davidson County, Tennessee has achieved a similar rearrangement. The reformation in Davidson was made feasible in part by a battle between two local leaders, one of whom had the misfortune to induce enough resentment to aid significantly in bringing about the change. Further development elsewhere of metropolitan reorganization may await similar powerful and colorful leadership.

LEE S. GREENE

The Changing Pattern of Urban Party Politics

By Fred I. Greenstein

ABSTRACT: Disciplined urban party organizations, capable of controlling politics and government in their communities, have been one of our more interesting indigenous political growths. This political form probably could not have arisen in the United States had it not been for certain broad cultural patterns, such as the absence of strong traditional authorities. These cultural patterns were necessary but not sufficient for the growth of party machines. The immediate determinants were the organizational requirements of urban growth, the inability of existing city governments to meet these requirements, the presence of a market—among both businessmen and voters—for the services of the old-style politician, and the existence of free suffrage. Old-style urban parties have declined only partly as a consequence of direct attacks upon them. A variety of social and political changes have sapped the resources of old-style parties and, in many communities, have reduced voter interest in those resources still available to the parties. Further insight into the functions of old-style parties may be had by looking at certain of their present-day alternatives—the politics of nonpartisanship and new-style reform politics within the Democratic party.

Fred I. Greenstein, Ph.D., Middletown, Connecticut, is Assistant Professor in the Department of Government at Wesleyan University. He previously taught at Yale University. He is author of The American Party System and the American People (1963), coauthor of Introduction to Political Analysis (1962), and a contributor to such professional journals as The American Political Science Review, The Journal of Politics, Midwest Journal of Political Science, and The Public Opinion Quarterly.

HIGHLY organized urban political parties are generally conceded to be one of America's distinctive contributions to mankind's repertory of political forms. Just as the two major national parties in the United States are almost universally described in terms of their *dis*organization—their lack of an authoritative command structure—the municipal parties have, until recently, been characterized by most observers in terms of their hierarchical strength. E. E. Schattschneider once summarized this state of affairs in the memorable image of a truncated pyramid: a party system which is weak and ghostlike at the top and solid at the bottom.[1]

This essay deals with the disciplined, largely autonomous local political parties which sprang up in many American cities in the nineteenth century. Much of the literature on these political configurations is heavily pejorative, concerned more with excoriation than explanation. Even the basic nomenclature, "boss" and "machine," is laden with negative connotations, although recently there has been a turn toward nostalgic romanticization of the "vanishing breed" of city bosses.[2]

Here, for reasons which I shall indicate, the attempt shall be to delineate rather than to pass moral judgment: What was the nature of old-style urban party organization? Why did this political pattern develop and how did it operate? What contributed to its short-run persistence in the face of reform campaigns? Under what circumstances have such organizations disappeared and under what circumstances have they continued into the present day—or even undergone renaissances? What are the present-day descendents of old-style urban party organizations?

Analytic delineation invariably involves oversimplification. This is doubly necessary in the present case, because our knowledge of the distribution of types of local party organization is scant. We have no census of local political parties, either for today or for the putative heyday of bosses and machines. And there is reason to believe that observers have exaggerated the ubiquity of tightly organized urban political parties in past generations, as well as underestimated somewhat their contemporary prevalence.

OLD-STYLE PARTY ORGANIZATION: DEFINITIONAL CHARACTERISTICS

Ranney and Kendall have persuasively argued that the imprecision and negative connotations of terms like "boss" destroy their usefulness. What, beyond semantic confusion, they ask, can come from classifying politicians into "bosses" versus "leaders"? Such a distinction leads to fruitless preoccupation with the purity of politicians' motives rather than the actuality of their behavior; it overestimates the degree to which figures of the past such as Richard Croker, William Tweed, and Frank Hague were free of public constraints; and it obscures the fact that *all* effective political leaders, whether or not they are popularly labeled as bosses, use quite similar techniques and resources.[3]

Granting these points, it still seems

[1] E. E. Schattschneider, *Party Government* (New York, 1942), pp. 162–169.

[2] Among the better known accounts are Frank R. Kent, *The Great Game of Politics* (Garden City, N. Y., 1923, rev. ed., 1930); Sonya Forthall, *Cogwheels of Democracy* (New York, 1946); Harold F. Gosnell, *Machine Politics* (Chicago, 1937); and the many case studies of individual bosses. For a recent romanticization, see Edwin O'Connor's novel, *The Last Hurrah* (Boston, 1956).

[3] Austin Ranney and Willmoore Kendall, *Democracy and the American Party System* (New York, 1956), pp. 249–252.

that a recognizable and noteworthy historical phenomenon is hinted at by the venerable terms "boss" and "machine." If the overtones of these terms make us reluctant to use them, we might simply speak of an "old style" of party organization with the following characteristics:

(1) There is a disciplined party hierarchy led by a single executive or a unified board of directors.

(2) The party exercises effective control over nomination to public office, and, through this, it controls the public officials of the municipality.

(3) The party leadership—which quite often is of lower-class social origins—usually does not hold public office and sometimes does not even hold formal party office. At any rate, official position is not the primary source of the leadership's strength.

(4) Rather, a cadre of loyal party officials and workers, as well as a core of voters, is maintained by a mixture of material rewards and *nonideological* psychic rewards—such as personal and ethnic recognition, camaraderie, and the like.[4]

[4] This last definitional criterion explicitly departs from the characterization of a "machine" in James Q. Wilson's interesting discussion of "The Economy of Patronage," *The Journal of Political Economy*, Vol. 59 (August 1961), p. 370n., "as that kind of political party which sustains its members through the distribution of material incentives (patronage) rather than nonmaterial incentives (appeals to principle, the fun of the game, sociability, etc.)." There is ample evidence that for many old-style party workers incentives such as "the fun of the game," "sociability," and even "service" are of central importance. See, for example, Edward J. Flynn, *You're the Boss* (New York, 1947), p. 22; James A. Farley, *Behind the Ballots* (New York, 1938), p. 237; and the passage cited in note 8 below. The distinction between "material" and "nonmaterial" incentives would probably have to be discarded in a more refined discussion of the motivations underlying political participation. So-called material rewards, at base, are nonmaterial in the sense that they are valued for

THE RISE OF OLD-STYLE PARTY ORGANIZATION

This pattern of politics, Schattschneider comments, "is as American as the jazz band . . . China, Mexico, South America, and southern Italy at various times have produced figures who played roles remotely like that of the American boss, but England, France, Germany, and the lesser democracies of Europe have exhibited no tendency to develop this form of political organization in modern times."[5] What then accounted for the development of old-style party organization in the United States?

The Crokers, Tweeds, and Hagues and their organizations probably could not have arisen if certain broad preconditions had not existed in American society and culture. These include the tradition of freewheeling individualism and pragmatic opportunism, which developed in a prosperous, sprawling new society unrestrained by feudalism, aristocracy, monarchy, an established church, and other traditional authorities. This is the state of affairs which has been commented on by countless observers, even before de Tocqueville, and which has been used to explain such disparate phenomena as the failure of socialism to take hold in the United States, the recurrence of popularly based assaults on civil liberties, and even the peculiarly corrosive form which was taken by American slavery.[6]

It also is possible to identify five more direct determinants of the form that urban party organization took in the nineteenth century, three of them

the status they confer and for other culturally defined reasons.

[5] *Op. cit.,* p. 106.

[6] See, for example, Edward A. Shils, *The Torment of Secrecy* (Glencoe, Ill., 1956) and Stanley M. Elkins, *Slavery* (Chicago, 1959, reprinted with an introduction by Nathan Glazer, New York, 1963).

consequences of the Industrial Revolution and two of them results of political institutions and traditions which preceded industrialization.

Massive urban expansion

Over a relatively brief span of years, beginning in the mid-nineteenth century, industrial and commercial growth led to a spectacular rise in the number and proportion of Americans concentrated in cities. A thumbnail sketch of urban expansion may be had by simply noting the population of urban and rural areas for each of the twenty-year periods from 1840 to 1920:

	URBAN POPULATION	RURAL POPULATION
	(in millions)	
1840	1.8	15.2
1860	6.2	25.2
1880	14.1	36.0
1900	30.1	45.8
1920	54.2	51.6

These statistics follow the old Census Bureau classification of areas exceeding 2,500 in population as urban. Growth of larger metropolitan units was even more striking. In 1840 slightly over 300,000 Americans lived in cities—or, rather, a single city, New York—with more than a quarter of a million residents; by 1920 there were twenty-four cities of this size, containing approximately 21 million Americans.

The sheer mechanics of supporting urban populations of this magnitude are, of course, radically different from the requirements of rural life. There must be extensive transportation arrangements; urban dwellers are as dependent upon a constant inflow of food and other commodities as an infant is on the ministrations of adults. A host of new administrative functions must be performed as the population becomes urbanized: street construction and maintenance, bridges, lighting, interurban transportation, sanitary ar-

rangements, fire-fighting, police protection, and so forth. Overwhelming demands suddenly are placed on governments which, hitherto, were able to operate with a minimum of effort and activity.

Disorganized forms of urban government

The forms of government which had evolved in nineteenth-century America were scarcely suitable for meeting the demands of mushrooming cities. Governmental structures reflected a mixture of Jacksonian direct democracy and Madisonian checks and balances. Cities had a multitude of elected officials (sometimes they were elected annually), weak executives, large and unwieldy councils and boards. The formal organization of the cities placed officials in a position permitting and, in fact, encouraging them to checkmate each other's efforts to make and execute policies. Since each official was elected by appealing to his own peculiar constituency and had little incentive to co-operate with his associates, the difficulties caused by the formal limitations of government were exacerbated. In a period when the requirements for governmental action were increasing geometrically, this was a prescription for chaos.

Needs of businessmen

A third aspect of mid-nineteenth-century American society which contributed to the formation of old-style party organizations was the needs of businessmen. There was an increasing number of merchants, industrialists, and other businessmen, licit and illicit, who needed—and were willing to pay for—the appropriate responses from city governments. Some businessmen wanted to operate unrestrained by municipal authority. Others desired street-railway franchises, paving contracts, construction work, and other transactions connected with the very growth of the cities themselves.

Needs of dependent populations

The needs of the bulk of the nineteenth-century urban population were not for profits but for the simple wherewithal to survive and maintain a modicum of dignity. It is difficult in the relatively affluent society of our day to appreciate the vicissitudes of urban life several generations ago: the low wages, long hours, tedious and hazardous working conditions, and lack of security which were the lot of most citizens. Even for native-born Americans, life often was nasty and brutish. But many urbanites were first- and second-generation immigrants who, in addition to their other difficulties, had to face an alien culture and language. Between the Civil War and the First World War, the United States managed somehow to absorb 25 million foreigners.

Unrestricted suffrage

Urban dwellers were not totally without resources for their own advancement. The American tradition of unrestricted male franchise was, in the long run, to work to their advantage. Although it doubtless is true that few city dwellers of the day were aware of the importance of their right to vote, politicians *were* aware of this. Because even the lowliest of citizens was, or could become, a voter, a class of politicians developed building upon the four conditions referred to above: the requirements of organizing urban life, the inability of existing governments to meet these requirements, and the presence of businessmen willing to pay for governmental services and of dependent voting populations in need of security from the uncertainties of their existence.

The old-style urban party leader was as much a product of his time and social setting as was the rising capitalist of the Gilded Age. Building on the conditions and needs of the day, the politician had mainly to supply his own ingenuity and co-ordinating ability in order to tie together the machinery of urban government. If a cohesive party organization could control nominations and elect its own agents to office, the formal fragmentation of government no longer would stand in the way of municipal activity. The votes of large blocs of dependent citizens were sufficient to control nominations and win elections. And the financial support of those who sought to transact business with the city, as well as the revenues and resources of the city government, made it possible to win votes. The enterprising politician who could succeed in governing a city on this basis was a broker *par excellence;* generous brokers' commissions were the rule of the day.

The importance of out-and-out vote-buying on election day as a source of voter support can easily be overestimated. Party organizations curried the favor of voters on a year-long basis. In a day when "better" citizens espoused philosophical variants of Social Darwinism, urban politicians thought in terms of an old-fashioned conception of the welfare state. In the familiar words of Tammany sachem George Washington Plunkitt:

What holds your grip on your district is to go right down amoi. the poor families and help them in the different ways they need help. I've got a regular system for this. If there's a fire in Ninth, Tenth or Eleventh Avenue, for example, any hour of the day or night, I'm usually there with some of my election district captains as soon as the fire engines. If a family is burned out I don't ask whether they are Republicans or

Democrats, and I don't refer them to the Charity Organization Society, which would investigate their case in a month or two and decide they were worthy of help about the time they are dead from starvation. I just get quarters for them, buy clothes for them if their clothes were burned up, and fix them up til they get things runnin' again. It's philanthropy, but it's politics, too—mighty good politics. Who can tell how many votes one of these fires bring me? The poor are the most grateful people in the world, and, let me tell you, they have more friends in their neighborhoods than the rich have in theirs.[7]

With numerous patronage appointees (holders not only of city jobs but also of jobs with concerns doing business with the city), party organizations could readily administer this sort of an informal relief program. And, unlike many latter-day charitable and governmental relief programs, the party's activities did not stop with the provision of mere physical assistance.

I know every man, woman and child in the Fifteenth District, except them that's been born this summer—and I know some of them, too. I know what they like and what they don't like, what they are strong at and what they are weak in, and I reach them by approachin' at the right side.

For instance, here's how I gather in the young men. I hear of a young feller that's proud of his voice, thinks that he can sing fine. I ask him to come around to Washington Hall and join our Glee Club. He comes and sings, and he's a follower of Plunkitt for life. Another young feller gains a reputation as a baseball player in a vacant lot. I bring him into our baseball club. That fixes him. You'll find him workin' for my ticket at the polls next election day. Then there's the feller that likes rowin' on the river, the young feller that makes a name as a waltzer on his

block, the young feller that's handy with his dukes—I rope them all in by givin' them opportunities to show themselves off. I don't trouble them with political arguments. I just study human nature and act accordin'.[8]

This passage reflects some of the ways in which party activities might be geared to the *individual* interests of voters. *Group* interests were at least as important. As each new nationality arrived in the city, politicians rather rapidly accommodated to it and brought it into the mainstream of political participation. Parties were concerned with the votes of immigrants virtually from the time of their arrival. Dockside naturalization and voter enrollment was not unknown.

But if the purpose of the politicians was to use the immigrants, it soon became clear that the tables could be turned. In Providence, Rhode Island, for example, a careful study of the assimilation of immigrant groups into local politics shows that, within thirty years after the arrival of the first representative of a group in the city, it began to be represented in the councils of one or both parties. Eventually, both of the local parties came to be dominated by representatives of the newer stocks. Thus, in 1864 no Irish names appear on the lists of Democratic committeemen in Providence; by 1876 about a third of the names were Irish; by the turn of the century, three-quarters were Irish. In time, the Republican party became the domain of politicians of Italian ancestry.[9] Perhaps the most dramatic example to date of urban party politics as an avenue of upward social mobility was in the antecedents of President Ken-

[7] William L. Riordon, *Plunkitt of Tammany Hall* (originally published in 1905; republished New York, 1948 and New York, 1963; quotations are from the 1963 edition), pp. 27–28.

[8] *Ibid.*, pp. 25–26.

[9] Elmer E. Cornwell, Jr., "Party Absorption of Ethnic Groups: The Case of Providence, Rhode Island," *Social Forces,* Vol. 38 (March 1960), pp. 205–210.

nedy, whose great-grandfather was an impoverished refugee of the Irish potato famine, his grandfather a saloon keeper and a classical old-time urban political leader, his father a multi-millionnaire businessman, presidential advisor, and ambassador to the Court of St. James's.

When the range of consequences of old-time party organizations is seen, it becomes apparent why moral judgments of "the boss and the machine" are likely to be inadequate. These organizations often were responsible for incredible corruption, but they also —sometimes through the very same activities — helped incorporate new groups into American society and aided them up the social ladder. The parties frequently mismanaged urban growth on a grand scale, but they *did* manage urban growth at a time when other instrumentalities for governing the cities were inadequate. They plied voters, who might otherwise have organized more aggressively to advance their interests, with Thanksgiving Day turkeys and buckets of coal. But, by siphoning off discontent and softening the law, they probably contributed to the generally pacific tenor of American politics. It seems fruitless to attempt to capture this complexity in a single moral judgment. One can scarcely weigh the incorporation of immigrant groups against the proliferation of corruption and strike an over-all balance.

WHY REFORMERS WERE "MORNIN' GLORIES"

Stimulated by high taxes and reports of corruption and mismanagement on a grand scale, antiboss reform movements, led by the more prosperous elements of the cities, became increasingly common late in the nineteenth century. Compared with the regular party politicians of their day, reformers were mere fly-by-night dilettantes—"mornin' glories." [10] · They lacked the discipline and the staying power to mount a year-long program of activities. Perhaps more important, the values of the reformers were remote from—in fact, inconsistent with—the values of the citizens whose support would be needed to keep reform administrations in office. Reformers ordinarily saw low taxes and business-like management of the cities as the exclusive aim of government. To the sweatshop worker, grinding out a marginal existence, these aims were at best meaningless, at worst direct attacks on the one agency of society which seemed to have his interests at heart.

THE DECLINE OF OLD-STYLE PARTY ORGANIZATION

Although in the short run old-style party organizations were marvelously immune to the attacks of reformers, in recent decades the demise of this political form has been widely acclaimed. Because of the absence of reliable trend data, we cannot document "the decline of the machine" with precision. The decline does seem to have taken place, although only partly as a direct consequence of attempts to reform urban politics. Events have conspired to sap the traditional resources used to build voter support and to make voters less interested in these resources which the parties still command.

Decline in the resources of old-style urban politicians

Most obviously, job patronage is no longer available in as great a quantity as it once was. At the federal level and in a good many of the states (as well as numerous cities), the bulk of jobs are filled by civil service procedures. Under these circumstances, the most a party politician may be able

10 Riordon, *op. cit.,* pp. 17–20.

to do is seek some minor form of preferment for an otherwise qualified job applicant. Furthermore, the technical requirements of many appointive positions are sufficiently complex to make it inexpedient to fill them with unqualified personnel.[11] And private concerns doing business with the cities are not as likely to be sources of patronage in a day when the franchises have been given out and the concessions granted.

Beyond this, many modern governmental techniques—accounting and auditing requirements, procedures for letting bids, purchasing procedures, even the existence of a federal income tax—restrict the opportunities for dishonest and "honest" graft. Some of these procedures were not instituted with the explicit purpose of hampering the parties. Legislation designed deliberately to weaken parties *has*, however, been enacted—for example, nomination by direct primary and nonpartisan local elections, in which party labels are not indicated on the ballot. Where other conditions are consistent with tight party organization, techniques of this sort seem not to have been especially effective; old-style parties are perfectly capable of controlling nominations in primaries, or of persisting in formally nonpartisan jurisdictions. But, together with the other party weakening factors, explicit antiparty legislation seems to have taken its toll.

Decline of voter interest in rewards available to the parties

Even today it is estimated that the mayor of Chicago has at his disposal 6,000 to 10,000 city patronage jobs. And there are many ways of circum-

[11] Frank J. Sorauf, "State Patronage in a Rural County," *American Political Science Review*, Vol. 50 (December 1956), pp. 1046–1056.

venting good government, antiparty legislation. An additional element in the decline of old-style organization is the increasing disinterest of many citizens in the rewards at the disposal of party politicians. Once upon a time, for example, the decennial federal census was a boon to those local politicians whose party happened to be in control of the White House at census time. The temporary job of door-to-door federal census enumerator was quite a satisfactory reward for the party faithful. In 1960 in many localities, party politicians found census patronage more bother than boon; the wages for this task compared poorly with private wages, and few voters were willing to put in the time and leg work. Other traditional patronage jobs—custodial work in city buildings, employment with departments of sanitation, street repair jobs—were becoming equally undesirable, due to rising levels of income, education, and job security.

An important watershed seems to have been the New Deal, which provided the impetus, at state and local levels as well as the federal level, for increased governmental preoccupation with citizen welfare. The welfare programs of party organizations were undercut by direct and indirect effects of social security, minimum wage legislation, relief programs, and collective bargaining. And, as often has been noted, the parties themselves, by contributing to the social rise of underprivileged groups, helped to develop the values and aspirations which were to make these citizens skeptical of the more blatant manifestations of machine politics.

VARIETIES OF CONTEMPORARY URBAN POLITICS

Nationally in 1956, the Survey Research Center found that only 10 per cent of a cross section of citizens reported being contacted personally by political party workers during that year's presidential campaign. Even if we consider only nonsouthern cities of over 100,000 population, the percentage is still a good bit less than 20.[12] This is a far cry from the situation which would obtain if party organizations were well developed and assiduous. But national statistics conceal a good bit of local variation. A survey of Detroit voters found that only 6 per cent of the public remembered having been approached by political party workers; in fact, less than a fifth of those interviewed even knew that there *were* party precinct officials in their district.[13] Reports from a number of other cities—for example, Seattle and Minneapolis—show a similar vacuum in party activity.[14]

In New Haven, Connecticut, in contrast, 60 per cent of the voters interviewed in a 1959 survey reported having been contacted by party workers.[15] The continuing importance of parties in the politics of this municipality has been documented at length by Robert A. Dahl and his associates.[16] New Haven's Mayor Richard C. Lee was able to obtain support for a mas-

sive urban redevelopment program, in spite of the many obstacles in the way of favorable action on such programs elsewhere, in large part because of the capacity of an old-style party organization to weld together the government of a city with an extremely "weak" formal charter. Lee commanded a substantial majority on the board of aldermen and, during the crucial period for ratification of the program, was as confident of the votes of Democratic aldermen as a British Prime Minister is of his parliamentary majority. Lee was far from being a mere creative creature of the party organization which was so helpful to him, but he also was effectively vetoed by the party when he attempted to bring about governmental reforms which would have made the mayor less dependent upon the organization to obtain positive action.[17]

Further evidence of the persistence of old-style party activities came from a number of other studies conducted in the late 1950's. For example, in 1957 party leaders from eight New Jersey counties reported performing a wide range of traditional party services, in response to an ingeniously worded questionnaire administered by Professor Richard T. Frost.[18]

SERVICES PERFORMED BY NEW JERSEY POLITICIANS

The Service	Percentage Performing It "Often"
Helping deserving people get public jobs	72
Showing people how to get their social security benefits, welfare, unemployment compensation, etc.	54
Helping citizens who are in difficulty with the law. Do you help get them straightened out?	62

[12] Angus Campbell, Philip E. Converse, Warren E. Miller, and Donald E. Stokes, *The American Voter* (New York, 1960), pp. 426–427. The statistic for nonsouthern cities was supplied to me by the authors.

[13] Daniel Katz and Samuel J. Eldersveld, "The Impact of Local Party Activity on the Electorate," *Public Opinion Quarterly,* Vol. 25 (Spring 1961), pp. 16–17.

[14] Hugh A. Bone, *Grass Roots Party Leadership* (Seattle, 1952); Robert L. Morlan, "City Politics: Free Style," *National Municipal Review,* Vol. 38 (November 1949), pp. 485–491.

[15] Robert A. Dahl, *Who Governs?* (New Haven, 1961), p. 278.

[16] *Ibid.;* Nelson W. Polsby, *Community Power and Political Theory* (New Haven, 1963); Raymond E. Wolfinger, *The Politics of Progress* (forthcoming).

[17] Raymond E. Wolfinger, "The Influence of Precinct Work on Voting Behavior," *Public Opinion Quarterly,* Vol. 27 (Fall 1963), pp. 387–398.

[18] Frost deliberately worded his questionnaire descriptions of these services favorably in

There was even some evidence in the 1950's of a rebirth of old-style urban party activities—for example, in the once Republican-dominated city of Philadelphia, where an effective Democratic old-style organization was put together. Often old-style organizations seem to exist in portions of contemporary cities, especially the low-income sections. These, like the reform groups to be described below, serve as factions in city-wide politics.[19]

Why old-style politics persists in some settings but not others is not fully clear. An impressionistic survey of the scattered evidence suggests, as might be expected, that the older pattern continues in those localities which most resemble the situations which originally spawned strong local parties in the nineteenth century. Eastern industrial cities, such as New Haven, Philadelphia, and many of the New Jersey cities, have sizable low-income groups in need of traditional party services. In many of these areas, the legal impediments to party activity also are minimal: Connecticut, for example, was the last state in the union to adopt direct primary legislation, and nonpartisan local election systems are, in general, less common in industrial cities than in cities without much manufacturing activity.[20] Cities in which weak, disorganized parties are reported—like Seattle, Minneapolis, and even Detroit (which, of course, *is* a

manufacturing center of some importance)—are quite often cities in which nonpartisan institutions have been adopted.

SOME NEW-STYLE URBAN POLITICAL PATTERNS

In conclusion, we may note two of the styles of politics which have been reported in contemporary localities where old-style organizations have become weak or nonexistent: the politics of nonpartisanship and the new "reform" factions within some urban Democratic parties. Both patterns are of considerable intrinsic interest to students of local government. And, as contrasting political forms, they provide us with further perspective on the strengths and weaknesses of old-style urban politics.

The politics of nonpartisanship

The nonpartisan ballot now is in force in 66 per cent of American cities over 25,000 in population. Numerous styles of politics seem to take place beneath the facade of nonpartisanship. In some communities, when party labels are eliminated from the ballot, the old parties continue to operate much as they have in the past; in other communities, new local parties spring up to contest the nonpartisan elections. Finally, nonpartisanship often takes the form intended by its founders: no organized groups contest elections; voters choose from a more or less self-selected array of candidates.

In the last of these cases, although nonpartisanship has its intended effect, it also seems to have had—a recent body of literature suggests [21]—a num-

order to avoid implying that respondents were to be censured for indulging in "machine tactics." Richard T. Frost, "Stability and Change in Local Politics," *Public Opinion Quarterly*, Vol. 25 (Summer 1961), pp. 231–232.

[19] James Q. Wilson, "Politics and Reform in American Cities," *American Government Annual, 1962–63* (New York, 1962), pp. 37–52.

[20] Phillips Cutright, "Nonpartisan Electoral Systems in American Cities," *Comparative Studies in Society and History*, Vol. 5 (January 1963), pp. 219–221.

[21] For a brief review of the relevant literature, see Fred I. Greenstein, *The American Party System and the American People* (Englewood Cliffs, N. J., 1963), pp. 57–60.

ber of unintended side effects. One of these is voter confusion. Without the familiar device of party labels to aid in selecting candidates, voters may find it difficult to select from among the some-times substantial list of names on the ballot. Under these circumstances, a bonus in votes often goes to candidates with a familiar sounding name—in-cumbents are likely to be re-elected, for example—or even candidates with a favorable position on the ballot. In addition, campaigning and other per-sonal contacts with voters become less common, because candidates no longer have the financial resources and per-sonnel of a party organization at their disposal and therefore are dependent upon personal financing or backing from interest groups in the community.

Nonpartisan electoral practices, where effective, also seem to increase the influence of the mass media on voters; in the absence of campaigning, party canvassing, and party labels, voters be-come highly dependent for information as well as advice on the press, radio, and television. Normally, mass com-munications have rather limited effects on people's behavior compared with face-to-face communication such as canvassing by party workers.[22] Under nonpartisan circumstances, however, he who controls the press is likely to have much more direct and substantial effect on the public.

Ironically, the "theory" of nonparti-sanship argues that by eliminating par-ties a barrier between citizens and their officials will be removed. In fact, non-partisanship often attentuates the citi-zen's connections with the political system.

The reform Democrats

The doctrine of nonpartisanship is mostly a product of the Progressive era.

While nonpartisan local political systems continue to be adopted and, in fact, have become more common in recent decades, most of the impetus for this development results from the desire of communities to adopt city-manager sys-tems. Nonpartisanship simply is part of the package which normally goes along with the popular city-manager system.

A newer phenomenon on the urban political scene is the development, es-pecially since the 1952 presidential campaign, of ideologically motivated grass-roots party organizations within the Democratic party.[23] The ideology in question is liberalism: most of the re-form organizations are led and staffed by college-educated intellectuals, many of whom were activated politically by the candidacy of Adlai Stevenson. In a few localities, there also have been grass-roots Republican organizations motivated by ideological considerations: in the Republican case, Goldwater con-servatism.

New-style reformers differ in two major ways from old-style reformers: their ideological concerns extend beyond a preoccupation with governmental effi-ciency alone (they favor racial integra-tion and improved housing and some-times devote much of their energy to advocating "liberal" causes at the na-tional level); secondly, their strategy is to work within and take control of the parties, rather than to reject the legiti-macy of parties. They do resemble old-style reformers in their preoccupation with the evils of "bossism" and machine politics.

There also is an important resemblance between the new reform politician and the old-style organization man the re-former seeks to replace. In both cases, very much unlike the situation which seems to be stimulated by nonpartisan-

[22] Joseph T. Klapper, *The Effects of Mass Communication* (New York, 1960).

[23] James Q. Wilson, *The Amateur Democrat* (Chicago, 1962).

ship, the politician emphasizes extensive face-to-face contact with voters. Where reformers have been successful, it often has been by beating the boss at his own game of canvassing the election district, registering and keeping track of voters, and getting them to the polls.[24]

But much of the day-to-day style of the traditional urban politician is clearly distasteful to the new reformers: they have generally eschewed the use of patronage and, with the exceptions of campaigns for housing code enforcement, they have avoided the extensive service operations to voters and interest groups which were central to old-style party organizations. For example, when election district captains and other officials of the Greenwich Village Independent Democrats, the reform group which deposed New York Democrat County Leader Carmine DeSapio in his own election district, were asked the same set of questions about their activities used in the New Jersey study, strikingly different responses were made.

[24] There is another interesting point of resemblance between old- and new-style urban party politics. In both, an important aspect of the motivation for participation seems to be the rewards of sociability. Tammany picnics and New York Committee for Democratic Voters (CDV) coffee hours probably differ more in decor than in the functions they serve. An amusing indication of this is provided by the committee structure of the Greenwich Village club of the CDV; in addition to the committees dealing with the club newsletter, with housing, and with community action, there is a social committee and a Flight Committee, the latter being concerned with arranging charter flights to Europe for club members. See Vernon M. Goetcheus, *The Village Independent Democrats: A Study in the Politics of the New Reformers* (unpublished senior distinction thesis, Honors College, Wesleyan University, 1963), pp. 65–66. On similar activities by the California Democratic Clubs, see Robert E. Lane, James D. Barber, and Fred I. Greenstein, *Introduction to Political Analysis* (Englewood Cliffs, N. J., 1962), pp. 55–57.

SERVICES PERFORMED BY NEW YORK
REFORM DEMOCRATS[25]

The Service	Percentage Performing It "Often"
Helping deserving people get public jobs	0
Showing people how to get their social security benefits, welfare, unemployment compensation, etc.	5
Helping citizens who are in difficulty with the law. Do you help get them straightened out?	6

The successes of this class of new-style urban party politician have vindicated a portion of the classical strategy of urban party politics, the extensive reliance upon canvassing and other personal relations, and also have shown that under some circumstances it is possible to organize such activities with virtually no reliance on patronage and other material rewards. The reformers have tapped a pool of political activists used by parties elsewhere in the world—for example, in Great Britain—but not a normal part of the American scene. One might say that the reformers have "discovered" the British Labor constituency parties.

It is where material resources available to the parties are limited, for example, California, and where voter interest in these resources is low, that the new reformers are successful. In practice, however, the latter condition has confined the effectiveness of the reform Democrats largely to the more prosperous sections of cities; neither their style nor their programs seem to be successful in lower-class districts.[26] The areas of reform Democratic strength are gener-

[25] Goetcheus, *op. cit.*, p. 138.
[26] DeSapio, for example, was generally able to hold on to his lower-class Italian voting support in Greenwich Village; his opponents succeeded largely by activating the many middle- and upper-class voters who had moved into new high-rent housing in the district.

ally *not* the areas which contribute greatly to Democratic pluralities in the cities. And, in many cities, the reformers' clientele is progressively diminishing as higher-income citizens move outward to the suburbs. Therefore, though fascinating and illuminating, the new reform movement must at least for the moment be considered as little more than a single manifestation in a panorama of urban political practices.[27]

CONCLUSION

The degree to which *old-style* urban party organizations will continue to be a part of this panorama is uncertain. Changes in the social composition of the cities promise to be a major factor in the future of urban politics. If, as seems possible, many cities become lower-class, nonwhite enclaves, we can be confident that there will be a continuing market for the services of the service-oriented old-style politician. Whether or not this is the case, many lessons can be culled from the history of party politics during the years of growth of the American cities—lessons which are relevant, for example, to studying the politics of urbanization elsewhere in the world.[28] In the nineteenth century, after all, the United States was an "emerging," "modernizing" nation, facing the problems of stability and democracy which are now being faced by countless newer nations.

[27] Probably because of their emphasis on ideology, the new reform groups also seem to be quite prone to internal conflicts which impede their effectiveness. One is reminded of Robert Michels' remarks about the intransigence of intellectuals in European socialist parties. *Political Parties* (New York, 1962, originally published in 1915), Part 4, Chap. 6.

[28] On the significance of the American experience with old-style urban politics for the emerging nations, see Wallace S. Sayre and Nelson W. Polsby, "American Political Science and the Study of Urbanization," Committee on Urbanization, Social Science Research Council, mimeo, 1963, pp. 45–48.

Boss and Faction

By James A. Riedel

Local parties tend to break into factions competing with each other in much the same way as political parties. The political charge "bossism" tends to have little effect in a stable political economy, such as Albany, despite its appropriateness. In politically unstable, economically depressed Schenectady, the charge "bossism" is used indiscriminately with some apparent effect. Political patronage, once the basic political cement, is still a focal point of political activity but is giving way to other bases of organization, such as faction. However, the growing division between the secure and politically unconcerned top as against the insecure and politically active bottom in the local economy is separating the traditional source of political leadership from the masses. In such a context, it is easier for an insurgent to build a personal political movement than it is to transform an existing factional split into a successful reform movement. Furthermore, the business community tends to adjust to an incumbent organization and in time to defend it regardless of party label and countless allegations of wrongdoing. Finally, general public unconcern approaches a condition of militant apathy against which no amount of campaigning has any effect. "The leader" becomes more meaningful than the issue.

James A. Riedel, Ph.D., Elnora, New York, is Professor of Political Science at the Graduate School of Public Affairs, Albany, a unit of the State University of New York, and has been since 1957 Chairman of the Department of Political Science at Union College, Schenectady. Previously, he taught at Purdue University, the University of Denver, and lectured at the University of Chicago. He is the author of Hoosiers Go to the Polls (1956) and The Urgent Need for Local Tax Reform (1960). He has been active in local politics, holding several party offices including City Chairman in West Lafayette, Indiana.

AMONG the many perennial problems of interest in local government, some of the more interesting have to do with the formation and dissolution of political machines. Nothing within the space of these few pages can be definitive, either of the problem or of the solution to these questions. Modern studies such as Robert Dahl's *Who Governs?* and the much older *Boss Rule* by J. T. Salter have shed light on aspects of the process, but many more will be necessary. Case studies build up data from which generalizations may more appropriately be made. All will recognize that each community is, in some particular, unique and that the variety of variables is enormous. What we hope now to add to what has been done is the product of several years' work on the characteristics of factions within the major parties of Schenectady, New York and the context in which they have developed. As for the latter, there is much evidence that the lines of political influence within each city in New York State's capital district are often part of a web that embraces the whole area, but, except as it is essential to this essay, no effort will be made to spell that out in detail.

No machine is so strong that it can withstand a genuine public uprising against its continued existence in power. Machines can, and probably do, "win the close ones" by hook or crook, but something has to be said about the very fact that the outcome is even close. Antimachine critics of Albany speak most fervently about the assessment power of the organization. There seems very little doubt that this has long been a trade-mark of that city. But, while fear of unfair assessment is undoubtedly an intimidation in primary enrollment, it is an unacceptable explanation for the consistent 3 to 1 victories in elections patrolled by the (Republican) State Attorney General's staff (1961

and 1963). One would have to assume that the voters feared more the possibility of reprisals from any alternative slate of candidates. That does not speak very well of the various opposition factions. I suggest the answer lies either in satisfying complacency—there is something about the *status quo* they actually like,[1] or else they do not sufficiently dislike it to want to be disturbed—or in voter apathy. In this case study of Schenectady, compared in part with Albany, the former has relatively high taxes and high unemployment, the latter has lower taxes and lower unemployment. When favorable, these could induce a sense of comparative well-being in an otherwise depressed area and serve to stabilize an existing political regime.

I have not yet run a test on voter interest in Albany, but, during the 1960 campaign, I did so in Schenectady, where the level of party and factional activity was unusually high.

During the last week of September, a sample of 450 people were asked (1) Can you name the offices that will be filled at the general election this year? and (2) Can you name the candidates running for these offices? Twelve did not know that it was a presidential election year, and the same number, but not the same people, could not identify either candidate. The third and fourth positions on the ballot were for judges on the state courts, and the percentage of correct identification fell to below 3 per cent, a total of four persons in the case of Democratic candidate for supreme court in the local district! These were the extremes, but not the more disquieting "typical" results. Beneath the vice-presidency, the greatest proportion of correct identification, given the name of the office, was Stratton for

[1] Warren Moscow supported this view as of 1921–1948. *Politics in the Empire State* (New York: Alfred Knopf, 1948), p. 140.

Congress, 43 per cent. His opponent scored next at 25 per cent. The former mayor, Owen Begley, running for state senate, was identified by 17 per cent and his opponent by 11 per cent. The state assembly candidates reached 12 and 7 per cent, and almost no one could think of the coroner candidates' names. One candidate who had spent most of his savings and a month of evenings campaigning muttered, "Why bother?" when he saw the results. Another borrowed $2,000 and plastered his name on all the city buses.

Until the results were broken down by socioeconomic group the figures were merely depressing. Then a new dimension was revealed. The bloc of voters who had scored best in the survey was from the poorest wards where a substantial number of city and county employees lived. The respondents who did least well? The high income group, the business and professional leaders of the community! I interpret this to mean that voting habits attached to party labels can be so strong that those people from whom a community might expect its leadership to come attach no great importance to individual candidates except at the top of the ticket. It could further mean that the scandalous performance of a particular officeholder is easily separated in their minds from the party which nominated him. In the absence of a generalized objection to the party in power, which could lead to development of a faction or swing to the opposition, the upper echelons of a community can, by their very apathy to politics, contribute to the perpetuation of whatever mode of government prevails locally. How to get this class to share its concern for personal achievement with a concern for civic development is the problem of our times.

During the summer of 1961, a nonpartisan group of citizens from the area formed an Eastern Mohawk Valley Development Study Committee headed by J. Herbert Holloman, later named Assistant Secretary of Commerce. In its final report, the dilemma of the capital district was thus described: [2]

However badly off a community may be at any given time, someone profits while the community remains in its present conditions. Someone owes his status to retention of the present conditions. Someone's plans and investment in the future depend on everything remaining the same. . . . Any change . . . will be more beneficial to some than others and, therefore, will change the relationships between individuals within the community. Man is by nature a conservative animal and government is his instrument for preventing rapid change. Changes in the law [and administration] take place when an overwhelming public sentiment concludes that the status quo is working an injustice on a significant part of the community.

Albany, Schenectady, and Troy form a central triangle of continuous metropolitan development in six counties and constitute the heart of the capital district market area embracing ten cities within twenty-five miles of the state capitol. It should not be at all surprising, then, that close commercial ties, heavy commuter traffic, and easy opportunity have led to competition and cooperation both among business and political organizations. Superficially, the contrasts among them appear greater than the similarities, but there is little ground for disputing the existence of machine politics in each of the major cities. Albany has a machine in the classic form, headed at the moment by seventy-eight-year-old Daniel P. O'Connell, whose Democratic organization took over in 1921 where the Republican

[2] Eastern Mohawk Valley Development Study Committee, *The Valley Tomorrow?* (Schenectady, September 15, 1961).

"Barnes machine" left off. Local historians assert that Albany has had one variety or another of autocratic government since it was founded, and each has seemed invincible until shortly before its collapse. The Troy and Schenectady machines have not been so closely identified with a single individual in the public eye, but, until recently, they have been just as durable. It is the fact that the Schenectady Republican machine began to crack in the late 1940's, finally giving way in a 1963 Democratic sweep that made the examination of Schenectady party politics timely and, I think, rewarding. The Troy machine has possibly "bought time" for itself by initiating a charter change and has this year installed city-manager government. The Albany machine has been challenged recently only by a synthetic coalition organized outside the major party framework, and this challenge was without success. Perhaps in examining some of the transitional stages in Schenectady's recent past and comparing them with Albany's, we can identify factors that have a wider significance than for this case study alone.

In rough outline, the Schenectady machine was made possible by a lopsided Republican majority which was virtually unchallenged for thirty years, following a brief Socialist interlude prior to World War I. A notable exception was the formation of a Charter League coalition in the mid-thirties which brought about city-manager government but affected no change in party balance. The League promptly went out of business, and a different faction in the Republican party took over control. That faction was led by James E. "Ed" Cushing who has remained the dominant figure up to the present moment, although the defeat last year may have precipitated a change. Cushing is a road and building-materials contractor. His lieutenants are business leaders in banking, real estate, and the practice of law, but the foundation of his organization has been an elected county committee made up in large part from public employees and their immediate relatives. The party had, until the 1950's, also been able to count on the nearly unvarying support of the voters of Italian extraction, the largest ethnic group in the county. The hard core of support for most political machines, Schenectady and Albany appearing not to be exceptions, is made up of those who personally profit from the continuation of the group in power, commonly called its patronage base. That patronage takes the form of jobs or favored treatment from government in the purchase of goods and services and in the administration of laws.

Political machines do not die easily and gracefully. Nor when they do is it simple to explain why they did. In this case study, we find at least three factors: (1) internal dissatisfaction, (2) a strong personality in the opposition camp (Sam Stratton), and (3) a shift in community political orientation which gave rise to factionalism in both parties.

DISSATISFACTION

The early signs of disintegration within the Republican party dominant in Schenectady stemmed from dissatisfaction with the distribution of favors through patronage and nomination, particularly felt in the Italian community. One peculiar characteristic of the Mohawk-Hudson Valley is that early Italian settlers became almost totally identified with the Republican party. Irish and Poles in earlier migrations had become as Democratic. However, unlike other minority groups except the Negroes, the Italians in the area even today seem to feel a strong lack of total acceptance and a competitive urge to hold, or to have held, every existing public

TABLE 1—NATIONALITY DISTRIBUTION ON COUNTY COMMITTEES, 1960

	DEMOCRATS			REPUBLICANS		
	TOTAL	CITY	TOWNS	TOTAL	CITY	TOWNS
Italian	53	38	15	59	52	7
Polish	36	23	13	18	13	5
Irish	76	53	23	58	36	22
German	27	17	10	26	14	12
English	13	8	5	37	18	19
Jewish	10	6	4	8	5	3
Dutch	5	1	4	15	4	11
Undeterminable	39	16	23	29	12	17
Other	16	6	10	25	12	13

Note: For purposes of comparison, The *U. S. Censuses of Population and Housing, 1960* (PHC (1)-3, for Albany, Schenectady, and Troy) reports the following distribution of first- and second-generation residents by national origin: Italian, 15,596; Polish, 8,062; German, 5,757; United Kingdom, 5,185; Canadian, 3,751; Irish, 2,507; Russian, 1,726. Care should be taken in interpreting these in light of the dates of migration among nationality groups which will not be revealed in these data.

office.[3] Despite their numerical strength in the county committee (See Table 1, Nationality Distribution on County Committees), the greater share of top positions in party and governmental affairs had always gone to the English, Irish, and Dutch. One Italian leader, Amedeo H. "Babe" Volpe, fought "Boss" Cushing for twelve years but could not bring himself to leave the party as so many have done in recent years. In 1953 Volpe declared himself to be an "Independent Republican" candidate for city council, with an accompanying blast charging that Cushing had attempted to "buy me off in 1951." [4] Volpe then urged the nomination of an insurgent candidate for sheriff over Cushing's man. When the challenger won in the primary, Volpe hailed it a "crushing defeat . . . of Cushing's handpicked candidate," and predicted that the Cushing "machine" would begin "to topple." "Mr. Cushing sent out the word to defeat Mr. Calkins and called

upon his followers to vote for the Democratic candidate, Henry Madigan, whom he always favored and who was financed by Republican headquarters." [5] Harold Calkins then went on to win that November, but the machine survived.

Volpe's troubles with the organization did not end there. In 1957 he announced that he would not seek city council nomination. "[I] will never seek Republican nomination for any office," as long as the Republican party is "dominated by one man—James E. Cushing . . . [He] handpicks his candidates without even consulting the opinion of the rank and file of the enrolled Republicans." [6] Volpe's pledge lasted two years. In 1959 he was given the formal endorsement of the Republican party to run for mayor. Shortly thereafter, an undertaker, named Malcolm Ellis, announced his independent candidacy in the Republican primary. Almost at once, Republican committeemen began reporting that they had "got the word" that Volpe was endorsed to

[3] Comment of State Supreme Court Judge Felix Aulisi in Amsterdam, New York, July 17, 1958 interview.

[4] *Schenectady Union-Star*, September 9, 1953, p. 22.

[5] *Ibid.*

[6] *Schenectady Union-Star*, August 1, 1957, p. 17.

shut him up and that Ellis was the organization's man. Ellis won easily, and grumbling in some sections of the Italian community increased, but not enough to bring victory to the Democratic candidate—an Italian converted-Republican dentist. However, in the predominantly Italian districts, selective voting in favor of Italian candidates increased significantly.

An earlier charge of bossism, from within the party, also involved an Italian who was Republican ward president in a downtown, low-income, transient section. In a dispute reputed to be associated with patronge dissatisfaction and a quarrel with Cushing, the Fourth Ward Republicans endorsed the incumbent Democratic supervisor in 1949. Cushing called the ward's committeemen together and persuaded six of the eight to withdraw their cross endorsement and back an Italian Republican tavern owner. The ward president, then also an insurgent primary candidate for sheriff, retorted strongly in the press, "They're trying to give me the works. That meeting was not legal. . . . They forced those fellows into doing what they did. The only thing that wasn't used was a shotgun!"[7] He took the disputed endorsement to court and won, but, in his own primary fight, the county organization soundly trounced him.

Another facet of the internal cleavage appears to be more whimsical, and parenthetically supplies one of the interparty, intercity links alluded to earlier. A highly successful criminal lawyer who had been closely associated with "Ed" Cushing was, in the late 1940's, assumed to be "next in line" for the county chairmanship when Cushing stepped out of titular control temporarily (until 1963). He was at the time, however, one of the attorneys employed by the Albany Democratic machine doing bat-

[7] *Schenectady Union-Star*, August 5, 1949, p. 9.

tle with Governor Thomas E. Dewey. According to the legend, when the governor learned that one of his Albany adversary's more effective agents was also about to become his own party's chairman in a key and neighboring county, he routed Cushing out of bed and summoned him to appear before him in Albany before breakfast, threatening dire consequences to Schenectady's patronage should the move be made as planned. Whatever the facts of the matter, the top party job in the county was handed over to a succesion of acknowledged figureheads with Cushing holding the strings, and the frustrated attorney engaged himself in backing a series of "insurgents" in each local election thereafter—almost invariably successfully. While some local Republican leaders say the split between the two men was always superficial, and maintained as a convenient illusion, others believe that it was genuine and that the practice of successfully running insurgents in the primaries contributed to weakening the machine internally. In the 1963 Democratic sweep of city and county control, the first in nearly half a century, only those Republican candidates who had been identified with the "rejected" attorney survived.

LEADERSHIP

Nearly all local parties are divided internally by a degree of factionalism, usually centering on differing conceptions or identifications of leadership, which leaders in turn may personify some ideological or issue differences. When factionalism becomes a public power struggle, well advertised in the news media, leaders in the dominant faction of the divided party tend to deplore the division and imagine that only the opposition party can profit from the split. Indeed, this is often true in the short run. A nasty primary fight often leaves the losers in no frame of mind to support the winners. If professional politicians know that it is best at least to appear to restore unity, the rank-and-file voter is under no such pressure and may desert to another party's candidate just to reinforce the point at issue. This is precisely what happened in Schenectady in 1951 when Sam Stratton, then a part of the Democratic majority on city council, launched an attack on his party's leadership. Election day produced a Republican sweep and control that lasted twelve years. The issues on which Stratton built his challenge to Schenectady County Democratic leadership attracted wide admiration, even from otherwise disenchanted and indifferent Republicans. In 1955, attacking Republican bossism, he was elected mayor while Republicans were winning all three vacant council seats and eleven of fourteen city seats on the county board of supervisors. By 1958 his strength had grown to the point that he defied the county chairman's ultimatum that he declare his own intention to run for Congress and let the Democratic "old guard" organization put up its "unbeatable Carroll 'Pink' Gardner" —whom he then swamped in the primary.

Running "against machine bosses" had become Stratton's stock in trade and had gained him so much popularity that in November he beat the Schenectady Republican county chairman to become the first Democratic Congressman from that district. At the organizational meeting following the primary of 1959, Stratton was able to dictate his choice for county chairman, a respected businessman and banker. But Stratton's party backing was shaky and the new chairman's even shakier. A monumental dispute threatened to dissolve the Stratton faction when it came time to nominate a postmaster for Schenectady. The chairman had his own man and rallied the party's executive committee (ward and town chairmen) behind the principle that all patronage be cleared through channels—stopping with the county chairman. But Stratton was not a party-organization man in the traditional pattern. In the rural counties of his district he recommended appointment of some Stratton Republicans to postmasterships. In Schenectady he nominated a professional postal employee who had been personally friendly but politically inactive. The end result of this pattern of behavior was the replacement of one chairman with an even more loyal "Strattonite" and even more intense devotion from unorganized Stratton supporters drawn from a wide spectrum of society.

The Stratton saga is still unfolding. In 1960 Stratton continued to run apart from his party. More than once burned, the Republican organization was beginning to treat him like "Pink" Gardner, ten-term county clerk whom it either endorsed or opposed only superficially. A tragically inadequate figure was nominated from a rural county to oppose Stratton in 1960, reputedly because he was willing to pay all of his own campaign expenses. The state legislature redistricted the state's congressmen after the 1960 census and pointedly placed Stratton on the horns of a dilemma. His home county, Schenectady, was included with Democratic-machine controlled and more populous Albany. His other four counties were distributed between districts overwhelmingly Republican. From these, Stratton chose the new Thirty-fifth District for his 1962 race. Once again Stratton was able to run against the "cynical manipulators," the political machines that "disregard the welfare of the people to serve their selfish partisan ends." To everyone's astonishment, he captured the district, most of which had been dominated for a life-time by powerful Congressman John Taber. His 1962 campaign was coupled with a try for the gubernatorial nomination, in which he lashed out against the mayor of New York City and his attempted "bossism" over the state convention.

PATRONAGE VERSUS POLICY

A phenomenon that has received some attention since the end of World War II in the Middle and Far West appears gradually to be taking effect in the capital district. Both parties began to split between those interested primarily in patronage and those interested in policy.

In Schenectady, the factionalism present in both parties was brought into sharp focus by the Stratton bandwagon. What he had to offer, besides an attractive political personality, was a verbal facility and quick wit (he entered politics while holding a temporary position on the philosophy faculty at Union College) which he used to formulate and identify issues, to badger inept public officials, and to be the "public's champion against the forces of evil at City Hall." In a city slowly and painfully eroding economically with the withdrawal of industry, there was in the public an abundance of latent hostility looking for an outlet. In 1956 Mayor Stratton staged a midnight raid on a gambling establishment "right in the shadow of City Hall" to prove his charges of "laxity." His image continued to grow in favor with the idealists and the common men of many partisan persuasions as he exploited situations that might otherwise have gone unnoticed: the discovery of a body weeks later frozen in the water of fire hoses used to extinguish a tenement blaze (apparently a drifter hiding in the building); the

sudden retirement of one police chief when a page disappeared from the police blotter and of his successor after a racketeer had complained to the city manager that he was not getting the police protection that he allegedly had paid for.

Resentment of Stratton's "antics" was not limited to the opposite party in power. Businessmen complained that he was giving the city a black eye and discouraging new business investment. Democratic leaders who had grown accustomed to accommodating themselves to patronage the opposition granted them objected doubly.[8] They were being held responsible for the constant harassment of Democrat Stratton, and they were losing ground to him in the party's struggle for leadership. Dissident Republicans who were unable to find common cause with Stratton found him a substantial distraction in their efforts to reform their own party. Damning Stratton was made a test of party loyalty. Once Stratton was seated in Congress, several of these factions breathed more easily, but the forces at work were not Stratton's creations, simply his vehicle. Strattonites settled down anxiously to consolidate their gains and to build an independent party.

Republicans representing approximately the same socioeconomic groups as the Strattonite leadership had a similar preoccupation with issues more than with patronage and set out to "rebuild the Republican Party on a more enlightened foundation." Calling themselves the "Grassrooters," they began hammering away at the "old guard" in their party. Under the leadership of

[8] A former Republican county chairman alleges that his party paid as little as $1,000 for the county Democratic party's endorsement for certain offices, a practice still common in areas of New York as an easy way of getting funds when chances of winning are slim.

such people as a Telephone Company official, a minor General Electric executive, and the wife of a General Electric scientist, the Grassrooters began quietly to organize after the party's disappointing performance during the 1960 elections, but more especially because of a change in party climate. They were rebelling against preoccupation with patronage and the surrendering of the initiative of program issues to the Stratton Democrats. The then Republican county chairman had decided to step down as county chairman after his loss to Stratton. He was succeeded by an attorney who could provide almost no personal strength and who was supplied with a full-time party executive secretary whose mandate was to shape up the organization. While the voices of Republican party authority were no longer party officeholders at the local level, they gave the new secretary a whip and told him to use it. Nominally a full-time public employee but actually a full-time party worker, he wielded the patronage club and quickly struck terror in the hearts of most committeemen and aroused the bitterness of many who joined the Grassrooters in opposition to his tactics.

Herein lies the basic split within both parties—emphasis on patronage versus program—but most dramatically illustrated in Schenectady Republicanism. In 1960 each party had 278 district committeemen (two for each district). A check of city and county payrolls revealed that seventy-nine Republican committeemen were employed along with seventy immediate relatives of committeemen (wives, husbands, brothers, sons, and so on).[9] Twenty-four committeemen held state or federal jobs. By way of comparison, eight Democratic committeemen held city or county government jobs, and eighteen state or federal positions. Relatives of many others held state and federal patronage appointments. Since civil service at the local level had been compromised by a party test, nearly every public position was regarded as a patronage opportunity. Shortly before the 1961 campaign, in which the city manager was the center of attack, a highly placed city official alleged publicly that the city government had completely lost control of the hiring function in city government. All appointments were being made at party headquarters from "civil service lists" to satisfy the law. Another high city officer stated that he found evidence in 1962 that promotions in the police and fire departments were still being recommended on the basis of party acceptability and suspected that there was some truth in an often-heard complaint that promotions were bought and sold. A situation so intolerable could only be a source of embarrassment to those Republicans who themselves were not dependent on patronage and who were actively interested in politics for some more abstract reasons, such as the direction of public policy.

By the fall of 1961, the Grassrooters were ready to challenge the old-guard organization. They had rallied to their support many of the very patronage-holding committeemen upon whom the "machine" had been built. Public employees privately and bitterly com-

---

[9] Several high party leaders asserted that if all jobs offering some compensation from the city or county during the year, including part-time, and honorific positions without compensation were included, the figure would be nearer 90 per cent, or roughly 250. Every ward and town chairman was interviewed to check on his own and opposition party committeemen, but the discrepancies were incalculable. Schenectady County ranks second to Albany as recipient of state patronage and receives many of the better opportunities since Albany is the primary source of custodial and low-skilled help.

plained that some of them were forced to take vacation leave to work for the organization against the Grassrooters in that primary and against the opposition party each November. At the party's postprimary organization meeting, the crucial motion was to vote by secret ballot. In the absence of a sympathetic chairman and protective rules, balloting was open and the Grassrooters lost their concealed support. Even so, one leader believes that had the chairman of one town not switched at the last minute the revolt would have succeeded.

There is a striking similarity between the geographic sources of support for the Democratic (Strattonite) and Republican (Grassrooter) factions. Both drew heavily from the silk-stocking wards, the towns, and those sections still able to muster some civic spirit. Both appealed to the intellectuals and idealists. The "old guard" factions, while in both cases backed by the more conservative business element, drew most heavily on the plight of the insecure and impoverished.

While Schenectady was witnessing two nearly successful party-faction uprisings, in 1961 a coalition of insurgent Democrats and Republicans took on the Albany "bosses" under the banner CURE (Citizens United Reform Effort). Despite a vigorous campaign, the election made hardly a dent on the usual three to one margin enjoyed by the machine. In reprisal for its campaign coverage and subsequent reporting of police work, Albany lifted a quarter million dollars in advertising from the two city dailies. This is also thought to be related to a 35 million dollar libel suit brought by Albany policemen against the papers and their editors, a suit growing out of reporting alleged instances of police brutality with racial overtones.

Leadership of the CURE campaign

lacked nothing in enthusiasm and energy. It lacked substantial support from the inside of both parties where it was needed, and it lacked sensitivity to the nature of the community, which has for nearly a century had a succession of tightly controlled machines of one party and then the other.[10] The role of spokesman was seized by a zealous young clergyman who became its candidate for mayor. The fact that he was related to a cosmetic fortune was a minor liability in impoverished Albany, and the fact that he was a Presbyterian cleric in heavily Catholic Albany was a major one. The 1963 election suggests that far from gaining ground, the insurgent factions lost ground in both parties. One Republican district worker told me that in 1963 he was instructed by his ward leader to cut the Republican turnout by 20 per cent! [11]

Discontent in the Albany County Republican party has become far more apparent than in the Democratic party, despite hearings before the State Investigation Commission (SIC) into county purchasing practices that ought to disturb anyone. Early in 1963, the entire Watervliet Republican committee resigned in protest against "indifferent performance and implied collusion" between the two parties' county leadership. The chairman of the Watervliet committee, Albany County, announced on January 14, 1964 the

10 "The people of Albany have always voted for the kind of machine government given them by the O'Connells." From Warren Moscow, *Politics in the Empire State* (New York: Knopf, 1948), p. 37.

11 CURE achieved a measure of victory on January 20, 1964, with the assistance of the State Attorney General. Gren Rand, Chairman of CURE, carried on the fight for grand jury reform and shared credit when the State Appellate Division, Third Department, announced new rules for jury selection in the area including Albany. See Albany *Times-Union,* January 21, 1964.

formation of a county-wide insurgent Republican organization called DRIVE (Determined Republicans In Victory Effort for Albany County) and tied it to an attack on the Republican County Chairman for remaining silent throughout the long and lurid SIC investigation of alleged corruption in Democratic-controlled Albany city and county government. The Albany *Times-Union* had editorially abetted the CURE campaign, but it defended Conway, Albany Republican chairman, in this case.[12]

The Albany machine is obviously a much tougher nut to crack. Differing from the Schenectady situation, the O'Connell machine has a solid Irish-nationalist foundation with very little noticeable opposition from competing ethnic groups. Dan O'Connell had personally broken the grip of the old Barnes machine by being elected assessor back in 1919. Two years later, the city changed party hands. Stories are rife about the techniques used to establish O'Connell's power, but one characteristic stands out today—iron-clad discipline. Like "Ed" Cushing, O'Connell likes to remain in the background, leaving the problems of direct contact to a strong party secretary. The O'Connell group is a straight patronage organization, trailing every other city in the area in the initiation of new programs. All of the evils that accompany underpaid police are commonly attributed to Albany, and the salary schedule there is so low that the state legislature intervened this year. Why then has there been so little support for a reform movement in Albany while barely ten miles away the political pot boils? In Schenectady, the factional cleavages in both parties are sharp; in the city of Albany they are barely detectable.[13]

One stage of this research was conducted by interviewing each of the identifiable prominent party leaders in Schenectady County who would agree to the interviews. These included five current or former county chairmen, most current ward and town chairmen, former candidates for major office, and the like. Those thought to be factional leaders, or their associates, were given 278 cards, each bearing the name of a committeeman from their party. Following a rather general discussion about the reasons people go into politics and the problem of maintaining party cohesion, the subject was asked to sort out the committeemen by name into piles according to any base of group affinity or similarity he thought appropriate. Upon completing the sorting, he was asked to identify the characteristics of the pile. The faction labels supplied hold some interest. Two Republican county committee officers merely divided people between "in" and "out." By this method they counted 139 "in" and 130 "out"—there were nine vacancies—which corresponds roughly with the test of strength several months later. A Grassroots leader chose "old guard," "do nothing," "insurgents," and "sympathetic to insurgents" (124, 12, 56, and 83). A former county chairman (Republican) counted 187 "old guard," 46 "young, new ideas," 8 "follow-the-leaders," 23 unknowns, 1 "self-seeker," and 10 "enigmas." A ward supervisor and top county official, who later in the year came within 150 votes out of 4,800 of losing a ward enrolled four to one in his favor, identified 81 in the "old guard," 24 in the "middle of the

---

[12] Albany *Times-Union,* January 16, 1964.
[13] In the city of Cohoes, Albany County, an insurgent faction of the Democratic party

labeled itself the Citizens party and captured control with some Republican support in 1963. Republicans control most of the towns in Albany County, and it has not been determined at this writing what the basis of its new factionalism is.

road," 10 "rebels," and did not know the other 160. Over on the Democratic side, the only differences were in the use of the terms "Strattonite" and "anti-Stratton" to designate new and old guard. Also, the man later to be elected county chairman demonstrated far too much discrimination in analysis of the committeemen (too many piles!) to make his judgment comparable to that of others.

The exercise revealed several interesting facts. Vertical communication (up and down the hierarchy) is far superior to horizontal. This is probably only another way of saying that people who succeed in rising to the top know more people and are known by them. Furthermore, the tendency to take for granted the "in" and "out" categories points up the *de facto* existence of a more complex pattern of political behavior than is described by the expression "two-party system." In the Schenectady example, the factions behave in many respects like independent parties. They caucus separately through representatives who organize sometimes formally (Grassrooters) and sometimes informally through social intercourse. Those politicians from the "old school," found in the old guard of both parties, appear to be far more preoccupied with formal organization having tight discipline. They also display a marked preference for opposition party politicians who share these values. A strong affinity was noticed among leaders of both old-guard factions for the Albany organization model, and in some instances even for its leaders, as well as for each other in gossipy support of their factional warfare. Insurgent factions in both cases challenged the "machine tactics" and "bossism" of the old organization, and not without reason. Once successful, however, insurgency becomes "establishment." In the Democratic party, the

roles were abruptly reversed last year in Schenectady.

SUMMARY

In summary, then, we find that even old and tough political machines can successfully be overthrown, either by internal factionalism, or by concerted effort from the opposition party if it can attract substantial public support. However, tight political machines are not necessarily vulnerable to verbal attack charging "bossism" and exposing "corruption," in the absence of one or more political preconditions of change. A machine can hasten its own downfall by failure to satisfy the expectations of a large element of its party support or by continually ignoring certain values (such as program preferences) of a major element of its formal base. Machines can be brought down from "the outside" when a particularly attractive and effective personality succeeds in gaining the sympathetic attention of party workers in either party and in the general public. The importance of support from within established parties should not be minimized. The "invasion" of existing political parties by idea-oriented, or program-oriented, people willing to do the routine chores of party workers can build factions strong enough to attract support even from those with a patronage interest. Such factions become a convenient platform from which to launch insurgency and reform campaigns with a reasonable chance of success because, by definition, they start with a portion of the organizational base of the machine or the indifferent opposition party. Machines can even be challenged by the objective facts of the community's economic condition, which is to say that, even in the absence of effective political opposition, depressed economic areas focus attention on the taxing power of government, and a sentiment for rejection of the "ins" can grow even without effective direction. A combination of these can topple even the most formidable machine, as in fact occurred in Schenectady. Recognition of these forces by those public-spirited citizens who have the time and courage to "do something" for their communities could be quite an advantage. Constant vigilance in exposing the wrongdoing, willingness to risk both legal and extra-legal harassment, and attention to the details of organization stretching into every segment of the community are the price of democratic reform.

Bosses, Machines, and Ethnic Groups

By Elmer E. Cornwell, Jr.

ABSTRACT: The boss and his urban machine, though products of many factors, were virtually unthinkable without their immigrant clienteles. These gave the machine its essential mass base. And the machine operated, in effect, as virtually the only agency facilitating the political—and economic—integration of the immigrants into the American community. This was done by soliciting—or "buying"—their votes with the familiar array of machine "services," bringing their representatives into the organization, offering a career ladder to some individuals, and giving general recognition to them as a group. Then the immigration flow virtually stopped during the 1920's. This, plus various urban reforms, the development of government-sponsored welfare services, and the like ended the era of the boss. Actually, two kinds of "immigration" have gone on since the twenties. The Negro has come in increasing numbers from the rural South to northern urban centers, and the Puerto Rican has sought wider opportunity in New York City. Though the present-day urban party has far less motive and ability to deal with these newcomers in the former manner, evidence suggests that they are finding their way into the party organizations and, hence, are to some extent being represented by them.

Elmer E. Cornwell, Jr., Ph.D., Providence, R. I., is Associate Professor and Chairman of the Department of Political Science, Brown University. He previously taught in various capacities at Williams College, Harvard University, and Princeton University. He is author of articles on urban politics and the American presidency which have appeared in Social Forces, the Midwest Journal of Political Science, the Public Opinion Quarterly, and the Journalism Quarterly, and of a forthcoming book on the President as leader of public opinion.

THOUGH the direction of the causal relationship may be difficult to establish, the classic urban machine and the century of immigration which ended in the 1920's were intimately intertwined phenomena. This fact is not always recognized as fully as it should be. Much of the literature on bosses and machines, beginning with the muckrakers, but not excluding more recent studies with less overt moralistic flavor, carries the implication that such factors as the dispersal of power in urban government—under weak mayor charters and through rivalries among state, county, city and special district authorities, all plowing the same field but none with full responsibility for its cultivation—invited the machine's extralegal reconcentration of power. It is also true that attitudes engendered by a business society whose prime movers characteristically had their eye on the "main chance"—and specifically on traction franchises and the like—also fostered the growth of the essentially entrepreneurial role and amoral attitude of the boss.

RELATION OF MACHINE TO IMMIGRATION

When all this has been said, however, the fact still remains that the classic machine would probably not have been possible, and certainly would not have been so prominent a feature of the American political landscape, without the immigrant. Essentially, any disciplined grass-roots political organization rests upon a docile mass base which has in some manner been rendered dependable, predictable, and manipulable. The rank and file of the Soviet Communist party is disciplined by a combination of ideological allegiance, fear, and hope of reward. The average party supporter in a liberal-democratic society cannot be so disciplined under ordinary circumstances, at least not for long. The newly arrived immigrant was a special case, however. He was characteristically insecure, culturally and often linguistically alien, confused, and often in actual want. Thus, even if he had valued the franchise thrust upon him by his new political mentors, its careful exercise would have taken a low priority in his daily struggle for existence. In most cases, he did not value or even understand the political role into which he was being pushed.

Thus, it was the succeeding waves of immigrants that gave the urban political organizations the manipulable mass bases without which they could not have functioned as they did. And, until immigration dried up to a trickle in the 1920's, as one generation of newcomers began to espouse traditional American values of political independence, there was always a new group, often from a different country of origin, to which the machine could turn. As long as this continued to be possible, machines persisted, and once the immigrant base finally began to disappear, so did most of the bosses of the classic model. In a very real sense, then, the one phenomenon was dependent on the other.

The argument can be made that there were other machines that clearly were not immigrant-based in this sense. All generalizations, especially those in the social sciences, are but proximate truths. At the same time, machines based on white, Protestant, "old stock" clienteles were not wholly unrelated in their motivation and operation to the factor of immigration. Platt's smooth-functioning organization in New York State [1] and Blind Boss Brayton's contemporary operation in Rhode Island [2] were both

[1] See Harold F. Gosnell, *Boss Platt and His New York Machine* (Chicago: University of Chicago Press, 1924).

[2] See Lincoln Steffens, "Rhode Island: A State for Sale," *McClure's Magazine*, Vol. 24 (February 1905), pp. 337–353.

based, in the immediate sense, on what
Lincoln Steffens called "the good old
American stock out in the country."[3]
And yet recall that both of these states
were highly urbanized even in the 1890's
and early 1900's when these two worth-
ies flourished and had ingested disproportionate numbers of immigrants. As
of 1920, when 38 per cent of the total
United States population was foreign
born or of foreign parentage, the corresponding percentages for New York
and Rhode Island were 64 and 71.[4]
These facts alone suggest what the political history of both makes clear: these
rural "old stock" machines existed
largely as means of political defense
against the newcomers and doubtless
would not have existed had there been
no immigrants.

The point, then, is that, whereas in
the cities the immigrants sold their political independence for the familiar
currency of favors and aid, their rural
native cousins were sometimes prompted
to do the same, in part out of desire for
cultural-religious as well as political,
and perhaps at times economic, self-
protection. Recollection of the Know-
Nothing era of militant nativist activity
a half-century earlier suggests that this
kind of cultural-religious antagonism
can be a very potent political force indeed. An analogous explanation could
even be offered for the existence of machines in the South like that of Harry
Byrd in Virginia, by simply substituting
the perceived Negro threat for the danger of engulfment by foreigners in the
North. And, curiously enough, the two
examples of reasonably thoroughgoing
machine-like organizations that flourished in the otherwise inhospitable English soil—Joseph Chamberlain's Bir-

mingham caucus [5] and Archibald Salvidge's "machine" in Liverpool [6]—also
were at least indirectly related to the
problem of Irish home rule, and, in
Liverpool, to actual rivalry with Irish
immigrants over religion and jobs.

In short, whatever else may be said
about the conditions and forces that
spawned the classic machine, this kind
of disciplined political entity must rest
at bottom on a clientele which has felt
it necessary to exchange political independence—its votes, in a word—for
something seen as more essential to its
well-being and security. In general,
such a group will be the product of
some kind of socioeconomic disequilib-
rium or cultural tension which finds its
members in an insecure or seriously disadvantaged situation. Thus, the immigrant was willing to submit to the boss
in exchange for aid—real or imagined—
in gaining his foothold in the new environment, and the old-stock machine
supporters, North or South, submitted
in part for protection against swarming
aliens or a potential Negro threat to
white dominance.

THE CLASSIC MACHINE IN OPERATION

It cannot be assumed that the process
of machine exploitation of succeeding
groups of newcomers was a smooth and
simple operation. Any formal organization, political or otherwise, must maintain a continuing balance among a series of often contradictory forces.[7] Its
very existence rests on the success with
which it achieves its objective—in the

---

[3] Lincoln Steffens, *Autobiography* (New
York: Literary Guild, 1931), p. 367.

[4] E. P. Hutchinson, *Immigrants and their
Children* (New York: John Wiley, 1956),
p. 27.

[5] See J. L. Garvin, *The Life of Joseph
Chamberlain* (3 vols.; London: Macmillan,
1932–34).

[6] Stanley Salvidge, *Salvidge of Liverpool*
(London: Hodder and Stoughton, 1934).

[7] For an elaboration of this approach to the
internal dynamics of the machine, see James
Q. Wilson, "The Economy of Patronage,"
Journal of Political Economy, Vol. 69, pp.
369–380.

case of a political party, the winning of elections and, thus, power. In the long run, this success depends on the organization's continuing ability to tap fresh sources of support as time goes on and old reliances dwindle and may at times depend on keeping newly available resources away from its rival or rivals. For the machine, this has meant wooing each new ethnic contingent. Yet this process of growth and renewal will inevitably threaten the very position of many of the proprietors of the organization itself by recruiting rivals for their roles. Any organizational entity must not only achieve its corporate goals but, to survive, it must also satisfy the needs and desires of its members as individuals. If it fails in this, its supporters will vanish and its own objectives remain unattainable. Specifically, for the machine, this fact of organizational life often tempered missionary zeal and tempted its members to protect even an eroding *status quo*.

Usually the machine did yield in the long run to the political imperative that all groups of potential supporters must be wooed, if for no other reason than to keep them from the enemy. The short-term risk to the present leadership often must have appeared minimal. The plight of the newcomers was so pitiful, their needs so elemental, and their prospects of achieving security and independence so problematical in the foreseeable future that they must have appeared like a windfall to the machine proprietors. Thus, after initial hesitancy, the Irish were taken into Tammany and found their way into the ranks of the clientele of other big city party organizations.

The ways in which immigrant political support was purchased are familiar and need no elaborate review here. They had at least three kinds of needs which the ward heeler could fill on behalf of the party leadership. Above

all, they needed the means of physical existence: jobs, loans, rent money, contributions of food or fuel to tide them over, and the like. Secondly, they needed a buffer against an unfamiliar state and its legal minions: help when they or their offspring got in trouble with the police, help in dealing with inspectors, in seeking pushcart licenses, or in other relations with the public bureaucracy. Finally, they needed the intangibles of friendship, sympathy, and social intercourse. These were available, variously, through contact with the precinct captain, the hospitality of the political clubhouse, the attendance of the neighborhood boss at wakes and weddings, and the annual ward outing.[8]

As has often been noted, these kinds of services were not available, as they are today, at the hands of "United Fund" agencies, city welfare departments with their platoons of social workers, or through federal social security legislation. The sporadic and quite inadequate aid rendered by the boss and his lieutenants thus filled a vacuum. Their only rivals were the self-help associations which did spring up within each ethnic group as soon as available resources allowed a meager surplus to support burial societies and the like. The fact that the politicians acted from self-serving motives in distributing their largess, expecting and receiving a *quid pro quo*, is obvious but not wholly relevant. At least it was not relevant in judging the social importance of the services rendered. It was highly relevant, of course, in terms of the political power base thus acquired.

Some of the later arrivals following the pioneering Irish were in at least as great need of aid. The Irish did speak

---

[8] One of the most readable depictions of these machine functions is to be found in Edwin O'Connor's novel *The Last Hurrah* (Boston: Little, Brown, 1956).

English and had had some experience with political action and representative institutions at home. This, plus the fact that they got here first, doubtless accounts for their rapid rise in their chosen party, the Democracy. The groups that followed, however, usually did not know English and bore the additional burden of a cultural heritage that had less in common with the American patterns they encountered than had been the case with the Irish. And, too, almost all groups, the Sons of Erin included, differed religiously from the basic Protestant consensus of their Anglo-Saxon predecessors.

As group followed group—not only into the country but into the rickety tenements and "river wards" reserved, as it were, for the latest arrivals—the processes of absorption became more complex. The Irish ward politicians doubtless had, if anything, more difficulty bridging the cultural and language gap to meet the newcomers than the "Yankees" had had in dealing with themselves some decades earlier. Also, while it may well be that the Yankees gave up their party committee posts fairly willingly to the Irish, because politics was not essential to their well-being either economically or psychologically, the Irish were in a rather different position when their turn came to move over and make room.[9] They had not fully outgrown their dependence on politics for financial and psychic security. Thus, the conflicting demands of the machine for new sources of support versus the reluctance of the incumbents to encourage rivalry for their own positions, produced tension. In the long run, however, most of the new ethnic groups found their place in the party system. In some cases, as with the Italians, the Republicans, generally less

skillful in these arts, won support by default when the Irish were especially inhospitable.

THE MACHINE AS SOCIAL INTEGRATOR

There is another side to the coin of machine dependence on the continuing flow of immigrants. The "invisible hand"—to use an analogy with Adam Smith's economics—which operated to produce social benefits out of the *quid pro quo* which the ward heelers exchanged for votes was at work in other ways, too. Henry Jones Ford noted in the 1890's, while discussing the role of party: [10]

This nationalizing influence continues to produce results of the greatest social value, for in co-ordinating the various elements of the population for political purposes, party organization at the same time tends to fuse them into one mass of citizenship, pervaded by a common order of ideas and sentiments, and actuated by the same class of motives. This is probably the secret of the powerful solvent influence which American civilization exerts upon the enormous deposits of alien population thrown upon this country by the torrent of emigration.

Again, in other words, the selfish quest by the politician for electoral support and power was transmuted by the "invisible hand" into the major force integrating the immigrant into the community.

This process has had several facets. In the first place, the mere seeking out of the immigrants in quest of their support, the assistance rendered in getting them naturalized (when it was necessary to observe these legal niceties), and so forth were of considerable importance in laying the foundation for their more meaningful political participation later. In addition, the parties have progressively drawn into their own

[9] See the author's "Some Occupational Patterns in Party Committee Membership," *Rhode Island History*, Vol. 20 (July 1961), pp. 87–96.

[10] *The Rise and Growth of American Politics* (New York: Macmillan, 1911), p. 306.

hierarchies and committee offices representatives of the various ethnic groups. The mechanics of this process were varied. In some cases, there doubtless emerged leaders of a particular group in one ward or neighborhood who, if given official party status, would automatically bring their followings along with them.[11] On other occasions, new ethnic enclaves may have sought or even demanded representation in exchange for support. Perhaps prior to either of these, the machine sought to co-opt individuals who could speak the language and act as a cultural bridge between the party and the newcomers. Depending on the situation, it probably was essential to do this and impossible for precinct captains of a different background to develop adequate rapport. It is at this point that ethnic group rivalry in the organization becomes difficult. Gratitude to the boss for initial admission into the lower ranks of the hierarchy would be bound to change in time into demands, of growing insistence, for further recognition of the individual and his group.

These general patterns can to some extent be documented, at least illustratively. The tendency for the urban machines to reap the Irish vote and later much of the vote of more recent arrivals is well known. The process of infiltration by group representatives into party structure is harder to identify precisely. With this in mind, the author did a study of the members of party ward committees in Providence, Rhode Island, the findings of which may reflect trends elsewhere.[12] Analysis of committee membership lists or their equivalent going back to the 1860's and 1870's showed initial overwhelming Anglo-Saxon majorities. For the Demo-

crats, however, this majority gave way, between the 1880's and 1900, to a roughly 75 per cent Irish preponderance, while the Republican committees stayed "Yankee" until after the First World War. Then, in the 1920's, both parties simultaneously recruited Italian committeemen to replace some of the Irish and white Protestants, respectively. Today, both have varied, and roughly similar, proportions of all major groups in the city population. In other cities, the timing of shifts and the ethnic groups involved will have differed, but the general process and its relation to local patterns of immigration were doubtless similar.

It is incredible, viewed now with hindsight, how reckless the American republic was in its unpremeditated policy of the open door and the implied assumption that somehow, without any governmental or even organized private assistance, hundreds of thousands of immigrants from dozens of diverse cultures would fit themselves smoothly and automatically into a native culture which had its own share of ethnocentrism. The fact of the matter was that the process did not operate smoothly or particularly effectively. There were tensions and incidents which accentuated cultural differences and engendered bitterness. These ranged, chronologically, all the way from the abuses of the more militant Know-Nothings to the Ku Klux Klan activity of the 1920's.

Economically, most occupational doors that did not lead to manual labor jobs were closed to the Irish and later arrivals and were only gradually pried open after much time had passed and many lasting intergroup enmities had been engendered. Here again, the party organizations represented one of the few mechanisms, public or private, that lubricated a process of integration which, in its very nature, was bound to generate enormous amounts of friction.

[11] *Ibid.*, p. 307.
[12] "Party Absorption of Ethnic Groups," *Social Forces*, Vol. 38 (March 1960), pp. 205–210.

Besides drawing group representatives into its councils, party work also was one of the few career ladders available to the immigrant and his ambitious sons. Here, status could be achieved, as well as a comfortable income, one way or another, when few other routes were open. This became not just status for the individual but a measure of recognition and acceptance for the group as a whole through the individual's success. In fact, not only did the newcomer use this alternative career ladder, but he carried over into the political sphere some of the "Horatio Alger" quest for success and other aspects of an essentially pragmatic, materialistic American culture as well.

Politics for the machine politician never was an ideological enterprise or a matter of beliefs and principles. As someone once said, the boss had only seven principles, five loaves and two fishes. Rather, politics was an entrepreneurial vocation like any other business. Banfield and Wilson have written: "A political machine is a business organization in a particular field of business—getting votes and winning elections. As a Chicago machine boss once said . . . it is 'just like any sales organization trying to sell its product.' "[13] The politician's aim was and is so to invest his supply of capital—jobs, favors, and the like—as to earn a profit, some of which he will take as "income" and the rest reinvest in quest of larger returns. In other words, the immigrant political leader took the one vocation open to him, politics, and made it into as close an approximation as he could of the more valued business callings in the society, from which he was effectively barred. He acted out the American success story in the only way open to him.

Obviously, the foregoing is not designed to portray the machine as a knight-errant rescuing American society from its willful folly. In the first place, the folly was not willful, and perhaps not folly. In the second, the boss's contribution toward making the melting pot melt should not be overrated. At the same time, many have testified—as does the record itself—to the almost unique ability of party as organization to bring people together across cultural and similar barriers. As Glazer and Moynihan have written of New York City: [14]

> . . . political life itself emphasizes the ethnic character of the city, with its balanced tickets and its special appeals. . . . For those in the field itself, there is more contact across the ethnic lines, and the ethnic lines themselves mean less, than in other areas of the city's life.

Ticket-balancing, or United Nations politics, as it is sometimes called, is perhaps symbolic of the ultimate step in the process of granting group recognition and confirming the fact that something approaching intergroup equality has been achieved. Either, as with the Manhattan Borough presidency and the Negro group, certain prescriptive rights become established to a particular office or to one place on a city-wide ticket or ethnic allocation is made using the background of the head of the ticket as point of departure.

In short, the classic urban machine rested upon the immigrants, while at the same time it fostered their integration into American life. It also made, in the process, a major contribution to the over-all American political style. It is true that politics as a pragmatic entrepreneurial vocation owes much in America to the contributions of Burr,

[13] Edward Banfield and James Q. Wilson, *City Politics* (Cambridge: Harvard and M.I.T. Presses, 1963), p. 115.

[14] Nathan Glazer and Daniel Patrick Moynihan, *Beyond the Melting Pot* (Cambridge: Harvard and M.I.T. Presses, 1963), p. 20.

Van Buren, Weed, Marcy (to the victor belong the spoils), and, in a sense, to Andrew Jackson himself. Thus, Richard Hofstadter's attribution of one of the two central systems of political ethics in America to the immigrants is only partially valid.[15] He is clearly correct, however, in suggesting that a political style which stressed "personal obligations, and placed strong personal loyalties above allegiance to abstract codes of law or morals"[16] was congenial to the machine politicians and their followers, and they made it their own, developing its full implications in the process. At the same time, the immigrant versus old stock cultural cleavage prompted the latter to espouse the more vigorously the typically middle-class, reformist style which stresses honesty, impartiality, and efficiency. These two styles or ethics, since the late nineteenth century, have, by their interaction, shaped both the evolution of urban politics and the machinery of urban government.

THE DECLINE OF THE MACHINE

The decline and fall of the boss as a political phenomenon has often been chronicled and explained. It is argued, *inter alia,* that reforms like the direct primary, nonpartisan systems of election, voting machines and tightened registration requirements, and city-manager schemes often dealt crippling blows. In the aggregate, they doubtless did, though many exceptions can be found to prove the rule. One particular contribution of the reformers which has had unquestioned importance—though circumvention has not proven impossible—was the elimination of patronage with the installation of civil service based on the merit principle. And,

[15] Richard Hofstadter, *The Age of Reform* (New York: Knopf, 1955), pp. 8 ff.
[16] *Ibid.,* p. 9.

generally, educational levels have risen, and occupational levels and incomes have risen as well. Even where patronage remains available, the latter development has rendered it less attractive, and to fewer people. Finally, and most often cited, there was the impact of the New Deal. Its installation of publicly sponsored welfare programs eliminated many of the rough-and-ready welfare functions of the precinct captain, though the more imaginative recouped part of their loss by helping to steer constituents through the bureaucratic maze, claiming credit for the benefits thus obtained.

Granting the importance of all of these developments, in the long run, the decline of immigration doubtless proved the most important blow to the traditional machine operation. New arrivals had been entering the country at a rate in excess of four million each half decade up to the First World War. The rate averaged barely more than one third of that between 1915 and 1930 and dropped to a mere trickle for most of the period down to the present. Sharply restrictive legislation passed in 1921 and 1924 was responsible. Obviously, the impact on the machines came in the form of a delayed reaction, but most of them gradually withered. The few that survived did so through shrewd adaptation to changed conditions, specifically through judicious self-administered doses of reformism, as, for example, with the Daley organization in Chicago.

Thus ended an era. Immigration may not have called the boss into being, but the two in most cases were closely linked. Two questions remain to be dealt with. What contemporary counterparts are there, if any, of the immigrant influx of yesteryear and how are the parties dealing with them? And what can be said of the current political behavior of the children and grandchildren of the former immigrants?

THE PARTIES AND THE NEW IMMIGRATION

There are, of course, two major groups that do represent close parallels with the earlier influx and at the same time carry important differences. These are the Negroes who have been migrating in increasing numbers from the South to northern urban centers since the First World War and the Puerto Ricans who began coming to New York City, for the most part, after the Second World War.[17] Both resemble their alien predecessors in the magnitude of their numbers, their basic and important cultural differences from the population into whose midst they are moving, an almost invariable need of assistance in adjusting to a new environment, and their potential impact on the political balance of forces.

The major points of difference are also worth noting. Both come bearing the credentials of American citizenship, which was not the case with the earlier groups. Though this factor should make for easier adjustment, other group characteristics operate to make acceptance more difficult. For the Negro, there is the fundamental problem of color, coupled with cultural characteristics which, though acquired ostensibly in the American environment, operate to make assimilation more difficult. These include all the long deposit of servitude and enforced inferior status: loose marital ties and correspondingly weak family ties generally, a poverty of leadership potential, low literacy and skill levels, and the like. For the Puerto Ricans, there is language, plus differences of culture, and a partial color barrier which

[17] Two recent books are especially useful discussions of these groups: Glazer and Moynihan, *op. cit.*; and Oscar Handlin, *The Newcomers: Negroes and Puerto Ricans in a Changing Metropolis* (Cambridge: Harvard Press, 1959).

operates to cause at least some Spanish Americans to be classified—against their will—as Negroes. On balance, it is probably true that, so far as these two groups are concerned as groups, they face higher barriers to integration into American life than almost any earlier group save, possibly, the orientals.

But the society itself has changed enormously from the society to which the Irish, Italians, and Jews sought entrance. Urban areas are now equipped with facilities to which the newcomer can turn for aid that counterbalance to some degree the particular hostilities which members of these two groups arouse. There are now elaborate public welfare programs, there is Aid to Dependent Children for the many fatherless families, there are numerous private agencies and charities which stand ready to help, and, in the case of the Puerto Ricans, their land of origin has taken a unique interest in the welfare of its emigrants. There have even been legislative efforts to ban the discrimination in housing or employment which they encounter.

Though these facilities stand ready to ease aspects of the economic and social integration of these latest immigrants, there still remains the question of political absorption. Here, too, the situation today sharply differs from the past. The political parties now have neither the incentive nor the means with which to perform the functions they performed for the earlier immigrants. The machine in most affected areas is gone beyond recall, and there remain in its place party organizations that are hollow shells of their former strength and vigor. Party in general, given the proliferation of both public bureaucracies and the mass entertainment industry, has been pushed to the fringes of the average citizen's attention span and often to the fringes of the governing process itself. The debilitating impact of reform legislation contributed to the same end, needless to say. Thus, in general, the new immigrants can look to the parties for little of the former assistance they once provided in gaining entrance and leverage in the political processes of their new homes.

There are partial exceptions here, as there are to all the foregoing generalizations. Mayor Daley's modern Chicago version of the old-style machine has been mentioned earlier. Within his over-all Cook County Democratic organization, there is the "sub-machine" comprising the Negro followers of Representative William E. Dawson.[18] Dawson, a former maverick Republican, shifted parties in 1939 and joined forces with Mayor-boss Kelly. Some twenty years later, he had put together a combination, under his leadership, of five or six Negro wards. This "organization within an organization" appears to bargain as a unit through Dawson and his lieutenants for patronage and other kinds of preferment in the gift of Mayor Daley and in turn tends to exert a moderating influence on the more aggressive elements in the Negro community. Trends suggest that this is not destined to be a permanent arrangement. The population of the Dawson-controlled wards has been declining as the more prosperous Negroes manage to settle in more desirable locations, and, as Dawson and his associates grow older, they become more conservative. Whether or not this latter is partly an illusion produced by the rapid rise in Negro militancy since 1954 would be hard to say. It is probably true that leaders of the Dawson type will get more "out of phase" with the civil rights movement as that movement gains further momentum.

New York City, almost by traditional right, is *the* locale for the study of the behavior of American parties in relation to the immigrant. The 1960 census reported just over a million Negroes in New York City and somewhat more than 600,000 Puerto Ricans. In broad terms, it can be said that, since the days of Al Smith and Boss Murphy, New York politics have been long on confusion and fragmentation and short on centralized, disciplined organization. There was, therefore, little possibility that a relationship such as Representative Dawson worked out with his Negro clientele on the one hand and the leaders of the Cook County Democracy on the other could be developed in New York. Especially in Manhattan—which we shall take for analysis—one finds exemplified the more typical contemporary party situation: no dominating borough-wide authority save that in the hands of the mayor himself, hence a series of local feudal chiefs who are rarely willing to exchange their relative independence for the rather meager supplies of patronage available, and the whole system wracked periodically by factional feuding.

The Negro in New York, in apparent contrast to the Chicago situation, has been more fragmented in his political organization, has found little borough-wide structure with which to associate, but has made more spectacular symbolic gains in the party and city government. Representative Adam Clayton Powell, the rather erratic champion of the city's nonwhites, reaps vastly more national publicity for his espoused cause than the publicity-shy Congressman Dawson.[19] How much this means in concrete benefits would be hard to determine. More significant is the fact that in 1953 a Negro, Hulan Jack, was

[18] This discussion of the Dawson organization draws particularly on James Q. Wilson, *Negro Politics* (Glencoe, Ill.: Free Press, 1960), pp. 50 ff. and *passim*.

[19] A useful source on Powell is David Hapgood, *The Purge that Failed: Tammany v. Powell* (New York: Holt, 1959).

elected for the first time to a major office in the city, that of Borough President of Manhattan. Powell had a major role in this, though he later broke with Jack. Since then, this position has become an accepted Negro prerogative. Other high positions have been filled by Negroes in the city administration in recent years.

REPRESENTATION ON PARTY COMMITTEES

A somewhat more useful basis for judging the reality of ethnic or racial group political absorption and power position than possession of some of these "commanding heights" (in Lenin's phrase) would be an analysis of the extent to which they had gained footholds in the lower and intermediate levels of the party organization. The ethnic proportions among Providence ward committee members cited above are a relatively accurate reflection of the nationality power relationships in city politics. For example, the fact that the Irish Democrats have held onto about half of the ward committee seats after yielding some places to Italians reflects the fact that they still have the dominant voice in the party. The rise of the Italians on the Republican side to the status of the largest single ethnic group also reflects their growing power.[20]

Table 1 shows the approximate percentages of ethnic/racial representation in the total New York City population and, in the second column, the background of the Manhattan Democratic Assembly district leaders and coleaders insofar as these could be determined.[21]

[20] "Party Absorption of Ethnic Groups," op. cit.

[21] Thanks are due the author's former student, Edwin Cohen, now active in Manhattan politics, and to George Osborne, himself a district leader, for tracking down the leadership data used.

TABLE 1—COMPARISON OF ETHNIC PROPORTIONS IN POPULATION WITH DEMOCRATIC DISTRICT LEADERS IN MANHATTAN

	APPROXIMATE PERCENTAGE OF NEW YORK CITY 1960 POPULATION[a]	PERCENTAGE OF DEMOCRATIC ASSEMBLY DISTRICT LEADERS (N = 66)
Negroes	14	21
Puerto Ricans	8	6
Jews	25±	38
Italians	17±	11
Irish	10±	9
Others	26±	15[b]
	100	100

[a] Population percentage estimates are from Nathan Glazer and D. P. Moynihan, *Beyond the Melting Pot* (Cambridge: Massachusetts Institute of Technology and Harvard Press, 1963). Only figures for Negroes and Puerto Ricans were given in the 1960 census. It was impossible to get ethnic group percentages for Manhattan alone.

[b] Includes Anglo-Saxon Protestants and others of unidentified background.

There are sixteen Assembly districts, but most are divided into two or three parts with a leader and coleader for each. There were some vacancies at the time the data were obtained. It can be seen that the Negro has done quite well by this measure of political integration in that the group has considerably more than the share of district leadership positions it would be entitled to on a strict population basis. The bulk of these Negroes preside over districts in or around Harlem, as might be expected—the 11th, 12th, 13th, 14th, and 16th Assembly districts. Of the eighteen occupied positions in these five Assembly districts, they hold twelve. There are two Negroes, one each in the 5th and 10th, to the west and east of Central Park, respectively, but none to the south of the Park at all.

In passing it might be noted that the other groups on the Table each have

TABLE 2—AREAS OF HEAVY PUERTO RICAN POPULATION[a]

AREA	ASSEMBLY DISTRICT	DISTRICT LEADERS	ELECTION DISTRICT CAPTAINS	
			TOTAL	PUERTO RICANS
Lower East Side	4th, South	2 Jewish	29	7
East Harlem	10th, North	1 Puerto Rican and 1 Negro	16	9
	14th, South	2 Puerto Ricans	17	8
	14th, North	2 Negroes	—[b]	—[b]
	16th, South	1 Italian and 1 Puerto Rican	—[b]	—[b]
Upper West Side	13th, South	1 Italian and 1 Negro	52	23

[a] Puerto Rican population location was determined by plotting location of census tracts with at least 15 per cent Puerto Ricans and coloring these in according to density. There are scatterings in a few other parts of Manhattan as well.

[b] Data could not be obtained.

something approximating their proportionate share of the leaderships. The Jewish contingent is disproportionately large, due in considerable measure to the fact that three-fifths of all the anti-Tammany "reform" leaders come from that part of the city population. True to what one knows about their situation in other cities, the Italians appear to be underrepresented. The Irish, however, even in view of the extreme difficulty in guessing their share of the city population, have far fewer positions than the prevailing myth of continuing Irish dominance of urban Democratic politics would suggest.

Turning now to the Puerto Ricans, they offer the best opportunity for assessing the ability of at least the Manhattan Democratic organization to absorb a genuinely new ethnic group. In Table 2, the backgrounds of the district leaders in the areas of heaviest Puerto Rican population are tabulated. Also included, in the last two columns, are figures on the personnel of the lowest level of "grass-roots" party organization, the election district captains. Out of the twelve district leader positions occupied at the time the data were obtained, four were held by Puerto Ricans, giving that group representation in three

of the six most heavily Puerto Rican districts. Though only firsthand knowledge would indicate how effective these individuals are in representing their ethnic group and bargaining on its behalf, there is indication here of rather significant infiltration into the party structure. The figures for election district captains, where these could be obtained, point to the same conclusion. Except for the lower east side, where the proportion is smaller, roughly half of these captains are also Puerto Rican, casting further doubt on common assumptions that the party in Manhattan is lagging seriously in making room for this latest group to arrive.

In general, both Table 1 and Table 2 suggest that the Puerto Ricans have secured, in the relatively short time since their arrival in large numbers, party offices roughly commensurate with their share of the population overall and in areas of high concentration. In addition, there are three state assemblymen from this group (two from East Harlem and one from the Bronx) and four or five with high positions in the city administration.[22]

[22] Layhmond Robinson, "Voting Gain Made by Puerto Ricans," *New York Times*, November 23, 1963.

These achievements, obviously, as well as the district leaderships themselves and election district captaincies, can only be taken as rough indicators of the political progress of the group as a whole and are doubtless far less significant than they could have been viewed in the political setting of forty or fifty years ago when parties were central to the governing process and urban life generally. At the same time, they must be evaluated in light of the fact that New York State will not accept literacy in a language other than English (such as Spanish) as qualification to vote, and, thus, only some 150,000 to 175,000 of the total Puerto Rican group are on the rolls.

Returning for a moment to the current status of descendents of earlier immigrants, the assumption that significant cultural distinctions and tendencies toward common political attitude and behavior would disappear in two or three generations has proven erroneous. Ticket-balancing, for example, in ethnic or religious terms is as prevalent, perhaps, as it ever was and shows few signs of disappearing in the immediate future. The election of an Irish Catholic President in 1960, if anything, enhanced the importance of such balancing tactics, as the discussion in early 1964 of Democratic vice-presidential candidates indicated. In psychoanalysis, it is well recognized that problems have to be clearly recognized and frankly made explicit before they can be eliminated. The same may in a sense be true of ethnic factors in American politics. Only the frank recognition of the once-potent barrier to a Catholic in the White House paved the way for the Kennedy election. At the state and local level, it is probably also true that only after various groups have achieved and enjoyed the recognition they feel they are entitled to and have done so for a long enough period to transform a privilege into a quasi right will it become possible, gradually, to choose candidates without these criteria in mind. The unfortunate thing is that American parties have decayed as organizations to the point that they can make far less contribution to this process of adjustment than they could and did in the past.

Organized Labor and the City Boss

By LOUIS L. FRIEDLAND

ABSTRACT: The expression "Keep politics out of the union and the union out of politics" indicates the minor concern with the political process that has long been considered a distinguishing feature of the American labor movement. Political action on the part of labor picked up during the Depression years of the 1930's and the advent of the New Deal. The nonpartisan approach first employed by the American Federation of Labor has been the dominant pattern of American labor in politics. The powers exercised by political machines and political bosses had dwindled by the time organized labor got around to political action at the local level. Labor's preoccupation with strictly economic goals and its increasing concern for a better civic posture produced sufficient internal conflicts to generate in many cities an antipathy between union leaders and municipal reformers. Yet labor was frequently skeptical of alignments with existing political machines or their fragments and so failed to support these waning institutions. Labor views depended on American Federation of Labor or Congress of Industrial Organizations affiliation in many instances, with the former more apt to line up with the political boss or his henchmen. The craft nature of the American Federation of Labor unions tied them more closely to local affairs.

Louis L. Friedland, Ph.D., Detroit, Michigan, is Professor of Political Science at Wayne State University. He is currently research consultant to the Michigan Commission on Legislative Apportionment. He has written extensively on state and local government issues.

UP to 1940 it was commonplace to find sizable numbers of union members in the United States who expressed in no uncertain terms their opposition to any participation by unions in political affairs. The expression "Keep politics out of the union and the union out of politics" aptly portrayed this attitude. On the whole, such remarks are rarely heard today.

This minor concern with politics has long been considered a distinguishing feature of the American labor movement. It is generally assumed, however, that organized workers were stimulated into a display of political consciousness and activity as a result of the Depression of the 1930's and the events of the New Deal years. Such assertions are, to a considerable extent, valid but also contain some misconceptions.

Any attempt to study the effects of an "awakened political consciousness" on the part of organized labor in a brief essay would barely skim the surface. The patterns of political behavior developed by organized labor have been at least threefold:

(1) Establishment and maintenance of independent parties at the local, state, or national level, either alone or in conjunction with farmers or others;

(2) Support given to radical political parties;

(3) Nonpartisan political action in which labor exchanges its votes for favorable government action, which in one sense is simply an extension of collective bargaining in the area of government.[1]

The nonpartisan approach first employed by the American Federation of Labor (AFL) has been the dominant pattern of American labor in politics.

Labor sought unsuccessfully during the nineteenth century, either independently or through coalitions with farmers, to form political parties. It is interesting to note that labor parties at the local level gave temporary promise of real strength in Philadelphia, Boston, and New York. The Jackson-Van Buren alliance during the 1830's found these to be a source of political support—for a time.

As fruitful as a continuing historical examination of this nature might prove to be, the focus of our interest in this essay is the relationship of organized labor to the municipal "boss." There is an assumption, of course, that such leadership types still exist. If not, what form of leadership has superseded the colorful boss and how does organized labor relate its goals and needs to the newer focuses of governmental authority at the municipal level? These are the questions we shall seek to answer.

The period from 1875 to 1900 has been characterized as being one of "unmitigated spoils" in American local government. It was charged by the muckrakers, a group of journalists of whom Lincoln Steffens was one, that, with very few exceptions, the city governments of the United States were the worst in the Western world, as well as the most expensive, the most inefficient, and the most corrupt.[2] This was certainly a reasonably accurate judgment if we are to accept the contemporary opinion of the era's reformers.

Echoing this judgment almost fifty years later, an appraisal of many of the same cities criticized by Steffens characterized "local government in America as a reeking shambles of corruption,

---

[1] J. B. S. Hardman and M. F. Neufeld (eds.), *The House of Labor* (New York, 1951), see especially H. David, "100 Years of Labor in Politics," pp. 91–104.

[2] Lincoln Steffens, *The Shame of Our Cities* (New York, 1904). See also Charles N. Gloab, *The American City—A Documentary History* (Homewood, Ill., 1963).

incompetence, waste and misrule" and claimed that we had made little fundamental progress in municipal government in the past fifty years.[3]

Repeating the charge of fifty years earlier, the authors went on to say, "Behind the pretentious facades of most American cities is a very different story. It is the same old story of boodling, bosses, and businessmen."[4] It is interesting to note that nowhere is labor mentioned, reflecting, without doubt, the extent of interest group participation in local affairs.

Whether charitable or not, most accounts of "boss rule" in America, and there are many, are willing to admit that political bosses and their organizations, the political machines, performed necessary functions both social and governmental. All authorities are generally agreed that they have outlived their usefulness and, as their functions have been absorbed, have been disappearing from the municipal scene.

It must be noted that the exposure by muckrakers of graft and corruption and the improved methods applied by industry had their effects on government organization and administration as well. Opportunities for the political machine and its leaders began to disappear.

THE WORKING CLASS IN MUNICIPAL POLITICS

The boss and the machine which he headed had found jobs, helped families in securing housing, provided advice, and had frequently come to the rescue with gifts of food or fuel. In return, the recipients of such favors were expected to support with their votes the candidates of the political machine. This favor on the part of the worker

could be given freely; it was free. The machine also served certain social functions as well which were of importance to the low-income, low-status worker. It provided a "route of social mobility for persons to whom other routes were closed and was an antidote to constitutional dispersal of authority."[5]

From 1870 to 1930, the working class, especially immigrants, were the mainstay of the machine. They gave freely the one thing they had to offer— the vote. In return, they received both material rewards and nonmaterial inducements, the latter mainly in the form of friendship and a feeling of acceptance extended them by the precinct workers.

As the immigrants were assimilated and public welfare programs expanded, the petty favors and friendship of the precinct captain declined in value, and the influence of the machine declined with them.

UNIONS AND THE MUNICIPAL BOSSES

In the rapid changes which occurred, particularly during the 1930's, the war years, and their aftermath, the political behavior which emerged inevitably assumed varied shapes and directions for people differently constituted and value oriented. Concomitant with the shrinking of the lower-income and immigrant voters, the worker became more amenable to labor-union political activity. So, too, did the machine politician become more dependent on support from groups and associations rather than a collection of individuals who could be reached through the precinct organizations. The rapid acceleration of union membership during the late 1930's, with membership estimated between 13 to 15 million at its high point, gave even more impetus in some instances

[3] Robert S. Allen, *Our Fair City* (New York, 1947), p. 3.
[4] *Our Fair City, op. cit.,* p. 4.

[5] R. K. Merton, *Social Theory and Social Structure,* (rev. and enl.; Glencoe, Ill., 1957), p. 71.

to efforts on the part of machine politicians to garner such support.

The increase in union membership and the acquisition by unions of considerable influence, if not power, served to upset the traditional balance of control in many cities. This occurred because there was a shift in the loyalty of many workers from the machine and its leadership. Accounting for this shift in no small degree was the fact that a more modern and professionalized approach to the problems of social welfare took away from the political machine its most powerful means for achieving the loyalty and support it had so long enjoyed. Professionalization was not confined to social welfare functions alone but applied across the board to a large share of local government personnel with the introduction of civil service practices based on merit provisions.

As we have already noted, the problems of the city provided a major impetus to the reform movement, beginning late in the nineteenth century and continuing throughout the first half of the twentieth. The emphasis initially had been on freeing the cities from "boss rule" and from the boss's main support, the immigrant voter; to the reformer, these two elements seemed to be basically involved in municipal corruption.

In the minds of labor and its leaders, municipal reform was considered to be an effort by businessmen to reduce the expenditures of government, frequently at the expense of service levels which they wished to maintain or increase. There is no doubt that many labor leaders knew that the reform movement had produced a more efficient type of local government. Yet, it was also felt that, simply to save the taxpayer's money at the expense of not solving the community's problems, many of which concerned the worker,

could not be supported. In some instances, this meant support of the machine politician in opposition to such reforms. In general, the supporters, as well as the program, of the reform movement confirmed labor's belief that a major part of the relief sought would have to come from the federal government. The experience of the 1930's, when both local and state governments had proved themselves unable to meet the needs of the inhabitants of the local communities, had been shattering for those who represented labor.

Labor's preoccupation with its goal of economic concessions from management and social welfare services for its membership produced in many cities an antipathy between union leaders and municipal reformers. In many instances, much that was of major interest to the reformers was largely irrelevant to the unionist. Yet, labor unions and their leaders did not rush to the support of the machine politicians where they still existed.

AFL AND CIO POLITICAL PATTERNS

Up to the early 1930's, the American Federation of Labor—roughly equivalent to organized labor—was little interested in political power as such and viewed it as secondary to the attainment of economic power. The impact of the Depression led to a considerably greater interest in political power, including the possibility of organizing politically at the local level to achieve labor's goals. Nevertheless, the AFL continued to maintain that its chief purpose for engaging in political action was to secure a favorable economic climate.

A major goal for the AFL had consistently been to achieve a monopoly of skilled labor and to make its members better and more prosperous members of the middle class. This objective has been characterized in several ways, but that most generally expressed is to identify such a goal as "business union-ism." The phrase involves no partic-ular social philosophy but can be de-fined as meaning, "the highest possible wages, the best possible working con-ditions, and the shortest possible hours."

The most important innovation in the AFL's political conduct came in 1948 in response to the Taft-Hartley Act. In order to combat in the halls of Congress what it considered to be restrictive legislation, the AFL set up Labor's League for Political Education (LLPE), financed by "private" sub-scriptions, as the Taft-Hartley Act had barred direct union contributions for political action. However, the LLPE did have as its goal the recruitment of trade-union political stewards to direct teams of political workers in every one of the more than 110,000 urban and rural voting precincts of the United States. This goal has not yet been realized. A national office was set up in Washington, with offices in every state capital and all principal cities. At the local level, LLPE representa-tives were named for many local unions and for union shops and plants. The local representatives of the LLPE have followed the AFL's practice of support-ing or endorsing local candidates on occasion, including those of political machines.

The rise of the CIO in the 1940's and the introduction of its Political Action Committee (PAC) in 1941 pro-vided, in some respects, a sharp con-trast to the political activities of the AFL's League (LLPE). The CIO's views differed much more sharply with the policies of an entrenched leadership at the local governmental level, which shared the views of business and a middle-class orientation. It certainly cannot be said that strong class diver-gencies exist in American cities, yet the CIO sought to inculcate into its membership the idea that the working class has a set of interests different from those of a business-oriented mid-dle class.[6] It was thus more logical to expect the CIO PAC would seek to challenge the existing government leadership and the business community for control of city government.

Political action committees were quickly established at both city and county levels. A committee was also established in each congressional dis-trict which generally coincided with party political organization. The city or county PAC usually was an integral unit of the industrial council at the same level. A national office was also set up in Washington.

With merger of the AFL and the CIO, a pooling of political action forces has also taken place by the creation of the Council on Political Education (COPE). Councils have since been established in most large cities. The number of union participants so far is not large.[7] It would appear that in many locals pressure for active local political involvement arises not from the desire of the membership as a whole but from requirements of the union activists from whose ranks of-ficers are selected and who set the standards by which the officers will be judged.[8]

There has been and continues to be a distinct difference in the political involvement of the industrial (CIO) and craft (AFL) unions. Craft-union members, who are generally well-paid

[6] Robert R. Alford, "Role of Social Class in American Voting Behavior," *Western Political Science Quarterly,* Vol. 16, No. 1 (March 1963), p. 186.

[7] See Harold Sheppard and Nicholas Mas-ters, "The Political Attitudes and Preferences of Union Members," *American Political Sci-ence Review,* June 1959, pp. 442–443.

[8] "The Political Attitudes and Preferences of Union Members," *op. cit.*

skilled workers competing in a local market, are concerned about the actions of local government in certain fields. They, therefore, seek access to the local bureaucracy as well as sympathetic treatment from the local police and display great concern for local wage rates and working conditions. The craft unions will emphasize enforcing work agreements, a check on work conditions, and the like.

The industrial unions, which contain large numbers of unskilled or semi-skilled workers and deal with highly organized although decentralized industry, are concerned about industry-wide or national wage contracts and controls as well as with state and federal welfare measures which favor lower-income groups. The industrial unions, therefore, are eager for alliances with parties or groups which will support the welfare measures it favors. Frequently, this means the CIO has its interest centered on Congress and the President while the AFL will be concerned with local parties or factions in control at that level.

However, industrial unions are also vitally concerned with the development of local welfare services, the provision of free legal advice, workmen's compensation laws, unemployment compensation, eviction, medical needs of members, sources of loans, police activities, and social events. As much of this activity is similar to that of the precinct captain in a "machine" organization, the CIO unions, especially, found it necessary to set up organizations paralleling that of the political party. As a result, many unions have gone the one step further into political action at the local level.

UNIONS AND THE NONPARTISAN BALLOT

One of the outcomes of the triumph of the reformer over the boss and his machine was the acceptance of such middle-class values as "honesty, efficiency, impartiality." With the weakening of the machine, the businessmen and others of influence, never a preponderant number at the polls, now had no effective way of reaching the voters. The result has been the acceleration of a drastic separation of numbers and wealth in the contemporary metropolis. Yet, these same businessmen and middle-class influentials continued to retain status in the core city. The politicians who remained, freed of the necessity for reliance on the business community, now concerned themselves with the votes of the workers and the ethnic groups left behind in the central city.

A change also took place in the politics of the central city in that the two-party competition was reduced, with the Democrats getting a marked advantage. In an effort to salvage at least a part of the control formerly enjoyed, under the guise of reform, the role of the local executive was strengthened, and a nonpartisan method for the election of local officials was introduced. Control of the mass media of communication, essential to the promotion of such innovations, had already taken place.

Developed by the reformers for the purpose of providing a corrective to the "evils" of party or boss control of nominating conventions, the direct primary system was basic to the nonpartisan pattern of election. Insofar as the primary system offered organized labor a means, at least in theory, of acting independently of the political parties and their leaders, or even of gaining control of one of the major political parties, it encouraged nonpartisan behavior on the part of labor.

The two major political parties at all levels, according to a majority of labor leaders, had generally been animated by opportunistic rather than ideological considerations. Whenever it was necessary to insure victory, the parties have shown themselves to be responsive to labor's demands. However, except for its bitter opposition to the passage of the Taft-Hartley Act and efforts to have it withdrawn or modified, the AFL has evidenced nonpartisan behavior in the past at local as well as at national levels.

Over the passage of time, the organized labor movement has demonstrated that it continues to be committed to the continuation of nonpartisan action. This is especially the case as American political parties have not yet demonstrated any firm ideological roots. The party's purpose is, instead, the uniting of the largest number of divergent interest groups in the pursuit of power. Its ability to retain its institutional character is due to the results of compromise, not the development of dogma.[9]

Labor in this context has supported slates of candidates at the local level only sporadically. It has operated in the nonpartisan situation as only one of many groups, generally behind the scenes, and without conducting active political campaigns except in specific instances.[10] As Adrian has noted: "The fact that the bread and butter issues of the worker are frequently a function of state and national, rather than local politics (partisan or non-partisan) has deterred such groups from voting in municipal elections."[11]

Curiously, as several of our case studies discussed briefly below will suggest, organized labor has had relatively little success in local politics. With the lessening of power of the machine as the monolithic nature of its organization crumbled, the underlying factionalism of the city came sharply into focus. Even though the businessman and the upper-middle-income whites fled to the suburbs which ringed the core city, the actuality and the myth of this group's influence was still present and felt.

In the vacuum which developed, organized labor could not take over control, even though it has tried to do so. For one thing, its political organizations were neither fully organized political parties nor good government groups. As representatives of a "class," organized labor and its PAC and COPE found themselves vulnerable to the charges of being "selfish" groups not concerned with the welfare of the total community.

Nonpartisanship was therefore the most effective pose which labor could assume. As already noted earlier, its political payoffs were not particularly at the local level except possibly for a few of the craft unions. Also important was the fact that segments of its membership, particularly white union members, had anxieties and fears of their own, stemming from racial tensions, which did not make them easily amenable to labor leadership in municipal politics.

Organized labor has, for the most part, taken nonpartisanship politically in stride at the local level. Its leaders have found that supporting candidates friendly to labor rather than putting up its own slate is more effective at this time. The nonpartisan pattern also is in keeping both with labor's historical pattern and with its current dilemma of preventing a facing off between two of its most ardent support groups, the low-income whites and certain white ethnic groups still living in the central

[9] Clinton Rossiter, *Parties and Politics in America* (New York, 1960), p. 58.

[10] Charles Adrian and Oliver P. Williams, "Local Politics Under Non-Partisan Ballot," *American Political Science Review*, Vol. 53, No. 4 (December 1959), pp. 1062–1063.

[11] *Ibid.*, p. 1059.

city and the equally low-income and increasingly militant Negro.

LABOR, BOSSES, AND MUNICIPAL POLITICS TODAY

The political machine had maintained its control through an exchange system. The boss dealt at the top level with the influential business leadership of the community. Utility franchises, public works contracts, permits and licenses of all types, relaxations and even evasions of municipal laws were granted or entered into. The price was either a payment of money or a reciprocity in favors needed by the boss or his political machine. The purpose of all this was to nourish both the machine and the boss. Lincoln Steffens has aptly described what this respectable segment of society bought from local government during the heyday of the American city boss.[12]

The continuing effects of technological change, the increasing size and bureaucratization of government at all levels, the radical changes brought about in the general character of the urban population, all have wrought the destruction of the old-time political machine and, with it, the arrangements between the political bosses and the businessman element of the community.

One consequence of the change was an enlargement of the powers of the mayor, formerly little more than a figurehead executive with the boss operating from behind the scenes. To many an aspirant who would not have thought of running for city office a generation ago, the office of mayor is now very much worth while. The contemporary mayor is given an ample salary, in many instances, with adequate expense allowances, and is expected to operate in visible, often spectacular fashion. He is expected to exert strong organizational leadership as well as to demonstrate comprehensive community consciousness. The modern city executive, or even boss, can no longer run the city anonymously from a smoke-filled room, and this fact has certainly had pervasive effects on the nature of political organization in the modern city.

Under these changing patterns, labor's participation in city politics has varied from city to city, depending on the local strength and political motivation of labor and the structure of its city politics. Of course, there are the differences of the metropolis or "core" city and the suburbs to consider, especially the impact of union organization on the politics of both. As this essay is concerned only with organized labor and the city "boss," the role of organized labor in the suburban communities is not considered. Few, if any, political machines have concerned themselves in any event with the suburb's political affairs, except to maintain as innocuous a pose in such areas as they could.

POLITICAL CASE STUDIES

Detroit

The passage of a reform nonpartisan charter for Detroit had been accomplished in 1918 before the rise of a strong labor organization there. The strongest political interest group at the time was business. Its nineteenth-century ideals of liberalism and individualism made it sharply antilabor in attitude. With increasing unionization, labor emerged as a potential political power but was confronted by hostile political forces very much in control. Given the CIO's ideological drive, or-

[12] *The Autobiography of Lincoln Steffens* (New York, 1931). See also slightly fictionalized versions in Theodore Dreiser, *The Financier* (New York, 1912), and *The Titan* (New York, 1914).

ganized labor here felt it necessary to adopt full-scale political tactics if it desired to achieve success in any degree. The United Auto Workers (UAW)-CIO in 1948, through its PAC, worked out an alliance with the "liberal" factions of the Democratic party at the state, county, and city levels. The coalition succeeded in taking over control of the state leadership of the Michigan Democratic party.

With the combining of the AFL-CIO and the setting up of COPE, about 40 per cent of all Democratic precinct delegates in Detroit came under its aegis. These, together with liberal non-COPE Democratic precinct delegates, have given the CIO clear control of the city and county delegations and, to a considerable extent, of the state party as well. In the Detroit city elections, these precinct captains work on behalf of nonpartisan labor endorsees. As a Detroit study noted: [13]

Between 1946–1955 CIO-PAC endorsees won 67.5 per cent of all primary and 91.2 per cent of all general elections for partisan offices in state, congressional and county level but less than 38 per cent of all contests for non-partisan municipal offices. The CIO failed three times (1943, 1945, 1949) to elect a mayor in Detroit.

By 1957 labor in Detroit no longer fought for the acceptance of a strong ideological stand but merely sought candidates to support at the local level who looked like winners and were at least "friends" of labor. This tactic in 1961 was unsuccessful in that a comparatively unknown candidate backed by Negroes upset the incumbent who was supported by labor. However, it is not likely that organized labor will change its political strategy in Detroit's nonpartisan climate. Thus, in one of the most heavily unionized areas in the United States, in which more than twice as many people belong to labor unions as to any other nonchurch organization, organized labor has sought in vain to elect its candidate for mayor. Yet, its leadership exhibits an acute awareness of the relationship between labor and the political process. The mayoralty results indicate both important defections of the rank and file and also differences in viewpoint on the part of AFL and CIO leaders. The fact that over 90 per cent of a sampling of union membership in Detroit are classified as Democrats and at least two known Republicans have been elected as mayors since 1943 further clouds the picture.[14]

However, apart from its failure to elect a mayor, COPE in Detroit has had a considerable measure of success and has in considerable measure rivaled the accomplishments of the great patronage-based machines in other cities. It has gone into the precincts of the central city slums and won the allegiance of the electorate there. The social welfare ideology of the UAW and COPE has enabled the union's precinct workers to organize sizable votes in support of their endorsees. At the same time, the program of COPE has also appealed to certain middle-class and professional groups which a traditional patronage-oriented organization could not do. That it has not had the success its numbers would seem to make possible has been due to its special-interest "posture" and the continuation of the myths of a middle-class business-oriented reformism. The dissipation of these myths and further

[13] Nicholas A. Masters, "The Politics of Union Endorsement of Candidates in the Detroit Area," *Midwest Journal of Political Science,* August 1957, p. 149.

[14] Samuel J. Eldersveld, Robert Friedman, Robert Dodge, Sam Belanoff, *Political Affiliation in Metropolitan Detroit* (Michigan Governmental Studies, University of Michigan; Ann Arbor, 1957).

political change in the core cities are distinct possibilities.

St. Louis

In contrast to Detroit's single-industry economy, St. Louis represents a city of diversified industry. Similar to many other core cities, its population declined between 1950 and 1960 by 13.6 per cent. It shares with other large American cities a sizable Negro population, approximately 30 per cent in 1960. Taking its cue from the prevailing community political value, labor's goal is one of moderation. Because its election system involves a primary which is open, in actuality a nonpartisan framework is present, even though officials are nominated in what purport to be Democratic and Republican primaries. By 1950 only four of the city's twenty-eight wards were voting Republican in all general elections, an indication of the effects of the general pattern of outward movement to the suburbs by its middle- and upper-income residents.

So many factions are involved in St. Louis politics that the mayor and the two other city officials elected at large have not had to be directly responsible to anyone. The political line-up has arrayed the mayor's group and "civic-progress" agencies and organizations against patronage-oriented ward machines, county officeholders, and their minions. St. Louis labor, when it took an interest in local politics, usually allied itself with the patronage-oriented ward and county-office groups. In 1957, the CIO-AFL and Teamsters joined with such groups in opposing charter reform proposals that would have increased the mayor's powers at the expense of the ward politicians.

With the major exception of the Teamsters, most St. Louis unions have shown little interest in local affairs.

The Teamsters have proved to be an active and effective interest group in city politics. They operate through a Community Action Stewards' Assembly which the Teamsters portray as an attempt to apply shop-level tactics to the ward and precinct. Each precinct "steward" in effect presents "grievances" to the Assembly for consideration and action. Some observers have noted that the stewards' group and the PAC are a challenge to the independent patronage machines in the wards. The Teamsters have been effective because of the attention given to the growing Negro community, although this tie-up shows signs of abating as Negroes organize in their own right.[15]

Houston

This Texas metropolis is an economic youngster industrially. As might be expected, local politics have been and continue to be dominated by big business and its ally, the press. Local government is not the battleground on which labor will risk its fledgling forces, as it has too little to offer with its contractual battles yet to be won.

Yet, it should be noted that, in 1959, of Harris County's 165,000 industrial workers, about 75,000 were unionists (AFL-CIO) with additional thousands in Teamster locals and railroad brotherhoods. In Houston, unions have not generally endorsed local candidates, although the Teamster locals have done so in recent elections. Labor strength is more likely to be reflected in voting at the state or national levels in the support of "liberal" candidates. City administrations have thus far failed to grant many concessions to organized labor in Houston.

[15] Kenneth E. Gray and David Greenstone, *Organized Labor in City Politics—Urban Government,* ed. Ed Banfield (Glencoe, Ill., 1961), p. 376.

Chicago

In Chicago, the only large city still run by a machine, the mayor has had to bridge the gap between the traditional machine-boss mayor and today's management-man mayor. This has meant operating in a way that would not run counter to middle-class political mores. Patronage and payoffs have had to be pushed in the background. Blue-ribbon candidates for important offices, combined with professional administrators, have given recent Chicago administrations considerable respectability. They have also permitted much of the machine organization to be preserved.

The PAC did not enter the Democratic party in Chicago. Instead, it attempted to set up an independent political organization among union members to influence the party from the outside. The lack of regular party patronage and the continuing strength of the Chicago organization because of the measures undertaken by the machine have limited the success of PAC. Labor here has needed the politicians more than the machine has needed labor.[16]

New York

In New York, labor has been more influential than in Chicago, because the Democratic party and the political machine developed considerable weakness during the reformist period. The internal dissensions which rent Tammany Hall cannot be recounted here. The influence of the garment workers rose markedly during the 1930's and 1940's. In 1959 the CIO and AFL unions merged into a Central Labor Council with a membership of approximately one and a half million. Although not too well structured, the Council was a political force of significant proportions.[17]

In 1961 the Central Labor Council demonstrated organized labor's frequent indifference to campaigns of reformers by showing itself largely indifferent to an anti-Tammany campaign, although it did back the reform group's candidate for mayor, Robert S. Wagner.

SUMMARY

The power exercised by political machines and political bosses had run its course by the time organized labor got around to political action at the local level. The impact of an improved technology, immigration curbs, the increasing bureaucratization and professionalization of industry and government had taken their toll of the highly personalized although opportunistic approach of the municipal "boss." In his place, an executive with managerial skill and broad community vision is now urgently required.

Labor's preoccupation with strictly labor goals and its increasing concern for a better civic posture produced sufficient internal conflicts so as to produce in many cities an antipathy between union leaders and municipal reformers. Yet, labor was frequently skeptical of alignments with existing political machines or their fragments and so failed to support these waning institutions. Labor views depended on AFL or CIO affiliation in many instances with the former more apt to line up with the political boss or his henchmen. The craft nature of the AFL unions tied them more closely to local affairs.

The CIO through its political action groups has evidenced greater likelihood

[16] Fay Calkins, *The CIO and The Democratic Party* (Chicago, 1952).

[17] See Walter S. Sayre and Herbert Kaufman, *Governing New York City* (New York, 1960), pp. 508–510.

of establishing independence at the local level. However, even in Detroit, where there is a militant union presumably able to influence a majority of the city's voters, the CIO has never succeeded in electing its own candidate to major office.

Underrepresentation in the politics of large American cities, especially those which are nonpartisan, does not prevent organized labor from strongly influencing civic action at times. It is safe to say that labor probably has less influence than businessmen collectively in determining what issues are important, what priorities should be given to those issues, and what should be done about them.

Leadership in a Large Manager City:
The Case of Kansas City

By STANLEY T. GABIS

ABSTRACT: Municipal leadership in Kansas City centers on the nonpartisan principle and the council-manager plan. Unlike many other cities with nonpartisan requirements, Kansas City has produced a nonpartisan system that has proved workable over a twenty-year period. But continuance depends on the viability of the Citizens Association, a nonpartisan—or bipartisan—group which has dominated Kansas City politics from its inception in 1941 to the present time, with a four-year break from 1959 to 1963. The Association has experienced some difficulty in keeping its leadership vital and in maintaining a sufficiently broad base to permit participation by the diverse elements of the community. The leadership responsibility of the Association, resumed in 1963, is of major importance in maintaining a stable source of power. Also, relations between the mayor and the manager are crucial, as experiences in the immediate past have shown. Under present arrangements, official and private groups are co-operating in achieving public objectives. A new sophistication is now being demanded of those to whom the manager is accountable.

Stanley T. Gabis, Ph.D., Kansas City, Missouri, is Associate Professor of Political Science in the Department of Political Science, University of Missouri. He previously taught at Michigan State University and University of Illinois, Chicago. He is presently Director, Graduate Program in Public Administration, located in Kansas City. He is author of Mental Health and Financial Management (1960).

ANY description or assessment of municipal leadership must take into consideration the larger governmental system of which the city is a part and the basic principles which underlie the frame of government. Our treatment moves in both of these directions. Kansas City has enjoyed a special brand of government for the past two decades. It has adhered, with only one major lapse, to a nonpartisan system. Kansas City's nonpolitical character is plausible enough if construed in a narrow sense.

One learns very soon that the city is regarded as a special case among seasoned politicians. It is a "chosen" city, scarcely approximating the "New Jerusalem" but partaking nonetheless of the virtue of a city that has been newly purged. One need only read the remarkable address of Governor Lloyd Stark to the Missouri legislature during the closing-out of the Pendergast system. In recommending that the state regain control of the Kansas City police department, Stark referred to the "arbitrary and despotic power of partisan politics" and "political slavery" and declared that "in the enforcement of law, politics is public enemy number one."[1] Even today the state retains control of the city police through a local board with members appointed by the governor. This is scarcely a negligible factor in city administration, for the charge on the general city budget for police services is slightly over 20 per cent and carries very limited budgetary review by the city. The purge some twenty-four years ago had major consequences for municipal leadership, for it created new jurisdictional relationships and a different style of direction. Some might hold that it merely allowed the principles of the charter adopted in 1925 to find expression after lying dormant for

[1] *Kansas City Star*, March 23, 1939, p. 8.

fifteen years under the heavy weight of unenlightened despotism.

The county, state, and nation are given over to politics in the full sense of the word. The city, under the dispensation of the early-twentieth-century reformers, can, because of its different nature, operate on a radically different theory. Nonpartisanship and the city-manager idea presuppose a unique quality and blend of rationality, personal detachment, and know-how which can find application in the municipality because its problems are thought to be mainly technical. We have interviewed experienced politicians who are deeply immersed in state and county politics. When the subject of Kansas City was raised, they drew a curtain between the city and the rest of the state. The city, they asserted, can be treated as a technical rather than a political problem. We understood this as a sincere act of faith, will, and intelligence. This is the art of government in the modern sense, for it represents an expression of man's vision and his intention to superimpose on a large human collectivity a set of principles with the full expectation of achieving a desired result.

This radical subordination of political passion and involvement to a dispassionate and technical attitude presupposes certain values and assumptions about the nature of local government. A consensus is more easily arrived at in the city. Voters can think of issues rather than party labels. The public interest is much more readily discernible in local government, for the voter can readily judge the effect of a proposed program. Local issues can be more readily resolved on their merits than by becoming mixed with questions of party organization, survival, and prestige. An individual's voting behavior can be neatly stratified so that he is encouraged to deal with local issues without getting involved with national or state matters. Individual perspectives derived from socioeconomic status or ethnic background do not seem to have the same relevance in the local setting where men are much closer together and therefore better able to understand each other. Because local government is primarily a technical problem, it is much easier to develop precise, formal criteria for the valid selection of experts to man the highest administrative posts. The professional city manager symbolizes a belief in the great value of technical know-how in solving the city's problems. The mayor can be reduced primarily to a ceremonial figure who propagates the faith and co-ordinates the consensual activities of the council. He should not be intimately involved with the manager's activities.[2]

This is a rough approximation and summary of the axioms which control nonpartisan government. Some of them are reasonable and, when acted on with prudence and understanding, are essential to making the system work. A few of the axioms are simply fictions which are used, as Eric Fromm says, "to catch mice." Several are self-deceptions sometimes believed by clever men who have suspended critical judgment where the "chosen" city is concerned.

Because we seek to describe leadership in Kansas City in relation to the larger governmental system and the underlying principles and axioms of nonpartisan government, we will try to tie the immediate past to the present and delineate actions which suggest both the opportunities and ambiguities

which arise as a result of this system or in spite of it.[3] About a decade ago, Paul Appleby made an interesting observation on leadership which reflects the orientation of this essay: [4]

Leadership roles . . . are exercised in influencing, identifying and operating within respective areas of discretion. While such areas of discretion widen and contract with particular leaders and with changes in time and circumstances, they are always confined within limits policed by the public and somewhat roughly made clear by history, institutions and custom.

THE PENDERGAST HERITAGE

Nonpartisan government incorporating the idea of a professional city manager was formally adopted in Kansas City in 1925 with the adoption of a new charter. Despite the letter and spirit of the charter, its central provisions did not become really effective until fifteen years later. The proponents of the new charter had not reflected sufficiently on the fact that all frames of government must operate within a political context with power and normative concerns defining the boundaries of possible action. At the time the charter was adopted, Thomas J. Pendergast controlled the Democratic organization in Kansas City. He apparently understood the realities of power infinitely better than the advocates of charter reform. Rather than oppose the new frame of government, he allowed it to pass, and, when it did,

[2] For a good discussion of nonpartisanship, see Edward C. Banfield and James Q. Wilson, City Politics (Cambridge, Mass.: Harvard University Press and the Massachusetts Institute of Technology Press, 1963), Chap. 12.

[3] Useful material on the recent background of Kansas City government and politics is found in Howard D. Neighbor, Metamorphosis of Non-Partisan Politics: Kansas City, Missouri (Kansas City, Mo.: Community Studies, Inc., 1962); and A. Theodore Brown, The Politics of Reform: Kansas City's Municipal Government—1925–1950 (Kansas City, Mo.: Community Studies, Inc., 1958).

[4] Paul H. Appleby, Morality and Administration in Democratic Government (Baton Rouge, La.: Louisiana State University Press, 1952), p. 102.

he and his organization simply embraced the new system. He controlled the votes and the council. Under the new plan, the council was easier to control because its numbers had been reduced. Because he controlled the council, he could ratify the selection of the manager. The manager served at the pleasure of the council and Pendergast could be assured that the first manager, Henry F. McElroy, would be responsive to the needs of the Democratic organization as well as his personal requirements. This is exactly how the affair turned out. McElroy was recruited shortly after serving a term as one of the three judges (administrators) of Jackson County.[5]

McElroy held the manager post throughout the period of Pendergast dominance, about fifteen years. During this time, his master gained almost total control of the various factions in Kansas City. His sphere of control during the 1930's included Jackson County, and eventually his influence was strongly felt at the state capitol in Jefferson City. His leadership was state-wide, and this in turn gave him an important voice in national party circles. Since the close of the Pendergast system, Kansas City has not been able to produce another leader with state-wide influence. Furthermore, because there is a tendency of a large unbossed city to generate a number of factions, it is fair to say that, with all its deficiencies, Pendergast rule regulated factional activity and made orderly government possible. When the Democratic factions—or Coalition—returned to power in 1959, there was no individual who had the power and authority to unify the activities of factional representatives in the council.

During this four-year period, there was, for all practical purposes, no effective government operating in Kansas City.

Pendergast operated with one-party government based on a deliverable vote. He spread the benefits wide enough so that he controlled the vote of the economically and socially depressed and also commanded the allegiance of a sufficient number of well-born and well-to-do to give his system a legitimate basis. His appointments were skillfully made to assure the continuance of his power and to accomplish the minimum requirements of local government. In exceptionally sensitive areas, such as the judiciary and school board, more than normal care was exercised and some good appointments were made. Pendergast operated as a political virtuoso, showing an enormously shrewd understanding in manipulating people and moving the levers of power. He held no official position, but his return was very large. It consisted of despotic power exercised behind the scenes. At a more mundane level, he benefited considerably from his connections. Firms he owned or in which he had an interest virtually monopolized city and county contracts in the construction field, and pressure was frequently brought to bear on private contractors to do business with his concerns. Probably his unofficial status facilitated this arrangement.[6]

Pendergast's great power and facility bred carelessness and perhaps even boredom. Ordinarily, in a competitive political system, sufficient excitement and variety are generated to keep the interests and attention of the participants at a fairly high pitch. The competitive element was absent from the system. In his later years, Pendergast

---

[5] Harry S. Truman served on the court with McElroy. Both were protégés of Pendergast. Truman's loyalty to Pendergast lasted until the end.

[6] See Brown, *op. cit.*, pp. 189ff. for results of audit of city records.

derived great pleasure from horse-race betting. His wagers were on a very large scale, which suggested a kind of addiction. In a curious way, his interest in horse racing seemed to overshadow his interest in politics. His trial and imprisonment in 1939 on the grounds of receiving large bribes in connection with insurance rebates came rather suddenly. Behind the breaking up of his power was the United States Department of Justice, indirectly the President of the United States, and more directly the governor of Missouri, for the state superintendent of insurance had collaborated with Pendergast in the payoff scheme.[7]

THE CITIZENS ASSOCIATION (1941–1963)

The fall of the Pendergast regime, accompanied as it was by a scandal of national proportions, was a shattering experience for the people of Kansas City and for the entire state. The Pendergast heritage still lingers more as a monument in ruins.

William Reddig suggests that the McElroy (Pendergast) regime was a businessman's government, that the machine was an instrument of the business community during most of its existence in the twenties and thirties. Observing that the reform group which followed Pendergast was a "businessman's government," he raises the question as to whether reform is compatible with the pursuit of private economic interests. Following Lincoln Steffens, he suggests the possibility "that private economic interests by their very nature required corrupt

politics."[8] This is surely an oversimplification and distortion of the political and business process. Human power, whether it be found in politics, business, or any other form of human activity, is subject to abuse. Business interests, because they are private, can prosper at the expense of the public interest and with indifference to it until gradually public qualities are destroyed, carrying private interests with them. There are businessmen who can function effectively in their public as well as in their private roles, and a number of them do. But his point carries weight, for a business oligarchy joined with political power might be more dangerous than a political oligarchy, for it can hide behind the cloak of respectability and call on massive economic power to discriminate against those who disagree.

In the Kansas City experience, the opposite happened. Businessmen with reform interests were prominent in organizing the Citizens Association in 1941. This nonpartisan or bipartisan group has dominated Kansas City political life from its inception to the present time, with a four-year break from 1959 to 1963. The Association was an amalgamation or coalition of a variety of different forces and interests. The professions were probably as widely represented as the business interests. Liberal Democrats, conservative and liberal Republicans, and even some members of the hard-core Democratic organization previously associated with Pendergast found their way into Association ranks. Mr. Thomas Gavin, who was well regarded by the administration during the fifties, was endorsed by the Association and is a good example of the latter. Reddig's concern notwithstanding, an important problem which has always faced the

[7] Extensively discussed in Maurice M. Milligan, *Missouri Waltz* (New York: Charles Scribner's Sons, 1948). Milligan was the United States District Attorney who investigated the vote frauds of the 1930's. At that time, Senator Truman attempted to block Milligan's reappointment. *Ibid.*, p. 160.

[8] William M. Reddig, *Tom's Town* (Philadelphia: J. B. Lippincott Co., 1947, p. 370.

Association is keeping capable businessmen interested and involved.

The gradual decline in the Association's effectiveness during the middle and late fifties was caused by two kinds of problems. The first characterizes all organizations—keeping its leadership vital and replenishing sources of supply. The second, which may be even more difficult, involves maintaining a wide enough base to permit broad participation by the diverse elements of the community. The tendency toward exclusiveness, either in the interest of maintaining purity of doctrine or perhaps even encouraging in a subtle way a social class distinction, limited the base. Labor, Negro, and Italian ethnic groups have, in the past, seldom found their way into the Association. This is beginning to change. Two Negroes were elected to the Council in 1963 and are active in the Association. The only holdover in the new Council, Mr. Sal Capra, has roots in the Italian community. He is a young, ambitious lawyer of the new Italian middle class. His sponsor and uncle, Mr. Alex Presta, was until very recently a major Democratic faction leader who controlled the first ward and relied on lower-class ethnic support. After the 1963 election, Presta retired and moved to the suburbs after admitting that his traditional basis for support was disappearing. The upward mobility of his constituents and major urban-renewal activities took their toll.[9]

There are other specific problems in maintaining the coalition. In the 1959

election, which brought the Democratic factions back into power, there was a serious defection in the Citizens Association which reflected a narrowing of the base. Professor Howard D. Neighbor has made a careful analysis of the defector.[10] He defines the defector as one who was in sympathy with the Citizens Association in 1955 but switched to the Democratic Coalition in 1959. In his sample, almost one fourth of these who voted for the Coalition fit the defector pattern. First, the defectors tended to middle or upper-middle income status. Second, the defector identified with the national Democratic party by almost three to one. Neighbor suggests that it is easier for a Democrat to defect than it is for a Republican, who is more likely to sacrifice his national party preference in the interests of the Citizens Association. This is rather ambiguous. It is true that, inasmuch as Missouri voting behavior is normally Democratic, the Association has been reluctant throughout its history to slate a Republican for mayor. Republicans are slated for the city council in a division with Democrats. Republicans usually require some kind of clearance with the Republican county committee. Doubtless, it is a sacrifice for Republicans to take a Democratic mayor each election year. Until 1963 this did not present any real difficulty. At this time, a defection took place among Republicans. Mr. Dutton Brookfield, a prominent businessman and conservative Republican, deserted the Association and formed a separate group known as the Independent Voters Association (IVA) because he failed to receive the endorsement for mayor. If the public had not been so deeply aroused as a result of the poor record of the Democratic Coalition during the previous four years, there could have

[9] Studying three precincts of the first ward in Kansas City, Richard A. Watson was able to show a definite trend away from the Democrats as a direct result of urban renewal between 1951 and 1959. See his *The Politics of Urban Change* (Public Affairs Monograph Series No. 3; Kansas City, Mo.: Community Studies, Inc., 1963). The trend has been accentuated since 1959.

[10] Neighbor, *op. cit.*, pp. 149 ff.

been serious consequences for the Association. Though the Democratic Coalition gave its support to Brookfield in an effort to defeat the Association, the public was sufficiently aroused to compensate for the Republican defection as well as Coalition support. The Democratic defector faces real dificulties. About the only place a Democrat can go locally is back to the Coalition camp. This is very difficult to do because of past associations. The only other possibility is to form a new grouping, which has the effect of adding another faction to the lengthy list. Recently, a new organization has emerged known as the Democratic Council, composed mainly of younger liberal Democrats who are no longer comfortable in the Association and who have little in common with the regular Democratic factions. Some of the 1959 defectors are to be found in this camp.

THE CITY MANAGER

H. F. McElroy's long tenure as manager depended upon a stable base of power. He had this in Pendergast and the boss-controlled council. The same principle applies to L. P. Cookingham, who succeeded McElroy in 1940 and served to 1959. His source of support was the Citizens Association and its representatives on the council. Cookingham took out an extra margin of insurance by establishing a network of Community Councils throughout the city. These are neighborhood organizations which meet periodically and which were originally established to provide a means for stimulating community interest in their neighborhoods. Professional staff was assigned to work with the Councils. There was no explicit political intention, but, over the years, the political implications of the Councils in helping to provide popular support for the manager became clear to anyone with sensitivity to these matters.[11]

After Cookingham resigned in 1959 there was, and continues to be, speculation as to the cause of his departure. The most obvious and probably most valid reason is that, with the defeat of the Citizens Association in that year, a new group took power and simply did not believe in the manager principle. There was additional speculation. Cookingham, it was asserted, had been in office too long; many petty grievances had piled up over the years; he restricted his activities to middle and upper income groups; he was mainly interested in the physical, and not the human, side of the city. Perhaps there is some degree of plausibility in all of these criticisms. No profession is without its limitations, and some of them are built into the profession. The city manager is no exception. But the complaints seem very minor when compared with Cookingham's outstanding record over nineteen years. We suggest that the crucial factor lay in the leadership of the Citizens Association and the type of men who were slated for the 1955 council. The decline in Cookingham's fortunes began with the 1955 mayor and council. The manager was fortunate in his first two mayors, John B. Gage and William E. Kemp. They understood that the value of the manager principle lay in the expertise the manager could bring to his job and the relative freedom he had in applying this expertise. Also, the profession adheres to rather well-defined standards and ethics which, if seriously violated, lead almost inevitably to the manager's resignation. H. Roe Bartle, who was mayor from 1955 to 1963, paid voluble lip service to the manager

[11] See A. Theodore Brown, "The Politics and Administration of Welfare," in Edward C. Banfield, *Urban Government* (New York: The Free Press of Glencoe, 1961), p. 552.

principle but never seemed to understand the quality of initiative which had to be left to the manager. If he understood, his personality and inclinations would not let him follow his understanding. He did not hesitate to eclipse the manager and was unable as leader of the council to restrain some of his more ambitious colleagues from upsetting the equilibrium on which the manager depends.

In the face of ambition and aggressiveness, the manager is defenseless and vulnerable, for he can easily be made to appear an authoritarian figure in a very negative sense. It was exactly this approach which was used very effectively in the 1959 election which led to the unseating of Cookingham. Personalities and attitude counted heavily in this unfortunate denouement of a distinguished public official. One must also add the mounting frustration at the intractability of the city's mounting financial problem, which by 1959 had reached the critical stage. There was no effective political leadership willing to grapple with the problem. The Citizens Association had defaulted on its responsibility. It was not until the city experienced four humiliating years of inaction and factionalism under the Democratic Coalition (1959–1963) that it was prepared to restore its mandate to the Citizens Association. By 1963 the Association had become revitalized and was prepared to reassume responsible leadership.

LEADERSHIP—THREE EXAMPLES

Financial crises

From the middle 1950's to the new administration in 1963, the handling of the financial question illustrated the lack of an effective center of leadership and discipline. In 1953 an earnings tax was recommended by consultants as a solution to the growing money problem. The same year the council refused to support state legislation providing for a distribution of a portion of the state income tax to the city. The question of an earnings tax was seriously considered by the council in 1956. A number of the councilmen immersed themselves in detail and, as a result, arrived at a variety of views that scarcely encouraged a unified approach. A positive decision, lacking in enthusiasm, was reached in February 1956, a month before elections. At that time the councilmen agreed that they would *not* carry the question to the voters but would rely on a citizen group. The earnings tax was decisively rejected.

In the 1959 election, the Democratic Coalition candidates pledged that they would not support an earnings tax if elected. They tied their hands very explicitly. Two years after the Coalition victory, one of its leading members on the council admitted he was mistaken and changed his position. In the 1963 campaign, both candidates for mayor advocated the earnings tax. Following the victory of the Citizens Association in the spring of 1963, Carleton F. Sharpe, a city manager of national standing, was hired. With the new mayor, Ilus W. Davis, and the manager working closely together, a systematic campaign for the tax was mounted. Members of the council devoted a large portion of their time over a period of several months addressing groups throughout the community on the question. The mayor and the manager provided strong leadership throughout the campaign. Almost immediately after his election, the new mayor, faced with a deadline, had proceeded to the state capitol and persuaded state leaders of the need for enabling legislation. Influential community leaders also added their voices.

The *Kansas City Star* gave unusually strong press support throughout the entire period, including a series of fairly detailed stories on the difficulties a number of departments were experiencing in their programs as a result of financial limitations. The general picture painted was one of a major city falling behind other cities, departments undermanned in crucial categories, city maintenance behind schedule and equipment in disrepair or increasingly obsolescent, inadequate vermin-control programs, underpaid personnel, the absence of an adequate pension plan and other standard fringe benefits. The picture drawn was very convincing. Powerful community groups which had been hesitant, opposed, or lukewarm in 1956 supported the mayor and manager with a new feeling of confidence that had been generated over a period of several months. Reluctant labor unions —the earnings tax was a flat half of one per cent with no exemptions—were brought into line with a frank appeal to self-interest. Without the tax, the mayor argued, major public construction would be delayed. Representatives of the construction unions listened, for they needed jobs for their members. Only a few unions failed to support the tax. City employees, firemen, and police were mobilized as far as etiquette would permit and perhaps even more. Again, self-interest was a key. Department heads went on the stump and several proved very effective in portraying in graphic detail what increased revenue would mean to their departments. The Negro councilmen who joined the government in 1963, after indicating an initial concern over the fate of pending proposals on public accommodations and after receiving reassurance that the needs of the Negro community would receive sympathetic consideration, supported the tax and devoted themselves energetically to persuading their constituents to follow suit. The public accommodations bill was passed prior to the earnings tax election but, as a result of a petition initiated by tavernkeepers, has to be submitted to a referendum as provided by charter. In the November 1963 referendum, the tax received a required two-thirds endorsement, although of five badly needed bond issues only one received the necessary two-thirds required under Missouri law.

Personnel crisis

The leadership and community esprit so completely lacking in 1956 was present in full force in 1963. Widespread public confidence in the new administration has permitted the mayor and manager to deal forthrightly with difficult situations. In one recent case, the firemen's union persuaded a councilwoman to propose a resolution providing for an increase in salary for firemen complementing an increase recently given the police, who are subject to state direction through a local police board and over whom the city has no direct control. This move in the council was very embarrassing for the manager. After finances, personnel improvements had been given the next highest priority. When Cookingham had left in 1959, department heads and highly trained staff personnel departed or were pressured into resigning by the new council. When Sharpe assumed his duties in June 1963, he found, with few exceptions, that the departments had been stripped of high caliber personnel, and inadequate city pay levels did not allow their replacement. As new department heads were added, salaries were raised for new heads. This could be done by ordinance in each case. But, below the top posts, the entire classification-pay structure was involved, and the need for a survey was strongly indicated. In the fall of 1963, a broad personnel survey was initiated. It was designed to study the entire range of personnel activity —recruiting, training, health and other fringe benefits—as well as classification and pay. The essence of the approach was a systematic and orderly attack on the entire personnel problem. The city's hand had been forced in the case of the police increase, but, if the firemen were given an across-the-board increase several months before pay adjustments for other city employees, any possibility of installing an effective and rational personnel program would be seriously jeopardized. But, perhaps even more important, the demands of the firemen represented a serious challenge to the authority and prestige of the new manager.

In two dramatic confrontations with firemen at their union hall, Sharpe pleaded with them that they await the personnel report due in March 1964. He assured them of his good intentions and pointed to his record in Hartford. The aggressive leader of the union, a city battalion chief, could not be persuaded, and, for several days, firemen demonstrated by circling city hall carrying placards expressing their grievance in terms unflattering to Manager Sharpe. Although the demonstrations were given wide publicity and the wives of firemen bombarded the manager's office with importunate phone calls, public opinion supported the position of the administration. Sharpe had gone on record at one meeting with the firemen declaring that a new manager would have to be found if the city gave in to the pressure. After several days of demonstration and a series of conferences with union leaders and their counsel, a former councilman who had been one of the leaders in bringing about the demise of Cookingham in 1959, the union decided to suspend its demonstration and await the findings of the personnel study and its implementation.

Kansas City Athletics crisis

Another matter, still unresolved at this writing, concerned the future status of the Kansas City Athletics. This major-league ball team had been brought to Kansas City in 1956 and housed in a refurbished municipal stadium amid great fanfare symbolizing a new stage in the development of the city. The previous council, in April 1963, immediately prior to its departure from office, had granted a new stadium lease to the owner, Mr. Charles O. Finley, on terms that were widely regarded as not in the best interests of the city. The new council, on assuming office, decided for reconsideration and negotiations began anew.

The intensity of public attention during various periods of the renegotiation far exceeded anything else of public importance. It is fair to say that the merger of the private University of Kansas City with the University of Missouri in August 1963 created less stir in the community than the prospect that Finley would take his team elsewhere, as he threatened to do repeatedly over the ensuing months. The news media, especially television, gradually developed a most unattractive picture of Finley showing him with a somewhat battered hat, an unshaved profile, and a grim mouth clenching a cigar stub. Finley became a villain in the eyes of the public. Mayor Davis assumed the burden of the negotiations, although Sharpe was deeply involved. Finley followed a procedure of calculated harassment and, as if by design, demanded meetings at odd intervals which insured the maximum disruption of city business. The climax was reached when the matter was appealed by the city to President Cronin of the American

League, who in turn called a conference of American League club owners to consider the matter. Before the issue was resolved in favor of the city, two United States Senators from Missouri, Edward V. Long and Stuart F. Symington, became directly involved. Senator Symington, together with city officials, attended the meeting of club owners in January 1964. The noted attorney, Louis Nizer, was retained by Finley, presumably to add to the efforts of regular attorney Mr. Tom Kean, a prominent Chicago politician. The case caused reverberations throughout the sports world and stimulated several members of the United States Senate to think seriously of re-examining the exemptions which organized baseball enjoys under antitrust laws. Throughout this difficult situation, Manager Sharpe received letters of commiseration from fellow city managers around the county.

What is the meaning of these examples? Several ideas are suggested. Each case had the potentiality of destroying the manager. If he had not received affirmative and thoughtful support from the mayor and council, as well as the news media, his situation might have become completely untenable. Provision for a fixed term of office gives some assurance that a strong wind will not endanger the survival of an official. However, the manager serves at the pleasure of the council. His special vulnerability has to be recognized and understood.

The cases also tend to show how it is possible for problems confronting municipal leaders to become deeply involved with larger political and administrative systems far beyond the purview of the city. In an important respect, it is inaccurate to discuss municipal leadership per se if this means disregarding relationships to the larger system, embracing not only the federal, state, and county jurisdictions but important private groups within the city as well.[12]

SUMMARY ANALYSIS

We return to Appleby's statement which provides the unifying thread of this essay. What he is saying suggests an expansive role for leadership contained in the words "influencing," "identifying," and "operating." There is an area of discretion which varies with individuals and situations. There are limits imposed by the public and traditions of society. We believe all of what he says is illustrated in our remarks.

Twenty-three years ago, the Citizens Association was a new creation. Now it has roots and a tradition. Although it can pass as a major local institution, the possibility of collision with longer established political entities is always possible. Recently, a candidate for Democratic nomination for governor of Missouri sought the endorsement of a major leader of the Citizens Association. The Citizens leader has refused to meet with the candidate for governor for fear of jeopardizing a forthcoming bond referendum. This leader is a liberal Democrat with a brilliant political future, but, for the time being, he has accepted the restraints which nonpartisan leadership place upon him. The former mayor, H. Roe Bartle, has agreed to serve as the candidate's campaign manager in Jackson County. Bartle no longer feels the need for adopting a nonpartisan role. The point

[12] Without the support of the *Kansas City Star* and the Kansas City Chamber of Commerce, the earnings tax would not have been passed. Without their continued support on important issues, the manager could not survive. It is instructive to note that both the manager and the executive vice-president of the Chamber of Commerce were recently recruited from Hartford, Connecticut.

is that we have two established systems in incipient conflict, for one refuses to supplement the other in the political sphere. Who can measure the consequences as far as future personal political fortunes are concerned?

The nonpartisan system seems theoretically impossible, yet it has worked with varying degrees of efficiency for more than two decades. It has a direct effect on strategies of public leadership. In interviews which we conducted to gather material for this essay, we attempted to discover whether the nonpartisan character of Kansas City hampered it in dealing with partisan state officials. The state and city officials thought there was no hindrance on this score. When the city has to deal with the state, its leaders are required to develop specific group support in the community. If this support is impressive, articulate, and united and its case is a good one, the city receives a sympathetic hearing and has good prospects of getting what it wants. There seems to be a basic reasonableness that transcends partisan considerations.

City-county relationships are different. The city and the county seem to operate in two separate worlds, although their headquarters confront one another on the same street. The Democratic factions control the county and are tied in directly to the state and national political system. None of the values which characterize nonpartisanship is in evidence in the county. Yet some of the most crucial problems confronting the city depend on close co-operation between the two jurisdictions. Law enforcement, property assessment, public health, prisons, and metropolitan area planning require a close relationship between the two. It may well be that the conflict in values is a major barrier to co-operation.

The relationship between the mayor and the manager emerges as an important point for consideration. The relationship between Pendergast and McElroy served to bring about an unusually stable balance. But it was a balance that was not effectively policed by the public. Cookingham achieved an excellent balance with his first two mayors and had a misfortune with the third. Davis and Sharpe have developed an excellent relationship in the new administration. Sharpe does not like the word "politics," but he regards "public relations" as being an exceptionally important function. Government for him includes not only the official side but also private groups that can co-operate with the city in achieving public objectives. This requires a dividing line to avoid having the private sphere control the public. Housekeeping responsibilities are important, but secondary to planning and public relationships. The rationale of the manager principle has shifted in emphasis. With this shift, the manager becomes more vulnerable but more valuable. His expertise is not so much technical as prudential in the classic meaning of the term. A new sophistication is now being demanded on the part of those to whom the manager is accountable.

Dade County: Unbossed, Erratically Led

By Thomas J. Wood

ABSTRACT: Personal political leadership in Dade County—Miami, Florida—when it does exist, tends to be short-lived and limited in scope—that is, confined to a particular area of the county or to a particular level of government. The elements of the political environment which produce a high degree of political atomization are ever-changing factions in a one-party state, failure of the multitudes of newly arrived residents to identify themselves with the governmental problems of the area, the predominance of suburban attitudes and values together with a lack of organization of minority groups whether or not they be disadvantaged, and local governmental forms stressing nonpartisanship and the short ballot. The newspapers, which have greater than normal weight owing to the peculiar dependence of the newcomers on the papers, wield substantial influence. No recent newspaper publisher or editor has attempted to develop personal political leadership. A newspaper in alliance with an attractive leader could become a potent political force.

Thomas J. Wood, Miami, Florida, is Professor of Government at the University of Miami, having served previously as instructor at Williams College. He has followed closely the development of metropolitan government in Dade County and has reported this for the National Civic Review.

FIFTEEN years ago, in discussing Florida politics, V. O. Key wrote "those [politicians] who deliver their home county are few. Florida is not only unbossed, it is also unled." [1] Ten years later, Dennis O'Harrow of the American Society of Planning Officials noted in a report on Dade County, "there is no clear and apparent leader or group of leaders as there is in most cities and metropolitan areas." [2] Today, while it may be argued that Dade County is sometimes led, it is still unbossed.

The factors creating an environment in which political atomization is encouraged are (1) the state pattern of amorphous factions in a one-party system, (2) the rapid increase in population from the end of World War II to 1960, (3) the overwhelming suburban character of most of Dade County, and (4) the nonpartisan character of most of Dade County politics.

WEAK PARTY SYSTEM

Although Florida has become a two-party state presidentially, in state politics and in most local politics it is still the exclusive preserve of the Democratic party. Since Reconstruction, the Republicans have elected neither a governor nor a senator; they have elected two congressmen and a number of local officials in a handful of counties. Republicans in Dade County, who now constitute one seventh of the registered voters, have not elected a county official in this century, although they did secure a majority within the county for their gubernatorial candidate in 1928. There are a sufficient number of hidden Republican voters to ensure almost any

Republican candidate a third or more of the total vote in a general election, but the Republican party does not constitute a sufficient threat to engender much cohesion within the Democratic ranks. Nor is the Republican vote large enough to encourage many Republican hopefuls to part with the qualifying fee. A nineteen-year-old student of the writer, attending a "screening" committee meeting of the Republican county organization recently, was importuned to run for the state legislature; pressure to run was removed only when he revealed his age.

Factional lines have always been difficult to discern in Democratic politics in Florida; the group which elects a candidate today may split half a dozen ways in electing his successor. Few political leaders have permanent followings; rather, they must regroup their armies for each battle, filling up the ranks with perhaps a majority of new recruits.

The Dade County Democratic organization is loosely held together and lacks influence. Composed of one man and one woman elected from each of forty districts, the executive committee chooses a county chairman who can derive no prestige from this position but, rather, may increase party prestige by bringing to this position power gained elsewhere. The county executive committee controls no patronage and generally plays only a small role in the conduct of general election campaigns. More likely than not, presidential, gubernatorial, and senatorial nominees will bypass the committee.

The lack of importance attached to the executive committee and the concomitant unsuitability of it as a power base may be illustrated by the fact that at the time of the most recent election of the members a twenty-one-year-old student of the writer, urged at the last minute to get into politics, won his race

[1] V. O. Key, *Southern Politics* (New York: A. A. Knopf Co., 1949), p. 82.

[2] Dennis O'Harrow, "Metropolitan Planning for Dade County: A Summary Report," Miami, December 1958, mimeographed, p. 51.

with little campaigning. Some positions are uncontested.

Thus, there is no Democratic organization for a boss to capture and to use and no really competitive Republican organization has appeared in opposition.

INCREASE OF POPULATION

The second factor tending to encourage political disorganization is the rapid growth of population. At the close of World War II, Dade had 315,000 persons; today, it is estimated that the population approaches 1,100,000. Comparatively few of today's voters were born in the county or even in the state. These voters have been slow to develop "traditional habits of action with respect to local personages, leaders, parties, and issues." Some never put down roots in the community, retaining, rather, loyalty to their former state to which they return each summer. Others build community ties very slowly because of frequent changes of houses. Dr. Reinhold Wolff, Dade research economist, states that in the first half of the 1950's Dade residents were among the most mobile in the country in terms of intracounty moving. Another measure of mobility is derived from the 1960 census which revealed that only 36 per cent of the 1960 population of Dade County over five years of age lived then in the same house they occupied in 1955.[3]

In a community thus composed, it is much more difficult for a political boss or leader to develop the bonds on which to build a reliable following. Many of the usual lines of communication between the leader and the led do not exist. In this state of flux, people are less likely to be members, much less attentive members, of the many neighborhood and community organizations

which serve as lines of communication for messages, whether they be political or otherwise. To an extent probably much greater than that noted in older, more stable communities, the residents of Dade County rely for their communications on the mass media, especially the newspapers. In the absence of an understanding between the would-be leader and the mass media, the political leader will have difficulty in reaching his potential followers or in retaining his organization if he is operating in an area larger than which he can supervise by personal contact.

POLITICS OF SUBURBIA

Like many of the newer communities in the Southwest, the Pacific Coast, and Florida, Dade County consists largely of one subdivision after another stretching from the ocean's edge to the Everglades. In this extended suburbia, middle-class virtues and values are dominant. There is a tendency to minimize political party and partisan political leadership and to extol nonpartisanship and good, clean, business management of public affairs. Although in other parts of the country in strongly suburban areas strong political leaders such as J. Russel Sprague of Nassau County, New York or Orville Hubbard of Dearborn, Michigan may appear, more usually suburban politics are characterized by a scramble of an ever-changing cast of amateur politicians for positions of leadership.[4]

A related factor contributing to the degree of political disintegration in Dade County is the fact that more than 400,000 persons live in the unincorporated areas of the county and have no easily understood and easily influenced unit of government with which to deal. They have only the county to look to

[3] *Congressional District Data Book* (88th Congress House Document 132; Washington, D. C.: U. S. Printing Office, 1964), p. 95.

[4] Charles Adrian, *Governing Urban America* (New York: McGraw-Hill Co., 1955), pp. 126–131.

for their services, whether these services are county-wide in nature or are municipal in type, such as trash collection or fire prevention. The county tends to be so big and so remote that the average citizen finds difficulty in relating to it or to any particular county political figure.

Since all metro commissioners are now elected on a county-wide basis, it will be difficult for a commissioner to find a sharply differentiated foundation on which to build his organization. During the first six years of metro, a portion of the commission was elected from districts and another portion from the larger cities of the county. The men thus chosen had an opportunity to build an organization based on reasonably narrow geographic limits. Some were sufficiently successful to cause alarm among the downtown businessmen and the newspapers who favored a greater degree of centralization so that a change in the method of commission representation was initiated late in 1963.

WEAK MINORITY GROUP ORGANIZATION

The suburban quality of most of the county is not compensated for by the existence of tightly organized disadvantaged groups within the core city (Miami). One group of significant size is the Negroes—who constitute 15 per cent of the residents, 9 per cent of the registered voters, and perhaps 5 per cent of those who actually vote. The Negroes have not yet become an important force in politics, although there are no official obstacles to their voting and very few unofficial barriers except perhaps in the agricultural southern reaches of the county where unorganized resident and migrant field workers are subject to mild forms of intimidation.

No single Negro political leader has emerged since the white primary was invalidated in 1944. Today, in the cen-

tral two-thirds of the county, four Negroes are regarded as sharing the political power in this community; each has a different power base. None can be regarded as a real "boss," and only one is known by many outside the Negro community.

The strongest has generally held a state patronage post dispensed by one of the successful candidates for state-wide office (the governor or one of the cabinet members); he is also a deputy constable. With more contacts with white political leadership than the others, he is the most influential in delivering votes but is important only in a very close county election or in an election in the smaller constituency of Miami. It is primarily his position as deputy constable which has enabled him to build up a following of persons grateful for flexible law enforcement.

The second most influential Negro leader is the public relations officer for the largest rental collection agency; formerly, he was the head of the local longshoremen's union. Intervention on behalf of tenants in arrears is the source of his political power. A third Negro leader is one of the two best-known Negro clergymen and an officer of the local National Association for the Advancement of Colored People (NAACP). His source of power is less tangible and the bonds with his followers more tenuous particularly now that Negroes desire more direct action and more immediate results than are usually obtainable via the normal NAACP law suit.

These three Negro leaders are decided individualists and have refused to consider a proposal to merge Negroes into one organization for political purposes. The fourth leader, the manager of a life-insurance company catering exclusively to Negroes, recognizes his relative weakness but has not been able to strike a bargain with any of the others. Despite the advantages they might derive from a united front, the Negro community has mirrored the disintegration of the whites.

The other large minority group, located mostly within the core city of Miami, is the Cubans, of whom there are now some 100,000 and of whom some 40 to 50,000 will remain after federal relocation efforts have ceased. Few of these have been in residence for a sufficiently long period of time to qualify for American citizenship and fewer now wish to relinquish Cuban citizenship, but, eventually, when special federal welfare funds are withdrawn, many of this group may be drawn into state and local welfare politics. At this time, they may produce a political boss as has the older Cuban community in Tampa.

Although there are nearly 100,000 Jews in Dade County, no county-wide Jewish leader has appeared. Mayor Aronovitz —whose role will be discussed later— had a following broader than that of the Jewish community and he never appealed to the Jews as such. Only in Miami Beach is there a noticeable cohesiveness of the Jewish vote in local elections. In the Miami Beach precincts lowest on the socioeconomic scale, blocs of votes have been delivered, but the operation is on a small scale.

No sufficiently large concentration of ethnic groups exists as a foundation for achieving significant political power within the county. One minor politician, who spent a dozen years attempting to develop a bloc of hyphenated groups, finally recognized the futility of his efforts and has recently turned to organizing the senior citizens for political purposes. Since these persons constitute 15 per cent of those over the age of twenty-one, and since many of them, having come here for retirement, identify themselves as retirees and in no other role, this group, too, may be the power base for a capable organizer.

SHORT BALLOT AND NONPARTISANSHIP

The fourth factor militating against strong political leaders is the preponderance of nonpartisanship in all but state and national elections. All but a few cities have council-manager government, and even the exceptions have nonpartisan elections. Of greater significance is the fact that many county officials, who elsewhere are elective, are appointive here under metro. Only the metro commissioner, the judicial posts, the state's attorney, and the school board are elective; of these, the metro commission is nonpartisan.

Also acting as a deterrent to the rise of local "bossism" in county politics is the recently adopted county-wide election of all members of the metro commission. When some commission members were elected from districts and cities, a politician well entrenched in a corner of the county could secure a seat and, by assiduously cultivating his own area, could retain such a seat. For example, the former mayor of North Miami created a small machine which, for a while, dominated politics in that city and was a determining factor in his successful race for a commission seat.

It was primarily to dislodge such local "bosses" as did exist that the newspapers and the downtown businessmen proposed and secured the adoption of the charter amendment abolishing the localized seats. When the commissioner from the North Miami area— and several others similarly situated— ran for the commission on a county-wide basis, they were defeated by comparatively unknown men backed by the newspapers and the businessmen.

A BOSS OF THE 1930's

In this unfavorable climate, the search for bosses is almost fruitless. Those who even approximate the description have tended to be short-lived in their careers, localized geographically within the county, or specialized as to the level of the governmental unit in which they acted. As a matter of fact, it may be argued that most of them are political "influentials" rather than "bosses."

Perhaps the only man who approached the status of a boss in Dade County was Dan Mahoney in the 1930's. As publisher of *The Miami News,* then the paper with the greatest circulation in South Florida, Mahoney combined the power of the press with control over a number of jobs, both governmental and semiprivate, such as those at the race tracks. He maintained a clubhouse for his followers, bankrolled frequent outings, and apparently delivered the votes of a large minority. But this organization was swamped in the rising tide of newcomers who streamed into Florida once the depths of the Depression had passed. The northwest section of Miami, where Mahoney's power had been centered, became only a minority of the city and an insignificant fraction of the whole county. In addition, *The Miami Herald,* purchased by the Knight interests in the late 1930's, soon rivaled *The News* in political influence. When State Senator William Graham, Mahoney's ally in local politics, ran for governor in the 1944 Democratic primary, he received only 57 per cent of the Dade County vote and failed to qualify for the runoff by 22,000 votes.

RECENT POLITICAL LEADERS

More recently, the individual possessing the greatest transferable political influence was Abe Aronovitz, one time mayor of Miami. His power was based on his reputation for complete honesty at a time when many Miami voters judged that this quality was in short supply in city politics. In a short period of two years, 1953–1955, he created an image of impeccability; this influence endured until his death in 1960 and even beyond that. After he left the Miami council, he sponsored one of the young men in his law office for mayor and was largely responsible for electing him. The latter has remained in that office and is currently a gubernatorial candidate. Aronovitz was influential in the election of three other persons to the Miami council during his lifetime, and, after his death, his reputation was at least a factor in the election of his nephew to the Miami council, first by the council to a vacancy and then by the voters to a full term. Another associate was elected to the metro commission primarily on the basis of the Aronovitz connection. This was Aronovitz's only venture into county politics; his success here was facilitated by the fact that the district from which his protege was elected was composed in large measure of Miami precincts.

Another localized political leader is Henry Milander, mayor of Hialeah since 1947. One of the very few strong mayors in Dade County, Milander has dominated politics in this lower-middle-class suburb for seventeen years, during which period the population has grown fourfold. In the face of contrary advice from the two Miami newspapers, his constituents have returned him to office eight times, usually with a complaisant council majority, and have rejected the establishment of a council-manager system. When Hialeah, by reaching the 60,000 mark in population, qualified for a seat of its own on the metro commission as constituted prior to January 1964, Milander persuaded Hialeah voters to elevate one of his most co-operative city councilmen to the commission post. Anyone who runs county-wide must reckon with Milander, who does interest himself in national, state, and county elections.

Milander's power is based on personal

contacts, personal favors, and fulfillment of suburban values. He is accessible to his constitutents, keeping long office hours and an open-door policy while allowing the town clerk to function as city manager. Prior to the advent of the metro traffic court, the mayor took care of thousands of traffic tickets and in other ways has eased the contact of the individual with his government.

By providing only a modest level of services and by relying heavily on taxes other than those on property, Hialeah under Milander has kept the homeowner's taxes low. In addition, property values have been protected. The tiny pre-Milander Negro enclave has been contained, and Negroes have not found a foothold elsewhere in the city despite the fact that the Negro community has been expanding rapidly in the northwest section of the county near Hialeah. It is interesting to note that Hialeah is the only city in the county which has been able to annex substantial numbers of persons in recent years. Few cities dare propose annexations, and usually those which are proposed are bitterly and successfully contested.

One of the most influential political leaders is the county campaign manager of the current governor. This person may have an important state office; he and his local committee have for patronage several hundred state positions, many of which are nonpaying, and, through having the ear of the governor, he can exercise a strong influence on the selection of men for positions filled on a state-wide basis. This, however, is a position of transitory importance. Since it is unusual for a man to manage two successive winners, the rate of turnover in this position is high.

The present successful gubernatorial campaign manager is Robert Morgan, head of a firm of auditors specializing in governmental auditing. Morgan is chairman of the state racing commission; undoubtedly he can find jobs for followers in the several tracks and *jai alai frontóns*. These jobs are in addition to those normally at his disposal as campaign manager in the largest county.

Morgan has for sometime been active in Democratic political circles. Candidates for state and county offices have sought his support not because he has a bloc of votes at his disposal but because he is a door-opener and a campaign fund-finder. He has also taken the lead in mobilizing a state-wide slate of delegates for the Democratic convention. Only once has he gone into politics on his own behalf; in 1958 he ran for the state party committee and for the county party committee and put up a slate of followers for the latter. He won both posts and his slate captured a majority on the county party committee, whereupon he was elected county chairman. Apparently, he had hoped to revitalize the formal party organization, but, before he could accomplish much, he became involved in gubernatorial politics and resigned as county chairman.

THE NEWSPAPERS AND POLITICAL LEADERSHIP

In his study of the advent of metropolitan government in Dade County, Professor Edward Sofen notes the central position of the editor of *The Miami Herald* in the political life of Dade County.[5] Without doubt, *The Herald* is the most important political force in the county. However, neither Mr. John Pennekamp, who had primary editorial responsibility during most of the 1940's and 1950's, nor his successor, Mr. Don Shoemaker, can be called bosses. Their power, and this applies especially to

[5] Edward Sofen, Miami Metropolitan Experiment (Bloomington, Ind.: Indiana University Press, 1963), p. 78.

Mr. Shoemaker, is institutional power, not personal power. Politicians believe that the endorsement of *The Herald* is worth 25 to 30,000 votes. In county contests in which the total vote does not exceed 150,000, such an advantage is more often than not the deciding factor.

A combination of the paper's influence and a political figure popular in his own right standing on a "good government" platform would be irresistible. But such a team has never come into being. It may be that the editors of *The Herald* are not comfortable with a man who has the ability to appeal successfully to the voters through other media. At the same time, such a politician might find that his area of discretion is too narrow when working in double harness.

In the most recent election of the metro commission, *The Herald's* choice for the new position of mayor was a commissioner of four years' experience, a businessman who had provided a large measure of the stability found in the old commission and who had led the defense of metro against crippling amendments in several campaigns. He and the editors of the paper saw eye-to-eye on all matters. But whatever his good qualities, and they were many, he was, in the words of one of his friends and supporters, "the world's worst politician." He was decisively defeated by a man whose metro qualities were unproved but whose ability to project himself personally and through the several media was overwhelmingly established.

Although seated in the most promising position in the county, the new mayor cannot hope to develop into a boss of any kind. Recent experience indicates that, while the newspapers cannot create a county-wide political leader, they can destroy those believed to be "bosses" or incipient "bosses" acting against the public good as defined by the papers. At the same time, the newspapers and particularly *The Herald* do not appear to be capable of sponsoring the development of a truly popular leader. Dade County is therefore destined to be unbossed and only erratically led.

Metropolitics and Professional Political Leadership: The Case of Nashville

By Daniel R. Grant

ABSTRACT: Adoption of a single metropolitan government for Nashville and Davidson County in 1962, at a time when many metro reform proposals have been rejected elsewhere, provides an opportunity to examine the role of professional political leaders in its formulation and adoption. Thirty years of Nashville suburban spillover without annexation led to the familiar pattern of a service vacuum, inequalities, rivalries, and confused responsibility. During the 1950's, two surveys by professional staffs, working closely with the Nashville mayor and a rival Davidson County judge, led to a proposal for major structural change (city-county consolidation) which was endorsed by both the mayor and the judge. Their support was undoubtedly helpful in the 1958 metro campaign, but it was rejected by the voters outside Nashville. Two windfall issues —annexation and an auto tax—and the opposition of the Nashville mayor contributed to a new and successful metro vote in 1962. The Nashville experience indicates that active involvement of rival professional political leaders in all stages of a metro reform movement is possible, is not necessarily a kiss of death, does not prevent "radical reform," and may actually constitute a tactical advantage for metropolitan reformers.

Daniel R. Grant, Ph.D., Nashville, Tennessee, is Professor of Political Science at Vanderbilt University. He served as consultant for the Nashville and Davidson County Planning Commissions in the formulation of the "Plan of Metropolitan Government" adopted in 1962 and is consultant for the U. S. Advisory Commission on Intergovernmental Relations. In 1958–1959 he was Visiting Professor of Municipal Government and Planning at the Institute of Public Administration, Thammasat University, Bangkok, Thailand. He is coauthor with H. C. Nixon of State and Local Government in America (1963), coauthor with Victor Jones and others of Metropolitan Surveys: A Digest (1958), coauthor with Lee S. Greene of Metropolitan Harris County (1957), and author of articles in various journals.

IN the search for scapegoats in the wake of unsuccessful "metro reform" efforts, eyes invariably turn to the professional politicians in the metropolitan area—the core-city boss and his "city hall crowd," the county boss and his "courthouse gang," and—or—the "parasitic suburban city officeholders." Many cases could be cited in which the professional politicians have been less than enthusiastic for metro reform proposals, and still others in which the public support of professional politicians amounted to a virtual kiss of death. The political boss is thus said to contribute to the defeat of metropolitan government reorganization proposals, *whatever* his stand on the issue.

While it is exceedingly difficult to pin the blame on any specific person or group for the rejection of metro reform, it should be helpful to look at the role of professional political leaders in the *adoption* of a major metro reform proposal. The newly adopted metropolitan government of Nashville and Davidson County provides such an opportunity. After rejecting in 1958 a city-county consolidation proposal supported by both the city and county political leaders, the electorate changed its mind and adopted a similar proposal in 1962 in spite of strong opposition from the mayor of the core city.

The role of professional political leaders in "metropolitics" should be illuminated by investigating the case of Nashville in four respects: (1) what was the relationship of the local political leaders to the growth of the "metropolitan-type" problems which seemed to call for major structural reform, (2) what was their relationship to early metropolitan reform strategy, (3) what was their role in the 1958 defeat and the 1962 victory for metro, and (4) what is the significance of having an *elective* metropolitan

mayor (rather than an appointive professional manager) in the process and problems of transition to a single metropolitan government for Nashville and Davidson County?

SETTING FOR METRO REFORM

Before considering these four questions, a brief look at the political setting of Nashville and Davidson County is in order as well as at certain relevant demographic and geographic factors. Located in the upper middle portion of the state of Tennessee, Davidson County covers 533 square miles and contains the state's capital city, located on the Cumberland River. Its historic sites include the Hermitage, home of Andrew Jackson, and the replica of the Parthenon. While Nashville is an educational and religious center of considerable significance and claims the title "the Athens of the South," it may well be better known as the home of the "Grand Ole Opry" and as the country-music capital of the nation.

Metropolitan Nashville has a diversified economy with a moderate amount of manufacturing—such as DuPont, Ford Glass, Gates Rubber, and Genesco —supplemented strongly by an above-average quantity of religious printing, insurance and banking establishments, educational institutions, and state and federal payrolls. Prior to the adoption of metropolitan government, the city's governmental form was a fairly strong mayor-council type, and the county was governed by a fifty-five-member "quarterly county court" and a county judge whose role was more that of titular head than genuine chief executive. Factional politics, rather than party politics, is the dominant theme at the local level, with Nashville Mayor Ben West and County Judge Beverly Briley heading rival factions for the decade before metro's adoption. Of equal or greater importance in the factional picture, the two daily newspapers in Nashville, the *Tennessean* and the *Banner,* have played strong and active roles in supporting the opposing factions.

Although the proportion of Nashville's population which is Negro (37.9 per cent in 1960) is comparable to that in many cities of the deep South, Nashville has earned a reputation as a moderately progressive city for its desegregation activities. In spite of bombings and other inflammatory incidents, it was able to carry out gradual desegregation of schools as well as desegregation of buses and of downtown eating establishments. Negroes had served on the city council and school board for many years, though not on the county governing body or county school board.

Core-city and suburban population trends are quite similar to those in metropolitan areas of comparable size. In the decade of the 1950's, Davidson County's population grew from 321,758 to 399,743, while Nashville's population dropped from 174,307 to 170,874, even after counting 4,587 residents annexed in 1958. While the core city did not lose population between 1940 and 1950, its 4.1 per cent increase contrasted sharply with the 64.1 per cent increase outside the city. Failure to annex any appreciable amount of territory after 1929 had kept the city's area down to less than twenty-three square miles as late as 1957. The rural portions of the county in 1960 contained approximately 53,000 persons, but only 5,874 of these actually lived on farms; the remainder apparently were urban-oriented in their means of livelihood.

POLITICAL LEADERSHIP AND "METROPOLITAN-TYPE" PROBLEMS

Nashville's "metropolitan-type" problems—those governmental problems uniquely related to the suburban spillover beyond the city boundaries—were similar in many ways to those of most other medium-sized or smaller metropolitan areas in the United States.[1] Beginning first as a trickle but ultimately assuming the proportions of a flood, old and new residents of Nashville settled in a massive fringe area outside the legal city and soon discovered that the urban service needs moved with them but urban government did not.

The "number-one problem" was generally conceded to be the absence of sanitary sewers in the suburbs with an uncertain dependence upon septic tanks in the limestone base of Davidson County and the resulting inhibitions on the attraction of new industries. Other service deficiencies were almost as serious, however, with suburban fire and police protection being provided in poor quality and quantity on a private subscription basis. Houses of nonsubscribers actually burned to the ground while firemen from a private department stood idly by, watching only to see that the house of the subscribing neighbor was safe. Some two hundred miles of suburban water lines of a size insufficient for fire hydrants were installed over a period of several decades. Thousands of acres of beautiful open space and woodland were cut up for residential subdivisions without reserving a single acre for public parks and playgrounds. County leaders declared they had no authority to operate suburban parks and city leaders declared they had no responsibility for such.

Suburban service deficiencies were

---

[1] For a description of the essentially same basic combination of governmental problems in metropolitan areas in the United States, see the writer's summary in *Metropolitan Surveys: A Digest* (Chicago: Public Administration Service, 1958), pp. 5–6.

not the only metropolitan problem.[2] No area-wide authority existed for coping with many area-wide problems, and duplications existed between city and county agencies in a variety of ways. City-county financial inequities, some serious and some only minor irritants, provided steady fuel for a running feud between in-city and out-of-city taxpayers and their respective political leaders. Charges of "suburban free-loading" and counter charges of "city tax-grabbing" were common parlance and tended to make city and county buck-passing the expected thing. The dismay and even cynicism of the citizen seeking to fix responsibility for governmental action or inaction may well have been the most serious problem of all.

This brief and, necessarily, oversimplified view of Nashville's metropolitan governmental problem in the 1940's and 1950's leads one almost inevitably to such a question as "Who was keeping the store when the merchandise fell into such disarray?" What was the relationship of the two principal political leaders in the area, the mayor and the county judge, to the emergence of these problems? Quite obviously, their roles were not the only ones of importance— a whole host of interests, individuals, and influences were involved—but the following observations should make it clear that the roles of the elective political leaders were of critical importance:

(1) The Nashville mayor and the Davidson County judge were significantly involved in certain "nondeci-

[2] For a more detailed treatment of these problems, see the writer's "Urban and Suburban Nashville: A Case Study in Metropolitanism," *The Journal of Politics*, Vol. 17 (February 1955), pp. 82–98; and Lee S. Greene and Daniel R. Grant, *A Future for Nashville, A Report of the Community Services Commission for Nashville and Davidson County* (Nashville, 1952).

sional causes" of the growth of metropolitan problems; that is, it might be said that their inaction and failure to anticipate consequences of inaction helped start the problems on their way. For example, when suburban spillover was only an initial trickle, the nontaxpaying suburbanites were permitted, primarily through inaction of city and county leaders, to initiate a financial inequity by receiving city water at the same rate as taxpaying city dwellers and to begin such suburban service deficiencies as laying water lines which were of inadequate size for fire hydrants. It was only during these early years of the 1930's that preventive measures might have been adequate rather than the more drastic and expensive curative measures being undertaken today.

(2) For the thirty-year period of virtually no annexation by the city of Nashville, it is the mayor, the political leader of the core city, who must bear major responsibility for the failure to annex. Actually, all mayors during this time expressed an almost glib willingness to annex any area interested in becoming a part of the city, but, to even the most casual student of suburban politics, it would not be surprising that there were very few "takers." As the unserved area outside the city grew larger and larger, the political risks became formidable to any Nashville mayor who might push through large-scale annexation. Experts reported that the core city would lose money, at least in the short run, by annexing residential areas; city councilmen were apprehensive about a drop in services in their districts while new services were being installed in the annexed areas; any realistic estimate of the time required to serve—particularly to sewer—the suburbs involved a serious time lag, which could only mean to the mayor a new and hostile group

of voters with, which to reckon at election time.

(3) While the mayor's failure to push annexation during the early years of suburbanization must be termed a cause of the growth of metropolitan problems, metropolitan reformers may have to credit this do-nothingism with providing important assistance toward eventual consolidation of Nashville and Davidson County. It is quite probable that the absence of a vigorous push for annexation resulted in less antiannexation pressure in the suburbs for separate incorporation of "satellite cities." Prior to 1950, there was only one incorporated city in the county outside of Nashville. Five others were incorporated during the fifties, but even the total of six is small by comparison with other metropolitan areas. It is quite possible that a mayor might have triggered an epidemic of separate incorporations around Nashville if he had pushed more vigorously for annexation, with the resulting proliferation of separate governments making it considerably more difficult and perhaps impossible to achieve consolidation.

(4) Finally, the relative balance of power in the factional rivalry of the mayor and county judge probably had the effect of militating against any major change in the *status quo* and, thus, in favor of continued growth and aggravation of the metropolitan problems. Throughout most of the forties and fifties an uneasy stalemate existed in the power struggle between the mayor and the judge, each having the support of one of the daily newspapers. Any major governmental change, such as annexation or city-county consolidation, was likely to run counter to fears of an unfavorable disturbance of this balance of power. It was only after it became obvious in the late fifties that the suburbs *must* be sewered by one means or another that the log jam against gov-

ernmental change began to break. The mayor and the judge then began to scramble for position.

Early Strategy and Leadership

The first comprehensive study of the over-all metropolitan problem in Nashville and Davidson County was that conducted by the Community Services Commission, created in 1951 by private act of the Tennessee legislature. With the assistance of a small, full-time, professional staff, the commission completed its study by June 1952 and recommended the extension of Nashville's boundaries to include the bulk of the suburban fringe area, some sixty-nine square miles and approximately 90,000 people. It further recommended that four functions being performed by the city of Nashville (public health, hospitals, schools, and welfare) be transferred to Davidson County and performed on a county-wide basis. City-county consolidation was not recommended at this time, primarily because it was felt that a constitutional amendment permitting a tax differential between urban and rural property would be required. In the absence of any strong push for carrying out these recommendations, either by citizens' organizations or the heads of city and county government, no annexation took place, and only a part of the recommended transfers to the county were carried out. Mayor Ben West took the initiative in abolishing the city's health department and letting the county assume responsibility in this field, with a city budgetary strain providing support for the move. In general, however, the role of the mayor and of County Judge Beverly Briley with respect to the 1952 recommendations seemed to be one of inaction rather than of either opposition or support in an active way.

Four years later, a second comprehensive study was made, this time by the city and county planning commissions with professional staff assistance from Vanderbilt University. This study was able to utilize the detailed information of the earlier report and to concentrate primarily on the administrative, legal, and political feasibility of particular proposals for metropolitan reform. Most of the assumptions of this study were the same as those of the 1952 study: (1) that some kind of area-wide government was necessary in order to co-ordinate urban services and to spread the tax burden equitably, (2) that single-purpose approaches such as special districts or authorities would inhibit rather than facilitate co-ordination, (3) that either annexation or city-county consolidation would meet the need for area-wide jurisdiction, but (4) that *political* feasibility was the major hurdle in either case because it was becoming clear that Judge Briley favored city-county consolidation and Mayor West was leaning toward the annexation approach. This did not become apparent until after 1952, but both in 1952 and 1956 it was felt that a proposal could not survive the opposition of either the city or county political faction, led by the mayor and judge respectively, and that it would probably require the active support of both.

The 1956 "Plan of Metropolitan Government" which was the product of the planning commissions' study was carefully tailored to elicit the endorsement of both Mayor West and Judge Briley. The original strategy of the research staff was to recommend immediate annexation while working ultimately toward a single metropolitan government for the city and county. This would permit the mayor to emphasize "phase one" and the judge to emphasize "phase two," with each conceivably thinking privately that the other phase either would never be

adopted or would be only temporary. During the period between March 1956, when the staff draft was first submitted to the planning commissions, and October 1956, when the finished report was released to the public, the proposal was subjected to painstaking analysis by both the mayor and the judge, serving as members of the commissions. As the report was released in final form, it gave much greater emphasis to phase two (city-county consolidation) than it did to phase one (annexation), and there was considerable speculation that Mayor West might have openly opposed the report had it not been for strong support for the plan from his newspaper ally, the Nashville *Banner*.

The report called for combining the functions and agencies of Nashville and Davidson County in a single metropolitan government, with provision for a higher level of services and taxes in an expandable "urban services district." The new government was to be neither a city nor a county but, rather, a new political entity. No more suburban incorporations could take place under the new government, but the existing cities outside of Nashville could retain their charters if they so desired. They must be a part of the "general services district," however, in the same manner as the unincorporated area. A recommended "plan of action" in the report called for the passage of general enabling legislation by the state legislature early in 1957, authorizing the creation of a "Metropolitan Government Charter Commission." Such an act was passed in March 1957, and, in view of the fact that opposition from either the mayor or judge could have killed it at that stage, its passage seems, in the light of hindsight, to be something of a political miracle. During this period and the months immediately following, the public position of Judge Briley was favorable to the idea of metropolitan government, while Mayor West maintained a kind of noncommittal "wait and see" policy. The charter commission consisted of five members appointed by the mayor and confirmed by the city council and five members appointed by the judge and confirmed by the county court. They completed their work in approximately one year, and a referendum was held in June 1958.

1958 DEFEAT AND 1962 VICTORY

It is obviously not possible here to give a full account of the events leading up to the adoption of metro in 1962. A brief summary or chronology of events is necessary, however, as a background for generalizations about the role of professional political leaders in metropolitan reform in Nashville.

With the filing of the proposed charter on March 28, 1958, less than three months of campaigning were allowed before the June 17 referendum. The campaign for the charter was in large measure a newspaper campaign, with the *Banner* and the *Tennessean* laying aside their usual political differences and going "all out" with editorials, news stories, and special features in support of metro. In addition, the charter had the endorsement of Mayor West and Judge Briley, the Nashville Chamber of Commerce and the great majority of business leaders, the Nashville Trades and Labor Council, Tennessee Taxpayers Association, League of Women Voters, and several other civic and professional groups, as well as the ten members of the charter commission, including its two Negro members. A citizens' committee for metropolitan government was created, but its principal work was supplying speakers for civic clubs and distributing a pamphlet summarizing the provisions of the charter.

Active opposition to metro was hardly visible until the final week before the referendum, when a flood of antimetro handbills appeared at bus stops throughout the city and at suburban and rural mailboxes and front doors. Newspaper advertisements and singing jingles on radio and television hammered away on the theme that metro meant bigger government, higher taxes, and a "virtual mortgage on your home." Joining in the attack on metro were the suburban private fire and police companies, the constables, about one half of the members of the city council and the county court, most of the operators of the small suburban business establishments, and a few Nashville businessmen.

The scare campaign appeared to be most effective in the lower-income suburbs and least effective in the higher-income suburbs. A plausible explanation of this would be that it was a result of the proponents' excessive reliance on newspaper publicity and civic club speeches and failure to develop a precinct and block organization. The suburban and rural alarm was reflected in a fairly heavy negative vote, 19,234 to 13,794, while the vote inside the city of Nashville was light but favorable, 7,797 to 4,804.

Not long after the rejection of the metro charter, the city of Nashville began to use for the first time the strong annexation powers which had been authorized by the Tennessee legislature in 1955. Without a vote in the affected areas, the city council annexed first seven square miles of largely industrial property and then forty-three square miles of residential area containing some 82,000 persons. These actions had the effect of tripling the previous area of the city and of causing many unhappy suburbanites to re-examine their earlier opposition to metro. Mayor West supported the industrial annexation but vetoed the residential annexation bill because it did not provide for a referendum. His own majority faction in the city council overrode his veto, however, giving rise to the charge that he had actually given an informal "green light" to the residential annexation. County school officials and teachers were especially upset by the confused status of the annexed schools, and the *Tennessean* showed no mercy in reporting those annexation developments which tended to embarrass Mayor West.

While many factors were involved, including the levying of a "green sticker" tax for use of city streets, the second effort to secure metropolitan government received its main impetus from this massive annexation move by the city of Nashville.[3] In brief outline, the events leading to the framing of a second proposed charter for metropolitan government were as follows: (1) passage of a resolution by the county quarterly court calling for the creation of a new charter commission, followed by an unsuccessful effort to secure passage by the city council; (2) election of a delegation to the state legislature pledged to give the people a second chance to vote on metro; (3) passage of state enabling legislation in 1961; (4) approval of the creation of the new charter commission in a referendum in August 1961 by a light but surprisingly favorable vote: 11,096 to 3,730 inside Nashville and 7,324 to 3,848 outside of Nashville; and (5) creation of a charter commission composed of identical membership to the

[3] For a more detailed discussion of the 1958 and 1960 annexations, see David A. Booth, *Metropolitics: The Nashville Consolidation* (East Lansing: Michigan State University Institute for Community Development and Services, 1963), pp. 71–93, and Daniel R. Grant and Lee S. Greene, "Surveys, Dust, Action," *National Civic Review,* Vol. 50 (October 1961), pp. 466–471.

1958 group except for two vacancies filled by appointments by the mayor and the county judge.

The charter which was filed in April 1962 was not appreciably different from the 1958 charter, although some changes were made. The metropolitan council was enlarged from twenty-one to forty-one members in deference to the local tradition of large legislative bodies in both the city and county. Because of the new annexation, the urban services district would begin with an area of almost seventy-five square miles instead of the 1958 area of less than twenty-five square miles. The metropolitan mayor's salary was increased to $25,000 from $20,000, and the earlier two-term limit was changed to a three-term limit. Strong pressure for an independently elected school board was resisted by the charter commission in a narrow vote. A companion proposal was accepted, however, to permit the school board by a two-thirds vote to secure a public referendum on the school budget if it is cut by the metropolitan council.

Two major differences may. be cited between the 1962 and 1958 metro campaigns. The first is the much more effective organization of the pro-metro forces in 1962 than in the earlier effort. As early as the summer of 1961, a fairly broad-based "Citizens' Committee for Better Government" was organized to support the creation of a charter commission. After the successful August referendum, it stayed in existence and built on this experience. A women's division enlisted more than 1,500 persons who worked zealously for metro with neighborhood coffees, telephoning, and doorbell ringing. Judge Briley and many of the same groups as before endorsed metropolitan government, and the *Tennessean* crusaded even more completely than in 1958, if such is possible. The county tax assessor and county trustee, whose elective jobs were protected in the charter, provided important support from some of the "organization politicians" in the county.

The second major difference in the 1962 campaign was the change-over of Mayor West, who campaigned publicly and vigorously against the charter. His reasons for the switch are disputed—he contended that the city's program of annexation should be given a fair chance before trying anything new, but his critics were unconvinced. They explained the cooling off on metro as a realization that his chances of becoming metropolitan mayor were not good in 1962, whereas they had been considerably better in 1958. Mayor West's opposition to metro permitted the *Tennessean* to adopt a "beat-the-city-machine" theme in contrast to the more educational but less colorful approach in 1958. Joining in opposition to metro in 1962 were the *Banner,* most of the city councilmen, many of the county magistrates and constables, perhaps one third of the members of the chamber of commerce board of governors, the officials of the six incorporated suburban cities, and a few right-wing extremists such as racist agitator John Kasper and a leader of the John Birch Society.

In the referendum on June 28, 1962, the consolidation charter received the necessary separate majorities inside and outside Nashville. Even though Mayor West was able to carry the "old city" to a close vote against metro, this was more than outweighed by the overwhelmingly favorable vote in the newly annexed areas. The totals in Nashville were 21,064 in favor and 15,914 against. Outside Nashville, 15,591 voted in favor and 12,514 voted against. Following an early court test favorable to the metropolitan charter, Judge Briley was elected metropolitan mayor in November 1962, over Tax Assessor Clifford Allen—Mayor West did not run. The new government went into effect on April 1, 1963.

MAYOR'S AND JUDGE'S ROLES IN DEFEAT AND VICTORY

With only this one case study to draw upon, what kinds of generalizations can be suggested about the role of professional political leaders in metropolitics? In addition to the broad assertion that Nashville's experience with metropolitics offers no support for any inclination of metropolitan reformers elsewhere to leave the professional political leaders out of their plans, the following more specific conclusions may be drawn from the Nashville events.

(1) Plans for major structural change in local government in a metropolitan area *can* be devised in such a way as to achieve support of the primary political leaders. In the two campaigns in Nashville, the support of three of the four top politicians was achieved (two in the first and one in the second), and this should be considered a rather high batting average in the difficult arena of metropolitics.

(2) As in the case of city-manager reform campaigns, major metropolitan government reform *can* be used by one political faction as a device to oust an opposing faction from power. It would be difficult to say whether the Nashville *Tennessean* was more enthusiastic at the prospect of getting metro adopted or of getting Mayor West ousted. It would not be correct to conclude, however, that the 1962 metro campaign was entirely an anti-West struggle. The factional battle undoubtedly controlled many developments in the 1962 campaign but by no means all of them.

(3) The unanimous endorsement and even active support of the major political leaders for a metropolitan reorganization proposal is not sufficient

to guarantee an affirmative vote of the electorate, even when an imposing array of the alleged "community elite" also support the proposal. The 1958 defeat of metro proved this and demonstrated the great depth of suburban and rural suspicion and distrust of the central city and of any "entangling alliances" with it. Also demonstrated was the ability of seemingly insignificant opinion leaders in the lower-income suburbs—barbers, filling station operators, cleaning and pressing shop operators—to remain virtually unaffected by the daily barrage of pro-metro newspaper publicity or by the endorsements of both the mayor and the judge.

(4) It is not always within the power of one of the chief political leaders to block a major metropolitan reorganization proposal. More specifically, the core city political organization *can* be beaten by metropolitan reform forces. But reformers in other metropolitan areas should not take too much hope or be misled by this statement, which is one of possibility rather than probability. The *probabilities* of winning over the opposition of the city machine are doubtless very poor. Mayor West's association with the controversial "green sticker tax" and annexation program made his opposition to metro in 1962 an asset for the pro-metro forces rather than a liability, especially in the annexed area and the suburban and rural areas.

(5) In spite of appearances, it cannot be concluded from the Nashville experience that the prospects for a metro victory are greater if the major political factions are divided (as in 1962) than if they are united in favor of it (as in 1958). It is this writer's opinion that the victory in 1962 would not have been possible without the foundation laid in 1958 when *both* political factions endorsed metro. Pro-

ponents of metro in 1962 were able to make Mayor West's opposition seem more petty and personal because his statements seemed to contradict everything he said four years earlier. The unified, highly rational, "high road" campaign for metro in 1958, which was made possible by the endorsement of the mayor and the judge, did not result in victory, but it made significant contributions to the ultimate victory. While the margin of victory probably came from the vote-switchers who cast an emotional protest vote against annexation and the "green sticker," the greater part of the "yes" voters in 1962 were those who had been sold on metro in 1958 and had stayed with the cause.

ELECTIVE POLITICAL LEADERSHIP AND TRANSITION TO METRO

One other question, which admittedly can be answered only in speculative terms, concerns the significance of having an *elective* executive rather than an appointive manager during the transition to the new metropolitan government. Before considering this question, it might be well to explain that the decision to have the elective mayor for Nashville's metro rather than the professional manager (such as Metropolitan Dade County has) was not a reflection of weighing the merits of the two plans. It was rather a reflection of the over-all strategy to confine the issues placed before the electorate to the single question of whether to consolidate the two governments or not. Thus, pet projects of various reform groups were resisted by the charter framers with the argument that other major changes should not be pushed until after metro had been adopted. This is not to say that the charter commission otherwise might have favored the manager plan—it is likely that the commission members would have favored the elective mayor on its own merits as well as for strategy reasons.

It might logically be assumed that the elective mayor would tend to be stronger at the politics end of the governmental continuum and weaker at the management end, with just the opposite being true for the professional city or county manager. Thus, if one were trying to *predict* the effects of the elective executive on the Nashville metro experiment—which only the foolhardy would attempt—the following conditions might logically be expected: (1) more vigorous leadership in the resolution of community conflicts, including—but not limited to—community conflicts growing out of the merger of two major governments; (2) a more intensified—but more personalized—public-relations program, jointly focusing attention on the work of metro and of the mayor; (3) councilmanic leadership and initiative primarily in the hands of the metro mayor, but with periods of conflict and stalemate between the two from time to time; (4) a tendency to neglect or downgrade the importance of problems of "internal" administration, including—but not limited to—administrative problems growing out of the consolidation; (5) a greater capacity to secure favorable (more politically sympathetic) court interpretations of the new metro charter; and (6) a greater capacity to absorb (or avoid) the postadoption political attacks on the metro plan itself which will almost inevitably occur.

At the time of this writing, Nashville metro is finishing its first year of operation, and this is hardly time to check on the fulfillment of any of the above "predictions" for the elective executive, if, indeed, one could ever really test them satisfactorily. Inasmuch as this is admittedly speculative, however, no harm is done by attempting some preliminary observations.

Community conflicts *have* been resolved with above average success during the first year, with renewed racial demonstrations subjecting the new government to one of its first tests in this respect. Peaceful desegregation of downtown hotels and of certain holdout eating establishments was achieved after the mayor appointed a committee on human relations.

Public relations activities have been stepped up tremendously under metro, and Mayor Briley was elected "Newsmaker of the Year" by a local group of newsmen. The highly personalized character of the publicity seems to link together the popularity level of metro with that of the mayor himself in a way that would not be true of an appointive manager. Conceivably, both the mayor and the metro form of government must sink or swim together.

One year is especially inadequate to judge mayor-council relationships, but at least it can be said that no serious conflict or open breach in relationships occurred during this time. By its very nature, a forty-one-member council may be more subject to external leadership than a smaller body, but Mayor Briley had already had more than a dozen years of experience in dealing with the fifty-plus members of the Davidson County quarterly court before becoming metropolitan mayor. In any case, the expected periods of conflict and stalemate have not occurred.

Administrative problems resulting from consolidation were overwhelming during the first year, beginning with a frantic and chaotic effort to formulate the first budget, an agonizing job of merging city and county accounting systems, and a mountain of work for the staffs of the planning commission and legal department concerning organization and functions of merged agencies. "Government by postponement" became the order of the day, with police, fire, education, personnel, and many other departments forced to delay operations in many fields because of pending studies by professional consultants. Transition to metro during the first year was considerably smoother in the mayor's various other roles—political, legislative, and ceremonial leader—than in his role as administrative leader.

Finally, the political experience and strength of the elective mayor have undoubtedly been significant in securing favorable court decisions for the new government and in warding off political counterattacks against the new form of government. With the consolidation experience of other American cities and counties as a basis for comparison, Nashville's metropolitan charter has received unusually favorable treatment in the courts. Only time will tell what may lie ahead in the matter of political battles, crippling charter amendments, and public favor in general, but it is quite likely that the new government will weather the storm of inevitable tax increases with less difficulty with an elective mayor than it would with an appointive manager.

A final word of caution should be added for the reader in appraising the experience of Nashville and Davidson County. Of the four questions asked at the beginning of this article, three relate to what happened *before* metro went into effect and the fourth to one highly speculative aspect of the transition and first year's operations. The task of recording and analyzing the postadoption experience is a tremendous one which is just getting under way. The preadoption experience makes it clear, however, that active involvement of rival professional political leaders in all stages of a metropolitan reform movement is possible, is not necessarily a kiss of death, does not necessarily prevent "radical reform," and may actually constitute a tactical advantage for proponents of metropolitan reform.

From Bossism to Cosmopolitanism: Changes in the Relationship of Urban Leadership to State Politics

By WILLIAM C. HAVARD

ABSTRACT: Political bossism in American cities developed as a pragmatic response to the rise of American urbanism. Its political style developed out of a combination of the new directions of American society as it entered the age of enterprise and of the existing political system which was geared to a rural, decentralized mode of life. The power structure of bossism was based on a twofold relationship maintained by the city machine: the patron-client relation with blocs of voters—particularly ethnic minorities—and a brokerage relationship with business. Relations with state government were directed more toward the maintenance of control over the city than to substantive government policy. The appropriate political response to an urban, technological society came with the reorganization of national politics by Franklin Roosevelt and the institution of New Deal economic and social reform. This change affected urban politics by making it increasingly pluralistic and program-oriented. The new style of urban politics may be called a cosmopolitan politics, and it strongly affected, if indeed it did not dominate, state politics in most places. The city of New Orleans is a special case of the development of a cosmopolitan style of urban politics out of an earlier bossism within a state which has not yet assimilated to cosmopolitan politics.

William C. Havard, Ph.D., Baton Rouge, Louisiana, is Professor and Chairman of the Department of Government, Louisiana State University. He previously taught at the University of Florida, where he was also Director of the Public Administration Clearing Service. He is the author of The Government of Louisiana (1958), Henry Sidgwick and Later Utilitarian-Political Philosophy (1959), coauthor with Loren P. Beth of The Politics of Mis-Representation (1962) and with Rudolf Heberle and Perry H. Howard of The Louisiana Elections of 1960.

IF the study and practice of politics are going, independent concerns, a political system must be said to be more than a sum of its efficient parts. As a product of a self-sustained form of activity, political organizations tend both to reflect the society out of which they developed and to influence the patterns of organization of private associations in the community. Political decisions likewise are simultaneously products of the goals—articulated and unarticulated—sought by individuals and groups and a major factor in determining those goals as well as the means to their realization. And the individual act of voting is at one and the same time socially conditioned and socially conditioning. Although individual political participation may fall far short of the simple rational processes which the liberal optimists of the nineteenth century visualized, it is not necessary to embrace Hegelianism to realize that the very existence of a working political system implies at least some degree of built-in order and consistency in the political arrangements themselves. All of the participants share in the regulative functions and the opportunities provided by the deliberately constructed media of participation. Insofar as their actions imply willingness to abide by the terms of authoritative decisions reached in the prescribed manner, individual participants are not merely using a rational means to realize individual and collective ends but are, in effect, giving tacit approval to—and thereby helping to sustain—the political system itself.

Despite the dispersal of power that was deliberately built into the institutional structure of politics in America —and, *ceteris paribus,* into the conditioned responses that may be expected from political participants—the processes of politics are heavily implicated in adapting the system to social change.

Although the integrative function of the political system is apparent in the case of minor modifications or adjustments that take place within the framework of a traditional and accepted set of political ends, standards, and expectations, changes necessitated by great shifts in the responsibilities and activities of government produce such dramatic impacts that the system itself must be changed or must be drastically adjusted in order to cope with the new conditions. If careful observers such as Samuel Lubell are correct, massive shifts are rare; yet, when they do occur, they force readjustments in the proximate ends toward which the loose political consensus is directed and consequently in the orientation of voters on issues, the patterns of political leadership, and the standards and limits of political criticism and movements for reform.[1] Even in the face of such changes, however, interpretations of events as well as the elemental structure of institutions may tend to lag far behind the social—and even the political—changes themselves. Presumably, if the adjustment fails to be made in the face of pressing demands, the system is in danger; but, if changes are made, their complications tend to impinge on all levels and conditions of the governmental order.

CITY AND STATE BASES OF BOSSISM

The rise of the American city (circa 1870) was closely related to changes in technology, successive waves of European immigrants after the middle of the nineteenth century, and the extension of a previously existing physiocratic conception of decentralization and *laissez faire* to manufacturing and commercial enterprise. The development of the American city to a promi-

[1] Reference is to Lubell's *The Future of American Politics* (New York, 1951), especially Chap. 10, pp. 198 ff.

nent place in politics, in other words, coincided with the social and political changes associated with the post-Civil War American industrial revolution, and the phenomenon of the boss was a part of the political response to new modes of life and to the political problems entailed by these socioeconomic changes. However, the special characteristics of the boss did not represent something entirely new in American life; many features of the system were adaptations to historical political experience and to the interpretations of political life which had grown out of this experience.

The functional aspects of bossism were in part products of the social conditions which produced the city and of the political system which preceded it. More than anything else, the boss resembled a buccaneering entrepreneur, a man of many parts and interests, skilled in manipulation, ruthless and systematic in eliminating competition, generous in his rewards for co-operation and fiercely demanding insofar as personal and organizational loyalty of subordinates was concerned.[2] The traits were not solely outgrowths of the business ethic. The personalism of the boss, his antipathy to systemization and bureaucratization, and his capacity for intermingling private and public spheres also had their roots in near-anarchic frontier individualism, the

[2] The bosses themselves were not drawn mainly from the entrepreneurial classes as such; they tended to correspond more, perhaps, to what Robert Dahl in *Who Governs?* (New Haven, 1961), pp. 32 ff., refers to as the "Explebes," a fact in keeping with the democratic necessity to maintain a touch of the common. The "entrepreneur in office" slightly preceded the appearance of the boss and often continued to hold the official positions while the boss maneuvered in the background. Nonetheless, the boss, too, accustomed himself quite well to the general direction in which society and government tended in the age of enterprise.

spoils heritage of Jacksonian democracy, and the oversimplification of the problems of public order and public services attendant on the earlier American political ethos generally.

The services performed by the boss were essentially those of a patron and a broker, with the respective functions carried out on two levels. The only real point of contact between the two was the boss in his dual role of patron and broker. If the services were adequate to maintain the system, they were also well compensated. For the new urban groups, and especially for the ethnic collectivities, the boss and his ward and precinct leader cohorts were patrons in the sense of providing personal favors necessary to enable the newly arrived to adjust to the impersonality of urban life. Jobs, minor welfare, the provision for access to officials who exercised formal power, and related types of public-private assistance were doled out. The fee exacted in this case was the bloc of votes regularly returned for the organizational candidates. Broken down into individual acts, even where "repeating" was involved, the price was rather small in proportion to benefits rendered but, from the standpoint of the effect on maintenance of power, the returns were impressive. The broker functions which comprised the boss's relation to business were of a somewhat different order. Contracts for public works, transportation and utility franchises, a checkrein on public regulation, and occasionally a helping hand in keeping labor in order were typical, but not exhaustive, of the services rendered. In this case, the charges were levied in cash, varying amounts of which had to be diverted to the other half of the operation—the maintenance of the mass basis of support necessary to control the public offices which could in turn supply special advantages to business.

But what of the central problem of the method by which urban bosses extended their influence to the state government? Here, too, the bosses had a vendible commodity—a bloc of organized and deliverable votes. And, again, their demands were not excessive in relation to the prevailing ethos and the accepted attitudes toward politics. The urban leadership wanted generally to be left alone in its management of municipal affairs, although occasionally it might need special legislation for the realization of certain of its more specialized purposes—for example, to secure and maintain local control over state patronage within the city—and it wanted a voice in legislation which might affect the interests which represented at least the brokerage part of the over-all enterprise. Given the looseness of American political organization, the prevailing climate of opinion, and the potential assets of the urban organization's support, the reciprocal demands were not excessive, although in some instances they extended eventually to control of much of the party machinery and even to the governmental institutions of the state.

Although much maligned, the pattern of bossism apparently served to the reasonable satisfaction of both sets of its clients for a long period of time, and vestiges of the system linger on. Given the conditions the organization was created to meet and the sociological and political limitations on conceivable alternatives, it may even be said to have satisfied the primary demands of the American political system during its heyday.

Bossism, of course, had to fend off recurrent waves of reform, a large part of which came from the reform movements which sometimes overwhelmed the state governments. In many instances the reformers were of the good government variety—goo-goos who urged more individual civic participation, a more enlightened electorate, and other nostrums reminiscent of the romantic liberalism of the eighteenth and early nineteenth centuries. Coupled with these were certain standard administrative prescriptions such as municipal civil service, better systems of budgeting and accounting, and the reorganization of the bureaucratic hierarchy. Although sharing the goals of this polite parlor reform group to some extent, other reform elements such as the Populists and the Progressives were much more concerned with substantive programs than with procedural devices. For the most part, however, the content of their programs related to a mode of politics and a style of American life that was simple, egalitarian, agrarian, and hence anachronistic insofar as the city and its immediate causal antecedents were concerned. The latter reform groups would probably have preferred to abolish the large municipality, along with big business and big finance, rather than seek to make the mode of life in big cities tenable and its politics compatible with a more firmly established political ethic.

The Boss in Decline

The decline of the boss-dominated city machine in American politics is almost invariably attributed to the reorganization of the basis of national politics by Franklin Roosevelt and by the undercutting of the patronage system by the various New Deal programs. The necessities arising from economic collapse and the Roosevelt triumph foreshortened the time element involved in the "adjustment" form of political change, transforming the process into a seemingly drastic reorientation of American politics. The shift of social-welfare functions from a private-public local relief system to a rationalized bureaucratic operation of state and national governments cut heavily into the sources of small favors. The adoption of long-standing reform recommendations, such as the merit system of personal administration on a grand scale, cut heavily into the amount of local patronage available and substituted—partially, at least—depersonalized hierarchical structure for the complex of personal loyalties and indefinite lines of authority that had previously dominated the style of municipal politics. Although many of the organizational features of the old machines remained, the implements of control were so dispersed that their functions were reduced to that of one among several key determinants of the political system.

These specific structural changes, however, were merely symptomatic of a transformation of politics at all levels that compared in scope with the shift from agrarianism to industrialism in the latter half of the nineteenth century. The outcome was a maturation of the political system which brought that system to a point of cosmopolitanism which enabled it to cope with the social and economic changes that had occurred. While the age of population and economic expansion was by no means at an end, the conditions of that expansion and the exploitative aspects of its initial period were to be subjected to a different set of influences and controls. The earlier impact of new groups into the society was being absorbed through the assimilation or acculturation of the ethnic minorities. While Roosevelt forged a new Democratic majority coalition largely out of these elements, their support was transformed from the patron-client relationship characteristic of boss rule to a new traditional voter orientation to the state and national Democratic party organizations that was institutionalized and related to a

broader sentiment of community welfare. The pluralism that had always been a vaunted attribute of American politics emerged from its somewhat fictional basis in the concept of the autonomous individual into a socially effective form with the broader differentiation of politically articulate urban groups in the 1930's and thereafter. Policy decisions increasingly were affected by a polyarchy of cooperating and competing groups that represented the actual diversifications of a complex, urban, industrial mode of national life. As a result of such changes, post-New Deal political leadership had to adjust to the necessities which arose from the coming of age of an essentially cosmopolitan society. The leadership of big cities and the holders of major state-wide offices were compelled to display a considerable urbanity both in political style and in their approach to policy in order to attract support from a cross section of the great variety of influential groups arrayed along the political continuum, just as they had to apply new political skills in developing and implementing policies designed to keep the socioeconomic system in balance.

Reform proposals, too, were becoming less structurally and more substantively oriented as a result of the new commitment to governmental activism. The problems of life in metropolitan areas were forced to the forefront of public issues by all sorts of activist groups both at the state and national level; the sheer scale and complexity of a technological society forced the (now articulate) demand for closer attention to expertise and planning; except in those (perhaps all too numerous) places in which malapportionment or other inducements to lags in the adjustment of the system existed, the emergent polyarchal urban leadership became the determining factor in state political organizations, in state policy, and in the creation of electoral mandates to which the government attempted to respond.

Although pragmatic and in many respects institutionally conserving in its basis and orientation, the Roosevelt revolution produced the major changes necessary to preserve the political tradition under visibly altered social conditions which had long rendered the ameliorative capacities of a political style adjusted to the age of uninhibited enterprise ineffective. Since Roosevelt, America has practiced a cosmopolitan politics in which the problems of the private collectivization of the economy and other fundamental social institutions have been accepted and the problems of social existence under such conditions at least partially confronted rather than ignored. The administrative functions of government have simultaneously increased at all levels, as have the interdependence and cooperativeness of the various levels of government themselves. Whether one wishes to apply the label "liberal consensus" or some other to the altered outlook on the general direction of American life and expectations that are generated as a result of the adjusted interpretation, it has manifested itself in electoral responses, the general thrust of legislative executive policy, and the posture of political leadership.

NEW ORLEANS STATE-LOCAL RELATIONS

Up to this point, this essay has been concerned with a somewhat abstract summary of the changing relation of urban politics to American politics in general. The generalizations and simplifications of the descriptions were based on a broad overview of a system which in its empirical details displays a mazelike quality of digressions and exceptions. In order to demonstrate

the trend in a more specific manner, as well as to take note of the more prominent type of exceptions to the general pattern, the remainder of the essay will concentrate on the manner in which this historical sweep of urban politics is exemplified by a single city—the city of New Orleans.[3]

New Orleans is probably the only Southern city whose politics has closely paralleled the historical experience of the larger municipalities in the United States during the rise and development of the urban area as a focal point of politics roughly since the 1870's. Because of this, it furnishes a useful example for appraising the characteristic features of the interrelation of metropolitan political leadership and state politics. At the same time, its location in the South allows ample scope for assessing the differences which may arise because of regionally imposed variations in the major components of the political system—the structures of political organization, the practice of politics, and the habitual responses of the voters to candidates and issues.

Although the settled population base of New Orleans in the nineteenth century differed from most of the other older cities of the United States, inasmuch as it was composed mainly of French and, to a lesser degree, Spanish elements, the fact that it was the second largest port in the country meant that it shared with the other great urban centers of the country the experience of several successive waves of foreign immigration. The city re-

[3] Much of the following material on New Orleans prior to the era of Huey P. Long draws heavily on George M. Reynolds, *Machine Politics in New Orleans 1897–1926* (New York, 1936). The essay on "Martin Behrman" in Harold Zink, *City Bosses in the United States* (Durham, 1930), pp. 317–333, as well as the general summary of the characteristics of bosses and their modes of operation also proved useful.

ceived its share of Irish and German immigrants in the middle years of the nineteenth century, and, in the 1880's and thereafter, it experienced an even larger than average influx of Italians. Thus, the melting-pot cosmopolitanism that was to play so important a role in the history of metropolitan-area politics in the United States was typified in New Orleans over the past century.

A second characteristic that has made its impact felt in the politics of this city—and of the state of Louisiana —is the fact that New Orleans has for upwards of a century contained between 20 and 25 per cent of the state's population. No other municipality in the state has even come close to rivaling it as a metropolitan area or as a cosmopolitan community. Although several American cities contain larger proportions of the populations of their respective states than New Orleans, its size and its unquestioned metropolitan pre-eminence virtually assure it and its leaders a special place in the over-all politics of the state.

Even though New Orleans is not the state capital, as the major metropolis of the state, as an important center of international trade, and as the principal location of most of the industry of the state until fairly recently, the city was bound to be the seat of many governmental installations other than those of a purely local nature. Therefore, just as its growing and diversifying population gave its political leadership an opportunity to organize the vote along ethnic lines in the manner characteristic of growing urban areas in other states, so also did its size, economic importance, and the presence in it of a variety of local, state, and national administrative agencies—which were potential sources of patronage— mark the city as a singularly important factor in the political life of the state.

Although an apparently less effective political organization had existed earlier, the dominant era of machine politics and boss rule in New Orleans dates from 1897. The machine originated in the Choctaw Club, which was organized in that year as a political association, and it continued thereafter to maintain the club as its home base and to provide leaders from among its membership. The initial motivation of the organization was to consolidate the political control of the local Democratic party over state and municipal affairs following the victory of the party in a hot gubernatorial contest against a coalition—or fusion—of Populists and Republicans in 1896. From the beginning, the association between state and municipal politics was quite close because of mutual interests in one-party oligarchical rule. Prominent Choctaws began to weld alliances with upstate planters at least as early as the Constitutional Convention of 1898, when they supported the move to eliminate a major threat of party opposition by disfranchising the Negro while making it possible for white ethnic minorities in New Orleans to vote. The arrangement was continued and enlarged upon from that point onward, and its effectiveness was broken only by Huey Long's success in state politics after 1928.

There is no need to labor the organizational methods and control techniques of the Choctaws at length; they correspond precisely to the prevailing pattern in the other machine-dominated cities. The city was divided into seventeen wards, and many of the electoral offices—including the city council —were returned on a ward basis, thus affording the usual advantages to a preexisting organization of concentrated areas within which to maneuver for control of the vote. Ethnic blocs constituted the most viable elements for the machine to work with, and the patron-client relation of precinct and ward leaders to these groups was the main method of manipulation. Patronage (which was plentiful), minor forms of welfare dispensed through the local leader, a mediatory function between the voter and the official at city hall, and other familiar practices were the normal means for solidifying electoral support. The leaders were also unusually adept at brokerage in relation to business interests; in fact, a sizable number of business leaders themselves were active members of the Choctaw Club. The usual arrangements on utilities, franchises, and contracts prevailed; regulation of co-operative businesses was minimal, and the machine showed no disposition to support either legislation favorable to labor or the implementation of a merit system.

From precinct leaders to ward leaders to the leader of the caucus (which was composed of the ward leaders), the hierarchy was strictly established and decisions were taken on appointive offices to be filled and on endorsements and the like at the level appropriate to the office or function concerned. Except for his defeat in 1920, Martin Behrman held the office of mayor from his first election to the post in 1904 until his death in 1926—he was re-elected mayor in 1925—and was accepted during virtually the whole of this time as the organization's boss. Most observers agree that Behrman was unusually free from the taint of personal corruption and that, within the framework of a limited vision, he was a competent administrator. Of his superior abilities as a political manipulator there can be little question.

The purposes and methods of influence on state politics by the New Orleans machine were clear. The city ring was less interested in the general affairs of the state than in maintaining a constitutional and statutory basis for continued control of the city; they also wanted the disposal of a sizable portion of the quite large body of state patronage within the city. In most, although perhaps not all, cases the state-wide interests of the business clients for which the machine performed the brokerage function coincided with those of the machine's upstate allies in state politics anyway; as a result, the machine was fairly free to concentrate even its points of access to state power on the affairs of the city. An endorsement by the machine for a state-wide elective office was a great boon to aspiring politicians. The usual practice of the city organization was to select a likely candidate for governor from outside the New Orleans metropolitan area and endorse him after being given standard commitments. The machine's capacity to deliver a plurality of votes in the city that was far too large to overcome elsewhere in the state is attested to by the fact that only twice prior to Huey Long's victory was the machine-endorsed candidate for governor defeated, and, on both occasions, the machine itself was the main object of attack and was also in something of a chaotic condition internally. As assurance of its status, the machine insisted on a membership proportional to its share of the state population in the state legislature, on the state Democratic committee, and on other boards and committees in which it had a special interest. In legislative committees or other bodies directly and almost exclusively concerned with the city, such as the long-standing Committee on the Affairs of the City of New Orleans, complete control rather than representation was maintained. Needless to say, the machine-selected members of such bodies could be counted on to vote in a bloc, and this bloc of 20 to 25 per cent was a highly negotiable instrument insofar as legislative and party bargaining was concerned.

HUEY LONG'S "REFORM" MOVEMENT

The "reform" movement which finally broke the hold of the machine over New Orleans was that of Huey Long.[4] And the nature of the Long movement was the most important factor in differentiating the post-New Deal relation between urban and state politics in Louisiana from the general pattern outlined earlier. The basis of Long's appeals and his style of politics were Populist. Thus, while the Long regime shared certain welfare-state goals with the New Deal, Huey's criticism of the prevailing economic power structure and of government programs was much more clearly related to the radical agrarian tradition of an earlier period than to the pragmatic cosmopolitanism represented by Roosevelt and his followers. In fact, the movement fed on a criticism of cosmopolitanism—that is, of urbanity, private collectivism in business and other organizations, institutionalism and rational bureaucratization of government functions. Even when the surviving Long organization later assimilated itself to the irreversible trend toward the development of Louisiana as an urban, technological state, the political style and many of the appeals of the Longs continued to be Populist.

Furthermore, Long superimposed a state machine on urban politics instead of allowing a changing system of urban politics gradually to make its impact felt on state affairs. From 1928 onward, Long used his gubernatorial powers over state patronage in New Orleans, together with a steadily enlarging area of power derived through ripper legislation, to break the control of the machine in New Orleans and to substitute his own organization—or in some cases his modified edition of the Choctaws—for the old local boss system. New Orleans politics ultimately came almost completely under Huey Long's domination, and it was a politics of patronage, spoils, and machine organization in much the fashion of the old days of the Choctaw hegemony, except that the real influence was now exerted from the outside through the complete control of the state machine over the institutions of state and city government alike.

As a result of this concatenation of historical circumstances, New Orleans was somewhat later than most cities in reaching the stage of political cosmopolitanism; in partial consequence, the state of Louisiana has been even further delayed in assimilating itself to political cosmopolitanism under the influence of New Orleans than might have been the case if the social changes effected by Huey Long had not had the ideological basis that they did.

POST-WORLD WAR II

The realignment of New Orleans politics in the direction of cosmopolitanism occurred only after World War II. The process was effected almost entirely through the reform mayoralty of deLesseps Morrison, which extended from 1946 to 1962.[5] Following a brief

---

[4] Some of the methods by which Long reduced the effectiveness of the New Orleans ring and in effect took it over as an adjunct of his state machine are discussed in Allan P. Sindler, *Huey Long's Louisiana: State Politics, 1920–1952* (Baltimore, 1956), especially Chap. 3.

[5] The assistance of Mr. Joseph B. Parker in allowing me access to the data he has collected on political leadership in New Orleans is warmly acknowledged. Although the generalizations which follow reveal very little of the rich details that Mr. Parker has assembled, without the confirmation they afforded for the thesis outlined here the writer would have been on extremely shaky grounds in touching

prewar state legislative career and a distinguished record of military service, Morrison was selected as the candidate for mayor by a municipal reform group which had the benefits of state support from the state reform administration of Governor Sam Jones—which had been swept into office in 1940 following the massive scandals of the heirs to the Long machine in 1939—and of Jones's successor in 1944, Jimmie H. Davis.

In terms of organization, political style, approaches to public policy, and methods of expanding his political influence beyond the city, Morrison was the cosmopolitan type of political leader. This does not mean, however, that he completely abandoned the older techniques of local politics that were still useful. The municipal organization that he constructed—the Crescent City Democratic Association—followed something of the pattern of the Choctaws in its development of ward and precinct leadership and its use of the patronage which remained even after the institutionalization of many of the city's administrative practices and functions. In fact, parts of the organization were built around defectors from the old ring, even though the latter survived both the scandals and reforms and continues to operate in a drastically attenuated fashion. But even the interrelations of the leadership reflected considerable change: the precinct captains and the ward leaders were more diversified political types than were the old-fashioned ward heelers; loyalty to Morrison was strong but was perhaps as much a commitment to the ideas and issues that he symbolized as it was to the person; the process of decision-making on both organizational and policy matters was subject to the more diverse influences of a polyarchy than on the present organization of New Orleans politics.

to the constrictive, hierarchy-affected apparatus of the machine. Of as much, if not more, importance was the fact that the formal organization was by no means exhaustive of Morrison's effective political support. The "good government" civic groups had been instrumental in his initial bid for office and the association was continued and in many respects expanded during his entire tenure. Morrison eventually drew support from each segment of the pluralistic composition of the contemporary metropolis.

The policies effected during Morrison's administrations furnish even stronger evidence of the extent to which his political practices tended toward cosmopolitanism.[6] Although a merit system of civil service for the city had already been developed as part of the state reform program of 1940, many of Morrison's early efforts as mayor were directed toward institutionalizing the rather chaotic structure of city government and administration. The culmination of this endeavor was a constitutional home-rule amendment for the city and the subsequent drafting and adoption of a new city charter, effective in 1954, which completely reorganized, tightened and rationalized the legal basis of government in New Orleans.

Under Morrison's leadership, the city embarked on planning and redevelopment programs that extended the service concept of the city far beyond its previous limits. In part, this reflected a group-based clientele far broader

[6] On the general structure of New Orleans government, see L. Vaughan Howard and Robert S. Friedman, *Government in Metropolitan New Orleans* (New Orleans, 1959); on the whole relation of political control through spoils and patronage and the efforts to forestall these practices through civil service reform (with considerable emphasis on New Orleans), see L. Vaughan Howard, *Civil Service Development in Louisiana* (New Orleans, 1956).

than the two main (and rather simplified) lines of political association engaged in by the Choctaws—the patron-client relation with the ethnic groups and the brokerage relation with business. Morrison's policies with regard to such diverse problems as labor and the Negro—who had been readmitted to political participation after 1944—also attest to the cosmopolitanism of the new approach to urban politics in New Orleans.

This cosmopolitanism of city politics was extended to the participation in state politics of the New Orleans legislative delegation, party committee members, and so on. Although still interested in securing the constitutional and legislative bases for effecting policy in New Orleans, the purposes and clientele that the policy was to subserve tended to overshadow the old exclusive aim of maintaining local control. The New Orleans delegations moved to the forefront of support for legislative programs designed to cosmopolize the state and to secure more effective state-local co-operation in the administration of newer government services; in general, they supported other liberalizing tendencies of contemporary government.

However, when Morrison attempted by seeking state office to enlarge local success in New Orleans and to enhance the indirect influence on state affairs that his urban leadership position provided him, the obstacles to the cosmopolization of state politics manifested themselves strongly. Morrison has sought the Democratic nomination to the governorship (tantamount to election) three times—in 1956, 1960, and 1964—and has failed (albeit by narrowing margins) each time. Significantly, he has lost each time to candidates whose appeals were anticosmopolitan and rooted in the older bases of Southern politics. Although the race issue, which continues to furnish the strongest diversionary obstacle to cosmopolitanism in the deep South, played an important role in his defeat in both 1960 and 1964, when Morrison was labeled as the "bloc-vote" candidate, other aspects of Morrison's cosmopolitan background and actions also counted heavily in mobilizing the protest vote against him in an almost purely personal sense. Morrison's Catholicism, his "progressive moderation" (which is apparently objectionable even to welfare-oriented populists), his very derivation from the metropolis, and, perhaps as much as anything else, his very urbanity were grounds for suspicion in large sectors of the state which were far from being assimilated to the cosmopolitanism that characterized New Orleans and a sizable portion of South Louisiana. Among the bitterest of the ironies for a three-time loser, but one which is easily explainable in terms of the thesis proposed here, is the fact that Morrison's success as a cosmopolitan in New Orleans politics could be much more easily translated into a high-level role in national politics—he resigned in 1963 as Ambassador to the Organization of American States to run for governor—than into the major elective office of the state government in a noncosmopolitan state.

Urban Leadership during Change

By Gladys M. Kammerer and John M. DeGrove

ABSTRACT: Bosses, and their followers and apologists, peren-
nially inquire how alternative sources for leadership may be
developed in lieu of a boss. A boss is the principal but not
the sole leader of a political clique or faction at the top of a
monolithic power structure in a community with a monopolistic
political style. Alternatives to a boss are a clique or faction, a
popularly elected mayor, a city manager, or a political party.
Some Florida communities exhibit a monopolistic political
style; others, a competitive style. Towns with a monopolistic
style show a narrow set of economic interests; the entrance of
competing economic interests leads to competitive politics.
Ruling cliques are of varying kinds and can exist in either a
monopolistic or competitive situation. A popularly elected
mayor also can function as the leader in either situation. A
manager is a source of policy leadership, but several factors
condition his leadership. The elected mayor often inhibits the
manager. The manager's scope may also be greatly restricted
in a monopolistic setting, for he usually has no political base
of his own in such a situation. He will often have more scope
when competition is the style. A few managers succeed by
forming their own bases, as, for example, that composed of city
employees. Party participation is a concomitant of competitive politics in a few Florida cities, but the rise of the Republicans may lead to some local monopolies. Alternative sources
of leadership are enhanced by competition.

*Gladys M. Kammerer, Ph.D., Gainesville, Florida, is Professor of Political Science
and Director of the Public Administration Clearing Service, University of Florida. She
previously taught at Wellesley College and the University of Kentucky. She is the
author of books in public administration and coauthor with John M. DeGrove of books
on city-manager politics. She has been active in local and state politics in Kentucky and
Florida, and has published articles and monographs in public administration and national,
state, and local government.*

*John M. DeGrove, Ph.D., Gainesville, Florida, is Associate Professor of Political
Science, University of Florida. He previously taught at University of North Carolina.
He is author of a case study in the International Case Series and author and coauthor
of monographs in resource administration and local government. He has been a member
of the planning board of Gainesville and has been active in local and state politics in
Florida.*

A PERENNIAL query by political bosses, their followers, and apologists is directed to the question of where and how alternative sources for leadership may be developed in lieu of a boss. On the basis of our research in municipal politics in Florida, we shall attempt to analyze the sources of political leadership available to a community. The application of modern research techniques, including field studies as well as analyses of various kinds of census data, industrial and commercial statistics, election returns, and the like, can help provide us with some answers to this question.[1]

LEADERSHIP DEFINED IN OUR CONTEXT

One of the knottiest problems in connection with any research into sources of municipal leadership is to develop a definition operational for research purposes.

Leadership may be regarded as the concomitant of formalistic or structural phenomena, that is, as evidenced by holding of certain positions or offices or as a derivative of certain material relationships. For example, the ownership of large amounts of property or possession of high social prestige are often assumed to confer leadership on the possessors. In contrast, however, leadership may be thought of as evidenced by possession of certain behavioral characteristics or skills, such as the ability to *influence* others to a particular course of action. Influence can be con-

sidered as the ability to persuade another person to decide as the influencer wishes. Leadership may go beyond influence to the exercise of *power* over others, which involves *authority* to obtain the *obedience* of others to one's command. Both small-group behavior studies and decision-making studies have served to alert us to the fact that a gap is often found between occupancy of an office, on the one hand, and the exercise of power, on the other.

Furthermore, power in one sphere of activity does not *ipso facto* assure power in another sphere. The manager of the local branch of a national industrial concern, although at the top of the local hierarchy of his company and in control of the selection, promotion, and dismissal of local employees of that firm, may lack skill or interest in local politics and exercise little political power. Or he may have skill but be forbidden by a company interdiction against political activity from participating in the political process, thereby losing all value from his skill. Conversely, a self-employed attorney of modest means may be very persuasive in manipulating what Schattschneider has called the "mobilization of bias" to determine the questions that are allowed to emerge into public discussion.

Without getting into the analytical questions of whether power is conceived of according to a dyadic or an n-adic relationship,[2] or an ego- or other-orientation, we wish to state that we assume that power to make community political decisions inheres in the principal officeholders of a community. We also assume that some power, at least to influence such office-

[1] For an excellent methodological analysis of possible variables in community studies, see Harry M. Scoble, "Some Questions for Researchers Regarding Economic, Political and Social Structural Variables Underlying Processes and Patterns of Community Decision-Making and Change," a paper prepared for a research seminar on Processes of Community Decision-Making and Change and Their Influences upon Education, University of Oregon, Eugene, Oregon, August 5–24, 1963.

[2] See William H. Riker, "Some Ambiguities in the Notion of Power," a paper delivered at the 1963 Annual Meeting of the American Political Science Association.

holders in certain directions in their decision-making, inheres in those most intimately associated with their election or appointment to office. In other words, we postulate that mayors and city councils and city managers, and sometimes department heads, by reason of their formal position in the structure of city government, actually possess some measure of power in the community system of power. We also postulate that those economic, social, and political groups that help them achieve their officeholding status enjoy an "access" to such officeholders which makes them participants in the exercise of power also. These persons, by reason of their being actors in various kinds of power relationships, we think of as "leaders" in the municipality.

The question of the existence or preservation of power at all times, whether exercised positively or negatively, leads to the second major problem, that is, the determination of the situations or contexts in a community in which power may be manifested by leaders. As many observers of community politics have pointed out, the power to prevent questions from emerging into public discussion as issues has as significant consequences for the city as the power positively to participate in decision-making.[3] Thus, discovery of what is a "non-issue" as well as what is an "issue" gives us a clue as to the "mobilization of bias" and is requisite to interpret community politics correctly.

Power in a governmental unit can be conceived of as a system of distribution in a continuous state of change involving the parties to the system, the

differential amounts exercised, and the matters over which power is exercised. Or, conversely, a change in the matters over which power is used or in the structure for decision-making permits new participants access to the distribution system. Also changes in other governmental and economic units with which a city has relations affect changes within the city's system either over matters at issue, participants, or power exercised by any of them. Thus, changes in the leaders occur.

The leadership or power structure of a city can be understood only when viewed over a time span in comparison with such power structures in similar cities. It is just this kind of comparative view over a time span that the University of Florida research team, of which the present authors are a part, attempted to provide in their studies of Florida urban politics.[4] From these studies, inferences are drawn as to possible interrelationships of style of politics and economic and social configurations as well as typology of issues relating to style.

BOSSISM AND THE RULING CLIQUE

Before moving into a discussion of possible sources of municipal leader-

---

[3] See Peter Bachrach and Morton S. Baratz, "Two Faces of Power," *American Political Science Review*, Vol. 61 (December 1962), pp. 947–952, for a critique of Robert A. Dahl's New Haven study in the light of this kind of analysis of "non-issues" as well as "issues."

[4] Under a Social Science Research Council group research grant to Gladys M. Kammerer in 1960, the following studies were done of politics in Florida council-manager cities: Kammerer, Charles D. Farris, John M. De-Grove, and Alfred B. Clubok, *City Managers in Politics* (Gainesville: University of Florida Press, 1962) and, by the same authors, *The Urban Political Community* (Boston: Houghton Mifflin Company, 1963). Under a Rockefeller Foundation grant covering a three-year study, beginning in 1961, the same team has concerned itself with Negro participation and leadership in nonmetropolitan communities in Florida, a type of analysis which has required an unraveling of the total group and leadership structure over time in each polity to identify and describe the Negro structure during the same period.

ship as indicated by our studies, let us attempt to clarify one other notion, namely that of the political boss. We conceive of a boss as the principal but not the sole leader of a political clique, faction, or group at the top of a monolithic power structure in a community characterized by a monopolistic style of politics and made up largely of a working-class population with a low level of education. Normally, the boss is thought of as a party leader, but we found a boss operating under the nonpartisan requirement where, in fact, there were no parties operating in municipal politics. Only cliques could be found. It would seem that even where political parties operate with a boss, a cohesive clique clusters around him. The boss is the major co-ordinating authority that exists to manipulate the party for clique control. We do not conceive of a boss as ruling in solitary splendor but simply as having a primacy in the clique due to his central position in the communications net.

Much more significant from the standpoint of identifying what may well be the most important independent variables in the boss-controlled town, we found that, despite some increase in population, the town obtained no new economic bases and no new or different social classes, nor did any outside-based groups attempt to inject themselves into decision-making in the town. In contrast, neighboring communities grew very rapidly, changing in their economic and social configurations, especially in the direction of getting a large proportion of higher income and more highly educated migrants and thereby changing in their political configurations.

In short, the concept of the boss is tied up with exercise of actual power and is not limited to mere persuasion or to reputational attributes. It is also tied up with a particular kind of town

as to economic and social flavor— predominately working class.

ALTERNATIVE SOURCES OF LEADERSHIP

Alternatives to bossism cannot be discovered without identifying other ways of allocating the exercise of power and responsibility for co-ordination among the chief decision-makers. The same amount of power remains in the municipality, as the total jurisdiction loses no power, in the transition away from a boss. It simply adopts a different system of distribution of power which may or may not actually be wider. Even before a different distribution of power can be undertaken, however, a middle-class and upper-class population must increase in proportion to working-class numbers in order to develop and articulate a new set of values and policy objectives. Out of such expression of competing values, competitive power groups or cliques emerge.

Four alternative sources of leadership can be identified. These are (1) a clique or faction, (2) a popularly elected mayor, (3) a city manager, and (4) a political party. Each of these will be considered in relation to the two polar styles of politics we found in the cities we studied: a monopolistic and a competitive style. A monopolistic style we define as one in which a single political clique continuously wins all, or almost all, elective offices over a period of at least several elections. Although it may be challenged from time to time by another clique or by "self-starting" opponents, such opposition is sporadic and lacking in continuity. A competitive style of politics we define as one in which two or more political cliques regularly compete over a considerable period of time for public elective office. One clique can win elections fairly consistently, but, if it is regularly challenged by the same opposition clique from one election to the next, a competitive style of politics prevails in the community. Our definition of clique does not require a formally organized leadership group but applies equally validly to informal, unstructured groups that share similar policy commitments and desire to acquire and maintain control of the local government in order to further their policy goals. Most cliques operate from an identifiable power base of economic interests or aggregates—perhaps also social groupings—able to achieve electoral support. Cliques, as we use the term, may be equated with "crowds" or "factions" as used by other authors.

Style of politics we found a more useful analytic tool with which to classify towns than that of stability or instability, which are very "fuzzy" concepts. If instability means change in political control and stability, non-change, the first may occur under a monopolistic style of politics through the process of "revolution." In such an instance, one clique with complete control is totally replaced by another clique with monopolistic control, and the town might be called "unstable" or changing. This actually happened in the one boss-controlled town we studied. Yet the style of politics had not changed, and this to us seems crucial. In one of the cities we studied, two cliques regularly competed; the regularity of their competition structured the politics of the town. Surely this was a "stable" town, but that term does not adequately or accurately describe the competitive style of politics that prevailed there.

The first alternative source of leadership without a boss, just as with the boss, is the ruling clique or faction. The significant difference between the town run in monopolistic style by a clique without a boss and one with a boss is that, in the first type, the clique leaders conduct their own mediation and co-ordination within government and between government and outside groups instead of acting through the boss. Usually a clique has one member whose role is somewhat more influential within the clique in the decisions the group must make, but his relationship is one of influence rather than of greater actual control over other clique leaders. The clique acts in a true sense collegially, insofar as we could discover in the towns we studied. Their cohesiveness enables them to conceal some policy decisions from public view for a long time, as in two towns we studied, where clandestine special assessment favors by the city council to major developers created a severe strain on city finance. To borrow a phrase from Peter M. Blau, the "prime beneficiary," the clique, through its privatization of power, is the same whether its power is channeled through a boss or exercised directly by a clique operating unchallenged in monopolistic style.

Towns with a monopolistic style of politics will be examined first to identify possible sources of leadership apart from the obvious and broad generic one of the ruling clique itself. In the first place, in each of these towns, economic opportunities were limited largely to a single aggregate or set of interests. To the extent that such towns developed alternative or competing economic bases or organized effectively to start building a competing base, they moved into a competitive style of politics. Also the development of a new economic base in some instances brought persons with a different life style and different social identification. The development of different social perspectives as well as new economic goals helped to induce change in political style.

Ruling leadership cliques may differ markedly, according to the environmental settings in which they operate, both in the kinds of people who constitute the clique and the procedures they follow, even if the substance of their decisions may be quite similar. For example, in one town in which were located a major educational center and a large state institution, the ruling clique was made up primarily of local university graduates who had remained "locals" in their orientation to the community despite involvement by a number of them in state-wide politics and business enterprise.[5] Their policy goals for that town were limited to maintenance of the *status quo* as to public services and expenditures and use of their power to vote business favors, investments opportunities, and rebates to themselves. In another town of much smaller size, the ruling clique was largely but not entirely one family clan which had remained narrowly rural in outlook, despite the high degree of urbanism in the county as a whole, and which included only two college graduates. This second clique also looked upon the city government as a source of business favors to itself; such favors were of a petty kind. In still a third town which was almost entirely upper middle class, made up of retirees and professional and managerial persons employed in the adjacent metropolitan core city, almost anyone in the town could get into the leadership group by indicating a willingness to dedicate the required time and energy to council service. This suburban community offered a very limited range of services and enjoyed consensus on rigidly enforced zoning against

multiple dwellings, businesses, industry, and even against churches and recreational organizations. We consider the latter small city by no means atypical of the one-class dormitory suburb. Still a fourth small city, which was essentially monopolistic in style of politics, experienced tensions as a result of a generational cleavage over the attraction of industry, with the parental group of businessmen less interested than their sons in expansion of the town's one-commodity market economy. Nevertheless, since the struggle in this last town was essentially within the family, the town was not subjected to competitive politics.

The first two of these towns furnish contrasts that are enlightening as to one manner in which new sources of leadership may be developed and the whole style of politics of the community may be changed. The university town during the decade of the fifties received a great influx of middleclass professional people as the university enrollment doubled; the state institution was increased and its program goals changed from a custodial to a professional level; a new industry in the electronics field was established which employed primarily research and technical employees. These middleclass newcomers brought a new set of values and perspectives on such issues as community planning, zoning, municipal services, and housing. Many of these people would be categorized as "cosmopolitans."[6] As a result of the frustrations they experienced from continuous rejection of their ideas and demands by the "old guard," which had long ruled in monopolistic style, they organized against the natives for control and developed a complete platform, contesting successfully for a council seat in 1961, and, when they gained majority control in 1963, they

[5] As Robert K. Merton uses "local" in his article "Patterns of Influence: Locals and Cosmopolitans," in *Social Theory and Social Structure* (rev. ed.; Glencoe, Illinois: Free Press, 1957).

[6] *Ibid.*

started pushing aggressively along a broad front for one item after another to assure translation of program items into ordinances and administrative actions.

The contrasting town dominated by a familistic clique is a low-income working-class community that also received an influx of new residents in the fifties, but almost all of the in-migrants were working-class retirees living on their social security pensions in trailer parks or inexpensive small homes. The ruling clique was indifferent to municipal services or capital improvements and confined its interest to maintaining the customary low level of taxes and dividing up the petty favors and city purchases among themselves. One of the strongest members of the clique, a son-in-law in the central family, was city manager for most of the eight years that another son-in-law served as mayor. A challenge to the clan developed in the late fifties from a newcomer businessman who proposed public improvements that would have been judged minimal in most communities but were virtually revolutionary to that town. A political "revolution" was effected through victory by the challenger's slate in 1959, but his ineptitude in trying to force through simple police record-keeping and dismissal of the police chief precipitated several crises including dismissal of a professional city manager and a police strike. The "old guard" clique retaliated by organizing a recall election which they won by a large vote. They not only regained all seats on the council and restored the fired police chief but they also put in as city manager the family son-in-law who had been mayor during the fifties and whose submissiveness insured faithful execution of clique decisions. Interestingly, however, the style of leadership changed with their return to monopolistic control, for the "old guard" adopted the capital improvements program of the ejected opposition and had to act vigorously and positively. Without the development of a new economic base and a large in-migration of people of a different social class and educational level, the ingredients were missing both for development of new leadership sources and a permanent political base.

Cliques may also provide the source for leadership where a competitive style of politics prevails. Contrasting issue orientations had their effect in developing contrasting styles of leadership in one of the cities we studied. One clique which clustered around a so-called "boardwalk" clique or small merchants in an old beach resort town stood for relaxed police enforcement, minimal municipal services, and low taxes. The rival clique was supported by middle-class dormitory suburbanites who worked in an adjacent large city, and it was led by a businessman with a state-wide clientele. Its goals embraced the attraction of large chain-operated motels and construction of capital improvements. The charter provision for election of all members of the council every two years pushed the dormitory suburbanite clique into "crash" programs of improvements every time it won a majority because of the fear of imminent defeat unless it could point to significant achievements. The "boardwalk" clique, in contrast, felt impelled to stop the opposition's programs and fire its manager.

The popularly elected mayor, even in council-manager cities, provides a source of leadership which structures council relationships around the mayor. The elected mayor brings his own set of role expectations, particularly expectations that he will enjoy a primacy in policy presentation and in shaping policy decisions by the council. The electorate and the press also expect an elected mayor to take the lead in making policy proposals. The elected mayor as leader may be found in conjunction with either a monopolistic or a competitive style of politics. Regardless of the style of politics which prevails in the city, the popularly elected mayor is tied to a clique and is the chief exponent of their politics.

In one town, a group of retired millionaires who held no offices themselves had dominated for well over a decade and used their local "cracker" agents as their surrogates in government. The elected mayor and some of the council were permitted by the millionaire clique to enrich themselves to a certain extent by engaging in conflict-of-interest activities and to dispense favors to their friends. But their major service was in voting property assessment favors to several of the millionaires who had become developers. The entire clique, including its "cracker" surrogates, was dedicated to preservation of a strict zoning system.

However, relaxation of the zoning ordinance to permit the construction of a set of co-operative apartments on the beach introduced a new social and economic configuration into the community, with important consequences. The new in-migrants were an upper middle-class retired professional, managerial, and military elite who objected on moral grounds to the conflict-of-interest practices and slovenly approach to administration of the "cracker" surrogates. They also objected to the rebates and tried to change the tax structure. From their group, a retired physician was elected to the council and then twice elected as mayor after the "cracker" mayor had been discredited by a lawsuit over his conflict-of-interest activities. Mayoral powers over the manager were increased by charter amendment. How-

ever, at no time did the mayor succeed in wresting majority control of the council away from the millionaire developer clique. As a result, council meetings were normally the arena for noisy and bitter strife between the mayor and his clique opponents, with the retiree followers of the mayor forming a claque to applaud and boo the clash of debate. Competitive politics had come with a vengeance to this town, swirling around the figure of the elected mayor, just as the monopoly control by the millionaire clique had concentrated attention on their "cracker" agent in the mayor's chair.

In another town which moved from a monopolistic to a competitive style of politics, the elected mayor provided the principal overt source of leadership under both styles. The main factor in helping to restructure the style of politics of the town was the establishment of a second commercial bank which pursued an aggressive business policy. Around that bank clustered a younger set of downtown merchants who became sufficiently influential in the Chamber of Commerce to reorient that group into an aggressive program to bring new industry to the town. This same group started open competition in council politics. Around the original bank clustered a group of older, more conservative businessmen who were cautious about industrial development. The collision between the two bank cliques first came into the open when the newer bank group successfully backed a young ethnic restaurateur for the council and later for mayor and also advocated, through the Chamber of Commerce, a program of control of industrial waste from existing industrial processing plants. For the first time in the history of the town, the group introduced a specific election platform. With the use of a platform for more spending and for identification of emerging problems, the entire style of leadership changed with the style of politics. The mayor was expected to be a "doer" and not merely a "reactor."

Another city with an elected mayor and a competitive style of politics had experienced during the fifties extreme turnover both among mayors and among city managers. Originally a millionaire retirees' "estate" town, it had long been dominated by an "old guard" group clustered around the original land-development company. However, new money came into the town after World War II to establish a new bank and other enterprises, and a group of developers and businessmen in various kinds of supply businesses clustered around the bank to form a clique that successfully challenged the old-guard "estate" group. The mayor ultimately elected by the bank group was the major developer in the town who almost immediately plunged into real-estate schemes for park and recreational development that proved costly to the city. A sizable group of dormitory suburbanites, made up of managerial and professional employees, came into the city in the mid-fifties after a major aircraft and missile plant was located nearby. This young group, pursuing a family style of life, was interested in additional recreation facilities, especially for swimming and boating on the lakes, hitherto a private preserve of the millionaire waterfront property owners. A professional man, independently employed, unseated the developer for mayor in 1957, only to be defeated himself in 1960 by an ambitious attorney affiliated with the bank group who used the mayor's office to launch himself on a congressional career in 1962. Then the job was filled by a young businessman who was identified with the dormitory suburbanites. However, because the mayoralty election is not timed with the election of a majority of council seats, the election of a mayor does not always guarantee that the policies he stands for will be effectuated. Indeed, it merely seems to increase the vehemence of advocacy of issue stands by mayoral candidates. The politics of this town, as of the beach resort town previously described, we call *regime* in nature because the very destiny of the city —that is, "what kind of town shall ours be"—is at stake in its electoral contests. The elected mayors, therefore, have remained the central figures in articulating notions of town destiny for their cliques.

The city manager, of course, is another major source of policy leadership and, therefore, of political leadership in council-manager cities, but the force and direction of a manager's leadership depend upon several important factors. The elected mayor constitutes one major institutional limitation on the various manager roles involving policy formulation and execution. A true role collision—that is, two persons trying to get into the same set of roles simultaneously—occurs with a fair degree of frequency in manager cities with an elected mayor.[7] The result is a higher dismissal rate for managers in such cities for reasons we describe as "palace" rather than electoral or power exchanges[8] in clique control of council. Consequently, the manager's actual range of role behavior of a leadership nature is considerably reduced in these cities over a period of time.

The prevalence of a monopolistic style of politics in a city also tends to reduce the city manager's scope for

[7] See article by Gladys M. Kammerer, "Role Diversity of City Managers," in *Administrative Science Quarterly*, Vol. 8 (1964), pp. 421–422.

[8] A power exchange is a transfer of majority control of city council from one clique to another as a result of an election.

political leadership. Even though managers in such cities were usually "local amateurs" [9] rather than "outside professionals" and also were members of the ruling clique, nevertheless they were regarded as faithful agents of the clique rather than prime originators of policy ideas. This is so by reason of the commitment of such cliques to maintenance of the *status quo* rather than vigorous search for issues and programs. Hence, the manager tends to become the chief "nay-sayer" in town on behalf of the clique. But even more significant is the fact that a manager in such a city has no political base of his own and no way to build one where the field for political activity is entirely pre-empted by his clique.

A competitive style of politics provides more opportunity for city-manager leadership, especially when a more liberal or free-spending clique has gained control. As was mentioned earlier in discussion of cliques, those dedicated to positive program goals sometimes institute "crash" programs and hire outside professional managers to move forward with actual construction before the next election. Consequently, the manager in such cities occupies a symbolic as well as an actual position of political leadership. The fact that this twofold position makes him especially vulnerable to immediate dismissal in the event of a power exchange does not seem to deter professional managers from accepting positions in this type of setting.

One especially skillful city manager whose influence as a policy leader was enhanced by his possession of an independent political base consisting of

[9] We defined "amateur" as nonuniversity-educated or educated in a field unrelated to city management and lacking relevant job experience of an administrative nature. "Local" we defined as having received all education and experience within the county where employed.

city employees managed to survive several power exchanges in a fourteen-year period. The changing leadership requirements heretofore mentioned, as between conservative or "penny-pinching" and liberal or free-spending cliques, are almost classically illustrated by the way this particular manager changed his own role expectations and style of leadership according to the clique in control of city hall. This is shown by his handling of the budget. When the liberal or free-spending clique was in power, he launched broad programs to expand and improve the quality of city services. Major street improvements, sanitary services, storm drainage construction, and expanded recreational and cultural programs were proposed and adopted. In addition, liberal spending provided the manager with the *quid pro quo* for his independent power base: salary increases to city employees. But when the conservatives gained control, he concentrated on improving the quality of administration in such ways as through position classification, purchasing procedures, and internal reorganizations. His own view of the needs of the community as to basic services never changed, but the vigor with which he proposed services did change according to the clique objectives that prevailed.

A political party, despite the nonpartisan requirement in the cities we studied, is another major source of political leadership. Parties may be the local wing of a national major party or a purely locally oriented party limited to community political activity alone and without ties to state or national groups. At this stage of Florida local politics, the rise of overt party participation is a concomitant of competitive politics in a few cities. However, with the overwhelming influx of Republican migrants into central and south Florida cities, it is not inconceivable that Republicans may gain a monopolistic position in the politics of many towns in this area in the foreseeable future. In two of the major Florida cities which have had high rates of power exchanges, manager turnover, fragmenting of cliques, and even disappearance of cliques with the rise of factions with entirely new bases, the slating of candidates by the Republican party in recent elections has provided the sole factor giving continuity to local politics. Such slating has been the result of the retiree influx into each city. In the city described above in connection with the elective mayor and extreme turnover among three cliques, the Republican party entered the 1960 mayoral election to provide workers but no real policy orientation. In none of these cities has party activity to date structured council politics into any greater coherence, because each city has extreme fragmentation of interest groups and economic bases, with "regime" questions of economic destiny of the city at stake in each case.

In the university city discussed earlier, the local party based primarily upon university professors and professional personnel from the new electronics plant has served as the major vehicle for development of a competitive style of politics based upon coherent issue articulation. The city is now organized politically into two clearly competitive political factions which embrace economic and class configurations. This appears to be a division that may have some permanence, especially as the cosmopolitan professional population of the town will probably show marked growth by 1970.

As a leadership source, a political party is far more open than a clique or faction. Although party organization is controlled by a small group at the top who may be considered the ruling clique, nevertheless it is easier to get into the party inner circle than into an economic or social clique. In one of our larger cities, birth, educational attainment, and economic affluence are, indeed, limiting factors on membership in the conservative clique. But, on the whole, it is still true that anyone of normal intelligence willing to accept the prevailing party ideology and spend sufficient time working for the party can usually rise fairly rapidly in a party hierarchy. In growing cities which have yet to settle into permanent, stable factional patterns, the local or national political party, therefore, is the easiest avenue through which to achieve political status quickly in the community because it is usually the most open political organization. Therefore, it is close to the other end of the continuum as to ease of entry, possibility of rise, and ultimate exercise of power from the ruling clique where a monopolistic style of politics prevails.

Through all these sources of leadership from the ruling clique to the party runs the common thread of clique orientation of leadership. The combining element is always a clique or a faction, and the truly divisive element is similarly clique fragmentation. In other words, we conceive it to be impossible except in a true consensus community to develop leadership apart from the development of cliques even in a political party context. This does not mean a frozen leadership because of its origin in a clique. In many of our cities, population growth has been so great that cliques rise and fall and change in almost kaleidoscopic fashion. New persons who threaten the electoral dominance of a ruling clique are co-opted into that clique and given office or status as unofficial decision-makers in order to maintain a monopolistic style of politics. Only in the static community or one which attracts exactly the same social and economic class are the clique and its leadership group stable. Therefore, the problem that confronts us is as to the relationship between typology of political styles and the various combinations of leadership sources with a clique.

The possibilities for alternative sources of leadership are much more limited where a monopolistic style of politics prevails. By the very nature of the case, the economic base of the community is restricted and controlled by the ruling clique, and one social class or a combination of two classes prevails. An elected mayor may provide a source of leadership in such a community so long as he is willing to serve as the pliant agent or surrogate for the ruling clique. He is, therefore, merely a symbolic vessel for the clique, as is a city manager. At this stage of Florida municipal development, political parties do not accord with this monopolistic style.

A competitive style of politics may also provide merely the two or more cliques as sources of leadership, but the sources are doubled, and the community has a choice between programs as well as personalities under this style. It may even have a choice as to destiny of the town, or regime. Furthermore, under a competitive style, the elected mayor may become a real leadership figure as the exponent of policy, although he will usually have limited survival value unless he can align himself to a fairly articulate and coherent clique. With this style, a city manager may also rise to prominence as a principal policy leader provided the mayor is chosen by the council and not by popular vote. If the manager has a political base of his own in the form of actual votes that can be manipulated in a council election, he may have great survival powers as a "third force" despite power exchanges between cliques. Finally, a political party may provide the city with a significant source of leadership and even structure local politics into a competitive style. Or it may at least bring a modicum of order and coherence into a fragmentation of cliques so extreme as to yield no coalitions or workable majorities among councilmen. Although the hazards of the competitive style of local politics are serious, running all the way to near chaos, nevertheless it is only through competition that any effective source of leadership other than a single dominant clique may be developed as an alternative to a boss.

The Decentralized Politics of Los Angeles

By FRANCIS M. CARNEY

ABSTRACT: Under the same formal governmental arrangements, characterized chiefly by nonpartisanship and decentralization, Los Angeles has known both good and bad municipal government. Undoubtedly, the decentralized politics together with the demographic and geographic diversity of the city have helped to keep Los Angeles from coming under the control of a political boss or a covert ruling elite. With abundant room to grow and a benign natural environment, Los Angeles has not suffered from the more obvious problems of urban density. One possible consequence of this is a low visibility for politics. Now, as the margin of safety against the problems of urban density diminishes, some observers doubt that the diffuse and decentralized politics and government are adequate to the problems facing the city. Proposals to change the charter in the direction of centralization and integration have not drawn impressive support. Informal integration of city politics through particular private groups, or even through a comeback of political parties, does not seem to be immediately forthcoming. Probably until acutely pressed by obvious civic needs, Los Angeles' citizens will not consider her decentralized politics too great a price to pay for an unbossed and scandal-free city.

Francis M. Carney, Ph.D., is Associate Professor of Political Science at the University of California at Riverside and is currently Visiting Professor of Political Science at the University of California at Los Angeles. He is author of The Rise of the Democratic Clubs in California (1958) and coeditor (with H. Frank Way) of Politics 1960 (1960) and Politics 1964 (forthcoming in 1964). He is a contributor of articles on politics to scholarly and popular periodicals and newspapers.

IS it a vagrant and mistaken impression one has that when sociologists study community political power they tend to see rule by types of informal elites but that when political scientists examine the same subject they are inclined to see pluralistic arrangements in which policy emerges from an intricate interplay of competing elites or democratically from the competition of roughly equal citizen groups? All students of community power, of course, cannot be simply labeled as elitist or pluralist. The suggested sociologist-political scientist distinction, moreover, is simply an impression, and, as noted, perhaps a foolish one, stemming possibly from the wholly adventitious fact that one man happened to study political power in Atlanta and another in New Haven.

Still, it is possible that the sociologist, bent by the traditions and preoccupations of his discipline, hunts for informal groups, latent structures, and real as opposed to apparent purposes. Perhaps also the central place of the concept of social class in the development of sociology leads the sociologist to think naturally of power, prestige, rewards, and security as differentially distributed along class lines, to think of political power as an attribute of a broader social power. The political scientist, for all of his recent sophistication, may be so hag-ridden by the ancient preoccupations and conceits of his own discipline that he cannot but look to a constitutional matrix when he comes to study political power.

All of this may be worth no more than five minutes or so of heady talk in a graduate seminar in politics, but it does come to mind when one examines political power in Los Angeles. The best available evidence indicates that political power in Los Angeles is exercised within a constitutional matrix. That is, public policy decisions are largely made by the constitutionally designated public officials responsible for the various policy jurisdictions. While these constitutional officers, furthermore, are the subjects of many by no means equal influences, the best available evidence again indicates that there is no "power elite" in any meaningful sense of that phrase. A true power elite would be a small, self-conscious, coherent group, with distinct interests of its own, which controls public policy in such a way as always to realize its own interests regardless of the interests and wishes of the majority of the citizens and—or—of the public officials chosen by the citizens.[1]

Charles R. Adrian has offered a typology for nonpartisan elections. Adrian ranks elections from I, in which major political parties integrate and control the process in all but name, through IV, in which there is no apparent party, slate, or overt group activity.[2] Los Angeles, it is suggested here, falls between Adrian's groups III and IV, although Adrian himself tentatively assigns Los Angeles to type III.[3] Similarly, if one were to take Robert A. Dahl's five-point "scale" of patterns of community leadership, which ranges from the more or less familiar "power elite" at the top to a genuine diffusion of power at the bottom,[4] he would have to place Los Angeles on a point between groups IV and V, at the "power-diffused" end of the scale. Winston W. Crouch and Beatrice Dinerman, who have done the most comprehensive

[1] For a full discussion, see R. A. Dahl, "A Critique of the Ruling Elite Model," *American Political Science Review,* Vol. 52, No. 2 (June 1958), pp. 463–469.

[2] Charles R. Adrian, "A Typology for Nonpartisan Elections," *Western Political Quarterly,* Vol. 12, No. 2 (June 1959), pp. 449–458.

[3] *Ibid.,* p. 456.

[4] Robert A. Dahl, *Who Governs?* (New Haven, 1961), pp. 184–189.

study to date of government in the Los Angeles metropolitan area, put it as follows:

There are almost no general-interest groups seeking to influence formulation or execution of policy at either the municipal level or the metropolitan area level. The grouping of aggregates of political interest is made according to a different pattern. The pattern is more nearly a grouping of interests according to functional concerns. Influence groups, composed of clusters of public and private representatives, tend to form around programs; for example, planning and zoning, harbors, air pollution control, flood control, indigent aid, and public health protection. . . . Although there is some overlap in the membership of the influence groups concerned with functions at the local and regional levels alike, there is no common aggregate. Because the membership of the influence groups surrounding functional organizations tends to vary, a pluralistic system has developed in which competition exists among groups who covet the prizes to be bestowed through the allocation of political and economic resources.[5]

Edward C. Banfield and James Q. Wilson also rank Los Angeles among the few really large cities in which there is little evident party activity or slate-making nonparty group activity.[6] Finally, graduate students at the University of California at Los Angeles have conducted dozens of interviews with Los Angeles city officials and the heads and officers of numerous businesses and business and trade associations. These interviews contain many references to alleged and supposed "elites" and "kingmaking" groups, cabals, consortiums, and shadow organizations, but the interviews reveal no evidence at all that such groups exist and perform as alleged. In other

[5] Winston W. Crouch and Beatrice Dinerman, *Southern California Metropolis* (Berkeley and Los Angeles, 1963), p. 17.
[6] Edward C. Banfield and James Q. Wilson, *City Politics* (Cambridge, Mass., 1963), p. 152.

words, Los Angeles is at present unbossed, is in the grip of no political machine, and behind its formal government there lurks no covert or semicovert "power elite."

This really does not tell us very much, however, and a number of further observations must be made in order to put into some useful context the claim that Los Angeles is without a boss, without a machine or power elite. Let me make those essential observations in brief form and then return to take up each in greater detail.

(1) Los Angeles now enjoys "good government," both in the sense of the traditional formal arrangements implied by that term and in practice as well. (2) Los Angeles has not always had good government in the latter sense. It has evolved to its present state from a recent past that was at least different and probably malodorous. This evolution has taken place without benefit of any significant change in formal structure. In other words, Los Angeles had a machine-ridden "bad" government under the same arrangements which characterize its present good government. (3) Political forms and styles are evanescent and political eras come and go rapidly. In the present politics of Los Angeles there are harbingers of further change, change in the direction of integration and rationalization. An alarmist might say that already he sees shadowy outlines of the boss and his machine. (4) One must look beyond the formal political and governmental arrangements to general social and cultural influences if he is fully to understand the politics of Los Angeles. The important general cultural influences are a great and diverse population, prosperity, tremendous mobility within a confused social system, a large proportion of relatively new residents, vast physical distances, multiple discrete localities, and, above all, a su-

perbly pleasant climate and terrain which turn one's thoughts incessantly to the pursuit of the sweet life. The principal effects of these influences that I want to stress here are the absence of a definite leadership stratum and a general nonsalience of politics and political solutions to problems. (5) The beneficence of nature and the rapacious foresight of an earlier generation of civic leaders and boosters have given Los Angeles a handsome though diminishing margin of protection against the swarming problems of most dense urban areas. As that margin shrinks, politics and government may become more important to the people of Los Angeles. (6) Political resources are unevenly allocated, but I believe that no major group is disarmed and without access. (7) Major research must yet be done before we can know fully the nature and distribution of political power in Los Angeles and understand the role of both constitutional and general cultural influences in determining the pattern of politics.

GOOD GOVERNMENT

Crouch and Dinerman speak of the "general high quality of performance" of Los Angeles city government and of the governments of the metropolitan area.[7] Banfield and Wilson list Los Angeles along with Minneapolis, Milwaukee, Detroit, and Oakland as cities "notable for 'good government.' "[8] Banfield and Wilson, and others also, use the term "good government" to characterize a set of legal arrangements as well as to describe the quality of a city's government. The classical good government arrangements are nonpartisanship in municipal elections, the council-manager form, at-large election of councilmen, pervasive civil service, and

[7] Crouch and Dinerman, *Southern California Metropolis*, p. 373.

[8] Banfield and Wilson, *City Politics*, p. 165.

initiative, referendum, and recall.[9] Los Angeles, along with other California cities, has nonpartisan municipal offices, a strong city council, a widespread civil service, and the three familiar vehicles of direct democracy. Los Angeles does not have a city manager and its fifteen city councilmen are elected from single-member districts by majority vote. California cities have been nonpartisan since 1911 [10] and Los Angeles has lived with her present charter since 1924. Yet the legacy of honest and efficient government, it is generally agreed, dates from the accession to the mayor's office of Fletcher Bowron in 1938. Bowron gave fifteen years of distinguished service, and there are people who believe that under him Los Angeles was the best governed major city in the United States. Bowron's successor, Norris I. Poulson, did not develop the prestige and command that were Bowron's, but he served two honest and useful terms, functioning generally in the Bowron tradition. The present mayor, the dynamic and controversial Samuel W. Yorty, defeated Poulson in a savagely contested election in 1961. Yorty has not yet made his record, but his restless energy and hunger for command have him straining at the limits of mayoral power—under the charter the mayor is relatively weak as opposed to the city council—and ensnarled in a rancorous, and some say paralyzing, running fight with the city council.[11] The whole point here is that from 1938 to

[9] See Banfield and Wilson, *City Politics*, chaps. 11, 12, 13 for an excellent discussion of the relations between "good government" and the quality of local government.

[10] See Eugene C. Lee, *The Politics of Nonpartisanship* (Berkeley and Los Angeles, 1960), for a good discussion of the history of nonpartisanship in California.

[11] For an account of the Yorty-council struggle, see James Phelan, "Trouble in Happyland," *Saturday Evening Post*, May 25, 1963, pp. 78–82.

1964, from the mild-mannered Bowron to the fiery Yorty, Los Angeles has had at least tolerably effective government. To what extent, then, is this quarter-century of good government due to the formal structure?

The answer, unfortunately, does not come easily or clearly. The nonpartisanship has certainly been thoroughgoing. Los Angeles, like the rest of California, is heavily Democratic insofar as voting registration goes. But Bowron and Poulson were Republicans, as were the majorities on the city council during the Bowron and Poulson tenures. Registered Republicans, moreover, dominated the other city offices both elective and appointive. Yorty is a Democrat but a party maverick, and more Democratic activists undoubtedly opposed his election than supported it. Until very recently, the parties have not been visibly active in city elections. The fact that Republicans held office out of all proportion to their voting strength in partisan elections led many of us once to suppose that there was a Grand Old Party (GOP)-Big Business-*Los Angeles Times* cabal really "running things" behind the nonpartisan facade. But one simply must conclude that that case is not made at all. There may well be a concert of interests among the Republican party leaders, the business community in Los Angeles, and the *Los Angeles Times*. But there is simply no evidence that such a concert was in any way formalized and even less that it may have been running things. As a matter of fact, there is some evidence to the contrary. In the first place, the *Times* bitterly opposed Bowron and supported his incumbent opponent in 1938. Though the *Times* and, I am sure, most Republicans supported Bowron in subsequent elections, the *Times* and, I am sure, most Republicans deserted him and supported

Poulson in 1953. In 1961 the *Times* strenuously opposed Yorty but could not prevent his election. In any case, there is now a Democratic majority on the council, a Democratic mayor, and heavy Democratic infiltration of the appointive boards and commissions of the city government. Business-GOP-oriented power elites do not let things like that happen. The *Times* and the business interests simply have not won often enough to let us say that they were the wheels of a machine which functioned behind the screen of non-partisanship.

But that is not to say that the honest and efficient and unbossed Los Angeles government is attributable to nonpartisanship alone. Crouch and Dinerman feel that the district system of electing the city council has been instrumental in preventing the growth of any machine or of a dominating elite behind the scenes. The literature on the question of at-large versus district election of city legislatures comes down softly for the view that district or ward elections tend toward diffusion of power under nonpartisanship and that at-large election under nonpartisanship offers a tempting opportunity to informal slate-making groups even while it offers representation for general city interests at the expense, presumably, of district or neighborhood interests. Certainly in Los Angeles the district system coupled with staggered terms for the fifteen city councilmen has had a diffusing, decentralizing effect on the distribution of power and influence. The members owe their elections mainly to forces or groups within their respective districts rather than to any city-wide or other single group or force. Until recently, there have been no consistent voting blocs on the council, and winning majorities have had to be put together anew with each issue. Since the accession of Mayor Yorty in 1961, there has emerged a stable and top-heavy "anti-Yorty" majority on the council, but one must say in all candor that the majority is apparently held together solely by its common antipathy to the aggressive mayor. So, although ward or district elections are often associated with "machine politics" and partisanship and although at-large election seems to go in the package with nonpartisanship, Los Angeles' system of coupling district election with nonpartisanship has contributed to a decentralized politics. Voters not only "vote for the man rather than the party" under nonpartisanship, they also vote for fifteen different men in staggered elections and elect a council of fifteen sovereigns.

The "boss potential" of the mayoral office in Los Angeles is slight. Actually, the mayor is chief executive of the city in name only. He can recommend legislation and veto (subject to council reversal), he must submit a yearly municipal budget to the council, and he has certain powers of appointment and removal which seem impressive at first glance but turn out to be mild or weak upon closer inspection.[12] The charter designates the mayor chief executive of the city and charges him to "exercise a careful supervision over all of its affairs" and to exercise a "constant supervision over the acts and conduct of all officers and employees." But, as Bollens notes, "having assigned such administrative responsibility to the mayor, the charter does not grant him authority equal to the assignment. His administrative authority is highly restricted and very indirect."[13] The

real heads of most of the city departments are the boards and commissions. These, it is true, are appointed by the mayor and are removable by him. But both removal and appointment require council approval. If the mayor is at odds with the council over some other matter or if a majority on the council is sympathetic to an officer who has offended the mayor or with whom the mayor simply cannot work, the mayor is essentially powerless to do much about it. It is precisely this sort of restriction under which Mr. Yorty now chafes so publicly. Bowron and Poulson were bothered by the charter limitations also, but neither was so combative a fellow as is Yorty, and, in their special circumstances, they had better opportunities for conciliation than does Yorty. I do not want to suggest at all that Yorty's now celebrated troubles with the city council arise wholly or even primarily from temperament. They do not. The present deadlock is a result of a combination of legal structure, temperament, and certain other elements present now but not present in the Bowron and Poulson tenures. These will have to be touched on below. What I want to stress here is that the people of Los Angeles have partially secured themselves against emergence of "the boss" by keeping the mayor "weak." Innumerable citizen groups, college professors, study commissions, and neutral observers have urged revision of the mayoral powers under the charter, but these have been unavailing against the power of the council and the will of the voters.

Another part of the "good government" package of the Progressive reformers was the provision of arrangement for direct democracy, or abundant use of the initiative, referendum, and recall. The old Progressives not only despised the boss and the party ma-

[12] See John C. Bollens, *A Study of the Los Angeles City Charter* (Los Angeles, Town Hall, 1963), pp. 149–187, for a detailed analysis of the inadequacy of executive power in Los Angeles. The discussion here follows Bollens generally.

[13] Bollens, *A Study of the Los Angeles City Charter*, p. 179.

chine, they also distrusted the representative process itself and felt that the public good was safe only when the people themselves could act directly. Los Angeles has made generous use of direct democracy. It would not do here to get into the controversy over the use and abuse of the referendum. Let us take note of that consensus which holds that some things are the proper subjects of referendums and some not and then note further that Los Angeles has not often bothered to make the distinction. The Angelenos, as they are called, have been prodigious legislators. This increment of power to the voters has been a further hedge against Caesar, without doubt. Questions must be asked about the ultimate utility of this almost promiscuous use of direct democracy. But here let it be noted that it is one more evidence of decentralization of power in Los Angeles, one more brick in the edifice of good government. Besides, it was through the recall that the scandal-ridden predecessor of Bowron was jettisoned and the fine mayor himself brought into office. Let us turn our attention briefly to that occasion.

THE OLD MACHINE

Los Angeles was not noted for "good government" in the 1930's even though it was government under essentially the same formal arrangements that prevail today. Was there a boss? A machine? The answer is not easy to give, and to try to untangle all the threads of power, scandal, protest, and crime, to say naught of maladroit administration in the years from 1933 to 1938, requires more space than is available here and requires for the telling the talents of a police reporter, a criminal lawyer, and a dramatist.[14] There

[14] The best fictional accounts of the semi-public life of Los Angeles in the 1930's are to be found in the "Marlowe" novels of the

are some facts, however, which can be set down.

Harry A. Raymond, a private investigator on the payroll of a private group inquiring into corruption in Los Angeles municipal government, was bombed in his automobile and all but killed on January 14, 1938. Subsequently, Captain Earl E. Kynette, head of the special intelligence squad of the Los Angeles police force, was tried and convicted of the attempt on Raymond's life. A routine big-city scandal, perhaps, but it spelled the end of the administration of Mayor Frank L. Shaw through a recall election which brought Superior Court Judge Fletcher Bowron into city hall. The Shaw administration's chief of police, James E. Davis, defended Captain Kynette to the end. Mayor Shaw defended Chief Davis to the end. The *Los Angeles Times* defended Chief Davis and Mayor Shaw to the end, fought the recall, and opposed Bowron. The *Times* had also supported Shaw for re-election, which he won handily a scant few months before Kynette tried to blow up Raymond, despite the fact that the other four Los Angeles daily newspapers were headlining nearly a scandal a day from the municipal government and the police. Two different interpretations can be placed on this sequence of events and relationships. (1) A bungling mayor and his equally bungling chief of police were betrayed by a brutal eager beaver of an intelligence squad captain, while a "boosterish" major daily newspaper, the owners of which had vested interests in Southern California land values, played Dr. Pangloss for the whole

late Raymond Chandler. The real nemeses of the incorruptible Marlowe were not the fancy babes and moronic bullies with whom he tangled routinely but corrupt cops and their corrupters from the worlds of politics and business.

dreary performance. (2) Big business interests—typified by the Chandler family with its holdings in land, oil, agriculture, transportation, and investments, and with the greatest newspaper in the western states, the Chandler family's *Los Angeles Times*, as their voice—sought to keep in power a hireling city administration which diligently protected business interests and kept taxes low and whose police fought ruthlessly to keep out "Red agitators" (labor-union organizers) and "welfare chiselers."

In the 1930's Los Angeles was not a "wide-open" town for vice, but it was considerably more tolerant than it has been for the past several years under the honest, efficient, and some say puritanical, police administration of Chief William Parker. Today, Los Angeles citizens would be shocked or amazed by a suggestion that prostitution and gambling flourish openly in their city. But in the thirties there was plenty of action at the gaming tables, and prostitutes were easily available from the fancy call houses of the west side to the cribs on the east side. Known hoods fought with guns and bombs over the division of the profits. Then, too, Los Angeles was well known as an open-shop city in the thirties, and the city police, led notably by their famous "Red Squad," co-operated in keeping it that way. Mayor Shaw's brother, reputed to be "the man to see at city hall," was indicted by a grand jury for, in effect, auctioning city jobs but escaped prosecution when the district attorney moved for dismissal of the indictment because the case against him vanished across the border with its bail-jumping chief witness. The Merchants and Manufacturers Association, an organization of middle-sized to big retail and industrial concerns in Los Angeles, and

the Downtown Businessmen's Association strenuously favored the open shop, lower taxes, and balanced city budgets and unquestionably were satisfied that the *Times* spoke for their interests. The Chandler family had huge and widespread business interests in the city and elsewhere in Southern California, fought unremittingly for the open shop, relentlessly "boosted" Los Angeles, advocated low taxes and the preservation of land values, and supported the Shaw administration and Chief Davis. All of this has led to whispers and rumors that will not be still that a "Shaw machine" was the front organization for big business interests led by the *Los Angeles Times*.

But these items must be considered also. The "Shaw machine" was in office for only five years and was quickly routed once Bowron took office. The *Times* opposed Shaw's election in 1933 though it supported his re-election in 1937. There is not a shred of evidence that the *Times* controlled a consistent majority on the city council. Neither the Shaw administration nor the *Times* could stifle revelations of scandal, secure the acquittal of Captain Kynette, or fight off the recall movement.

The *Times*, furthermore, together with the Downtown Businessmen's Association and the Merchants and Manufacturers Association, was not all-victorious in the days of Mayor Shaw, no more than it has been since. Although more *Times*-endorsed candidates for councilman have been victorious than have been defeated, there is no clear evidence from a study of the council voting records that the *Times*-endorsed candidates vote consistently as a bloc now or that they did in the days of Mayor Shaw. Finally, if we can view the *Times* as speaking consistently for the preservation of real-estate values, low taxes, and balanced municipal budgets, there is not any evidence at all that these positions are opposed by the majority of the people who voted in Los Angeles municipal elections in the past and who vote today. In my judgment, the most that can be said is that in the pre-Bowron days the *Times* and the local business interests for which it speaks enjoyed a disproportionate influence over the municipal government and over the electorate but that they did not control either the government or the electorate. I believe also that the conclusion is warranted that the influence of the purely local or regional business interests and of the *Times* has been decreasing since World War II. Yet, a kind of "inside dopesterish" legend persists—and commands particular credibility among liberals and Democrats—that the *Times* veteran City Hall reporter sits in the council chamber during sessions and flashes the signals to the hireling legislators, one finger for yea and two for nay.

Still, if there was no machine in the Tammany Hall sense and no controlling business elite behind the scenes, Los Angeles' experience with the Shaw regime is proof that the "good government" arrangements do not always insure honest and efficient government. Nonpartisanship, ward elections, a weak executive, and decentralization to the voters, nevertheless, are barriers to integration—whether the integration of the boss and his machine or that minimum necessary for concerted, planned address to the riotously growing problems of urbanism. There is some reason to believe that the current governmental problem for Los Angeles is the problem of integrating this loose, decentralized, and unbossed city with its pluralistic population. There are possibly, too, some candidacies on the horizon for the role of integrating or aggregating agents.

THE PROBLEM OF INTEGRATION

Los Angeles is a city of over 2,700,000 souls, the third largest in the United States. It is the central city of a metropolitan area of over 7,000,000. The city's population is strewn with increasing density over its 452.6 square miles of territory. The city has always had a downtown center, but there is an ancient wheeze which goes, "Los Angeles is no city; it's a bunch of suburbs in search of a center." Many Angelenos are foggy about the political jurisdiction they live in, or know that they are "county" if they pay their light bill to the Southern California Edison Company, "city" if they pay it to the Department of Water and Power. Los Angeles County is a mad patchwork of seventy-four incorporated municipalities laced by bleak stretches of unincorporated county territory. The other seventy-three cities are forever fearful of Los Angeles imperialism. Housewives in the other cities and in the Los Angeles city suburbs boast that it has been three, four, or five years since "I've been downtown." An odd phenomenon of Los Angeles life is the fact that while her citizens enjoy the sunshine, the beaches, the mountains, open spaces, broad boulevards, the patios and *lanais* of their "ranch" houses, the prosperity, the shops and restaurants, and the ubiquitous ethic of pleasure, very few of them *like* Los Angeles. It is popular to run down the city and the region, to say, "San Francisco, now there's a real town," or to make invidious comparisons with the way it was "back East," which can mean Montana or Idaho as well as Vermont or Virginia.

Everybody knows that a large proportion of Los Angeles's population is made up of newcomers, migrants to the state. Less well-known is the fact that the mobile Americans who have come to Los Angeles continue to move around at an astonishing rate once they have arrived.[15]   The Los Angeles homeowner may be intensely proud of, indeed, wrapped up in, his home. He may even be proud of and concerned about his neighborhood. But there is not much sense of place among the people. Los Angeles has a low quotient of civic feeling. As a political community, it is highly attenuated. As a body politic, it is gangling and loose, and the nervous system which coordinates that sprawling body is haphazard and feeble. There are two major daily newspapers and seven television stations. The more popular newscasters have large audiences, and they do discuss municipal and county issues regularly. But one feels that the Angelenos are drawn together more on one of those sorrowing nights when the Giants bomb Koufax early in the game than they are on a day of a municipal election.

Los Angeles voters turn out in very respectable numbers for state and federal general elections. If we drop the World War II years, the average turnout for general state and national office elections from 1935 to the present is 79 per cent.[16]   But, in general municipal elections from 1935 to 1951, the turnout for the city of Los Angeles averaged only 40.3 per cent. The turnout in the highest year for the period was 48.9 per cent; for the lowest year (barring the war years), it was 32.1 per cent.   In the general state election of 1962, nearly 80 per cent of those eligible in Los Angeles voted.

But in the municipal election of 1961, with its hot mayoral contest between Yorty and Poulson, only 49.8 per cent of the eligible voted. In the municipal election of 1963, with no mayoral contest but four council district seats, four charter amendments, and two bond issues at stake, only 41.8 per cent of the eligible actually voted. All of these figures represent percentages of those actually registered to vote. If we took the percentage of those legally qualified to register but who for one reason or another have not registered, the figures would be much lower. One study shows that, for the municipal elections in 1941 and 1951, only 24.5 per cent of the *potential* voters (those who would be qualified to vote if they registered) actually turned out.[17]   With such figures to conjure with, who can speak of a mandate?

Ordinarily, this would be the place to begin speaking of alienation, but somehow the word and the sense that it conveys are not, I think, proper here. It may be possible to get out of the idiom of pathology in trying to generalize about Los Angeles. Politics simply has a low visibility in Los Angeles. This is partly due to that relentless pursuit of the pleasures the area offers. Partially it is due to the frantic and distracted pace of urban life generally and to the particularly exhausting battle for status within the confusing social system of Los Angeles, where the young man who buses your dishes at Frascati's climbs, after work, behind the wheel of a 3.8 Jaguar and tools off to his high-status neighborhood. The low visibility of politics is undoubtedly also partially produced by the lower key of nonpartisan campaigning. Finally, it is also due to the foresight of that earlier buccaneer generation of civic leaders who ravaged a

[15] See Crouch and Dinerman, *Southern California Metropolis*, p. 4.

[16] This figure and most of the turnout figures which follow are based on the reports in Lawrence W. O'Rourke, *Voting Behavior in Forty Five Cities in Los Angeles County*, Bureau of Governmental Research, University of California at Los Angeles, 1953.

[17] O'Rourke, *Voting Behavior in Forty Five Cities in Los Angeles County*.

beautiful valley hundreds of miles to the north to bring water to the city and annexed vast tracts of suddenly useful land to give the city space. Space and water and sunshine have been instrumental in providing that margin of safety against the myriad obvious problems of urbanism. It is not that politics seems futile or ugly or threatening to the Angelenos. To most of them, politics seems unnecessary.

But the people of Los Angeles may have to turn to politics as the margin of safety diminishes—and it is diminishing. Even the farflung precincts of the city are getting crowded. Public transportation in the city, as in the metropolitan area generally, is contemptible. The ever-growing population must, perforce, take to the automobile—which it does with zest anyway—and the result is an almost constant nerve-racking traffic jam on the freeways and the surface roads. On too many days of the year, the entire Los Angeles basin is overhung by an evil, eye-stinging, throat-burning, and possibly deadly roof of smog. The task of providing an educational system that can satisfy the needs of so diverse a society is simply mountainous. The drive of the "unassimilated" ethnic minority groups (14 per cent of the population are Negroes, and there are more persons of Mexican descent living in Los Angeles than in any city of Mexico save the capital) for a full share of the "good life" poses agonizing problems in housing, zoning, education, employment, and political districting. The city, like the area as a whole, is frighteningly dependent upon the golden stream of defense dollars for its prosperity, and no one really knows what its responsibilities are and what its resources are if automation produces some of its feared short-run effects. Neighborhood and other partial inter-

ests—with representation in the council and access to the decentralized administration and fortified by the traditional American sense of the rightness of "making a buck"—frustrate the development of a city-wide view. This makes for a pluralistic politics, a politics of trading, bargaining, and compromising, but it also contributes to urban sprawl and jumble and to the postponement of action until the problem becomes overwhelming.

In the context of the present and approaching problems, the judgment that Los Angeles enjoys good government may have to be revised. John C. Bollens clearly believes that the existing governmental arrangements are no longer adequate. He has called for extensive revision of the charter and most of his revisions point toward centralization or integration. Specifically, Bollens urges amendment of the charter to provide significant increases in both the administrative and legislative powers of the mayor, a drastic reduction in the administrative powers of the boards and commissions, "extrication of the Council from the heavy volume of administrative detail," and, although he would retain nominations from districts in all cases, at-large election of five of the fifteen members of the council.[18] If these revisions were to be adopted, the mayor would be a far more powerful figure than he is at present. Thus far, however, there seems to be little public support for any increase in mayoral power, and the past history of similar proposals for charter revision leaves little room for expectation that such recommendations as Bollens' will bear early fruit.

Crouch and Dinerman, though their focus is on the governmental problem of the whole metropolitan area, clearly are scanning the horizon for possible

[18] Bollens, *A Study of the Los Angeles City Charter*, pp. 149–201.

agencies of integration. Their general conclusion, however, is that integration will have to emerge from those very pluralistic processes which give the area its decentralized character. Integration, they feel, will come when the many groups, forces, political units, and elected officials involved realize that it is in their interests to integrate.[19]

Los Angeles' confusing social structure has been mentioned repeatedly here. The city is truly a system in which "you can't tell the players without a program," and the program has not yet been printed. That is a fascinating story in itself, but what must concern us here is the absence of a subjectively coherent upper class. There are "old families" and the "very rich" and a world of "celebrities," and their bazaars, cotillions, balls, hunts, and betrothals are duly chronicled on the society pages, most especially of the *Times*. But nobody really cares what this stratum does and no one is under the illusion that it constitutes a powerful class. More important than that is the fact that this stratum does not provide Los Angeles with a corps of disinterested leadership dedicated to civic betterment and the common interests.[20] That is not to say that one day, when the area has settled down and lost its "boomtown" ethos, such a stratum will not emerge. But, for the present and the immediate future, Los Angeles cannot look to class leadership as the integrating or aggregating agent.

The minority groups, of course, are inherently particular and, in any case, are only just now developing their own leadership and political effectiveness. This is especially true for the Negroes, who now have members on the city

council and are displaying an aggressiveness and willingness to use politics to achieve their special goals. The Mexican-Americans are more passive, more nearly alienated from politics, and do not have the political effectiveness that their numbers alone could win for them. The other ethnic minorities are too small to be of consequence.

Organized labor has still the stigma of the parvenu. Los Angeles can never go back to the "bad old days" of the open shop and the "Red Squad," even though the *Times* still proclaims from its masthead that it stands for "true industrial freedom." But labor has not been a major power in the city either. At best, labor has been one of the competing influence groups. It is good to have the support of American Federation of Labor and Congress of Industrial Organizations if some civic project is to be undertaken, but labor has not led or initiated or integrated. The numerical strength of labor, moreover, has not been growing apace with the population, and one has the sense that labor's influence is stable or declining rather than on the increase.

The old group of local businessmen, with purely local interests in property values, low taxes, and a good civic "image"—that group for which the *Times* was, and still is, the spokesman —has lost influence to labor, to the organized minority groups, to the far-flung voters who have their own and often divergent local interests. World War II, moreover, brought vast new industries to Los Angeles, and the managers of these new industries, while they share a desire for low taxes, also have interests that conflict with those of the old local barons. For one thing, the new industries look outward, to Washington and New York, for capital, for ideas, for stimuli. They have, moreover, a distinct interest in the living conditions of their employees and

[19] Crouch and Dinerman, *Southern California Metropolis,* pp. 363–411.

[20] Crouch and Dinerman have commented perceptively about this. See *Southern California Metropolis,* p. 393.

cannot simply embrace that low municipal budget which is the ideal of the old property or real-estate-oriented businessmen. The businessmen have a real differential in their favor with respect to political skills and resources, but they do not monopolize political resources and they are not themselves sufficiently cohesive to constitute the integrating or aggregating group.

The *Times* itself, a legend of power in Los Angeles, seems less influential today when it is one of but two major daily papers in the city than it did a generation ago when the readers could choose among five dailies. The paper still prints its mock ballot with its own choices clearly marked on the day before municipal and state-wide elections. But a more diversified electorate seems unmoved by the *Times*'s choices. The paper itself has undergone some remarkable changes since World War II and especially since the management of the paper was taken over by Otis Chandler, the fourth generation of the family. No longer does the paper speak in the hoarse rages of dinosaur Republicanism. It is now moderate and even liberal in some of its editorial policies. It offers a wide range of opinion on its editorial pages, reports local and national events fully and honestly, and covers world news better than any newspaper in the west and as well as all but two or three papers in the nation. The crude "boosterism" of the earlier days has been replaced by a mature major concern for local news and issues. The hard core of vested interest the *Times* still jealously guards is, I think, the interest in the real-estate market and property values. But I think that it is clear now that the *Times* is one influential voice for interests and groups that are themselves influential but not dominant in the city.

The most interesting potential agency of integration of the diffuse politics of the city is the political party. As noted above, Los Angeles would have to be ranked low on any scale of nonpartisan cities in which covert or informal integration is, nevertheless, performed by political parties. The old domination of municipal offices by registered Republicans was not due to any concerted action by the Republican party as such. Rather it was due largely to the fact that in the class which has the time, money, and skills for public office there were, and are, so many more Republicans than Democrats. The atmosphere of nonpartisanship with its peculiar issue "blandness" and the support of the newspapers for conservative candidates contributed also to the Republican ascendancy. Since the early 1950's, however, there has been a noticeable increase in party activity in the municipal elections.

The official agencies of the parties, the county central committee for each party, remain scrupulously aloof in conformance with the law. But unofficial or auxiliary groups, most notably the Democratic clubs, have entered the field repeatedly. In the case of the Democratic clubs, ideology has combined with the needs of organizational morale or sense of purposefulness to impel the clubs into municipal politics. They do not, yet, participate openly as Democratic clubs. But the club membership and machinery are mobilized behind candidates who may have themselves come out of the club movement. Eleven years ago, in the earliest years of the club movement, one organization in the San Fernando Valley not only made an intensive search for a councilmanic candidate, but, when he had been found, voted to support him and did so to the extent that his entire campaign was managed by the club and its leadership. This has happened in at least half-a-dozen subsequent councilmanic races since 1953. No candidates have openly avowed that they are all-but-official party nominees, and Democratic club leaders are careful to point out that the clubs do not "officially" enter the campaigns—whatever the disclaimer "officially" may mean.

While I hesitate to identify this surge of partisan activity as a distinct trend toward partisanship in the municipal elections, especially because there has been no matching effort on the part of Republican organizations, some additional evidence may be offered. In several recent school-board elections, both the Democratic clubs and such Republican-allied organizations as Pro-America, an organization of conservative women, have been active in turning up candidates and serving as campaign vehicles. School-board politics, of course, can be intensely ideological and emotionally provocative. It is natural to assume that liberal Democratic club members and the conservative women of Pro-America would be drawn as individuals into school-board politics. But the participation of recent years has been on an organizational basis, again especially in the case of the Democratic clubs. Then, too, there has long been strong sentiment among Democrats in the state officially to return partisanship to local elections.[21] Although the Republicans, the press in the state, and, undoubtedly, most voters right now are opposed to the partisan ballot for local elections, it is conceivable that the Democrats with their big legislative and electoral majorities could succeed in amending the constitution and ending the long experience with nonpartisanship.

The Yorty-Poulson contest of 1961 had distinct partisan overtones for the

[21] See Lee, *The Politics of Nonpartisanship*, pp. 110–116.

electorate in Los Angeles, though, ironically enough, most Democratic activists undoubtedly opposed Yorty, whom the activists consider a renegade for his open support of Nixon in the 1960 presidential election as well as for the mercurial Yorty's history as a maverick. Intra-Democratic party strife now complicates and exacerbates the struggle between Yorty and the city council, a majority of whom are Democrats. The best-known member of the council is Mrs. Rosalind W. Wyman, a Democrat and wife of Eugene Wyman, state chairman of the Democratic party. Mrs. Wyman is perhaps Yorty's keenest rival on the council. Yorty and some of his supporters hint of the threat of a putative "machine" stemming from an alleged alliance among the Wymans and Assembly Speaker Jesse Unruh of Los Angeles, the famed "Big Daddy" and only person remotely resembling a "boss" in California politics. The reason for mentioning all of this here is to try to indicate the degree to which partisan questions and considerations, a partisan *ambience* so to speak, have invested the traditionally nonpartisan politics of the city. Just now the alienation of Yorty from almost all other elements of the Democratic party's activist cadre frustrates the potential of the parties to play that integrating and aggregating role most observers feel is desirable. But the potential is there and one may expect that Los Angeles' politics will grow more rather than less partisan in the years ahead.

A more partisan politics, however, is no guarantee that the decentralized and diffused character of the city's politics will be seriously altered. The city charter almost insures tension between mayor and council despite a possible party bond. The district system of choosing the council insures representation for parochial neighborhood interests and the sprawling diversified population of the city insures that the neighborhood interests will be multiple or diverse. In a pluralistic politics, concerted action against serious and general problems is difficult before the problem has become acute or even disastrous. The problems of Los Angeles do not seem disastrous or even potentially so to the Angelenos. So long as this happy condition continues under the present arrangements and the city continues to be honestly governed, politics will continue to have a low salience, and decentralization and diffusion of power will continue as the pattern.

Recent Developments in Latin-American History

By ROBERT N. BURR *

THE field of Latin-American history has shown vigor during the past five years. Among other indications of this fact has been the willingness of publishers to reissue basic works which originally appeared in English and to publish translations of important studies by Latin Americans. Among the former were Cline's study of Mexico, Crawford's on Latin-American thought, Freyre's on Brazilian society, Haring's on the Spanish empire, and Whitaker's on the independence movement and on the enlightenment. Among the latter were the works of Chevelier on colonial Mexico, of Picón-Salas on colonial intellectual life, and of Romero on Argentine political thought.[1]

There was, moreover, an impressive number of new publications. In its volumes for 1959–1963, the *Handbook of Latin American Studies*—an important multidisciplinary annual bibliography—listed some five thousand books and articles in the field of Latin-American history alone, among which were several valuable additions to research tools, including Cline's brief but comprehensive general bibliography in the American Historical Association's *Guide to Historical Literature*.[2] Several good specialized bibliographies also appeared. For Mexico, there was the final volume of the revised edition of Roberto Ramos' basic three-volume bibliography on the revolution and a three-volume bibliography of sources of

---

[1] Howard F. Cline, *The United States and Mexico* (rev. ed.; Cambridge, 1963); Rex Crawford, *A Century of Latin American Thought* (rev. ed.; Cambridge, 1961); Gilberto Freyre, *The Masters and the Slaves: A Study in the Development of Brazilian Civilization* (New York, 1964); C. H. Haring, *The Spanish Empire in America* (New York, 1963); Arthur P. Whitaker, *The United States and the Independence of Latin America, 1800–1830* (New York, 1962); Arthur P. Whitaker (ed.), *Latin America and*

the *Enlightenment* (Ithaca, 1962); François Chevelier, *Land and Society in Colonial Mexico* (Berkeley, 1963); Mariano Picón-Salas, *A Cultural History of Spanish America: From Conquest to Independence* (Berkeley, 1962); José Luís Romero, *A History of Argentine Political Thought* (Stanford, 1963).

[2] Howard F. Cline, "Latin America," in *The American Historical Association's Guide to Historical Literature,* ed. George Frederick Howe and Others (New York, 1961).

Robert N. Burr, Ph.D., Los Angeles, California, is Professor of History at the University of California, Los Angeles. He is chairman of the SSRC-ACLS Joint Committee on Latin American Studies, vice-chairman of the Conference on Latin American History of the American Historical Association, and United States member of the Commission on History of the Pan American Institute of Geography and History. He has written on the history of Latin America's international relations.

* I thank my research assistant, Robert R. Smith, for collecting much of the material on which this article is based.

recent Mexican history.[3] Useful specialized bibliographies for Brazil, Venezuela, and Argentina were also compiled by Moraes, Grases, and Furlong Cárdiff and Geohegan.[4] Finally, two surveys of Russian writings on Latin-American history were published.[5]

The historian's resources were enriched also by publication of several greatly needed guides, such as Gómez Canedo's of depositories for colonial Latin-American history in Latin America, the United States, and western Europe; [6] Harrison's analysis of Latin-American materials in the National Archives of the United States; [7] and the extensive survey of archival materials on Mexico both within Mexico and in foreign depositories by Millares

Carlo.[8] Also of use are the three guides to the periodicals and periodical literature of Latin America prepared by Zimmerman, Leavitt, and the staff of the Columbus Memorial Library of the Pan American Union.[9]

Another indication of vigor in the field of Latin-American history has been the spurt of inventory-taking among its practitioners. The results have taken the form of historiographical or bibliographical essays and statements of research needs. Among the former are book-length surveys of Brazilian seventeenth-century historical writing, of the literature about colonial Paraguay, of Cuban history to 1898, interpretations of the May Revolution in Argentina, and evaluations of Venezuelan historiography as well as of Soviet historical work on Latin America.[10] Also noteworthy were Whitaker's discussion of new trends and interpretations in Latin-American history and Haring's review of literature on "Trade and Navigation between Spain

[3] Roberto Ramos, *Bibliografía de la revolución mexicana,* Vol. 3 (Mexico, 1960); Luís González y González, Guadalupe Monroy, and Susana Uribe, *Fuentes de la historia contemporánea de México* (3 vols.; Mexico, 1961–1962).

[4] Rubens Borba de Moraes, *Bibliographia Brasiliana: A bibliographical essay on rare books about Brazil published from 1504 to 1900 and works of Brazilian authors published abroad before the independence of Brazil in 1822* (2 vols.; Amsterdam and Rio de Janeiro, 1958–1959); Pedro Grases, *Nuevas temas de bibliografía y cultura venezolanas* (Maracaibo, 1960); Guillermo Furlong Cárdiff and Abel Rodolfo Geohegan, *Bibliografía de la Revolución de Mayo, 1810–1828* (Buenos Aires, 1960).

[5] Leo A. Okinshevich and Cecilia J. Gorokhoff, *Latin America in Soviet Writings, 1945–1958* (Washington, 1959), lists approximately fifty historical works. Warren Schiff, "An East German Survey Concerning Recent Soviet Historical Writings on Latin America," *Hispanic American Historical Review,* Vol. 40, No. 1 (February 1960), pp. 70–71, analyzes Manfred Kossok, "Zum Stand der sowjetischen Geschichtsschreibung über Lateinamerika," *Zeitschrift für Geschichtwissenschaft,* Vol. 7, No. 2 (1959), pp. 426–441.

[6] Lino Gómez Canedo, *Los archivos de la historia de América* (2 vols.; Mexico, 1961).

[7] John Parker Harrison, *Guide to Materials on Latin America in the National Archives* (Washington, 1961).

[8] Agustín Millares Carlo, *Repertorio bibliográfico de los archivos mexicanos y de los europeos y norteamericanos de interés para la historia de México* (Mexico, 1959).

[9] Irene Zimmerman, *A Guide to Current Latin American Periodicals: Humanities and Social Sciences* (Gainesville, 1961); Sturgis E. Leavitt, *Revistas hispanoamericanas; índice bibliográfico, 1843–1935* (Santiago de Chile, 1960); Pan American Union, Columbus Memorial Library, *Index to Latin American Periodical Literature, 1929–1960* (8 vols.; Boston, 1962).

[10] José Honório Rodrigues, *Historiográfia del Brasil: Siglo XVII* (Mexico, 1962); Efraím Cardozo, *Historiografía paraguaya; I, Paraguay indígena, español y jesuita* (Mexico, 1959); José Manuel Pérez Cabrera, *Historiografía de Cuba* (Mexico, 1962); Enrique de Gandía, *Historia del 25 de mayo: Nacimiento de la libertad y de la independencia argentina* (Buenos Aires, 1960); Germán Carrera Damas (ed.), *Historia de la historiografía venezolana* (Caracas, 1961); Juan A. Ortega y Medina, *Historiografía soviética iberoamericanista, 1945–1960* (Mexico, 1959).

and the Indies" following the publication of his classic work on the subject.[11] Combining the historiographical essay and the analysis of research needs was the series of excellent and extensive articles in the *Hispanic American Historical Review* by Barager, Stein, Potash, Griffith, and Arnade which dealt with Paraguay and Uruguay, Argentina, the Brazilian Empire, Mexico, Central America, and Bolivia after independence.[12] Dealing primarily with research needs and opportunities was an article by Stein and an issue of the *Americas* to which contributions were made by Helguera, McGann, and Naylor.[13]

Over one hundred new volumes of primary source materials have been made available to the historian since 1959, most of which added detail to traditional themes rather than opening new areas of research. The bulk of the materials on colonial Latin America, for example, was concerned with either the sixteenth-century conquest and settlement or the history of the eighteenth century,[14] while few sources were published for the little-known seventeenth century. Another well-worked theme which also accounted for an extremely large volume of source-materials publication was the independence movement. Noteworthy contributions were eight volumes of Argentine documents and thirty of materials published by the Venezuelan National Academy of History in celebration of the 150th anniversary of Venezuela's independence.[15] For the history of Latin America since independence, published source materials reflected continuing interest in the politics and personalities of the nineteenth century.[16] A notable contribution to the

---

[11] Arthur P. Whitaker, *Latin American History Since 1825* (Washington, 1961); C. H. Haring, "Trade and Navigation between Spain and the Indies: A Re-view—1918–1958," *Hispanic American Historical Review*, Vol. 40, No. 1 (February 1960), pp. 53–62.

[12] Joseph R. Barager, "The Historiography of the Río de la Plata Area Since 1830," *Hispanic American Historical Review*, Vol. 39, No. 4 (November 1959), pp. 588–642; Stanley J. Stein, "The Historiography of Brazil, 1808–1889," *ibid.*, Vol. 40, No. 2 (May 1960), pp. 234–278; Robert A. Potash, "Historiography of Mexico Since 1821," *ibid.*, Vol. 40, No. 3 (August 1960), pp. 383–424; William J. Griffith, "The Historiography of Central America Since 1830," *ibid.*, Vol. 40, No. 4 (November 1960), pp. 548–569; Charles W. Arnade, "The Historiography of Colonial and Modern Bolivia," *ibid.*, Vol. 42, No. 3 (August 1962), pp. 333–384.

[13] Stanley J. Stein, "The Task Ahead for Latin American Historians," *Hispanic American Historical Review*, Vol. 42, No. 3 (August 1961), pp. 424–433; J. Leon Helguera, "Research Opportunities in Modern Latin American—The Bolivarian Nations," *Americas* (April 1962); Thomas F. McGann, "Research Opportunities in Modern Latin America—Southern South America," *ibid.*; Robert A. Naylor, "Research Opportunities in Modern Latin America—Mexico and Central America," *ibid.*

[14] For example of valuable contributions to sources of these periods, see Raúl Porras Barrenechea (ed.), *Cartas del Perú (1524–1543)* (Lima, 1959), and Ricardo R. Caillet-Bois (ed.), *Documentos para la historia argentina, Tomo X: Padrones de la ciudad y campaña de Buenos Aires (1726–1810)* (Buenos Aires, 1959).

[15] Biblioteca de Mayo, *Colección de obras y documentos para la historia argentina* (8 vols.; Buenos Aires, 1960); Venezuela, Academia Nacional de la Historia, *Biblioteca de la Academia Nacional de la Historia* (30 vols.; Caracas, 1959–1960). For a listing and analysis of the Venezuelan item, see Jane de Grummond, "The Venezuelan Sesquicentennial Celebration Publications," *Hispanic American Historical Review*, Vol. 42, Nos. 1 and 4 (February and November 1962), pp. 29–36 and 544–557.

[16] Examples are Francisco Javier de Luna Pizarro, *Escritos políticos*, Recopilación prólogo y notas de Alberto Tauro (Lima, 1959); Bartolomé Mitre, *Correspondencia Mitre-Elizalde* (Buenos Aires, 1960); D. Pedro II, *Diario de 1862*, Introduction and notes by Helio Vianna (Rio de Janerio, 1960); and Universidad Nacional del Plata, Instituto de Historia Argentina, *Archivo del*

study of the period's political thought was the fifteen-volume collection edited by Grases and Pérez.[17] For the twentieth century, a continuing interest was shown in sources on the Mexican Revolution and also worthy of note were memoirs of the secretary of Getulio Vargas of Brazil and of a participant in the recent Cuban revolution.[18]

Three new general histories have appeared since 1959 [19] but most recent historical writing has been limited in scope. The colonial period continued to attract attention but broad general synthesis was attempted only in Zavala's comparative study of American colonial enterprises of Spain, Portugal, England, France, and Holland.[20] Work on the colonial period fell generally into two categories: syntheses of the history of specific areas for restricted periods of time, and monographic treatment of aspects of colonial life. Among the former were studies of colonial Panama, of the roots of

nationality in Paraguay, and an important work on eighteenth-century Brazil.[21] Monographs were published on a wide variety of more specialized topics.

For the history of the conquest, of interest were a solidly documented study of the discovery and conquest of New Granada, biographical studies of three conquerors, and an account of the conquest from an Aztec point of view.[22] Indian-Spanish relations were the subject of several studies: Forbes and Spicer investigated the Indians of the Southwest United States; Hanke dealt with racial prejudice; Borges analyzed methods of converting the American aborigines; and Giménez Fernández contributed a two-volume biography of the "Protector of the Indians." [23]

Several contributions on religious activity in colonial Latin America were

Coronel Doctor Marcos Paz (2 vols.; La Plata, 1959–1960).

[17] Pedro Grases and Manuela Pérez Vila (eds.), Pensamiento político venezolano del siglo XIX; textos para su estudio (15 vols.; Caracas, 1960–1962).

[18] Isidro Fabela (ed.), Documentos históricos de la revolución mexicana (3 vols.; Mexico, 1960–1962); J. Trinidad Núñez Guzmán, Mi infancia en la revolución: Apuntes de un muchacho pueblerino (Mexico, 1960); Luis Vergara, Fui secretário de Getulio Vargas: Memórias dos anos de 1926–1954 (Rio de Janeiro, 1960); and José Pardo Llada, Memorias de la Sierra Maestra (Habana, 1960).

[19] Helen Miller Baily and Abraham P. Nasatir, Latin America, the Development of its Civilization (Englewood Cliffs, N. J., 1960); Donald Marquand Dozer, Latin America: An Interpretive History (New York, 1962); John Edwin Fagg, Latin America: A General History (New York, 1963).

[20] Silvio Zavala, The Colonial Period in the History of the New World (Mexico, 1962).

[21] Rubén Darío Carles, 220 años del periodo colonial en Panamá (Panama, 1959); Elsa Mercado Sousa, El hombre y la tierra en Panamá según las primeras fuentes (Madrid, 1959); Efraím Cardozo, El Paraguay colonial: Las raíces de la nacionalidad (Buenos Aires—Asunción, 1959); C. R. Boxer, The Golden Age of Brazil, 1695–1750 (Berkeley, 1962).

[22] Juan Friede, Descubrimiento del nuevo reino de Granada y fundación de Bogotá (Bogotá, 1960); C. Harvey Gardner, The Constant Captain: Gonzalo de Sandoval (Carbondale, Ill., 1961); Vicente Murga Sanz, Juan Ponce de León (San Juan, 1959); Juan Friede, Vida y viajes de Nicolás Féderman. Conquistador, poblador y cofundador de Bogotá (Bogotá, 1961); and Miguel León-Portilla (ed.), The Broken Spears: The Aztec Account of the Conquest of Mexico (Boston, 1962).

[23] Jack D. Forbes, Apache, Navaho and Spaniard (Norman, 1960); Edward H. Spicer, Cycles of Conquest: The Impact of Spain, Mexico and the United States on the Indians of the Southwest, 1533–1960 (Tucson, 1962); Lewis Hanke, Aristotle and the American Indians: A Study in Race Prejudice in the Modern World (London, 1959); Pedro Borges, Métodos misionales en la cristianización de América (Madrid, 1960); and Manuel Giménez Fernández, Bartolomé de las Casas (2 vols.; Seville, 1960–1961).

published. Vargas Ugarte completed the fourth volume of his fundamental study of the church in colonial Peru, and José María Vargas wrote on the church in Ecuador. Both Shiels and Gómez Hoyos wrote on the patronato real, and Greenleaf and Lewin each studied aspects of the inquisition. Aspects of Jesuit and Franciscan activities were investigated by Pacheco, Pradeau, and Millé; and Hugo produced a two-volume work on the role of the missionary in the expansion of Brazil's frontiers. Also worthy of note was a biographical study of a missionary in New Granada.[24]

Colonial administrative history has also attracted interest during the last five years. Viceroyalty studies were published by Rubio Mané and Bobb, while Navarro García provided a valuable study of the intendency system in the Spanish colonies, and the Guatemala City cabildo was dealt with by Chinchilla. Ots Capdequí contributed to an understanding of Spanish land policy and Phelan investigated the

imperial bureaucracy. Particularly noteworthy was Zorraquín's history of the Spanish administrative system in the Río de la Plata region. Portuguese colonial administration in Brazil was analyzed in a general study of Portuguese colonization.[25]

There were relatively few studies of colonial economic and social life. Of major importance were, however, the three interpretive volumes of Chaunu's "dynamic and quantitative" analysis of the Seville monopoly. Significant also were the basic demographic studies on Mexico by Borah and Cook, and articles by Morse and McAlister on urban history and social structure respectively. Worthy of note were books on two American consulados by Rodríguez and Tjarks and a monograph on the Cuban economy by Ely.[26]

[24] Rubén Vargas Ugarte, *Historia de la iglesia en el Perú* (4 vols.; Burgos, 1953–1961); José María Vargas, *Historia de la iglesia en el Ecuador, durante el patronato español* (Quito, 1962); W. Eugene Shiels, *King and Church: The Rise and Fall of the Patronato Real* (Chicago, 1961); Rafael Gómez Hoyos, *La iglesia de América en las leyes de Indias* (Madrid, 1961); Boleslao Lewin, *La inquisición en Hispanoamérica* (Buenos Aires, 1962); Richard E. Greenleaf, *Zumárraga and the Mexican Inquisition, 1536–1543* (Washington, 1961); Juan Manuel Pacheco, *Los jesuitas en Colombia (1567–1654)* (Bogotá, 1959); Alberto Francisco Pradeau (ed.), *La expulsión de los jesuitas de las provincias de Sonora, Ostemuri y Sinaloa en 1767* (Mexico, 1959); Andrés Millé, *Crónica de la órden franciscana en la conquista del Perú, Paraguay y el Tucumán y su convento del antiguo Buenos Aires: 1212–1800* (Buenos Aires, 1961); Vitor Hugo, *Desbravadores* (2 vols.; Sao Paulo, 1959); and Mario Germán Romero, *Fray Juan de los Barrios y la evangelización del Nuevo Reino de Granada* (Bogotá, 1960).

[25] J. Ignacio Rubin Mané, *Introducción al estudio de los virreyes de Nueva España, 1535–1746* (3 vols.; Mexico, 1955–1961); Bernard E. Bobb, *The Viceregency of Antonio María Bucareli in New Spain, 1771–1779* (Austin, 1962); Luís Navarro García, *Intendencias en Indias* (Seville, 1959); Ernesto Chinchilla Aguilar, *El ayuntamiento colonial de la cuidad de Guatemala* (Guatemala, 1961); José María Ots Capdequí, *España en América: El régimen de tierras en la época colonial* (Buenos Aires, 1959); John Leddy Phelan, "Authority and Flexibility in the Spanish Imperial Bureaucracy," *Administrative Science Quarterly,* Vol. 5 (June 1960), pp. 47–65; Ricardo Zorraquín Becú, *La organización política argentina en el período hispánico* (Buenos Aires, 1959); and A. da Silva Rego, *Portuguese Colonization in the 16th century: a study of the royal ordinances* (Johannesburg, 1959).

[26] Pierre Chaunu, *Seville et l'Atlantique (1504–1650); Deuxième partie: partie interpretative; Structures et Conjoncture de l'Atlantique espagnol et hispano-americain* (3 vols.; Paris, 1959); Woodrow Borah and S. F. Cook, *The Population of Central Mexico in 1548: An Analysis of the Suma de visitas de pueblos* (Berkeley, 1960); Sherburne F. Cook and Woodrow Borah, *The Indian Population of Central Mexico, 1531–1610* (Berkeley, 1960); Richard M. Morse, "Some Characteristics of Latin American Urban History," *American Historical Re-*

Nor was there much work published in the field of colonial intellectual and cultural history. Monographs appeared on European attitudes toward the "new world" and on the "black legend." There were studies of the ideas of the Spanish reformer, the Conde de Campomanes, and of political thought in colonial Argentina. Attention was given to the work of the scientist Tadeo Haenke in South America. Two outstanding contributions were Leonard's interpretation of seventeenth-century Mexico and the study by Kubler and Soria of art and architecture in Spain and Portugal and in their colonies.[27]

Griffin's *"Outline"* provided a useful overview for the national period as a whole, and several writers surveyed the history of individual nations in that period. For Argentina, Levene and Scobie emphasized economic and social history while Lizando discussed cyclical interpretations of its history. Vianna dealt with the broad sweep of Brazil's history while Holanda edited the first volumes of a history of Brazilian civilization. Caballero Calderón surveyed the social and political history of Colombia while there appeared two separate volumes on Venezuela: one a cooperative work by Venezuelan scholars; the other by Lieuwen. Important also was Cline's able synthesis of recent Mexican history.[28] However, the great bulk of historical writing was on a more limited topical basis.

The topic of independence continued to attract attention. Interest was shown in analyzing the causes of independence movements from new perspectives as well as in dealing with their social and economic aspects.[29] However, there

view, Vol. 67, No. 2 (January 1962), pp. 317–338; L. N. McAlister, "Social Structure and Social Change in New Spain," *Hispanic American Historical Review*, Vol. 43, No. 3 (August 1963), pp. 349–370; María Encarnación Rodríguez Vicente, *El tribunal del consulado de Lima en la primera mitad del siglo XVII* (Madrid, 1960); Germán O. E. Tjarks, *El consulado de Buenos Aires y sus proyecciones en la historia del Río de la Plata* (2 vols.; Buenos Aires, 1962); Roland T. Ely, *La economía cubana entre los dos Isabelas, 1492–1832* (Habana, 1960).

[27] Antonello Gerbi, *La disputa del Nuevo Mundo* (Mexico, 1960); Edmundo O'Gorman, *The Invention of America: An Inquiry into the Historical Nature of the New World and the Meaning of its History* (Bloomington, 1961); Swerker Arnoldsson, *La leyenda negra, Estudios sobre sus orígenes* (Göteborg, 1960); Ricardo Krebs Wilckens, *El pensamiento histórico, político y económico del conde de Campomanes* (Santiago de Chile, 1960); Enrique de Gandia, *Historia de las ideas políticas en la Argentina, T. 1°, Las ideas políticas en la época hispana* (Buenos Aires, 1960); Josef Kühnel, *Thaddaeus Haenke* (Munich, 1960); Charles Arnade and Josef Kuehnel, *El problema del humanista Tadeo Haenke: Nuevas perspectivas en la investigación haenkeana* (Sucre, 1960); Irving A. Leonard, *Baroque Times in Old Mexico, 17th Century Persons, Places and Practices* (Ann Arbor, 1959); George Kubler and Martin Soria, *Art and Architecture in Spain and Portugal and their American Dominions, 1500–1800* (Baltimore, 1959).

[28] Charles C. Griffin, *The National Period in the History of the New World: An Outline and Commentary* (Mexico, 1961); Gustavo Gabriel Levene, *La Argentina se hizo así* (Buenos Aires, 1960); James R. Scobie, *Argentina: A City and a Nation* (New York, 1964); Manuel Lizando Borda, *Temas argentinas del siglo XIX: Estudios históricos* (Tucumán, 1959); Hélio Vianna, *História do Brasil* (2 vols.; São Paulo, 1961–1962); Sérgio Buarque de Holanda (ed.), *História geral da civilizaçao brasileira* (2 vols.; São Paulo, 1960); Eduardo Caballero Calderón, *Historia privada de los colombianos* (Bogotá, 1960); Mariano Picón-Salas, Agusto Mijares, Ramón Díaz Sánchez, Eduardo Arcilla Farías, and Juan Liscano, *Venezuela Independiente, 1810–1960* (Caracas, 1962); Edwin Lieuwen, *Venezuela* (London, 1961); Howard F. Cline, *Mexico: Revolution to Evolution 1940–1960* (New York, 1963).

[29] Hernán Ramírez Necochea, *Antecedentes económicos de la independencia de Chile* (Santiago de Chile, 1959); Sérgio Villalobos, *Tradición y reformaen 1810* (Santiago de Chile, 1961); Tulio Halperin Donghi, *Tradición política española e ideología revolucionaria de Mayo* (Buenos Aires, 1961); C. W. Arnade, A. P. Whitaker, B. W. Diffie, "Causes

was mounting concern in the last five years with the political and military history of independence movements. There were monographs on "loyalist" Peruvian reaction to the Napoleonic invasions of Spain and on seapower and Chilean independence. Detailed studies were published on early revolutionary movements in Ecuador and Paraguay. There also appeared a number of books on such revolutionary heroes as Egaña, Morelos, Saavedra, and Bolívar. Outstanding among these is Street's *Artigas*.[30]

For the history of Latin America since independence, publications have appeared in all major fields during the past five years. In economic and social history, there have been significant studies of the Chilean merchant marine, of the role of pressure groups in Brazil's industrialization, of British in-

vestment in Latin America, and of the government finances of mid-nineteenth-century Argentina. Attention was given to labor in a general study by Poblete Troncoso and Burnett, as well as in a monograph on the origins of the inquilino in Chile, and in Marxist and non-Marxist interpretations of the history of slavery in southern Brazil. Freyre continued his analysis of Brazilian society in a work on the nineteenth and twentieth centuries, while economic and social conditions in Mexico at the beginning of independence and during the rule of Díaz were the subject of two additional works.[31]

In the less prolific field of intellectual history, Whitaker explored the little-known area of Latin-American nationalism. Barros and Lemmo wrote on segments of the educational history of Brazil and Venezuela. Heliodoro Valle broadly reviewed the history of ideas in Central America. And from Mexico came three contributions: a history of social ideas, a study of the German image in Mexican periodical

---

of Spanish American Independence," *Journal of Inter-American Studies*, Vol. 2 (1960), pp. 125–144, and Charles C. Griffin, *Los temas sociales y económicos en la época de la independencia* (Caracas, 1961); for a variety of approaches to the various independence movements, see Venezuela, Academia Nacional de la Historia, Mesa Redonda de la Comisión de Historia del Instituto Panamericano de Geografía e Historia, *El movimiento emancipador de Hispano-américa* (5 vols.; Caracas, 1961).

[30] Armando Nieto Vélez, *Contribución a la historia del fidelismo en el Perú (1808–1810)* (Lima, 1960); Donald E. Worcester, *Seapower and Chilean Independence* (Gainesville, 1962); Alfredo Ponce Ribadenevia, *Quito, 1809–1812, según los documentos del Archivo Nacional de Madrid* (Madrid, 1960); Luís Vittone, *El Paraguay en la lucha por su independencia* (Asunción, 1960); José Luís Busaniche, *Bolívar visto por sus contemporáneos* (Mexico-Buenos Aires, 1960); Raúl Silva Castro, *Egaña en la Patria Vieja, 1810–1814* (Santiago de Chile, 1959); Alfonso Teja Zabre, *Vida de Morelos, nueva versión* (Mexico, 1959); Enrique Ruíz-Guinazú, *El Presidente Saavedra y el pueblo soberano de 1810* (Buenos Aires, 1960); John Street, *Artigas and the Emancipation of Uruguay* (Cambridge, 1959).

[31] Claudia Véliz, *Historia de la marina mercante de Chile* (Santiago de Chile, 1961); Nícia Vilela Luz, *A luta pela industrializaçao do Brasil (1808–1930)* (São Paulo, 1961); J. Fred Rippy, *British Investments in Latin America, 1822–1949: A Case Study in the Operations of Private Enterprise in Retarded Regions* (Minneapolis, 1959); Horacio Juan Cuccorese, *Historia de la conversión del papel moneda en Buenos Aires (1861–67)* (La Plata, 1959); Moisés Poblete Troncoso and Ben G. Burnett, *The Rise of the Latin American Labor Movement* (New York, 1960); Mario Góngora, *Origen de los "inquilinos" de Chile central* (Santiago de Chile, 1960); Fernando Henrique Cardoso, *Capitalismo e escravidão no Brasil meridional: O negro na sociedade escravocrata do Rio Grande do Sul* (São Paulo, 1962); Octavio Ianni, *As metamorfoses do escravo: Apogeu e crise da escravatura no Brasil* (São Paulo, 1962); Gilberto Freyre, *Ordem e progresso* (Rio de Janeiro, 1959); Catalina Sierra, *El Nacimiento de México* (Mexico, 1960); Moisés González Navarro, *El Porfiriato: La Vida social* (Mexico, 1960).

literature, and a substantial study of liberalism.[32]

By far the largest number of publications for the postindependence period was on political and military history and the history of international relations. For political history, there were cross-national studies of two types: Lieuwen and Johnson each made important contributions concerning the role of the military, while Karnes studied the unsuccessful attempts at Central American union.[33] The bulk of the remaining political studies were written within a national framework.

Valuable contributions to the history of the Mexican revolution were Quirk's study of the Aguascalientes convention, Dulles' *"Chronicle,"* Blaisdell's monograph on the revolution in Baja California, and Valadés' biography of Madero.[34] Schneider provided a well-documented study of communism in Guatemala, and there were monographs on early-nineteenth-century regional rebellions in Peru, on Ecuadoran politics of the 1850's, social conflict in Brazil, and early-twentieth-century Venezuelan political history. In addition, political history was a major theme of a number of biographies of Latin-American leaders, noteworthy among which were studies of Batlle of Uruguay, Ballivián of Bolivia, Facundo and Roca of Argentina, Mariño of Venezuela, and García Moreno of Ecuador. Significant military histories were Zook's study of the Chaco war, and Best's history of Argentine conflicts.[35]

Numerous studies on international relations included general diplomatic histories of Brazil and Colombia. In the field of intra-Latin-American diplomacy, there were works on Brazil's relations with four South American nations—Paraguay, Chile, Bolivia, and Argentina; on power politics during the War of the Pacific; and on Mex-

[32] A. P. Whitaker, *Nationalism in Latin America, Past and Present* (Gainesville, 1962); Roque Spencer Maciel de Barros, *A ilustracão e a ideal de universidade* (São Paulo, 1959); Angelina Lemmo, *La educación en Venezuela en 1870* (Caracas, 1961); Rafael Heliodoro Valle, *Historia de las ideas contemporáneas en Centro América* (Mexico, 1960); Victor Alba, *Las ideas sociales contemporáneas en México* (Mexico, 1960); Marianne Oeste de Bopp, *Contribución al estudio de las letras alemanas en México* (Mexico, 1961); Jesús Reyes Heroles, *El liberalismo mexicano* (3 vols.; Mexico, 1957–1961).

[33] Edwin Lieuwen, *Arms and Politics in Latin America* (New York, 1960); J. J. Johnson (ed.), *The Role of the Military in Underdeveloped Countries* (Princeton, 1962); John J. Johnson, *The Military in Latin America Society* (Stanford, 1964); Thomas L. Karnes, *The Failure of Union: Central America, 1824–1960* (Chapel Hill, 1961).

[34] Robert E. Quirk, *The Mexican Revolution, 1914–1915: The Convention of Aguas Calientes* (Bloomington, 1960); John W. F. Dulles, *Yesterday in Mexico: A Chronicle of the Revolution, 1919–1936* (Austin, 1961); Lowell Blaisdell, *The Desert Revolution* (Madison, 1962); José C. Valadés, *Imaginación y realidad de Francisco I. Madero* (Mexico, 1960).

[35] Ronald M. Schneider, *Communism in Guatemala, 1944–1954* (New York, 1959); Dante F. Herrera Alarcón, *Rebeliones que intentaron desmembrar el sur del Perú* (Lima, 1961); Wilfredo Loor, *La victoria de Guayaquil* (Quito, 1960); Evarado Dias, *História das lutas sociais no Brasil* (São Paulo, 1962); Rafael Gallegos Órtiz, *La historia política de Venezuela de Cipriano Castro a Pérez Jiménez* (Caracas, 1960); Milton I. Vanger, *José Batlle y Ordóñez of Uruguay: The Creator of His Times, 1902–1907* (Cambridge, 1963); Manuel Carrasco, *José Ballivián, 1805–1852: Estampas históricas* (Buenos Aires, 1960); Pedro de Paoli, *Facundo: Vida del brigadier general don Juan Facundo Quiroga* (Buenos Aires, 1960); José Arce, *Roca, 1843: Su vida —su obra* (2 vols.; Buenos Aires, 1960); Caracciolo Parra-Pérez, *Mariño y las guerras civiles* (3 vols.; Madrid, 1960); Benjamín Carrión, *Garcia Moreno, el santo del patibulo* (Mexico, 1959); David H. Zook, Jr., *The Conduct of the Chaco War* (New York, 1960); and Félix Best, *Historia de las guerras argentinas de la independencia, internacionales, civiles y con el indio* (2 vols.; Buenos Aires, 1960).

ico's relations with Central America.[36]

Much was written on relations between Latin- and non-Latin-American nations, including British relations with Argentina and with Mexico and the diplomacy revolving about British Honduras. Monographs were published on Spain and Spanish America and on Brazil and Africa. However, most numerous were the studies of United States-Latin-American relations. Both Wood and Dozer analyzed the good-neighbor policy. Pike described a relationship between Chile's domestic problems and United States diplomacy, while Smith discussed business interests in pre-Castro Cuban-United States relations. Attracting the greatest attention in this category were, however, United States-Mexican relations and inter-American co-operation.[37]

Two generalizations may be offered in summary. First, although during the last five years there have been contributions to Latin-American history from several European nations and almost all of the nations of the Western hemisphere, those countries which were most productive in quantitative terms were Mexico, Venezuela, Brazil, Argentina, and the United States. In the second place, while heavy publication continued on traditional topics, such as the conquest, the church, the independence movement, and politics, the appearance of research on economic, social, cultural, and intellectual history and of new approaches to traditional subjects indicated that historians of Latin America were seeking to probe Latin America's past in new and more productive ways.

---

[36] Carlos Miguel Delgado de Carvalho, *História diplomática do Brasil* (São Paulo, 1959); Raimundo Rivas, *Historia diplomática de Colombia, 1810–1934* (Bogotá, 1961); Olympio Roboré Guilhereme, *A luta pelo petróleo boliviano* (Rio de Janeiro, 1959); R. Antonio Ramos, *La política del Brasil en el Paraguay bajo la dictadura del Dr. Francia* (Buenos Aires-Asunción, 1959); Robert N. Burr, *The Stillborn Panama Congress: Power Politics and Chilean-Colombian Relations during the War of the Pacific* (Berkeley, 1962); Daniel Cosío Villegas, *El Porfiriato: La vida política exterior, Parte primera* (Mexico, 1960); Juan José Fernández, *La república de Chile y el imperio de Brasil: Historia de sus relaciones diplomáticas* (Santiago de Chile, 1959); José Antônio Soares de Souza, *Honório Hermeto no Rio da Prata: Missão especial de 1851–52* (São Paulo, 1959).

[37] Henry S. Ferns, *Britain and Argentina in the 19th Century* (Oxford, 1960); Alfred Tischendorf, *Great Britain and Mexico in the Era of Porfirio Díaz* (Durham, 1961); R. A. Humphreys, *The Diplomatic History of British Honduras, 1638–1901* (London, 1961);

Mark J. Van Aken, *Pan-Hispanism; Its origin and development to 1866* (Berkeley, 1959); José Honório Rodrigues, *Brasil e África, outro horizonte; relacões e política brasileiro-africana* (Rio de Janeiro, 1961); Bryce Wood, *The Making of the Good Neighbor Policy* (New York, 1961); Donald Dozer, *Are We Good Neighbors? Three Decades of Inter-American Relations, 1930–1960* (Gainesville, 1959); Frederick B. Pike, *Chile and the United States, 1880–1962: The emergence of Chile's social crisis and the challenge to United States diplomacy* (Notre Dame, 1963); Robert F. Smith, *The United States and Cuba* (New York, 1960); Carlos Bosch García, *Historia de las relaciones entre México y los Estados Unidos, 1819–1948* (Mexico, 1961); Daniel Cosío Villegas, *La vida política exterior, Parte segunda* (Mexico, 1963); Robert E. Quirk, *An Affair of Honor: Woodrow Wilson and the Occupation of Mexico* (Lexington, 1962); Edmond David Cronon, *Josephus Daniels in Mexico* (Madison, 1960); Harry Bernstein, *Making an Inter-American Mind* (Gainesville, 1961); J. Lloyd Mecham, *The United States and Inter-American Security, 1889–1960* (Austin, 1961).

Report of the Board of Directors to the Members of the American Academy of Political and Social Science for the Year 1963

MEMBERSHIP in the Academy has increased steadily in recent years. These are the end-of-the-year figures:

1963	15,890
1962	14,736
1961	14,145
1960	13,538
1959	13,442
1958	13,254
1957	12,919

During the calendar year 1963, 4,430 new members (the highest figure in our history) were enrolled, but 2,859 withdrew. A high rate of member turnover, ranging from one sixth to one fifth of the total membership, has obtained for the past generation.

FINANCES

The Academy income was $19,592 higher in 1963 than in 1962. Dues increased by $16,350, advertising by $2,645, royalties and donations by $177, miscellaneous income by $1,756, and income from investments by $869. In addition, there was an income of $3,855 from the sale of monographs. Sales decreased by $1,431.

The Academy outgo was $11,281 higher in 1963 than in 1962. The cost of meetings rose by $1,171, new members' costs by $5,209, printing of THE ANNALS by $9,090, sales costs by $1,778, advertising costs by $557, and miscellaneous expenses by $1,496. In addition, an expenditure of $14,977 was made for monographs. General overhead costs decreased by $1,795, accounts and finances by $1,854, and member records' costs by $63.

All nonprofessional employees with a service of one year or more (all but five) received a bonus of 4 per cent of annual salary.

Our bank balance at the end of the year was slightly in excess of $19,000.

The auditors report that we had an operations surplus of $6,026 for 1963. Also, we realized a profit on the sale of securities of $7,201. At the end of the year, the cost value of our securities was $334,581 and the market value $415,891. This comparison is to be evaluated in the light of our policy of investing approximately one third of our funds in bonds and of emphasizing yield rather than growth. It gives us satisfaction to report that we have been able to maintain a small operating surplus each year and also to keep our annual dues to a modest $8.00.

Our total cash income for 1963 was $179,970 and our cash outlay $161,502. These figures do not include changes in the value of securities, or gains or losses from the sale of them, or changes in the value of inventory, real estate, or equipment.

The totals on the Operations Report do not agree with those in the Auditor's Report. They should not agree, because the Auditor's Report reflects the depreciation of building and equipment, whereas our Operations Report does not deal with these matters.

The two reports have been completely reconciled in a conference between the Auditor and your President.

FINANCIAL STATEMENT OF OPERATIONS FOR THE
MONTH ENDED DECEMBER 31, 1963

INCOME FROM OPERATIONS	MONTH	YEAR	BUDGET
Dues and Subscriptions	$17,376.92	$126,879.02	$100,800.00
Sales	1,314.77	22,474.04	25,000.00
Advertising	848.22	10,586.14	11,200.00
Royalties and Donations	—	803.86	500.00
Miscellaneous	55.80	4,127.99	2,000.00
	$19,595.71	$164,871.05	$140,500.00

INCOME FROM INVESTMENTS			
Dividends and Interest	$ 844.97	$ 15,898.42	$ 14,000.00
Cost of Securities Management	42.25	799.48	700.00
Net Income	$ 802.72	$ 15,098.94	$ 13,300.00

TOTAL INCOME	$20,398.43	$179,969.99	$153,800.00

DISBURSEMENTS FOR OPERATIONS			
General Overhead	$ 1,321.21	$ 17,321.58	$ 16,500.00
Meetings	263.92	8,473.39	6,500.00
New Members	2,560.11	25,226.37	20,000.00
THE ANNALS	1,464.63	72,615.77	67,000.00
Accounts and Finance	769.82	6,728.26	7,000.00
Member Records	619.30	8,868.54	9,000.00
Sales	1,554.26	10,840.03	9,000.00
Advertising	94.00	3,717.05	3,000.00
Miscellaneous	2,041.06	7,711.08	6,000.00
TOTAL DISBURSEMENTS	$10,688.31	$161,502.07	$144,000.00

SPECIAL ACCOUNTS FOR MONOGRAPHS			
Income	$ 337.35	$ 3,855.45	$ 3,855.45
Expense	119.47	14,977.44	16,186.12

CASH BALANCE

Bank Balance, December 31, 1963	$ 19,080.81
Petty Cash	300.00
Postage Meter	94.69
TOTAL December 31, 1963	$ 19,475.50

Surplus from 1962 Operations Used for Purchase of Securities. $12,525.00

STATEMENT OF INCOME AND EXPENSE FOR THE YEAR
ENDING DECEMBER 31, 1963

REVENUE

Dues and Subscriptions

Membership Dues	$83,801.88	
Subscriptions	42,911.74	$126,713.62
Sales of Publications	22,474.04	
Monograph Sales	3,855.45	
Advertising and Royalties	11,316.44	37,645.93
		164,359.55
Interest and Dividends		14,509.71
TOTAL REVENUE		$178,869.26

EXPENSE

Membership—Records	$8,565.20	
Promotion	23,336.10	$31,901.30
THE ANNALS—Production Costs		68,795.38
Sales Costs		9,609.04
Accounting and Finance Costs		11,452.40
Office Operation		17,919.06
Philadelphia Meeting		5,797.18
Advertising		3,696.71
Monographs		14,977.44
Gifts		1,484.31
Refunds		632.60
Payroll Taxes		1,870.60
TIAA		618.53
TOTAL CASH EXPENSE		168,754.55

EXCESS OF CASH REVENUE OVER EXPENSES OF OPERATIONS......... 10,114.71

Less: Depreciation

Buildings	$ 330.00	
Improvements	1,523.44	
Office Equipment	2,235.00	4,088.44

NET PROFIT FROM OPERATIONS.. 6,026.27

OTHER REVENUE

Profit on sales of investments....................................... 7,201.05

NET INCOME TRANSFERRED TO SURPLUS............................ $ 13,227.32

PUBLICATIONS

During 1963 the six volumes of THE ANNALS dealt with the following subjects:

January   *Transportation Renaissance*, edited by George Fox Mott, Managing Partner, Mott of Washington and Associates, Washington, D. C.

March   *Medicine and Society*, edited by John A. Clausen, Professor of Sociology and Director, Institute of Human Development, University of California, Berkeley, California, and Robert Straus, Professor and Chairman, Department of Behavioral Science, University of Kentucky Medical Center, Lexington, Kentucky.

May   *Combating Organized Crime*, edited by Gus Tyler, Assistant President and Director of the Departments of Politics, Education, and Training, International Ladies' Garment Workers' Union, New York City, New York.

July   *The New Europe: Implications for the United States*, edited by James C. Charlesworth.

September   *Communist China and the Soviet Bloc*, edited by Donald S. Zagoria, Research Fellow, Research Institute on Communist Affairs, Assistant Professor of Government, Columbia University.

November   *The Crisis in the American Trade-Union Movement*, edited by Solomon Barkin, Deputy to the Director for Manpower and Social Affairs, Organization for Economic Cooperation and Development, Paris, France, and Albert A. Blum, Associate Professor, School of Labor and Industrial Relations and Social Science Department, Michigan State University.

Special supplementary articles have been published in some of these volumes. They are "Recent Developments in United States History," by James H. Soltow, Assistant Professor of History, Michigan State University, in the May 1963 volume; "American Government and Administration: Recent Develop-

ments," by William H. Young, Professor of Political Science and Assistant to the President, University of Wisconsin, in July 1963; "Some Recent Developments in Socialization Theory and Research," by William H. Sewell, Professor of Sociology, University of Wisconsin, in September 1963; and "Recent Trends in the Study of Minority and Race Relations," by Milton M. Gordon, Professor of Sociology, University of Massachusetts, in November 1963.

As planned so far, the publication program for 1964 includes, in addition to the January volume on *The Changing Cold War*, edited by D. F. Fleming, Emeritus Professor of International Relations, Vanderbilt University, the following volumes:

March   *Urban Revival: Goals and Standards*, edited by Robert B. Mitchell, Professor of City Planning and Director, Institute of Urban Studies, University of Pennsylvania.

May   *City Bosses and Leaders*, edited by Lee S. Greene, Professor of Political Science, University of Tennessee.

July   *Africa in Motion*, edited by James C. Charlesworth.

September   *Child Welfare*, edited by Alan Keith-Lucas, Alumni Professor, School of Social Work, University of North Carolina.

The rotating summaries of social science disciplines, established in 1961, is being continued.

In addition to the regular six volumes of THE ANNALS, the Academy published the following monographs:

June   *Mathematics and the Social Sciences: The Utility and Inutility of Mathematics in the Study of Economics, Political Science, and Sociology*, edited by the President of this Academy. Copies were distributed to all members of the American Economic Association, the American Political

Science Association, the American Society for Public Administration, and the American Sociological Association. In addition to this distribution, about 635 have been sold up to the date of this report.

August — *Achieving Excellence in the Public Service*, edited by the President and First Vice-President of the Academy. Copies were distributed to all members of the American Municipal Association, the American Political Science Association, the American Society for Public Administration, the International City Managers' Association, and the Public Personnel Association. In addition to this distribution, about 616 copies have been sold up to the date of this report.

The following two monographs are planned for the coming year:

Leisure in America: Blessing or Curse?, edited by the President of this Academy.

Functionalism and Its Limits in the Social Sciences, edited by Don Martindale, Professor of Sociology, University of Minnesota.

During 1963 the Book Department of THE ANNALS published 429 reviews. The majority of these reviews, 330, were written by college or university presidents, deans, professors, or lecturers, 33 by members of private and university-sponsored research organizations, 18 by government and United Nations officials, active or retired, and 48 by others. Most reviewers were residents of the United States, and some were residents of Africa, Australia, Austria, Canada, France, Great Britain, India, Iraq, Lebanon, The Netherlands, Pakistan, Portugal, Puerto Rico, Thailand, Turkey, and Vietnam. Eight hundred and twenty-seven books were listed in the Other Books section.

One hundred and forty-five requests were granted to reprint material from THE ANNALS. Eighty-nine of these were to professors and other authors for use in books under preparation, and ten were to journals. Twenty requests were granted for class room and adult education programs and eight for company training or independent organization programs. Eighteen requests came from various departments of the government, including eleven from the armed forces.

MEETINGS

The 1963 Spring Meeting, organized around the theme *The New Europe: Implications for the United States,* sustained the traditions of our meetings in respect of size of audiences, the interest displayed, and the great diversity of organizations represented by delegates. Twenty-three countries sent official delegations, also 6 missions to the United Nations, 11 public jurisdictions, 7 federal governmental agencies, 152 American and foreign universities and colleges, and 143 international, civic, scientific, and commercial organizations. Approximately 800 different persons attended one or more of the sessions. A typical attendance for a session was between 500 and 650.

The subject of the 1964 Spring Meeting (April 10 and 11 in the Benjamin Franklin Hotel, Philadelphia) will be *Africa in Motion.* We expect to have public figures (government officials and ambassadors), but we shall also continue to rely heavily on scholars and writers. We expect the tone of the meeting to be exposition and analysis, rather than criticism and contumely. Following the example of the 1963 Spring Meeting, we shall have five sessions with two speakers each. The July volume of THE ANNALS, in which the speeches are published, will contain complementary essays by outstanding writers in international affairs.

OFFICERS AND STAFF

Messrs. Sellin and Palmer were re-elected to three-year terms as Directors. Also elected were Donald R. Young, Carroll V. Newsom, and John Fischer. Joseph H. Willits was elected Vice-President, and Henry W. Sawyer, III, Counsel.

(Young, a sociologist, was previously associated with this Academy as Assistant Editor. More recently he has been president of the Russell Sage Foundation. Newsom, a professional educator, served until recently as president of New York University, and is presently Vice Chairman of the Board of Prentice-Hall, Inc. Fischer, a writer and government official, is now editor-in-chief of *Harper's Magazine*. Sawyer, a lawyer, is a part-ner of a prominent Philadelphia law firm and a civic leader.)

Respectfully submitted,

THE BOARD OF DIRECTORS

M. Albert Linton
Thorsten Sellin
Stephen B. Sweeney
Norman D. Palmer
James C. Charlesworth
James P. Warburg
Howard C. Petersen
Roy F. Nichols
Loren C. Eiseley
Donald R. Young
Carroll V. Newsom
John Fischer

13 March 1964

Philadelphia, Pa.

Book Department

POLITICAL SCIENCE AND GOVERNMENT

HAROLD D. LASSWELL. *The Future of Political Science.* Pp. x, 256. New York: Atherton Press, 1963. $6.50.

Scholars in any field are more effective if they can clarify for themselves such matters as the general scope of their subject, methods by which their studies can be advanced, and the relationship of their field to others adjacent to it. Such knowledge is not easy to come by; it is the slow accretion of study, experience, perspective, and insight.

This is why this book on the future of political science is a piece of good fortune for political scientists. Probably no one could bring to the subject a wider range of study and experience or more original and penetrating insights than does Professor Lasswell. With a brief account of the historical development of political science, the author moves swiftly into an analysis of factors which the rapid expansion of government and the increasing complexity of politics have forced upon the political scientist's attention. Advancing beyond the conventional description of political organization, events, and phenomena, the author employs his own

unique vocabulary to compel a fresh attention to the understanding of ordinary political matters—terms which sound strange to the ears of those whose training in political science has been rooted in law and bounded by formal descriptions of governmental machinery.

Most of the methods which the author wants political scientists to use in the future development of their field come from the areas of social analysis, particularly psychology, individual and social. Political scientists will be compelled to think anew about some of their problems when told that a "syndrome of boredom" can be as much a part of the raw data of revolution as tyranny, or that drugs can be more effective than rhetoric in creating a climate for peace. Once convincingly pointed out, however, such suggestions can never be comfortably ignored. Yet the book does not rely upon sensational suggestions to direct the attention of political scientists to the future. It proposes hard-headed demonstrations of the usefulness of experimentation, of "social models," and of the methods of social analysis.

The author rightly and generously gives credit to Charles S. Hyneman, as a former president of the American Political Science Association, for pressing a searching

137

inquiry into the prospects and future responsibilities of political science as a field of study and practice, an inquiry to which Profesor Hyneman has himself given much time and thought. But this acknowledgment in no way detracts from Professor Lasswell's achievement, for he has brought to the subject his own exceptional qualifications. No brief review can do justice to the result, but it can point out that future political scientists now have a new starting point for their studies.

HAROLD W. STOKE
President
Queens College
City University of New York

W. G. RUNCIMAN. *Social Science and Political Theory.* Pp. 200. New York: Cambridge University Press, 1963. $3.95.

MAURICE COWLING. *The Nature and Limits of Political Science.* Pp. vii, 213. New York: Cambridge University Press, 1963. $4.75.

These are two very different little books coming out of Cambridge. Mr. W. G. Runciman believes that to start by looking for any general theory of society is likely to remain a waste of effort. The one general question, however, that must be answered is whether social science is science. As between positivists, who assert that human events can be dealt with like the natural sciences, and intuitionists, who stress the uniqueness of human acts, each is partly right. The author believes that Max Weber's consideration of the need for both "internal comprehension" and "external confirmation" points to a middle solution, just as does the use of a particular vocabulary represent some presumptions. Analysis may be more important than prediction in social science, and prediction in any case is never enough. The fetishism of quantitative techniques the author rejects, and also allowing the issues to depend upon the form in which the fetishists would like to phrase them. Social scientists must accept the fact that some sciences will always remain more scientific than others.

Marx's concept of alienation of man, emerging more clearly from the recent recovery of fuller aspects of the early Hegelian stage of Marx, and Weber's concept of charismatic authority, provides illustrations of generalizations which send investigation in new directions. A chapter on elites and oligarchies, considering the "minor patriarchs," Mosca, Pareto, Michels, and Sorel, concludes that from this group, the startling query cannot be pushed away as to whether democratic government can escape oligarchic control any more than other governments of the past. A chapter on voting studies suggests that the emergence of the fact of a large element of apathy in the electorate has implications for any easy democratic ideal. The value of Weber's distinctions between class, status, and power is considered in one chapter.

The author differs from Weber in considering it possible to relate the "is" and the "ought." Some consensus of values exists—H. L. A. Hart's "minimum content of natural law" furnishes an example—analogous to the starting point for belief in the canons of natural science. Paying heed to the fact that all sociological generalization possesses "a necessary and irremediable tentativeness," there must remain a close connection between the search for how societies behave and how they ought to behave. This is a book with much calm illumination, a clearing of some cobwebs, allowing one to see the heart of the matter.

The book by Mr. Maurice Cowling is quite different. He contends that it is confusion to think that truth can be discovered in contemporary politics, as basic actions are embedded in secrecy not available to the scholar. Scholars have no business urging activity in public affairs, in being laureates of the Welfare—or any other—State; they must avoid the use of large words like "freedom," "social justice," "the national interest"; they must not try to choose the ends of government. He rejects much of recent British political studies for their transgressions, on grounds also widely applicable elsewhere. Among his own broad generalizations, we have an assertion that "societies can be governed as effectively with little public discussion as with much." He suggests that a society is better off if the citizens are "deceived and peaceful, in place of bursting with truth and burning with resentment." After driving academicians to their towers, a belfry full of bats fly out.

DALE PONTIUS
Associate Professor of Political Science
Roosevelt University

Parliaments: A Comparative Study on the Structure and Functioning of Representative Institutions in Forty-one Countries. Pp. xv, 321. New York: Frederick A. Praeger, for the Inter-Parliamentary Union, 1963. $7.00.

The Inter-Parliamentary Union, established in 1889, aims to promote good international relations by providing a forum and clearing house for the members of national legislatures. The organization has an Annual Conference, held in different parts of the world, and a permanent headquarters in Geneva where its Inter-Parliamentary Bureau is located. The 52nd Annual Conference took place in Belgrade, in September 1963, and was attended by approximately 500 lawmakers who came as delegates from the parliaments of 57 countries.

The book here reviewed is in large part the work of the Inter-Parliamentary Bureau. The text is a synthesis of the replies received from 41 countries in answer to a questionnaire sent to member legislatures. The replies gave the relevant data as of January 1, 1957. Subsequent changes, such as occurred in France with the advent of the Fifth Republic, are not taken account of in the text.

The volume is divided into four parts: "Structure and Organization of Parliament"; "Legislative Function of Parliament"; "Powers of Parliament in Financial Matters"; and "Control of the Executive by Parliament." Details are supplied on numerous subjects relating to the organization and functioning of legislatures. The Index is unusually full—twenty-three pages.

In essence, *Parliaments* is a well-written handbook, based upon the constitutional and legal provisions and the formal rules of legislative assemblies. It will not give much help to students of political process whose first question is: "Just what actually happens?" Admittedly, the authors had a difficult task in covering so many diverse countries, Communist and non-Communist, developed and underdeveloped. It is obviously easier to compare the salaries and allowances of lawmakers than to probe deeply into the roles of political parties and groups in legislative bodies. Indeed, the Conclusion states: "Throughout this study, in attempting to describe what Parliament is, we have endeavored to separate it from the political, economic and social context in which it functions within each country" (p. 298). But, the reviewer is moved to ask, will not the result be a kind of taxidermy?

Notwithstanding this limitation arising from the nature of the Inter-Parliamentary Union, the study has substantial merit and should be read by delegations to the Annual Conference. It contributes to the development of "dialogue" between members from divergent types of legislatures and thus aids the basic purposes of the Inter-Parliamentary Union.

ROGER H. WELLS
Visiting Professor of Political Science
MacMurray College
Jacksonville
Illinois

ROY C. MACRIDIS and ROBERT E. WARD (Eds.). *Modern Political Systems: Europe.* Pp. xiv, 575. Englewood Cliffs, N. J.: Prentice-Hall, 1963. $8.95.

Both the editors and the publisher should be congratulated for producing a superb two-volume series on *Modern Political Systems*. Not only do the volumes on Europe and Asia supplement each other and blend into a harmonious whole, but they also satisfy the professional reader in terms of successfully accomplishing the editors' objectives. These goals are clearly stated at the outset of the volume on Europe. Professors Macridis and Ward conceive of modern politics "as a system for the identification and posing of problems, and the making and administering of decisions in the realm of public affairs" (p. viii). Thus, their dual goal assumes a challenging combination of the static method of studying government —a descriptive identification of structure, forms, constitutional details—with the dynamics of modern politics, including pressure groups, behavioral factors, the use of public-opinion polls, and a study of the ever-shifting battleground of political parties.

This volume covers four countries: Great Britain, France, the German Federal Republic, and the Soviet Union. Although clearly guided by the editors' expectations and assumptions, the individual authors have attacked their problem-areas differently and with varying success. To this reviewer, the sections on France and the Soviet Union seemed to be the most useful and comprehensive in their coverage, while certain methodological and other details might arouse dissent from, if not criticism of, the British and German chapters. The former relies far too heavily on such fugitive and quickly aging materials as local Gallup polls and trade-union statistics; the latter—while admirably presented on the whole by Professor Karl W. Deutsch—tends to paint overexuberantly the current picture in the West German Federal Republic. In view of the recent Eichmann trial and more-or-less professional analyses of the German "national character" ranging from William Shirer to Hannah Arendt, it is surprising to read that in Germany "there is steadfastness in the face of difficulty, and great courage and discipline in the face of danger. There is a tradition of selflessness, of readiness to sacrifice and suffer, of solidarity with one's group; . . . there is a serious concern for justice and a deep well of imagination" (p. 310).

Professor Aspaturian draws a brilliant picture not only of the gradual evolution of a Soviet-Communist ideology, but also of the current domestic and foreign scene in the Soviet Union. His recurring references to the contrast between a "Soviet model" and a "Western model" of political- and state-building are useful and will serve as eye-openers to our often naive and overoptimistic students. Indeed, in view of recent world developments, this reviewer must agree with the author's realistically gloomy and strongly stated conclusion that "unless the Western world, led by the United States, is able to renovate and export the values and institutions it cherishes . . . , then the attractiveness of Communism, and with it its international impact, will grow" (p. 407).

ANDREW GYORGY
Professor of Political Science
Boston University

GABRIEL A. ALMOND and SIDNEY VERBA. *The Civic Culture: Political Attitudes and Democracy in Five Nations.* Pp. xi, 562. Princeton, N. J.: Princeton University Press, 1963. $8.50.

Professors Almond and Verba have produced an exciting book examining the political cultures of the United States, Great Britain, Germany, Italy, and Mexico. It is a book for professionals alert to distinguish hypotheses and suggestions from description. Handled by the semi-skilled, the findings are prone to misuse. The authors are explicit that their data, presented more effectively in 129 tables expressed in percentages and 11 graphs than in repetitious verbalization, need integration with other types of materials and that their explanations are inadequate and unsatisfying. But here lies the source of the excitement conveyed by the study, as it points the way to a host of other studies, some in depth, others more general and integrative.

Political cultures are conceived as composed of parochial, subject, and participatory elements present in varying proportions in the more advanced societies. "Civic culture" is a model of attitude patterns most closely approximated by the United States and the United Kingdom, with, roughly, Germany unbalanced toward subject competence, Italy toward parochialism, and Mexico toward participatory aspiration. Both model and its two historical approximations are fusions of the three elements. A balance, posited as contributing to democratic stability, exists only in the model but, since only the approximations can offer measurable dimensions, not in determinate proportions.

Political culture is viewed as a bridge between individual and political system, hence as an integrating object of study. The present study represents a bridge foundation, an investigation of the individual's perception of the system, of his role, and of his perceived capacity to influence if he chose. The view is unidirectional, toward, not from, the political system. Much of the data crosses no gap, for it relates to the individual's perception of himself.

Many criticisms can be rendered. Information is often not extracted from tables. On occasions verbalization and tables do not harmonize. For example, the statement (p. 340) that there is little regular pattern of change in Mexican family participation fails to extract the tabular information that not only family but also school authority patterns are of one sort between the Carranza and Cardenas regimes and of another sort since Cardenas. Moreover, the statement that school and family patterns in all five countries show changes in the "same direction" (p. 341) is not supported by the Mexican family pattern, beginning with the 1919–1924 birth group, or by the Italian, beginning with the 1929–1934 group. (Table 10, p. 339). In general, preoccupation with participatory facets, overindulged between page 202 and page 294 in a fashion almost suggesting the hand of a third author, allows much of the positive evidence for parochialism and for subject competence to remain in the tables awaiting pertinent articles based on the tabulated data and upon other extractions from the data cards at the Inter-University Consortium on Political Research at Ann Arbor.

Lapses and occasional verbal errors are to be expected whenever research is creative and exploratory. Travel over worn paths is always much more neatly done. Cross-national application of systematic survey research methods, hardly a worn path even after this study, gives rise to serious problems. Both the Appendix and a chapter on method guide and forewarn future researchers. The study needs no defense except professional production of subsequent studies generated by what the authors have said and have left unsaid.

WESLEY L. GOULD
Visiting Professor
Northwestern University

JAMES MACGREGOR BURNS. *The Deadlock of Democracy: Four-Party Politics in America.* Pp. 388. Englewood Cliffs, N. J.: Prentice-Hall, 1963. $5.95.

This book is rich in the material of American politics, and abundant in originality and incisive analysis. It should be of interest to anyone who wishes to acquaint himself with the American political system and to delve deeply into those facets of it that pertain to the role of political parties.

Burns's thesis is that the American political system is not really a two-party system, but rather is composed of four distinct political parties. Namely, both the Democratic and Republican parties are split into presidential and congressional wings, with the former representing the liberal elements in both parties while the latter are highly conservative. This system is largely the result of the Madisonian system of checks and balances, which not only gives different powers to each branch of the government but, what is even more important, provides for different constituencies for the President and Congress. Congress does not depend upon the President for election, and this prevents the President, who is the logical focal point of party leadership, from controlling his party in Congress.

Burns feels that the result of this fragmentation of our party system is irresponsible government. The vote of the people does not count in a meaningful way, for there is no effective leadership. The majority of voters may choose a liberal Democratic president only to find him perpetually frustrated by the Southern wing of his party that controls Congress. This nullifies the people's choice. Similarly, a liberal Republican will confront a conservative Congress even if his party has a majority in that body. Burns feels that not only does our fragmented party system diminish popular government, but also it deadlocks the national policy-making machinery, making it necessary for the President to rely upon his emergency powers to pull the country out of crisis. Congressional action, sometimes effective, is frequently too late to achieve the best results.

In conclusion Burns proposes a number of changes to remedy the "deadlock of democracy." He wants to bring the constituencies of Congress and the President closer together, and break the conservative grip on the machinery of Congress. The party should become the vehicle of presidential co-operation with Congress, and thereby the channel through which popular aspirations are expressed in American government.

Burns's case is convincing. His exposition of the need for more effective political parties is the best one in print, and everyone will be richer for having read it. It is possible to argue, contrary to Burns, that our democracy has not foundered because of the growth of and change in other institutions to fill the gap created by the deadlock between the President and Congress. Also, there are those who say constitutional democracy requires that the Madisonian checks and balances system be maintained, for the fragmentation of political power is a good thing. But the existence of such views in no way detracts from the excellence of Burns's book, and in fact it is up to those who may disagree with him to put forth their views as persuasively and articulately as does *The Deadlock of Democracy*.

PETER WOLL
Assistant Professor of Political Science
University of California
Los Angeles

CATHERINE ANN CLINE. *Recruits to Labour: The British Labour Party, 1914–1931*. Pp. ix, 198. Syracuse, N. Y.: Syracuse University Press, 1963. $5.00.

It was a happy inspiration that brought Professor Cline to the study of the "recruits," as she calls them, who joined the Labour party during and after World War I from the upper and middle classes.

Most of them were Liberals—a few were Conservatives—and a number had already been members of parliament; two, Lord Haldane and Christopher Addison, had already held cabinet office. Dr. Cline's study, perhaps inevitably, concentrates on recruits of some public standing, in politics or journalism. She makes no attempt to analyze the shift of Liberal voters to the Labour cause; nor does she suggest how the character of the Liberal party, a loose alliance of radicalism, protest, and nonconformity, inevitably encouraged an exodus of members whose normal frustrations had been compounded by the wartime policies of the party and the opportunistic methods of Lloyd George as prime minister.

Dr. Cline brings out excellently the immediate causes of the exodus, and its effects upon the Labour party. War was, as so often, the midwife. Many Liberals were pacifists; others were distrustful of secret diplomacy and undefined war aims. For many, the Union of Democratic Control was the bridge, bringing them in touch with Labour men like MacDonald and Snowden. Fiscal policy was another cause of changing allegiance: the wobbling record of the Liberals over the taxation of land and the maintenance of free trade. The new recruits were not ardent Socialists, but accepted socialism as a means to social reform and a weapon against warborn wealth. Their influence on the Labour party reflected this: they brought support for free trade and for a capital levy, and strengthened the party's adherence to these objects. Their greatest influence, however, was on Labour's foreign policy: criticism of the Versailles settlement and the postwar treatment of Germany, and support for the League of Nations and collective security, owed much to them. Even here, however, their effectiveness waned once Labour held office and MacDonald, not E. D. Morel, became foreign secretary. In the second Labour government, two of the recruits, Sir Oswald Mosley and Sir Charles Trevelyan, resigned over issues of policy, but by then the recruits were indistinguishable from other members.

Their number was quite large. Dr. Cline

lists 67 in her useful biographical appendix. This, unfortunately, contains a number of misprints and errors: Hoyton for Hoxton, Denbeigh for Denbigh, for example. Siegfried Sassoon was at Marlborough College, not the grammer school, and the Royal Naval College—not Academy—was never at Winchester. But these are small flaws in a useful and workmanlike study.

C. L. MOWAT
Professor of History
University College of North Wales
Bangor
England

WILLIAM E. LEUCHTENBURG. *Franklin D. Roosevelt and the New Deal, 1932–1940.* Pp. xvii, 393. New York: Harper and Row, 1963. $6.00.

This is a welcome addition to the New American Nation Series. The author, already favorably known for his *Perils of Prosperity,* has concentrated in the volume under review upon what is essentially the decade of the 1930's. The result is a stimulating book, well written, rising at times to brilliance of interpretation. In the words of Professor Leuchtenburg, the six years from 1933 to 1938 marked a greater upheaval in American institutions than in any similar period in our history, save perhaps for the impact on the South of the Civil War. It is the upheaval—the "Roosevelt Revolution"—that is the subject of this book.

Given such a clear-cut statement as to the field of the book, it is incumbent upon the reviewer to appraise the author's performance—how well did he do what he said he was going to do. This judgment will have to be set forth upon two phases of Professor Leuchtenburg's treatment of the New Deal period: (1) How well does he describe the events of the period or, in other words, the relation of facts, the telling of the tale, the bounding of the forests and the marking of the trees? (2) What does the author do interpretatively when it is necessary to shape the forest which must include trees or else it is not a forest? The verdict is distinctly on the favorable side on both of these counts. For one who

lived through the Roosevelt period of 1932 to 1940 and who has some frame of reference by which to judge the presentation of data and the exposition of event, Leuchtenburg's performance is good. Though age has dimmed memory's store, Leuchtenburg serves to recall with acute nostalgia and occasional pain the course of events of the troubled 1930's.

In the matter of interpretive acumen, Leuchtenburg scores well. Roosevelt appears as an inspiring, driving leader during his first term; then as a groper, trying to find something with which to lead, or what might be led, during his second regular term until singleness of national purpose again brought sureness of touch as war drew near. Carefully and with calm and dispassion, Leuchtenburg follows the gees and haws, the whoas and the giddyups of events of his assigned period without seeming to vent spleen or crack his whip in exasperation. This is indeed a good book by which to test the New American Series or any other American history of recent concern.

CHARLES W. SHULL
Professor of Political Science
Wayne State University

LUCIAN W. PYE (Ed.). *Communications and Political Development.* Pp. xiv, 381. Princeton, N. J.: Princeton University Press, 1963. $6.50.

It takes only a little exposure to contemporary literature to discover that the idea of "modernization" has given to much political discussion an implicit framework in which the notions of "linearity," "progress," and "advancing historical stages" are firmly embedded. To the American mind, always happy with the idea of "progress," this hardly seems strange—except, currently, as humanistic scholars, alienated from the scientific tradition, find themes of alienation and *anomie* more felicitous. Yet the non-European ambivalent hunger for, and spread of, Western culture and institutions make this concept of modernization plausible, and the cultural relativist is swept along on the tide; it is a counter to the Marxian dialectic—with some of the same intellectual apparatus—and proves so useful in discussion, and is so well supported by what is now an ocean of evidence, that one must accept the framework and its elaboration, even with a little gratitude to those who have thought and written about it so persuasively. This book deals with political development—modernization—in a multifaceted and nondogmatic way.

Its other leg, "communications" is a sturdy support, even an instrument for rapid forward movement. The various treatments of communication rely very little on formal communications theory of the Shannon and Weaver variety; they eschew the format of the earlier institutional studies of *The One Party Press* or *The Washington Correspondents,* and they have a broader focus than the many studies on the social impact of television, the comics, and so forth. There is very little content analysis of the more formal kind, although there is careful attention, in some of the articles, to the messages that the mass media carry. What then does the book speak of?

First, there are a number of theoretical pieces which attempt to formulate the ways in which various kinds of communications institutions—including the less formal ones, like conversation—and various kinds of messages, first, emerge from certain social situations and, second, affect the growth, stability, and integration of political processes. Pye's introduction, providing "Models of Traditional, Transitional, and Modern Communications Systems," and his introduction to many of the specific studies in the book are notable for their imagination and clarity of thought. Ithiel Pool's piece on "The Mass Media and Politics in the Modernization Process" is one that surely will be often referred to by scholars interested in political communication. And, as always, Daniel Lerner gives a graceful and penetrating theoretical article at the end of the book, entitled "Toward a Communication Theory of Modernization." There are a number of works which present analyses of how communications processes affect political life in certain countries: Mosel's piece on Thailand and Yu's on Communist China are especially good, for

they give insightful detail in a meaningful "dynamic" analysis. There are some specialized treatments of certain aspects of communication, specialized by process rather than by country. Here I would mention Shil's discussion of demagoguery, Hyman's piece on the "packaging" of political content in the media, and especially Herbert Passin's excellent imaginative study of linguistic problems and the role-interpretations of writers and journalists in the less developed nations.

Taken together, these articles answer such questions as the following: (1) What economic and social base is necessary for the development of a mass-communications industry? How do certain deficiencies thwart or bias this development? (2) What are the latent functions of the creation of a mass-communication industry? How does the provision of an economic base for journalists, critics, and propagandists affect political life? (3) What are the social functions of mass communication in terms of the nationalizing of taste and language, the creation of demands, the changing of images, and the alteration of "empathic" skills? (4) How do governments use these media and what are the social and political effects of various patterns of usage? (5) What kinds of strategies of communications development are most useful for political development? (6) What kinds of skills and predispositions affect the reception of various messages? (7) How are the mass media related to the more traditional interpersonal forms of communication?

That reviewers' cliché for collections by many authors, "uneven quality," does not leap to the mind here: the selection is good and the quality is almost consistently high. What one misses, perhaps, is a major integrative effort, but the reader who attempts his own will find the enterprise supremely worth while.

ROBERT E. LANE
Professor of Political Science
Yale University

J. EDWARD GERALD. *The Social Responsibility of the Press.* Pp. vii, 214. Minneapolis: University of Minnesota Press, 1963. $5.00.

There are few problems in the emerging institutions of mass communications more important than the professionalization of their elites. And the present author, professor at a major journalism school in the mid-West and specialist in the interplay between constitutionalism and the press, is well qualified to comment on issues which are essentially about how media, governmental agencies, and publics define freedom and self-restraint as they variously participate in the production and consumption of news. Professor Gerald divides his book into seven sometimes overlapping chapters: the nature of mass communication—containing an amazingly succinct sketch of press history; journalism as big business—where the role of advertising is graphically portrayed through the rise of Wanamaker's department store; the natural habitat of the press—where the pressure to expand is brilliantly revealed in a career profile of a hypothetical publisher, the best single thing in the book; the proprietorship role—basic economic trends; mass communication content—"passive non-involvement in critical problems is journalism's outstanding quality"; freedom's new community—the ethical stake of the press in meeting the community's new problem; and professional organization of mass communicators —the nurture of the professional *intra* and *extra muros*. There is no bibliography to this long, sometimes too rambling essay, but the full footnotes at the back of the book strike a note of heterogeneousness, as Gerald cites from trade papers, scholarly journals, speeches, law cases, and secondary sources. The Index is limited.

My chief complaint is a lack of focus, which I believe comes from inadequate organizing concepts. This seems evident to me on the important question of the role of the journalism school in catalyzing professionalism in the media. In Chapter IV, for example, Gerald cites from an unidentified issue of *Journalism Quarterly* that 105 journalism schools enrolled 11,766 in 1959, 11 per cent being graduate students. Picking up the same theme in the last chapter, the year cited is 1958, with an enrollment of 11,263 in 100

institutions, but 23.7 per cent are graduate students. One is curious about such a fluctuation. These figures do not really mean much either, unless some effort is made to distinguish among the several traditions in journalism education. Much of the economic data did not seem to explain a great deal to me either. And I believe that the book is too skewed to print media, especially newspapers, to get at the slippery question of how you prod people constantly sweating over deadlines to become more philosophical about their social roles. The best technique I have seen so far is a book that remains quite superior, Wilbur Schramm's *Responsibility in Mass Communication*. In that book Schramm cites a number of case histories which are crises for the professional's conscience. This combines an authenticity dear to the journalist with an inductive kind of moralizing or philosophizing that he can assimilate as part of his experience. Better one vividly articulated conflict for the professional to analyze than pages of high-level abstractions about the need for press improvement. A series of such incidents carefully analyzed leads to a predisposition to respond in a certain way; predispositions over time become traditions; traditions provide institutionalized self-control. And that is what we are after, if we can get there fast enough.

PATRICK D. HAZARD

Beaver College
Glenside
Pennsylvania

MARK SHERWIN. *The Extremists*. Pp. viii, 242. New York: St Martin's Press, 1963. $5.00.

This is an impartial, temperate, well-balanced discussion of the people and organizations usually included in the categories called ultraconservatives, right wing, radical right, right-wing extremists, and the like. It is written in a popular and informal style, not for the specialist, but for the general public, which, since President Kennedy's assassination, wishes to know more about both ends of the American political spectrum.

The book begins by describing the extremists on the left—the Communists. This chapter serves many purposes: it convinces the reader that the author understands both shades of extremism; it points out similarities in methods of thinking and acting between the two groups as well as a certain amount of infiltration. And it leads the reader to the conclusion that, even though the extremists on the right claim their main enemy is communism, they frequently lose sight of their main objective in favor of side issues that are unrelated to communism, thus raising the question of their true sincerity. This book describes all of the well-known individuals and groups, including a separate chapter on Senator Barry Goldwater, called "The Urbane Right."

The author, as have others who have tried to understand the extremists on the right, devotes a chapter to what he calls the intellectual right, a position occupied rather exclusively by William F. Buckley, Jr. and Russell Kirk. Mr. Sherwin finds Mr. Buckley a rather elusive subject to define and leaves the reader, quite justifiably, it seems to me, with the feeling that perhaps Jack Paar summed up the attempt very properly, after their television appearance, by saying: "I listen to him and I don't know what the hell he's talking about. It's my shortcoming."

The basic question of whether the extremists are more accurately characterized by the body of their beliefs than by their manner of thinking and acting is not dealt with in much depth by this book.

RALPH E. ELLSWORTH
Director of Libraries
Professor of Bibliography
University of Colorado

WILLIAM PRESTON, JR. *Aliens and Dissenters: Federal Suppression of Radicals, 1903–1933.* Pp. viii, 352. Cambridge, Mass.: Harvard University Press, 1963. $6.75.

Professor Preston's book almost accomplished something I had thought impossible. He very nearly made me sympathetic with the way in which both the alien and the radical problems were dealt with in this period. I continue to be critical of our attitudes and our procedures, but he has forced me to realize that the issues involved were more complicated and the answers less clear than I had assumed. The first element of confusion in the book is revealed in the title. It should be obvious that his two terms are far from coterminous. Few aliens were dissenters, and only a minority of radicals were aliens.

Much of the indictment of the policies of the United States government is based on the ruling of the Supreme Court in *Fong Yue Ting* v. *U.S.* (1893). I too wish that the majority of the Court had decided that judicial protection for aliens accused of deportable offenses be required, but the scholarly opinion of Justice Gray for the Court is a long and careful analysis, worthy of more than deprecatory references. And the decision of May 24, 1954 in which a seven-to-two majority of the Court adhered to the same doctrine—an opinion written by Justice Frankfurter, once an alien, who came to national attention by his defense of two alien anarchists, Sacco and Vanzetti—is not adequately dealt with by an out-of-context reference (p. 273) to it based on a news story in the Washington Post for May 25, 1954. The case is *Galvan* v. *Press,* not *U. S.* v. *Galvan,* and the phrase from the majority opinion here quoted fails to reflect the philosophy of that opinion: respect for the principle of representative government as evidenced by repeated Congressional statutes plus long adherence by the judiciary to the doctrine of Fong Yue Ting. The Galvan decision came, by the way, just a week after *Brown* v. *Board of Education,* the public school integration case, and seven of those who ruled for the rights of Negroes in Brown were of the majority in Galvan.

Perhaps my chief difficulty with the book is Professor Preston's puzzling attitude toward what he refers to, under several terms, as radicalism, and his unclear conception of constitutional democracy. That conception, as I understand it, is based upon the substitution of reason, discussion, and orderly procedures for force and unlawful conspiracy. Perhaps the author does not believe that anarchism should be tolerated even when there is incitement to violence, but I do get that impression. Just how far should we go in allowing either open or secret conspiratorial attacks on the processes which are the essence of constitutional democracy, on the elected officers of government, or, for that matter, on minority groups? The conceptions of "dangerous" speech and of "inflammatory and incendiary" speech need careful definition. And what of sabotage? Is this the method of democracy? Indignant narrative does not answer such fundamental questions.

The essentials of constitutional democracy cannot be preserved by well-intentioned but blurred attacks upon long continued policies made by elected or duly appointed officers of government. Both the right and the obligation to dissent and to state that disagreement should be beyond question. Scholars who engage in such enterprise are obligated to be equally secure in their facts and in their comprehension of the concepts and principles involved.

BENJAMIN F. WRIGHT
Professor of Government
University of Texas

OLIVER P. WILLIAMS and CHARLES R. ADRIAN. *Four Cities: A Study in Comparative Policy-Making.* Pp. 334. Philadelphia: University of Pennsylvania Press, 1963. $6.00.

"The relationship between policy, the policy process, and general community characteristics," as the authors phrase their concern, has challenged political scientists and political sociologists in a long line that stretches back to the Lynds' pioneering *Middletown* (1929). In method, the authors chose to investigate four cities so selected as to coincide in a number of basic respects but to differ in regard to the key variables directly under scrutiny. For this purpose the selected cities are all in a single state, within the same 50,000 to 75,000 population range, governed by similar council-manager charters, based mainly on manu-

facturing economies, located away from the direct influence of any larger metropolis, and, most important, faced with essentially the same urban issues. They differed mainly in regard to three groups of elements: (1) policies, as exemplified by action or lack of action in such fields as downtown improvement, urban renewal, industrial promotion, and civic amenities; (2) the policy process, as expressed in the working of governmental institutions; and (3) such general community characteristics as patterns of industrial and land ownership, ethnic structures, and the nature of the surrounding hinterland.

The observations about the four cities that occupy much of the book are interesting in themselves. They afford a wealth of data to any future researcher. So are the many comments of the authors on how the new materials appear to reinforce or to refute recent theories related to decision-making, community power structure, and the like, as well as the older concepts on which the city-manager movement has been based. But the success of the research is to be judged mainly, I think, first, by the validity of the analytical framework developed by the authors in the course of the studies and, second, by the plausibility of this first major test of the framework as a device for perceiving, explaining, and predicting the substance of policies from the nature of the community and its political processes.

The new vital element in the analytic framework proposed is what the book calls a "typology of local political values." Four different roles for local government are characterized: "(1) promoting economic growth; (2) providing or securing life's amenities; (3) maintaining (only) traditional services; (4) arbitrating among conflicting interests." The establishment of these types and the constant reference of materials descriptive of the four cities to them are what the book is about. I found the demonstration convincing. It not only was internally consistent, but it coincided also with my own experiences elsewhere. Of course, there is no simple one-to-one relationship of the four cities to the four types of local political values.

In profiles of the cities examined, it was clear that a city might rate high, for example, in both the promotion of economic growth and the provision of the amenities. Each type is, in fact, one pole of a distinct continuum along which a particular city may be placed with regard to a crucial factor of public policy. No doubt, in future studies of other places, additional significant continuums will be identified and with them additional policy types. The importance of *Four Cities* is to get this process started.

One note of mild criticism: during the reading I was reminded occasionally of the nineteenth-century Russian novel with its bewildering array of names that one has to absorb in the first twenty pages only to learn on page 100 that Sasha is also Misha who is also sometimes called Kolshka by one of the other characters. In the interest of protecting their sources of information, the authors use the code names Alpha, Beta, Gamma, and Delta for the four cities, which they describe in general detail almost from the very beginning of the book. The problem is that until each city has developed a personality of its own, one finds it difficult to remember which characteristics belong to which place. For two cities that have "strong" personalities, this occurs reasonably soon, but the other cities never quite "come to life" as literary critics like to say. My suggestion for the next edition would be an extended table at the back, where it could be pulled out, with a column for each city in which each item of significant description would be briefed and set down in the sequence developed in the text. In the meantime, a tip for the reader—do it yourself.

"We are under no illusions that the task we set out to accomplish has been completed," say the authors at the end with refreshing candor—and perhaps an eye to a larger research grant. My own judgment is that they have made substantial progress and that investigators in the fields of urban politics and metropolitan prediction will want to study the book, ponder the typology proposed, and benefit from the lively report on new experience gained.

HENRY FAGIN
Professor of Planning
University of Wisconsin

CHARLES S. HYNEMAN. *The Supreme Court on Trial*. Pp. xii, 308. New York: Atherton Press, 1963. No price.

Charles S. Hyneman, who is Distinguished Service Professor of Government at Indiana University, here presents an expanded version of his 1961 Shambaugh Lectures in Political Science at the State University of Iowa. In the four parts of his book, he surveys the critical estimate to which the country has always subjected the Supreme Court; especially he describes the popular judgment of the 1954 segregation cases. He examines the legitimacy, or lack of it, of the Court's function in refusing effect to Acts of Congress it deems unconstitutional. He analyzes the judicial duty of attributing meaning to constitutional language which is not self-defining, such as "commerce among the several States." And he surveys the ideas of "activists," and of their critics, concerning the proper role of the Court in the democratic system of the United States.

In the first of these four parts, Professor Hyneman speaks to the beginner in political science—usefully, for the adept should never forget that, to large groups of hearers, the recurring hostility evoked by this or that judgment of the Supreme Court is a novel and disturbing phenomenon. The author's second part, again, treads old paths. But one has only to associate with modern university students to realize how continually surprising for them is the initial discovery that a non-popular group of nine men performs its occasional public duty of disregarding Acts of Congress without any clause in the Constitution stating, in so many words, that the Court, when it finds conflict between an Act of Congress and the Constitution, should follow the latter and disregard the former. Dr. Hyneman examines the question of "usurpation" with detachment, and if he finds the evidence more evenly balanced than I would, this may only indicate my lawyer's prepossession that a constitution subject, in substance, to amendment by ordinary Act of Congress would not have satisfied the draftsmen of 1787, the ratifying conventions, or the proponents of the Bill of Rights; nor would it satisfy any substantial proportion of the American people in 1963.

The third part concerns the recurring mystery of meaning in words. "Due Process," of course, does not clearly say what actions of government lack this quality, with its vague contours, its ill-definable application to procedure or substance—if, indeed, these two terms are themselves clearly helpful! Surprisingly, Dr. Hyneman feels that "economic due process" might conceivably return to the Supreme Court (p. 185). The fourth part will most attract the adept; it scrutinizes the process of policy-making in contrast to adjudication—a difficult distinction at the borderline, a difficulty which Professor Hyneman makes quite clear in his discussion of the relation between judicial setting of policy and popular qualms about the legislative process.

ARTHUR E. SUTHERLAND
Bussey Professor of Law
Harvard University

RICHARD D. YOUNGER. *The People's Panel: The Grand Jury in the United States, 1634–1941*. Pp. 263. Providence, R. I.: Brown University Press, 1963. $5.00.

One need not agree with Mr. Younger's sanguine and laudatory analysis of the institution of the grand jury to applaud him for a detailed and scholarly work on that controversial "arm of democracy." *The People's Panel* is pre-eminently a work of history, not of jurisprudence; within that limitation it fills a gap and performs a service. It does so by chronicling the power and function of grand juries from their British origin and their adaptation to Colonial America, on through the Revolution, the "New Nation," the Civil War era, through the heyday of *laissez faire* and into the dawn of the gradually evolv-

ing new positive state of the present century, ending just prior to World War II.

In his chronological presentation Mr. Younger skillfully illustrates the changing character and preoccupations of the grand jury, and he does not shun an analysis of the controversy that has characterized its life throughout history. He demonstrates how the functions and powers of grand juries have fluctuated from state to state and from crisis to crisis, always endeavoring to justify their existence as a vital element in the democratic process of government. Although he would seem to pretend not to take a "position" vis-à-vis its value in that process, his bias is readily evident, and leads him to the rather expansive conclusion that the grand jury "is the one institution that combines the necessary measure of disinterestedness with sufficient authority to investigate effective malfeasance and corruption in public office" (pp. 245–246). Indeed, he characterizes it as "the one body . . . [that] remain[s] potentially the strongest weapon against big government and the threat of 'statism' " (p. 246). This reviewer confesses that he retains some doubts—indeed, very serious ones: Mr. Younger's enthusiasm for his subject has blinded him to some rather obvious deficiencies, which would hardly lend themselves to a rosy prognosis! As a matter of fact, England and France abandoned grand juries in 1933, and in more and more parts of the United States the rapid easy method of "information" has replaced Mr. Younger's favorite institution.

Admittedly, grand juries have performed valuable services in a host of areas, especially in those of juvenile delinquency, waterfront crime, corruption, and narcotics traffic. As such they represent a potentially powerful arm of direct democracy. But they have also shown themselves to be cumbersome, amateurish, time-consuming, annoying, emotional, and occasionally utterly disdainful of rudimentary aspects of the rule of law. Be that as it may, *The People's Panel* is a welcome addition to the library of legal history.

HENRY J. ABRAHAM
Professor of Political Science
University of Pennsylvania

WAR AND FOREIGN POLICY

WALTER MILLIS and JAMES REAL. *The Abolition of War*. Pp. xvii, 217. New York: The Macmillan Company, 1963. $4.50 clothbound; $1.95 paper-bound.

Since 1931, when Walter Millis wrote *The Martial Spirit* about the Spanish-American War, he has been explaining to Americans how and why they got into their past wars. Now he has been joined by a young expert in the interpreting of modern technology to the public, James Real, in explaining to Americans how and why—if they choose—they will be able to prevent future wars and indeed to abolish the war system.

The Abolition of War is as radical intellectually as it is moderate and cautious politically. It cuts far beneath the accumulated myths of pacifists, internationalists, militarists, and nationalists. Yet by the very act of creating radically new ideas about government, conflict, and violence, it suggests the possibility of abolishing war without radically changing our national or international institutions. The central thesis of the book, abhorrent to pacifists and militarists alike, is that in the thermonuclear age war can be, should be, and will probably be abolished not because it is too terrible to contemplate or too horrible to conduct—which pacifists would like to believe—but because it is too useless to bother with—which militarists would like to disbelieve. Millis and Real argue that modern war in general, and thermonuclear war in particular, cannot be used by national governments to win particular disputes or to register a generalized triumph in the search for world power. Hence the war system has become irrelevant to the foreign policies of the various nation-states.

As a crucial corollary to this, Millis and Real suggest that the warless world could be organized without setting up a world government—as internationalists frequently argue would be necessary—but without leaving nations utterly free to resume making war whenever they chose—as nationalists have demanded. They suggest that, as national governments absorb the facts of the impotence of war, they will search both for ways of exerting their power without war and for ways of eliminating arms so that war ceases to be a danger. The first search is likely to light upon such techniques as the space race and competitive aid to the underdeveloped world as substitutes for war; the second, to light upon a small-scale world police empowered to enforce disarmament and do nothing else, as a substitute for the hyperarmed deterrence system as a means of preventing war. In short, Millis and Real are reversing the old Clausewitzian dictum and seeking to show that international politics can be made an extension of war by other means. Once that is done, war itself can be abolished.

ARTHUR WASKOW
Peace Research Institute Fellow
Institute for Policy Studies
Washington, D. C.

JOHN STRACHEY. *On the Prevention of War*. Pp. ix, 334. New York: St Martin's Press, 1963. $5.95.

In this, his last book, the late John Strachey, M.P., former British Secretary for War in the Labour Government and subsequently one of the defense spokesmen of the Parliamentary Opposition, set out to provide a more comprehensive and more realistic study of the nature of war in general, and of nuclear war in particular, than has yet been undertaken. He divided his subject into four parts: "The Strategy of the Balance," "Disarmament," "Communist and Western Intentions," and "Possibilities of Survival." The book starts on a somber note: "War has become intolerable while remaining inevitable"; it ends with a demonstration of the "Three Forces of Hope": "First there is a tendency for the economic and social systems of the advanced, industrialized nation-states to approximate to each other, whether they are organized in the communist or capitalist way. Secondly, there is the sheer dread of nuclear war. And thirdly, and in the long run most important, a new attitude of mind is emerging, an attitude transcending both national and ideological loyalities; an attitude of mind essentially concerned to find a way in which the human race may hope to continue to inhabit its narrow planet." These three kinds of social forces, given time, "may be relied upon to erode or to override the immense obstacles which today stand in the way of the establishment of even the most limited degree of world authority."

The book discusses many questions raised in the American and British literature on deterrence, defense, disarmament, and effective international authority, and provides sensible answers to these questions. Space limitations permit only one important point to be brought out here. The author supported the widely held view that the North Atlantic Treaty Organization (NATO) must have more conventional forces, in fact, so many that it could meet even a large-scale conventional attack with conventional means. Yet neither in the book nor anywhere else in the literature has the question been discussed in detail whether NATO can, without undue risk, fight a war conventionally on a battlefield which might at any time become nuclear, and whether it can switch, if necessary, from conventional to nuclear war without thereby causing its own disorganization and defeat. Unless both questions can be answered in the affirmative, NATO cannot afford to fight a conventional war against a nuclear power; it would have to fight with nuclear means right from the start.

The book, agreeably free from nuclear jargon, is highly stimulating and undoubtedly one of the finest contributions to the debate on the most important subject of our time.

OTTO HEILBRUNN

Gerrards Cross
Bucks
England

MORTON H. HALPERIN. *Limited War in the Nuclear Age.* Pp. ix, 191. New York: John Wiley & Sons, 1963. $2.95.

In this fine volume, one of the youngest of Harvard's military intellectuals combines the lessons of the "historical clashes in Korea . . . and elsewhere" with cur-

rent theories on "the role of force in the nuclear age . . . to predict the likely evolution of such future conflicts" (p. viii) "in an era in which limited means are used despite the fact that both the United States and the Soviet Union have vastly greater means of destruction, and the latter has far-ranging objectives" (p. vii). This last phrase seems to take an American "no-win" policy as given, and to assume that its chief aim is to force a similar policy on the Soviet Union. While this is the most intelligent and systematic examination of limited warfare in print, it has to oversimplify its problem by the assumption that the chief dangers to peaceful coexistence come from the Soviet bloc and tends to ignore the forces of blackmail, ineptitude, and drift in the various states in the increasingly inchoate camps which the two superpowers are supposedly leading.

Dr. Halperin is particularly good on the dangers of tactical nuclear warfare, but his book is already dated on the North Atlantic Treaty Organization (NATO). In November 1962 it was still possible to feel that the NATO states might be prodded into raising "the necessary divisions to successfully engage in a local war in Europe" (p. 126). Dr. Halperin did not consider the possibility that one value of an independent French nuclear force was that it gives France the power to touch off a nuclear war and American intervention against threats which might otherwise be "too ambiguous, too obviously successful, or too near the brink of central war [the current jargon for general nuclear war] for the United States to be willing to intervene, no matter what its capability and declaratory policies" (p. 129).

Dr. Halperin's fine chapters on "Nuclear Weapons and Local War," "Arms Control and Local War," "The Limitation of Central War," and "American Local-Defense Strategy" do not really convince this reviewer that the present "mix" of cold, conventional, tactical nuclear, and strategic nuclear armaments has really increased our range of choices. For "the losing side in a local war may [still] conclude that the consequences of defeat are so great that it has to unleash a central war" (p. 38).

THEODORE ROPP
Professor of History
Duke University

EDVARD KARDELJ. *Socialism and War: A Survey of Chinese Criticism of the Policy of Coexistence.* Translated from the Serbo-Croatian by Alec Brown. Pp. 238. New York: McGraw-Hill, 1963. $4.50.

In this small volume Edvard Kardelj, Vice-President of the Federal People's Republic of Yugoslavia, attempts to answer two questions: (1) Do Chinese Communist conceptions of international policy really derive from Marxism-Leninism? And (2) What exactly is the Chinese policy and where does it lead?

Chapter One, "Chinese Ideology and Chinese Reality," contains an accurate statement of the Chinese position regarding the policy of peaceful coexistence. The author also faithfully presents the Chinese condemnations of "Yugoslav revisionism, opportunism, and cowardice." Throughout the remaining fourteen chapters, Kardelj dutifully cites chapter and verse from the writings of Marx, Engels, and Lenin to refute these condemnations. In building his case, Kardelj is ponderous, windy, and terribly dull. Taken as such, the author merely adds to the increasing body of Communist exegetical writings which show an awareness of reality and a consequent erosion of the neat images of theory.

However, Kardelj is most impressive when he rises above the strictures of dogma. Even when the Chinese theoreticians score a point—and they do on several occasions, as Kardelj himself readily admits—the author is unimpressed. "What does matter here," he states, "is whether peaceful development is or is not feasible." In Chapter Ten, entitled "What Is Revolutionary and What Is Not," Kardelj criticizes the Chinese for not understanding that "any aim one strives for should be a practical one." It is this failing that has caused the Chinese to become subjectivists, as they believe that "it is possible to build up communism simply by the further elaboration of political forms, quite independently of the development of the forces of production." Thus, Kardelj concludes that the Chinese are Trotskyites who believe that "nothing has changed in the world since Marx or Lenin's day."

Kardelj fires his main salvos at the Chinese for their views on just and unjust war (Chapters Three, Four, and Seven): "Here in fact the theory of just and unjust wars is brought to the ridiculous conclusion that any war which *I* wage is a just war" (author's emphasis). Yet Kardelj himself defines "progressive, just wars" as including "a defensive war of the socialist world against aggression, . . . people's liberation and internal revolutionary wars." The author does not comment on the ingredients in this vague definition, although he does state that "even very just wars can have a reactionary effect."

Finally, it must be mentioned that the translation by Mr. Brown is awkward, stilted and, on occasion, unintelligible. This reviewer noted many sentences of over 60 words, three of 88, and one monstrosity of 131 words. The book has some merit, but it takes a determined reader.

DENNIS J. DOOLIN
Acting Assistant Professor of
   Political Science
Stanford University

EMILE BENOIT and KENNETH E. BOULDING (Eds.). *Disarmament and the Economy.* Pp. x, 310. New York: Harper & Row, 1963. $5.75.

This volume represents the final report of the Program of Research on Economic Adjustments to Disarmament (READ), sponsored by Michigan's Center for Research on Conflict Resolution. There may be major obstructions along the path to disarmament, but the participants in this study are collectively optimistic about the removal of one obstacle: the economic hazards that are presumed to be a consequence of substantially reduced defense spending. Their analyses imply that the economic impact of disarmament may be less severe than commonly assumed and, in any case, that the period of adjustment can be managed without economic disaster.

All assumptions concerning pace and magnitude of disarmament hinge upon the READ disarmament model, a contrivance which is roughly consistent with the general and complete disarmament formula proposed by the United States at Geneva in 1962. The READ model postulates a progressive abandonment of national military capabilities and their transfer to a world authority, the stages of the process to be spread over a twelve-year period. Within this admittedly speculative framework each contributor analyzes a critical economic aspect of disarmament as it pertains to the American economy. Whether or not one takes issue with the relevance of the READ model in terms of practical political possibilities, the fifteen economists whose analyses are produced in this volume do provide the reader with a rather coherent set of discussions about the interrelationships between national defense and the over-all economy of the United States.

Neither the editors nor the contributors argue that disarmament will be easy to achieve or that only economic problems need to be solved for disarmament to become a practical possibility. There is general agreement that disarmament, even when phased out over a twelve-year period, will cause serious economic stresses, although Leslie Fishman maintains—in a chapter entitled "The Expansionary Effects of Shifts from Defense to Nondefense Expenditures"—that "the low expansionary effect of defense spending has been generally ignored," resulting in a . . . widespread tendency to exaggerate the deflationary impact of cuts in defense spending" (p. 173). Several authors point to the potentially powerful deflationary effect that a propensity to offset defense outlays by a reduction in the national debt will have, especially if this is the primary fiscal reaction to substantial reductions in defense expenditures. Recent evidence of popular and congressional preference for a debt retirement policy over tax cuts and unbalanced budgets suggests that the prospects for sound economic management of the transition of our economy from its current state to one in which the defense industries—for all practical purposes—will have been eliminated, are not as bright as the authors seem to imply. Moreover, none of the contributors directly consider the psychological impact of disarmament on the American economy. As a technical question the elimination of America's armaments industries is probably quite feasible, but would such a program undermine confidence in the system?

One suspects that the major quarrel with this book will not be with the economic analyses but with the relevance of the study to the political universe in which disarmament is to be carried out. Kenneth E. Boulding tells us in a highly imaginative, yet other-worldly analysis of the ' 'World War Industry" that "disarmament is now no longer a dream of the idealist, but has become a matter of intense practical concern" (p. 18). The concern may be intense and, as this study indicates, there are many "practical" considerations to be examined by the peace-researchers, but what is being proposed here is the substitution of a totally different and radical system of international politics—general and complete disarmament—for the currently imperfect system in which we live.

DAVID W. TARR
Assistant Professor of Political Science
University of Wisconsin

F. H. HINSLEY. *Power and the Pursuit of Peace: Theory and Practice in the History of Relations Between States.* Pp. 416. New York: Cambridge University Press, 1963. $6.95.

This book, written by a Lecturer of History in Cambridge University, is a study of the nature and history of international relations, an attempt to rationalize the long history of the state system. It covers a wide field, perhaps too wide; it requires careful reading. The author argues his case with assurance, frequently criticizing others for not distinguishing between the myths and the realities of history. It is an arresting analysis. The outstanding failure of recent times, says the author, is that of a civilization which has broken through barriers in almost every other direction but still retains the views on international relations which it held in its youth. He outlines the peace proposals of the past 600 years and analyzes the modern state system, ending with a prediction of probable developments.

Many people believe that the present deadlock between the great powers arose in the 1950's, out of nuclear parity. Not so, Hinsley says; this only recognized an existent fact. Nuclear weapons were the "logical culmination of that growth of technological deterrents against irresponsible policy, hasty decisions and war which has been so rapid since the beginning of the century" (p. 347). The great powers, now aware of the fatal consequences of using these weapons, have determined not to do so. Even without nuclear weapons there would have been no danger of general war since 1945, because of the new stability in the world-wide distribution of power which has developed in the twentieth century.

Hinsley asserts that Russia has not strongly pressed her quite limited demands since 1945. "The American position contained her long before the policy of containment was invented. It would have contained her if the weapons had never been invented" (p. 353). Russia and the United States constitute an "all-pervasive" check upon each other; coexistence was the only real alternative long before it became the announced policy of the Soviet government.

Far more important, Hinsley believes, are the internal social conflicts in both countries, which have produced classless "middle-class" societies led by technicians. This "mutual interpenetration" offsets their ideological differences. Even more important is the present disparity between the more advanced and the less developed parts of the world, which will probably dominate international relations for at least the rest of this century. Since no power can insulate itself from this turmoil, the great powers should, in view of their own stability, try to limit the extent and the bitterness of the coming struggle of the backward countries against each other and with the great powers.

DONALD G. BISHOP
Professor of Political Science
Syracuse University

ROBERT STRAUSZ-HUPÉ, JAMES E. DOUGHERTY, and WILLIAM R. KINTNER, with STEFAN T. POSSONY, ROBERT L. PFALTZGRAFF, JR., and FRANCIS B. HOEBER. *Building the Atlantic World.* Pp. xiv, 400. New York: Harper and Row, 1963. $6.00.

The authors of this book are well known for their previous studies of East-West strategy in a bipolar world. Their analysis in this new work on the Atlantic community is unencumbered by the more complex approaches employed by specialists in international relations: decision-making, action-reaction, image-perception, and game theory, among others. The world situation, in their view, has not changed: the Sino-Soviet bloc is the implacable enemy which will engage the West for some time to come in a protracted conflict. Thus they give little credence to the Sino-Soviet rift, to de-Stalinization, and to the possibility of a *détente* (p. 233). To forestall the threatening success of world communism they prescribe dynamic United States leadership within the Atlantic community. Specifically, they would have the United States make available to its North Atlantic Treaty Organization (NATO) allies, for their unilateral and collective use, nuclear weapons. The French would then renew their active co-operation within NATO, and the Soviet Union would be confronted with the difficult task of explaining why it did not share nuclear energy with its allies.

Nothing less than the institutionalization of political decision-making is required to revive the Atlantic Alliance: the authors argue that the development of regional economic institutions will not evolve towards political collaboration, and they admit the temporary nature of military alliances built upon mutual fear: Stalin, they declare, was the best ally of NATO. They oppose the concept of a European third force, of Fortress America, which is not militarily viable, and of the United Nations, with its solicitous concern for sovereign equality.

But the re-invigoration of the Atlantic Alliance is confronted with difficulties even more imposing than the authors are willing to admit. Their failure to recognize these difficulties compelled them to add a postscript which accounted for de Gaulle's rejection of Britain from the Common Market. Their faith in de Gaulle's policies—given their view of the Sino-Soviet menace—is all the more surprising since they are not in sympathy with his determined effort to create a third force, nor do they share his image of the emerging world situation as he describes it in his autobiography. Perhaps a second postscript for their book would now be in order to explain the French endorsement of neutralism in Southeast Asia, the French-Communist China negotiations on recognition and trade, and the recently expressed French tolerance of the Castro regime in Cuba. A more sensitive regard for decision-making processes within the respective countries might have led them to view the developing problems within the Common Market as more serious; the succession of Erhard in West Germany and the emerging role of the Labour Party in Britain will not necessarily contribute that required dimension of increased co-operation within the Atlantic Alliance the authors deem necessary.

This book can be considered timely only in the sense that the authors have foreshadowed the doom of the Atlantic Alliance as they would have it. Subsequent events have undermined the abundance of hortatory prescriptions which the authors outline. Their model for a Grand Design is farther from realization than it was a year ago. Apostles of the Atlantic Alliance will have to look elsewhere for a realistic rationale for this regional organization in a world of diminishing tensions, of growing equilibrium, and of resulting independence in national decision-making. A larger role can indeed be attributed to regional organization in a time of cold war, while lesser, but nonetheless important functions can be assigned to them in a more stable, secure,

and nationalistic world. The concept of sovereign equality is reasserting itself in the developed as well as the underdeveloped countries, and it is this realistic premise which gives renewed importance to the United Nations.

MARTIN B. TRAVIS
Professor of Political Science
State University of New York
Stony Brook

BRUCE M. RUSSETT. *Community and Contention: Britain and America in the Twentieth Century.* Pp. viii, 252. Cambridge, Mass.: M. I. T. Press, 1963. $7.00.

HERBERT NICHOLAS. *Britain and the U. S. A.* Pp. 191. Baltimore: Johns Hopkins Press, 1963. $5.00.

Both these books are about Anglo-American relations, but they differ greatly in content and treatment. Dr. Russett is concerned primarily with public opinion and uses the methods of the statistician or market-researcher; Mr. Nicholas is concerned primarily with governments and deals with his subject more like a historian or a student of current affairs.

The bulk of Dr. Russett's book is taken up with an analysis of economic and social factors which, he suggests, may affect the closeness of the tie between the peoples. He acknowledges that the results are not conclusive, but he seems to attach particular importance to the alleged evidence of a decline in mutual mass approval over the last seventy years. Having completed his analysis, Dr. Russett rightly observes that it is necessary to show its relevance to the making of political decisions, but instead he goes off at a tangent and discusses the effect on the attitude of individual members of Parliament or senators in one country of economic or personal ties to the other. Finally, Dr. Russett examines the military link and reaches the conclusion that the degree of military co-operation achieved in the 1950's was midway between those achieved in the two world wars; he observes, however, that military integration in the face of external danger is not in itself sufficient for the maintenance of an alliance. The point is a fair one, but he does not make clear what, in his view, is the relative importance of military and social or economic interdependence. In a postscript dealing with the years between 1954 and 1961, Dr. Russett examines the problems arising from the British governmental policy on an independent nuclear deterrent and the minority movement in Britain towards unilateral nuclear disarmament, both of which seem to him to have disruptive potentials. It is doubtful whether he appreciates all the complexities of the former, and most observers will probably think that he exaggerates the significance of the latter.

Mr. Nicholas' book deals with the ups and downs of British and American diplomacy in various trouble spots in the world between 1946 and 1962. He shows that he realizes the difficulty of assessing the importance of nuclear developments in defense co-operation, and he draws attention to some political factors not mentioned by Dr. Russett. The narrative part of his book is best when he resists the temptation to deliver judgment; his occasional departures from objectivity—for example, in referring alike to the British Suez operation and the American U-2 incident as "fiascos"—are not appropriate to the treatment of contemporary history. Mr. Nicholas suggests that "when it comes to the conclusions reached by the ultimate decision-makers in London and Washington there has been much less to choose than the publics of each country have sometimes assumed." In this respect he takes a more optimistic view than Dr. Russett, but it is no criticism of either of them to say that the evidence available to readers for forming their own judgment is incomplete, for this is bound to be the case in dealing with contemporary events. But it is perhaps not an unfair reflection on both books to suggest that material of this kind tends to be out of date as soon as it is published, and may therefore be more suitable for the pages of a periodical than for the more permanent form of a book.

A. S. HUTCHINSON

Tunbridge Wells
Kent
England

JAMES N. ROSENAU. *National Leadership and Foreign Policy: A Case Study in the Mobilization of Public Support.* Pp. xiii, 409. Princeton, N. J.: Princeton University Press, 1963. $8.50.

In the last decade or so, political scientists have become increasingly preoccupied with (1) the group basis of politics, (2) the "mobilization of public opinion" in creating a so-called "consensus," and (3) the use of the case method and statistical data as key weapons of analysis. One of the beauties of Professor Rosenau's *National Leadership and Foreign Policy* is that he has combined all three in a readable empirical study heretofore ignored yet known to exist: "one that lies somewhere between officialdom and the citizenry," one that concerns itself with "the role which [national] nongovernmental leaders play in shaping the contents and effectiveness of American foreign policy." What Professor Rosenau postulated is that such a study, to be meaningful, necessitated the "convening of [a] 'third chamber' . . . sponsored by an important agency of the federal government—[composed] of national leaders . . . to mobilize public opinion behind a proposed policy . . . on an issue of great national importance, . . . large enough to include a sample of all major segments of the leadership structure . . . [capable of] meeting together in one place . . . subjected to the same stimuli . . . [lasting] at least a day . . . [with] speeches delivered by the top leaders of both political parties . . . [who] should take a united and firm position on the issue . . . [toward the end] that those in attendance should exercise the full limits of their opinion-making capacities on behalf of the recommended policy."

Since "every detail of this scientific fantasy actually occurred on February 25, 1958" when the White House called together a "National Conference on the Foreign Aspects of the U. S. National Security"—which was another way of saying the foreign-aid program—it was possible for Professor Rosenau "exactly three months after the Conference" to send out an 8-page, 71-item questionnaire to the 1,067 who attended "soliciting in-

formation [about] backgrounds, . . . reactions, . . . and subsequent behavior"
of the conferees. Sixty-one per cent
responded and this study "is devoted to
an analysis of the findings yielded by the
647 returned questionnaires," the possible
interpretations of such data, the "major
tendencies [that] can be discerned with
sufficient clarity," possible shortcomings,
and future directions of continuing research to the end that, on any given issue
of major importance in foreign policy, "it
should be possible to isolate the variables
which lead to strong or weak consensuses,
to temporary or enduring ones, and to
ones which are narrowing or widely
based."

It would have been possible in a study
of such magnitude to bog the reader
down with trivia, with statistics, with
mathematical percentages and the like, to
the point that the major question of
whether "a foreign policy consensus [can]
be fashioned among the diverse groups
presently active in America" would be
lost completely or else create a "who
cares anyhow" attitude. Such is far from
the case, however. And this is due not
alone to the feeling that Professor Rosenau
is completely the master of these facts
and details, but to the grace of language
and style with which they are presented.

BENJAMIN MUNN ZIEGLER
Bertrand Snell Professor of
Political Science
Amherst College

BERNARD C. COHEN. *The Press and
Foreign Policy*. Pp. ix, 288. Princeton,
N. J.: Princeton University Press, 1963.
$6.00.

The press may influence foreign policy
by influencing the government officials in
Washington, or by influencing its readers
at the grassroots. Professor Cohen's book
is based largely on interviews with government officials and newspaper correspondents and reporters, and is more concerned
with the relation between the press and
government officials than with the relation between the press and the general
public. However, he is concerned with
the problem faced by the press in covering

foreign-policy news for the general reader
and opinion elites at the same time, and
he suggests improvement to better meet
the needs of elite readers.

The author stresses the importance to
government officials of the "prestige"
papers, particularly the *New York Times*.
He probably does not exaggerate the
extent to which State Department officials
read such papers, but he may exaggerate
their influence on congressmen. He suggests that congressmen pay more attention to what is in the *New York Times*
on foreign policy than to what is in their
own area papers. Undoubtedly most
congressmen get their first press reports
on foreign-policy developments from the
New York and Washington papers, but a
reader may be forgiven a bit of skepticism
regarding the idea that a member of
Congress from Missouri, for instance,
would give more weight to what they say
than to what the *St. Louis Post-Dispatch*
and the *Kansas City Star* say.

The author's picture of the relation
between the newspaper men and government officials is one of mutual dependence and mutual suspicion. The official
and the reporter depend upon each other,
but each suspects that the other is trying to "put something over" on him.
Doubtless there is much truth in this
picture, but efforts to "put something
over" vary at different times and with
different men.

The author makes several interesting
suggestions for improving press treatment
of foreign affairs. One is that, since many
people are supposedly not interested in
the subject, "it could be handled like
other materials that have few customers,
like financial news" or "materials like
comics and sports that have many customers." Another suggestion is that
foreign correspondents should be given
training comparable to that given foreign-
service officers. The latter suggestion is
an indication of the importance which the
author attaches to the contributions of
the press to foreign-policy formation.

This is an informative and useful book.
That it stimulates thinking and occasionally some disagreement is perhaps testi-
mony both to its interesting nature and

to the desirability of further research in this field.

CHARLES W. SMITH, JR.
Public Opinion Analyst
Arlington
Virginia

JOSEPH ALEXANDER SZIKSZOY. *The Legal Aspects of the Hungarian Question.* Pp. 219. Ambilly, France: Les Presses de Savoie, 1963. No price.

Revolutionary upheavals, consisting in the extralegal transfer of governmental power from one regime to another, are apt to raise two questions of international law. One concerns the recognition of revolutionary regimes as the lawful representatives of their countries. The other arises when foreign powers intervene with military force in support either of the insurgents or of the incumbent government. The two questions are interrelated: whether foreign intervention constitutes "aggression" depends on the legal status of the side requesting it and benefiting from it.

Neither question can be resolved in terms of purely legal criteria. The power factor plays a decisive role, since legal titles to governmental authority, however unobjectionable, can be voided by the loss of effective control. The gain of effective control, on the other hand, does not constitute a sufficient legal title in and by itself: to be legitimate, governmental authority must rest on something more than force. Since powers in an ideologically divided world differ as to their concepts of legitimacy, they will judge the claims of effective power-holders differently; thus the status of revolutionary regimes may remain controversial for a considerable time, and there will be much confusion about such questions as the justification of intervention or the *de facto* and *de jure* recognition of existing regimes.

The legal aspects of the Hungarian revolution of October 1956, discussed with admirable clarity and erudition in Dr. Szikszoy's thesis, display more than the usual degree of complexity and ambiguity present in revolutionary events accompanied by foreign intervention. A revolutionary regime arose in Budapest, ending

the Communist one-party regime and taking the country out of the Warsaw pact system. The Soviet army intervened in force, removing the revolutionary government of Imre Nagy and installing that of Janos Kadar, which restored Communist totalitarianism and steered the country back into the Soviet orbit. The United Nations, taking up the matter, questioned the legitimacy of the Kadar government, holding that it owed its tenure to armed aggression by a foreign power. The Soviet side, on the other hand, claimed that its intervention was requested by a legal Hungarian govenment threatened by counterrevolution.

This would be a straightforward controversy if the Communists asserted that the Nagy regime was an illegal, insurgent one. But as Dr. Szikszoy shows, this is not what the Communists say. They go to great lengths in arguing that there has been no breach in constitutional continuity in Hungary at all. The Nagy government was established legally under the Communist constitution, and so was the Kadar government which succeeded it. The point which this thesis is supposed to establish is that the United Nations had no legal basis to concern itself with the Hungarian question. The whole story boiled down to domestic incidents within a regime which had never ceased to exist.

The author demonstrates the fallacious nature of this reasoning: if the Nagy regime was legal, the Soviet intervention against it did amount to aggression, and the transfer of power to Kadar was extralegal. Kadar's control, at first, rested only on force, and foreign force at that. The United Nations challenged him, but to no avail, proving that this body is no effective instrument in stopping aggression. Kadar, on the other hand, not only consolidated his control, but also legalized it under Hungarian municipal law, since the parliament on May 23, 1957, confirmed his tenure *ex post facto*. All foreign powers now deal with the Kadar government as the legal representative of Hungary, in spite of the extralegal and even extranational origin of its power. The United Nations took a different stand, but its refusal to admit the Kadar regime's delegation was essentially based on the regime's noncompliance with United Nations resolutions. The status of the Kadar government could not be effectively challenged on this basis.

PAUL KECSKEMETI

The Rand Corporation
Washington, D. C.

ROBERT H. FERRELL. *The American Secretaries of State and Their Diplomacy,* Vol. XI: *Frank B. Kellogg—Henry L. Stimson.* Pp. ix, 360. New York: Cooper Square, 1963. $7.50.

The inauguration of an important new historical series deserves some felicitous comment. The revival of a distinguished series is a cause for even greater gratification. The ten volumes in *The American Secretaries of State and Their Diplomacy,* edited by the dean of American diplomatic historians, Samuel Flagg Bemis of Yale University, and published between 1927 and 1929, have long been indispensable, particularly for students just beginning to find their way through the maze of American diplomatic history. Now the publication of Professor Ferrell's eleventh volume marks the rebirth of the series, after many years, under the general editorship of Professor Ferrell himself and the advisory editorship of Professor Bemis. Four additional volumes, covering Secretaries of State from Cordell Hull through Christian A. Herter, are also being prepared.

The author of the volume under review is a professor of history at Indiana University and, appropriately, one of Professor Bemis's most productive and distinguished students. Dr. Ferrell's earlier books, *Peace in Their Time: The Origins of the Kellogg-Briand Pact* (1952) and *American Diplomacy in the Great Depression* (1957), have made him the pre-eminent authority on men and events covered by *Frank B. Kellogg—Henry L. Stimson.* Like earlier volumes in the series, it combines biographies of Coolidge's and Hoover's Secretaries of State with resumés of diplomatic developments during their tenure.

The author obviously had severe limitations of space, but his descriptions of Kellogg and Stimson are always satisfactory and sometimes lively, and he deals judiciously if briefly with the major problems of American foreign policy between 1925 and 1933: war debts, the Kellogg-Briand Pact, Latin America, disarmament, and, most thoroughly, the Manchurian crisis of 1931–1932. Although Dr. Ferrell has worked through the contemporary sources, he presents no new findings in this volume. These have already been embodied in his two earlier books and in L. Ethan Ellis's excellent *Frank B. Kellogg and American Foreign Relations, 1925–1929,* upon which Professor Ferrell relied heavily. Advanced students will no doubt think that the Bibliography is the most significant part of the book. It is a superb review, not only of published materials, but also of manuscript collections and archival sources.

This reviewer noticed few important errors. Admiral von Capelle made something like the remarks attributed to him (pp. 148, 310, n. 14) before the Budget Committee of the Reichstag, not the Reichstag itself; his remarks are incorrectly quoted. The author's discussion of Bryan and the origin of the nonrecognition doctrine (p. 237) is curiously inadequate in view of the evidence presented in the present writer's *Wilson: The Struggle for Neutrality* (pp. 304–307). It is doubtful that Nicholas Murray Butler's account of Ambassador Jusserand's conversation with President Wilson (p. 15) is entirely reliable. Finally, it might be observed that Professor Ferrell seems at times to have adopted an odd literary style for historical writing.

ARTHUR S. LINK

Princeton University

LAWRENCE E. GELFAND. *The Inquiry: American Preparations for Peace, 1917–1919.* Pp. xiv, 387. New Haven and London: Yale University Press, 1963. $8.75.

Developments in the application of increasingly specialized knowledge to policy are a key to understanding the structure and strains of contemporary public bureaucracy. Since the establishment of the Office of Strategic Services (OSS), American national-security and foreign-policy makers have had an institution continuously devoted to providing extensive background research and projections of developments and consequences of behavioral alternatives, on which to take decisions. Indeed, several departments and agencies have felt impelled to develop independent sources of intelligence, partly to provide information to meet their specific needs and partly to reduce their dependence on other departments. Increasingly policy discussions use such phrases as "intelligence production" and include speculation on the motivation and co-ordination of the "intelligence community." Next to this development, the work of the Inquiry, the subject of Lawrence Gelfand's book, is amateurish and a trifle comic-operalike.

The Inquiry was established in September 1917, by Colonel House at the suggestion of President Wilson. Like his present-day counterparts, Wilson wished to avoid too great a dependence on the Allied Powers for information and to obtain an independent evaluation of America's interests in the peace negotiations. Hence, the range of problems considered by the Inquiry included, among other things, studies of the territorial, economic, and ethnographic problems of Europe, the Middle East, Asia, and even Latin America. Participating in the group, which assembled under the leadership of Sidney Mezes and, later, Isaiah Bowman, were several individuals who had then attained or were soon to attain public or professional importance, for example, Walter Lippmann, Robert Lord, Charles Haskins, James Shotwell, Manley Hudson, and others. Professor Gelfand's study includes an analysis of the structure and functioning of the Inquiry and its relations with other governmental bodies, especially the Department of State, and an assessment of the work of the Inquiry.

And it is with the assessment that this reviewer registers dissent. Even Professor Gelfand is unsure how to evaluate the Inquiry (p. 225 and chapter 11). The central role of the Inquiry in the formulation of the Fourteen Points cannot be disputed. Nor can the role at Paris of certain members, although the record shows persistent refusal on the part of Wilson to accept the advice of his "experts." Without an indication of the relationship of the work of the Inquiry to the American position in Paris—an effort, incidentally, promised by Professor Gelfand—one must conclude, on the basis of Professor Gelfand's evidence that (1) the Inquiry was staffed with a mixed lot at best; (2) few participants had previous experience in the areas of their research; (3) many of the studies involved extreme "special pleading"; (4) much of the research was based on readily available secondary sources and was useless in the form provided; (5) major problems, such as the influence of socialism in various European countries, were untouched; and (6) a wholly unexplained and disproportionate share of the Inquiry's funds went to support a cartographic study of Latin America. If *The Inquiry* was a study in the history of the changing role of expertise to government, if *The Inquiry* explicitly identified the areas of changing content of America's foreign interests, if *The Inquiry* would have made "more comprehensible the means and ends of Wilsonian foreign policy" (p. xii), then Professor Gelfand's book would have been an excellent contribution to our knowledge of World War I. As it stands, the Inquiry must await Professor Gelfand's next volume even to be assessed.

WARREN FREDERICK ILCHMAN
Assistant Professor of Political Science
Williams College

IVO J. LEDERER. *Yugoslavia at the Paris Peace Conference: A Study in Frontier-making.* Pp. xiv, 351. New Haven, Conn.: Yale University Press, 1963. $8.00.

To the recent studies in English on the formation or enlargement of Rumania, Czechoslovakia, Poland, and Lithuania during and after the Peace Conference of 1919 should be added this painstaking and straightforward account of the birth of Yugoslavia, its negotiations in 1919–1920 for recognition and extensive boundaries, and the settlement reached with Italy in the Rapallo Treaty of November 1920. Firmly based on newly available documents—especially the papers of Yugoslav Foreign Minister Ante Trumbić, and, above all, the minutes of the Yugoslav Conference delegation—this study begins by touching briefly on the growth of the Yugoslav unification movement after 1914. This stirred opposition both among those Serbs favoring an expanded Serbia and among the many Italians who feared a strong Yugoslavia which might block their imperial ambitions in the western Balkans. Matters came to a head at Paris, since the boundaries hurriedly established by Serbian troops and pro-Yugoslav councils after the armistice and the dissolution of Austria-Hungary had not achieved international recognition and were, indeed, contested not only by the vanquished—Austria, Hungary, and Bulgaria—but by Rumania and Italy, Serbia's wartime allies. The Italo-Yugoslav conflict over Istria, Fiume, and Dalmatia was certainly the most dangerous of these conflicts, and Lederer shows clearly how the Yugoslavs countered Italian military and diplomatic pressure by invoking Wilsonian principles of national self-determination. Since France and Great Britain refused to fulfill the territorial pledges made in the Treaty of London, Italy found herself isolated, while Wilson's immense prestige, backed by an American financial power essential for European reconstruction, lay on the Yugoslav side. The situation began changing late in 1919, however, as a new Italian government showed greater flexibility, while American prestige began to ebb, and Lloyd George and Clemenceau pressed harder for a settlement during the Adriatic tension. Without firm support, shocked by Wilson's electoral defeat, and fearful lest the Italians bow to nationalist pressure at home by snatching Fiume, Yugoslavia finally accepted unfavorable terms at Rapallo.

On the whole, Lederer follows traditional canons of diplomatic history by chronicling the notes, proposals, and other components of diplomatic tactics. His real contribution, however, stems from his description of how the Yugoslav delegation, frequently cut off by poor communications from its home government, and riven by discords among its Serb, Croat, and Slovene members, formulated these tactics to meet an ever-changing situation. Unfortunately, this approach largely ignores both the general situation at Paris, and the ideological and strategic factors which shaped Yugoslav strategy. The result is a conventional monograph, knowledgeable, specialized, but only rarely enlightening.

LEONARD BUSHKOFF
Instructor
Department of History
Carnegie Institute of Technology

JOSEF KORBEL. *Poland Between East and West: Soviet and German Diplomacy toward Poland, 1919–1933.* Pp. xi, 321. Princeton, N. J.: Princeton University Press, 1963. $6.50.

It would be valuable for the student of interwar Polish diplomatic history to read Roman Dębicki's *Foreign Policy of Poland, 1919–1939* (New York, 1962), before starting on the volume under review. As the title indicates, Professor Korbel has restricted his study both in time and in context. His book ends with the Declaration of Non-Aggression between Poland and Germany on January 26, 1934.

The author has made a thorough use of Polish, Russian, and German primary language sources in his excellent treatise. For the first time, possibly, in English one encounters the fascinating account of secret talks between emissaries of Marshal Józef Piłsudski and V. I. Lenin at Mikaszewice which resulted in the Polish decision not to aid the White Russian army of General A. I. Denikin (pp. 22–26). These events had been discussed previously by Stanisław Mackiewicz, *Zwycięstwo prowokacji* (Victory of Provocation), published in 1962 at Munich, Germany.

The attitude of the Weimar politicians and military, especially seen in General Staff Chief Hans von Seeckt's 1919 plan to attack Poland and in the 1920 ban on transit of war matériel to that country (pp. 71–75, 87–88) when the Red Army had reached the gates of Warsaw, is again illustrative of how chauvinism blinded German policy-makers to the main danger from the East. The Polish barrier to communism would have been sacrificed willingly by the Germans in return for the 1914 border with Russia.

Indeed, the Rapallo Treaty, as part of foreign minister Gustav Stresemann's "grand design" to isolate Poland and expose her to Soviet-German pressure (p. 147), provides an object lesson for today. Those "exponents of *Realpolitik*," who claim that more contacts with the Soviet Union —as did Weimar ambassador to Moscow, Count Ulrich Brockdorff-Rantzau—and its puppet regimes in eastern Europe will make the Communists more peaceful, should read Professor Korbel's book first and then Bohdan Budurowycz's *Polish-Soviet Relations, 1932–1939* (New York, 1963) to find out why the fourth partition of Poland took place.

One inaccuracy does appear in this scholarly book, where the author refers to the 1926 "Communist Party of Poland and Lithuania" (p. 227). There did exist a Social Democracy of the Kingdom of Poland and Lithuania—SDKPiL (Socjał-Demokracja Królestwa Polskiego i Litwy) —founded in the 1890's. However, this organization fused with the left-wing of the Polish Socialist Party and a few persons from the Poalej Sjon party on December 16, 1918, at a conference in Warsaw, to establish the "Communist Workers' Party in Poland," renamed the Communist Party of Poland in 1925 at its third congress.

One would also have expected that a university press might order special type with all diacritical marks or else not use any. As it is, some letters have the marks, but others in the same word do not. Also the "z's" are marked incorrectly, with a slash instead of a dot above them. Both marks do exist. The foregoing, of course, should not reflect upon the author of this excellent book.

RICHARD F. STAAR
Chester W. Nimitz Chair of Social
    and Political Philosophy
United States Naval War College
Newport
Rhode Island

ASIA

RICHARD D. LAMBERT. *Workers, Factories, and Social Change in India.* Pp. xiii, 247. Princeton, N. J.: Princeton University Press, 1963. $5.50.

There are very few careful studies of the characteristics and job experience of factory workers in economically underdeveloped countries. This book, by a professor of sociology in the Department of South Asian Regional Studies at the University of Pennsylvania, has partially filled this gap and established a high standard for similar studies in the future. The title of the book is broader than its coverage. The data are drawn from a 10 per cent sample—856 workers—of production and maintenance workers, supervisors and clerks in five privately owned factories in Poona, India—a city of half a million people, west of Bombay. Detailed interviews were conducted in Marathi—the regional language—at the worker's home by Indian college students associated with the author, who was a visiting scholar at the Gokhale Institute of Politics and Economics in Poona.

Some of the possible limitations of the study are suggested by the Director of the Gokhale Institute, Professor D. R. Gadgil, in his foreword. Poona is not a highly industrialized Indian city; it grew gradually and afforded "scope for the migrant population to make adjustment in easy stages." There may also be alternative explanations for some of the conclusions. But despite these *caveats*, Lambert's data do raise doubts about some of the sweeping generalizations—my own included—on recruitment and commitment of industrial workers in developing countries. It is clear that a vast majority of the workers in his sample were committed to factory employment, and that the present job was not the first factory job for most of them. I think his results might have been different if he had interviewed workers in some of the new enterprises in expanding industrial centers in India, but this is only a hunch.

A useful typology of factories at different stages of development is suggested.

Three of the five factories in the sample were Type A—fairly simple processes, mostly unskilled workers as in the paper, biscuit, and rubber factories; one was Type B—repetitive, semi-skilled, machine-paced operations, as in cotton textiles; one was Type C—more skilled operations and workers, as in the factory producing oil engines. Only Type C was similar to a modern industrial factory in the West. Much of the data is analyzed according to this typology. In particular, an interesting occupational profile of each factory, showing the differences between the types, is developed in Chapter IV on "Internal Structure." Another conclusion which impressed me was that caste seemed to be much less important in accounting for the hierarchy within the plant than was educational attainment, although the two were not easily separated. The author's data indicate clearly the high educational aspirations of Indian factory workers, despite the fact that on their present jobs many workers apparently have more education than they need.

A brief review cannot do justice to the wealth of data and the provocative conclusions drawn from them. But the reader must remind himself that these conclusions apply to the restricted sample studied in one Indian city—which may or may not be typical of Indian industrial cities. The author is pessimistic about the modernization process, largely because only one factory in his sample—Type C—represented a sharp break with the past. But in present-day India, there are a growing number of Type C factories, both in the public and private sectors.

CHARLES A. MYERS
Professor of Industrial Relations
Massachusetts Institute of Technology

D. T. LAKDAWALA, V. N. KOTHARI, J. C. SANDESAR, and P. A. NAIR. *Work, Wages, and Well-Being in an Indian Metropolis: Economic Survey of Bombay City.* Pp. xxvi, 863. Bombay: University of Bombay, 1963. Rs. 36.50.

Ten years ago the Indian government, facing a mountain of literature on village India and practically nothing on the rapidly expanding cities, sponsored a series of city surveys. Each of the city surveys, including the one under review, has its value as a descriptive document. However, their cumulative effect is somewhat lessened by the fact that no common definition of terms or categories for statistical analysis were used. Of the more than a dozen already released, the survey of Bombay is the most extensive both in bulk and in the number of topics covered. Inevitably, there are many more facts here about Bombay than most people would care to know. For instance, to the general reader, the precise number of tenements with their own water taps in Bombay is of somewhat less than earth-shaking importance. The book will, however, be extremely useful in several ways.

First, perhaps its most common use outside of India, scholars will go to it for bits and pieces of information to be used in some cross-national topical comparison, for instance, the number of square feet of floor space per person in Dar es Salaam, Toronto, and Bombay. For this purpose, the crucial question is the adequacy of the sample and the clarity of the definition of terms. As to the former, this is a sample of tenements housing some 13,000 familes with 63,000 members taken at random from the electoral rolls. It tends to underestimate pavement-dwellers, those who live in shops, factories, and the like, and fresh migrants.

Second, the study will serve as a benchmark for comparisons over time. For this purpose, its comprehensiveness will be the most useful characteristic, since the domains in which important changes will occur cannot be fully anticipated. The study covers in depth the usual demographic bookkeeping variables: sex, age, mother tongue, family characteristics, migration history, and certain economic characteristics of the sample—income and expenditure, indebtedness, occupation, unemployment history, special studies on employers and the organized sector of the economy, and, finally, a detailed section on housing.

Third, at least theoretically, the book will serve as a policy guide for so-called "practitioners" in that it presumably highlights problem areas. In point of fact, the problems are so many and so overwhelming that even that rarest of policy-makers—one who has time to read, will read, and will act on the basis of what he has read—is likely to be stunned into total inaction.

Finally, there is the perverse reader who is a connoisseur of the intrinsically interesting bit of exotica or of the anomalous finding that contraverts the easy assumptions upon which many of our social-science generalizations are based. Some that are surprising and/or intriguing are the following: only 23 per cent of the heads of households are illiterate, and almost half of them have had some secondary education. The size of the family is generally a function of the number of females in it. Income and family size are positively correlated. More than half of the families are making some regular saving. Muslims have a higher percentage of their members in trade and commerce than Hindus. The most prosperous occupational group is the professionals.

In general, the survey is well done and well presented. For a change, percentages instead of sample frequencies are often reported, two- and three-way breakdowns instead of simple tabulations are often given, and even an occasional hypothesis is tested. At the end there is a digest of the primary substantive findings that is useful for the running reader; for pedestrians this is a full and competent survey.

RICHARD D. LAMBERT
Professor of Sociology
University of Pennsylvania

OM PRAKASH. *The Theory and Working of State Corporations, with Special Reference to India.* Pp. 272. New York: Frederick A. Praeger, 1963. $6.50.

Government enterprises under India's budding socialism have taken three major forms: (1) undertakings run directly by governmental departments as in the case of ordnance factories and gold mines—railways, posts, and telegraph can be considered a subcategory of this type since the boards running these services are so closely linked to their appropriate ministries; (2) statutory public corporations; and (3) government limited companies. This study deals with the last two types, examining their structure and functions, their control and accountability, and their performance.

The statutory public corporation was the chosen instrument for government enterprises in the first few years after independence. Parliament passed a special act establishing each corporate enterprise, hoping to gain the flexibility of private enterprise along with the financial backing of government. The Damodar Valley Corporation, modeled after the Tennessee Valley Authority, is probably the most famous example of this structure, but the State Bank of India and the Reserve Bank of India probably are the most successful ventures of this type. Most of the eleven public corporations formed by the central government have been in the financial field. These corporations have been more subject to the control of both parliament and the ministries than has been true of nationalized industries in Great Britain.

To gain more freedom from parliamentary control but assure more dependence upon ministerial control, the government more recently has turned to the third form of structure: the government limited company. Here the government establishes its public enterprises under the general incorporation statutes, usually as "private" corporations which require only two incorporators, do not issue equity shares on the open market, and need not issue financial or other annual reports. The central government, as sole or chief share-holder, has established forty-six limited companies which today run much of the public sector of industry in such fields as steel, machine tools, coal, oil, shipbuilding, fertilizer, insecticides, shipping, and newsprint. Each of these companies, although presumably "autonomous," is, in fact, dominated by one of ten ministries of the government. In 1956, parliament demanded greater accountability of these companies to the legislative branch, requiring annual reports and answers from the responsible ministers on company policy. This reversed, or at least modified, the tendency for the executive branch to run government enterprises as its own secret preserve.

This is a solid book; it gives the reader a good picture of the structure and control of government enterprises run by state corporations. It also makes useful comparisons with Britain, the United States, and, occasionally, other countries. The best chapter is that on the governing boards and their relationship to the ministries and to parliament. There are two major weaknesses of the study. (1) The picture is painted in all its detail and complexity; the reader is forced to construct his own simplifying categories and generalizations. (2) Although considerable space is devoted to evaluating the performance of these public enterprises, one finishes the book with very little light shed on this admittedly difficult question. Seven possible tests of efficiency are discussed, but only that of profits is applied with any consistency to the corporations under study.

WILLIS D. WEATHERFORD

Swarthmore College

F. G. BAILEY. *Politics and Social Change: Orissa in 1959.* Pp. xviii, 241. Berkeley and Los Angeles: University of California Press, 1963. $5.00.

Of the considerable number of studies of contemporary Indian political and social behavior, F. G. Bailey's three books on Orissa must be regarded as outstanding contributions. Relying entirely on his own field work, rather than on other people's ideas—there are practically no footnote references—he has managed in this latest book to capture in commonly used words the changing life of a little-studied region of India. The intimacy of the descriptive sections of the volume, coupled with an unbiased, objective analytical approach, results in writing of great credibility.

Part I centers on elections in two villages, the study of which can teach us much about democracy in India. Bailey's judgments are provocative, for example: "I do not think that the majority, as yet, have any conception of the meaning of 'responsible' government; their hori-

zons are too narrow for this. Accordingly a vote is a 'little thing'—not a valued and sacred responsibility" (p. 32). They are also honest, for example: "In some cases it is quite clear why people voted as they did. In other cases their behavior is inexplicable (to me at least)" (p. 39). Part II looks at vote-getting from the politicians' viewpoints and exposes the problem of winning elections in the rural areas, where "voters by habit are not common . . . and it is difficult to concentrate upon known supporters and marginal voters" (p. 111). To me, the most exciting chapter here is on the functions of caste groups in politics. Bailey concludes that the traditional caste is not effective in getting votes or in exerting political pressure, but when it becomes a caste association these functions may be open to it; yet he found no evidence that candidates in Orissa have yet systematically used these associations to promote their elections, as they have elsewhere in India. Part III is on state politics and is the shortest and probably the least valuable section; it is dominated by a rather pedantic account of a decade of Orissan politics, which centers on the congress and its main opponents, the Ganatantra Parishad.

The book provides a minimum of self-conscious theorizing—most of it is left to the final chapter—but an adequate amount of perceptive intuitions linking events and trends. Mr. Bailey's conclusions are modestly set forth, and the voters and politicians of Orissa, whom he knows from close association, are allowed to behave in his pages as they really are, not as a comprehensive scientific model would like them to function. The study breathes life into political processes at the village and constituency levels. A reader is taken into the author's confidence, so to speak, as Bailey asks him to look at the evidence, ponder its complexities, and then try one and another possible explanations for the facts. The author's preference in explanations, which gives the greatest meaning to the facts, is the idea that there are three "arenas" of political action—village, constituency, and state—whose interaction reveals the dynamics of social and political change now taking place. And again we learn that the most effective means of transforming Indian society is politics.

CHARLES H. HEIMSATH
Associate Professor of South
  Asian Studies
American University

MARGARET W. FISHER, LEO E. ROSE and ROBERT A. HUTTENBACK. *Himalayan Battleground: Sino-Indian Rivalry in Ladakh.* Pp. viii, 205. New York: Frederick A. Praeger, 1963. $6.00.

How many border disputes of the last century have cited treaties dated 930, 1684, 1842, 1852, or relied on travelers' notes, or used "marches" to measure distance? Detailing just such a situation, this small, highly concentrated work on the Sino-Indian border dispute is a useful addition to the literature of the Himalayan fringe area, an area too long neglected by scholars. Anyone who has tackled the *Report of the Officials of the Government of India and the People's Republic of China on the Boundary Question* will appreciate the need for this work which hews a clear path through the maze of conflicting evidence, claims, and charges characterizing the dispute. The authors make a noble effort to present the historical basis of the claims of each side, using, *inter alia*, the Ladakhi chronicles, journals of travelers, British, Indian, and Chinese official records, and, significantly, the rare *Hsi-Tsang Tsou-shu (Tibetan Memorials and Reports)* by the Chinese Imperial Resident at Lhasa 1839–1844.

Two chapters are worthy of close study —one an analysis of conflicting border claims, segment by segment, the other an analysis of recent developments and trends. In the former, the authors "found it necessary to supply not only the general lines of argument but also an explanation of the distortions—to put it kindly— the Chinese practised" (p. 99). The latter chapter not only analyzes the possible motives of the Chinese, but also places the dispute in a broader context in which "the dispute has become inextricably entangled with the most serious political problems facing the world today" (p. 138).

Unfortunately, there are several areas in which one could wish for further amplification. Although largely a work concerning the geographical complexities of the problem, the book includes only two maps. The text liberally uses place names, but it is a tiresome task to orient oneself on the maps as provided. Furthermore, the text does not discuss several interesting aspects of the problem, particularly the Indian political milieu of the 1950's. Although not a primary objective of the study, these aspects have relevance for an understanding of the Indian case, for example, the impact of the Panch Shila on policy vis-à-vis China, the role of Krishna Menon in policy-formation, and the general climate of opinion in India. As the authors point out, the problem is far from settled; the "Chinese aims have by no means been fulfilled" (p. 146). That the "nibbling" tactics will continue seems certain—hence such valuable studies are essential.

CATHERINE TISINGER
Mt. Jackson
Virginia

IAN STEPHENS. *Pakistan.* Pp. ix, 288. New York: Frederick A. Praeger, 1963. $6.95.

Such is the dearth of reliable studies on Pakistan, that any new book on the subject is welcome. When the book is a good one, as in the present instance, it is doubly welcome. This is a popular study rather than a scholarly treatise, hence rigorous documentation is lacking. A bibliography of secondary sources and three maps are included in the volume. Despite its genre, the book is generally reliable and well balanced, and, probably because of its genre, its style is felicitous and clear.

Stephens begins his study with a rather unusual chapter—"The Idea"—in which he seeks to set right certain misconceptions. First is the peculiar dual relationship which the Muslims of the subcontinent have with other Indians and with Muslims of the Middle East. The predominantly secular nature of the state, despite protestations of being Islamic, is the second issue, which is strengthened by some very apt references to the theocracy of Israel. There follows a chapter describing the physical character of the land and another on social problems. Social problems are somewhat unevenly treated. Sectarian differences within Islam and religious minorities are well handled. The problems of refugees, polygamy and population growth are satisfactorily analyzed. But the major problem of all—linguistic and cultural cleavages among Punjabis, Bengalis, Pathans, Sindhis and Baluchis—is analyzed in a curiously misleading way. The major cleavage, that is, Bengalis-non-Bengalis, is not given the prominence it deserves. It is far more than a linguistic problem; it involves ethnic differences and profound differences in temperament and way of life. Moreover, the Bengali problem should be posed in the context of traditional Punjabi dominance in government and commerce. Unfortunately, Stephens does not do this, and the analysis is thereby weakened.

The second part of the book, consisting of some one hundred pages, deals with the factors before 1947 which led to the creation of Pakistan. Stephens mentions the all-but-forgotten fact that it was W. W. Hunter, an Englishman, who pleaded for a separate Muslim state as early as 1871, four years before Syed Ahmed Khan established Aligarh University.

In the third part dealing with the post-1947 period, Stephens quite rightly devotes a full chapter to Kashmir. He handles the tribal incursions into Kashmir with skill and a sense of perspective, although not as fully as might be hoped. The Pathans of the Northwest Frontier were whipped to a frenzy by reports of Hindu atrocities against Muslims both in Kashmir and in East Punjab. Thinking themselves on *jihad* or Holy War, they crossed into Kashmir. Stephens, citing Lord Birdwood, states that "it seems clear that Pakistani politicians and civilian officials must have connived at this, helping the tribesmen to get vehicles and petrol and supplies, and ensuring that preparations were kept secret" (p. 202). In a brief paragraph, he then indicates that it would have been impossible for the new government of Pakistan to have stopped the Pathan incursion. This treatment of the key issue in the Kashmir affair is inadequate. Stephens should have shown how difficult the Pathans were to control and how uncertain Pakistan was that the Pathans would remain in Pakistan rather than create a separate state of Paktuhnistan. Then the role of Pakistan in that delicate situation would be appreciated.

The treatment of the 44-month period of martial law is generally satisfactory, although there are significant events which are omitted. For example, the role of the judiciary is omitted, although the supreme court's legitimation of martial law in Dosso's case is of immense significance and the restitution of the court's jurisdiction is equally important. The seizure of the *Pakistan Times* and the litigation involving its owner, Mian Iftikaruddin, is not mentioned. Finally, the recommendations of the Constitution Commission headed by Justice Shahabuddin should have been compared with the 1962 constitution which was eventually promulgated.

RALPH BRAIBANTI

Duke University

FRED R. VON DER MEHDEN. *Religion and Nationalism in Southeast Asia: Burma, Indonesia, the Philippines.* Pp. xvi, 253. Madison: University of Wisconsin Press, 1963. $5.00.

In this interesting study, Professor von der Mehden examines the relationship between religion and nationalism in Buddhist Burma, Moslem Indonesia, and the Christian Philippines. In general, he discerns a development from early traditionalist xenophobia to the rise of incipient nationalist organizations using religion as a unifying force, the infusion of a vigorous nationalism into the religious organizations, the formation of sectarian political parties, the decreasing influence of religion in politics as the nationalist movements grew, the conflict between religion and secularism and Marxism, and finally the strange role which religion at present plays in these young states.

Developments in the Philippines vary considerably from this pattern. In Indonesia and Burma, the dominant religion was different from that of the alien ruler, but in the Philippines, the vast majority of the people had accepted his religion, hence religion could not well be used as a unifying force against him. In this country, the nationalists became anticlerical and secular. The American principle of the separation of church and state reinforced this earlier trend.

Professor von der Mehden explains the reasons for the peculiar developments in the relation of religion and nationalism in these countries. There is little room for quarrel with his explanations. In the West also, it has been amply evident that people with similar religious connections may differ widely in their political views. Religion cannot be effectively used to prevent political fragmentation, especially not after the shift from opposition to control of the government. Moreover, the nationalist leaders were Western in their outlook.

If one cannot argue with the main outlines of this study, one can point to some weaknesses in the presentation. Britain and the United States had no religious political parties, but the Netherlands did. This Dutch political development deserves greater attention than it receives in this study, for it played an important role in colonial policy and administration. Von der Mehden follows the Dutch in their political terminology, which was largely determined by the bitter struggle over the past century between the secular and religious political parties for control of the government. The terms "right" and "left" have strange meanings in the Netherlands. A Dutch Liberal is generally not a liberal, and some Antirevolutionaires are. Certainly, the Antirevolutionaire Idenburg and the Christian Historical van Limburg Stirum as governors general were far more liberal than the Liberal Fock. Nor does the author adequately deal with the influence of Christian missionaries on the nationalist movements. Men like Vavinck and Kraemer not only were sympathetic with the movement, but their views were eagerly sought by its young leaders.

This study is based on wide reading and extensive research. It is a significant book on an important subject.

AMRY VANDENBOSCH
Director
Patterson School of Diplomacy
  and International Commerce
University of Kentucky

CLIFFORD GEERTZ. *Peddlers and Princes: Social Change and Economic Modernization in Two Indonesian Towns.* Pp. viii, 162. Chicago: University of Chicago Press, 1963. $5.00.

The Committee for the Comparative Study of New Nations at the University of Chicago is sponsoring a new series of publications on aspects of social, political, economic, and cultural change in the new states of Asia and Africa. *Peddlers and Princes* is the first to appear. Geertz asserts that a country can undergo "a great proportion of the social transformation we associate with industrialism" and yet progress only slightly towards the creation of such an economy—as Tokugawa Japan, pre-1917 Russia, and 1750 England on the brink of economic take-off.

To what extent has Indonesia undergone such a social transformation? A wide section of society has experienced an alteration in world view and ethos, in political and economic organization, in education, and even in family structure. Commercialization of agriculture is well advanced, nonfamilial business concerns are being organized, technical skills are gaining in prestige, and industrialization has become an explicit national goal. But Indonesia is a diversity, and Geertz examines the process of socioeconomic modernization in two widely different towns: Javanese Modjokuto, population 24,000, long exposed to Dutch economic exploitation, and Balinese Tabanan, population 12,000, occupied by the Dutch only in 1906, still deferential towards its traditional aristocracy.

In Modjokuto the petty trading economy of the market place has spawned some innovating and specialized shopkeepers from the devout Moslem minority with historical links to the trading towns of the north coast. In Tabanan the more dynamic among the aristocrats have drawn upon the collectivism of the Balinese village and on their own oligarchic traditions to institute a fundamental reorganization of the town's whole economic system. But Modjokuto's firms now fail to prosper, Tabanan's fail to rationalize. They are hamstrung by the very mentalities which produced them: that of the peddler, that of the prince.

How can Indonesia make the breakthrough to what Geertz calls the mentality of the professional manager, which alone can assure economic take-off? Geertz leaves the question unanswered, though he does state realistically that "whether—or perhaps better, when—it [modernization of society] will be completed is far from certain." The present rulers of Indonesia scorn private enterprise, at the same time giving no indication that they want, or are able, to provide any rational scheme for the economy. Meanwhile the Communist party waits in the wings. One wonders what it could do as an authoritarian, economy-oriented, modern-oriented ruler on the basis of the socioeconomic changes that have already occurred.

Peddlers and Princes is, like much of Geertz's other writing, eminently rewarding. It introduces the people under study as individual human beings; it views them as members of social, economic, and political groups; and it provides plausible and substantiated analyses of how they are adapting themselves, as products of history, to the tremendous changes of the twentieth century. In short, case study and broader theory are brought together in an illuminating marriage.

DONALD HINDLEY
Assistant Professor of Politics
Brandeis University

YONG SAM CHO. *"Disguised Unemployment" in Underdeveloped Areas, with Special Reference to South Korean Agriculture.* Pp. xiv, 163. Berkeley and Los Angeles: University of California Press, 1963. $3.75.

The relationship between the extended family system and disguised unemployment has attracted much attention from writers on underdeveloped areas. Although the extended family provides a kind of social insurance system, it is usually claimed that it results in surplus farm labor which, if removed, would not cause any reduction in total farm output. Additional members of an extended family share not only in the family income, but also in the work to be done. As a result, each member of the family has less work to do and becomes partially unemployed. Since the extended family system is deeply rooted in Korean traditions, an analysis of its effects there is of interest.

The principal conclusion of this study is that surplus agricultural labor in underdeveloped countries is far less extensive than usually assumed. The author estimates that in South Korea in 1959 technical underemployment—largely seasonal —amounted to only 12· per cent of the total labor available. Although this is a source of surplus labor that could be used in off-seasons for local development projects, underemployment of this type is not caused by the extended family system.

Underemployment resulting from the traditional family system is estimated to amount to 19 per cent of the total labor available, but the author believes that it does not provide an unused source of labor available for other purposes. This is because the sharing of family income reduces the caloric intake of the family members and thus the amount of labor that each member is capable of performing. The author has probably overemphasized the importance of the low per capita food consumption in Korea. While it is lower than in some Western countries, the caloric intake per person in South Korea is approximately as high as in Japan.

The author's estimates of underemployment are based on a survey of 600 farms by the Research Department of the Bank of Korea. The amount of underemployment was obtained by subtracting the number of hours of labor employed— shown in the survey—from the number of hours of labor available. Estimates of the latter were made by assuming a certain number of work days per year, an eight-hour day, an average number of farm workers per family, and a 60 per cent efficiency ratio of women to men. The results of the survey show a much higher percentage of underemployment for family farm workers than for wage farm workers. Because the social obligations of the extended family do not apply to wage workers, the author believes that the underemployment of such workers is primarily seasonal or technical. The author attributes the difference in the rates of underemployment of family workers over wage workers to the traditions associated with the extended family system.

COLIN D. CAMPBELL
Associate Professor of Economics
Dartmouth College

YUAN-LI WU, with the assistance of H. C. LING. *Economic Development and the Use of Energy Resources in Communist China.* Pp. xv, 275. New York: Frederick A. Praeger, for the Hoover Institution on War, Revolution and Peace, 1963. $7.50.

This is a full and authoritative study of the development of fuel and power utilization in Communist China, on which China's industrial and general progress so greatly depends. Professor Wu has analyzed abundant data at length, but with clear conclusions; his study is of the highest factual and indicative value. The vastness and variety of China's terrain, and the enormous channelling of its human efforts, lead generally to optimism about the impending industrialization of China. A vast and purposeful propaganda exerts itself to heighten great expectations. Professor Wu cuts right down to all the facts, and right across to all the difficulties of applying potential resources successfully for full, efficient, and balanced development. He adds useful comparisons with corresponding successes and failures in the Soviet Union and elsewhere.

Mainland China—he concludes—undoubtedly contains all the basic fuel reserves to support a highly industrialized economy—with some reservations about workable oil and natural gas deposits.

These, and some other circumstances, impose presently and prospectively a somewhat excessive and limiting dependence on coal. "The Chinese economy runs on coal" (p. 190). Of total energy production in 1960—other than from wood— 94 per cent was from coal, 3 per cent from petroleum, less than 3 per cent hydroelectric, and natural gas negligible. These proportions cannot be expected to change substantially for many years. Technically, it is rather an old model of Industrial Revolution that China is straining to catch up with; not so much world 1960 patterns, essentially, as those of Britain in about 1850, the United States in about 1890, and the Soviet Union in about 1930.

Despite tremendous efforts, and great statistical increases, the population and the needs tend to rise more than output. Power-developments and factory-developments are poorly co-ordinated, in a rigid planning (p. 195). Intersectoral balance has not been maintained between power-development and other developments. Within the power sector, equally, there have been serious inbalances; industrial power supply has been maintained largely at the expense of the domestic sector's share. Wasteful underefficient methods characterize not merely "backyard" coal production, but the more modern installations. There is "indeterminateness of policy" as to the proper proportion between hydro- and thermal-plants. It has not been possible to reshape at all significantly the regional distribution of power and industry in China, to go much beyond short-term improvisation into long-term and large-scale national planning in this field, to lessen basic dependence on imported equipment, or to raise the rationality of decision-making very significantly.

These limitations, largely inherent in the Communist planning, are unlikely to be outgrown even in the more distant future (pp. 200–203).

E. STUART KIRBY
Professor and Head
Department of Economics
University of Hong Kong

GERMANY

LUDWIG ERHARD. *The Economics of Success*. Pp. vii, 412. Princeton, N. J.: D. Van Nostrand, 1963. $6.50.

Publication of this substantial volume virtually coincides with the long-expected elevation of its author to the chancellorship of the German Federal Republic. The book brings together more than fifty addresses and papers covering the period from 1945 to 1962. Readers thus can conveniently review Professor Erhard's earlier pronouncements as guides to current West German policies. The principal architect of the "economic miracle" presents himself as the voice of economic freedom within the limits of national and international realities. As he says in the Foreword: "Freedom is too precious a thing to be jeopardized; and yet the perils are too great and the threats to freedom too powerful for a single people or a small group of peoples to attempt to withstand them alone." The panorama of subjects includes economic initiative and planned economy, safeguards of foreign trade, the economics of reunification, European functional integration, and Atlantic cooperation. Consistently, Erhard shows himself a resourceful advocate of his views with a fine sense of popular resonance.

As early as 1946, he established his vantage point by declaring: "The real contradistinction is not between free and planned economic systems . . . but between a market economy with free price-level adjustment on the one hand and an authoritarian economy with state controls extending into the sphere of distribution on the other" (p. 9). But he did not aim at a self-contained island: "We wish . . . to continue . . . cultivating free and unrestricted relations with all countries and particularly with our partners in Europe. To my mind, Europe is not an ultimate concept but simply a mould in which economic and political integration can take shape" (p. 93). This position carried over to his attitude toward cartels. As "a happy Europe cannot be a centrally controlled economic body," so "it is just as unthinkable that the eco-nomic unity of Europe could be achieved by coordinating international cartel agreements" (p. 136).

Inevitably, one of Erhard's chief efforts was to resist organized group demands, "one of the crucial problems of our time." He confessed in 1961 that in meeting with representatives of various groups, he seldom felt that they were aware of their personal responsibility: "On the contrary, I hear talk of nothing but a unilateral responsibility to the interests they are representing. In such cases, if the concept 'responsibility' is not turned upside-down, it is at least so devalued and falsified that one can only speak of rank misuse" (p. 379).

His cautious optimism obviously has not lulled Erhard into an easy assumption of world-wide solidarity throughout the free world. To him, "this Europe of ours has a character of its own," different from the United States. He senses a kinship of spirit with the American people, "and yet there is no denying that, in the final analysis, the Americans cannot understand us and we must accept this fact." Europeans are "burdened with a thousand years of history and with a countless variety of pronounced characteristics that play a significant part in our daily lives" (p. 406). Despite this reservation, however, he closes the book on an almost American note: "I feel most profoundly that we are called upon either to endure the future or to concentrate all our energies on moulding it" (p. 412).

FRITZ MORSTEIN MARX
Professor of Comparative
   Administrative Science and
   Public Law
Hochschule für Verwaltungs-
   wissenschaften
Speyer
Germany

EDWARD L. PINNEY. *Federalism, Bureaucracy, and Party Politics in Western Germany: The Role of the Bundesrat*. Pp. vii, 268. Chapel Hill: University of North Carolina Press, 1963. $5.00.

The author analyzes the constitutional and legislative role of the Bundesrat, one of the two chambers of West Germany's legislature. Pinney arrives at three major conclusions which, though tentatively presented as hypotheses, are well supported by an examination of specific legislative acts. The conclusions are: (1) The Bundesrat, the legislative chamber which represents the separate *Länder* (states) of Germany, does in fact promote federalism in Western Germany and advances the cause of the separate states of the Bonn Republic. (2) The bureaucracy of the different *Länder* plays a part in the legislative process by its representation in the Bundesrat and by its participation in the staff work of its committees. The Bundesrat is thus an effective channel for the expression of the views of the career civil servants, and it adds a high degree of professionalism to legislative deliberations. (3) The third conclusion, which the author presents most convincingly, is that the Bundesrat acts as a conservative or restraining influence in the legislative process. This conservatism refers primarily to delays caused in the formulation of laws or changes in the laws rather than the influence of particular economic groups on the policy of the Bundesrat.

Pinney's conclusions are based on an examination of a series of instances of the legislative behavior of the Bundesrat. Though one cannot be certain, as the author admits, that they are wholly representative of the role of the Bundesrat, they do appear to be a significant sample of the functions of the Bundesrat. The case histories are well documented.

Pinney's suggestion that some strength against a unitary state is provided by federalism remains to be proven. The statement in the Preface, "The ultimate concern of this study is democracy in Germany," is not supported by the contents of the book. There is a logical hiatus between this examination of the German Bundesrat and a study of democracy. The Bibliography is extensive and most informative, though marred slightly by minor errors in German spelling. The book carries an unusually good index. Pinney's book, together with the one written by Karlheinz Neunreither, *Der Bundesrat zwischen Politik und Verwaltung,* is among the most important contemporary studies on the Bundesrat.

ERIC H. BOEHM

Editor
Historical Abstracts
Santa Barbara
California

JAMES H. WOLFE. *Indivisible Germany: Illusion or Reality?* Pp. x, 130. The Hague: Martinus Nijhoff, 1963. Guilders 15.30.

PETER H. MERKL. *The Origin of the West German Republic.* Pp. xviii, 269. New York: Oxford University Press, 1963. $5.50.

These two books by young political scientists—Mr. Wolfe is an assistant professor at the University of South Carolina, while Mr. Merkl holds the same title at the University of California, Santa Barbara—appear at first glance to complement each other. Up to a point they do, the former treating the origins and implications of the split in post-Hitlerian Germany, the latter examining the processes by which the larger and stronger of the present German states was created fifteen years ago. Unfortunately, however, the studies themselves are so dissimilar in aim, in tone, and in quality of analysis that they cannot be bracketed in any but the most superficial sense.

It is not clear to this reviewer why Mr. Wolfe's offering was deemed publishable at all. Based on reading in published documents, especially those released by our own Department of State, on secondary works, and on newspapers and magazine articles—most of them in English—this summary of the former Allies' wartime decisions and of their postwar disagreements really adds very little to a well-worn narrative. Certain points, it is true, receive useful emphasis. One such is the complete reversal of American and Russian positions regarding nationwide elections for Germany, favored by the Soviets against Western opposition during the early stages of the occupation, only to be dropped by Moscow and increasingly urged by Washington as prospects shifted in the 1950's. Such observations, however, while sound in themselves, can be briefly stated and, in any event, are practically self-evident to any thoughtful student of the past two decades' history.

Even if we were to concede that Mr. Wolfe's exercise has some potential value, there would still be reason to deplore the fashion in which it has been carried out. Numerous typographical errors are not surprising in a work published on the European continent, but no Dutch printer can be blamed for the author's frequent stylistic lapses and apparently helpless addiction to the split infinitive. Finally, what *is* the message of the book? It would seem to be that whereas wiser Allied leadership at the end of World War II might have prevented the current division of Germany, that division is now rooted in economic, political, and strategic conditions which make reunification a practical impossibility for the foreseeable future. And yet, Mr. Wolfe announces, we cannot tolerate German disunity! On page one he warns that "Berlin must become the capital of a reunited nation," then proceeds to demonstrate why it cannot become any such thing. In few books known to me is the disjunction between the data presented and the author's commentary so nearly complete.

One turns to Mr. Merkl's thoughtful and compact monograph with relief. He, too, has used published documents, secondary accounts, and periodicals, but many of the items in each category have previously been inaccessible to American readers. Furthermore, the author has pulled together his voluminous and disparate sources to produce a closely argued analysis. Starting from "Point Zero"—the spring of 1945—Mr. Merkl moves through the early arrangements introduced by the occupying powers, the gradual re-emergence of German political interest and interests, the stages by which the Parliamentary Council was called into existence at Bonn in 1948, and the debates and compromises through which that body, over the course of a year, finally hammered out the Fundamental Law under which the Federal Republic now governs itself.

The author is at his best in elucidating the clashes of principle and of self-regard among German factions. While he pauses from time to time in order to examine, often critically, the interventions of American, British, and French authorities, he maintains the Germans' own angle of vision with laudable empathy. An introduction by Professor Carl J. Friedrich, a map frontispiece, a chronological chart of relevant events during 1948–1949, and the official English translation of the Basic Law itself all add to the value of this work. It is sure to prove extremely useful to college classes in German history, as well as to those in comparative government.

FRANKLIN L. FORD
Professor of History
Dean
Faculty of Arts and Sciences
Harvard University

HERBERT JACOB. *German Administration since Bismarck: Central Authority versus Local Autonomy.* Pp. xviii, 224. New Haven: Yale University Press, 1963. $7.00.

This book is one of a series of excellent studies in field administration stimulated by Professor James W. Fesler, Chairman of the Department of Political Science at Yale University. Professor Jacob has set for himself the task of analyzing the development of German field administration over the past century from the founding of modern Germany in 1871 through the first decade of the German Federal Republic. He pays special attention to the conditions that promoted or weakened administrative responsiveness under Germany's remarkably varied regimes. He devotes his research to relationships between administrative techniques and the social and political contexts in which field agencies have operated under different regimes. Mr. Jacob examines four successive German national governmental systems, treating them separately and comparatively almost as if they were four different national governments operating simultaneously in different countries. However, his work was eased by the fact that in Germany some of the most difficult independent variables were held relatively constant, such as the people, the geography, the resources, the culture, and the occupational status of such pursuits as public administration.

The theme of this book is that of German history itself—the unresolved clash between centralism and particularism, between federal authority and local autonomy. After discussing the social and governmental context and origins of modern German field administration, Mr. Jacob examines its development in the conservative Second Reich (1871–1919). He shows how the Prussian government maintained control over its field administration despite the reforms it initiated under pressure from the liberals. In the Weimar Republic (1919–1933), the Prussians encountered such barriers as the disloyalty of field officials and communication obstacles which impeded co-ordination of Land and Reich programs at the local level. In the Third Reich (1933–1945), the Nazi regime achieved a high degree of administrative concentration, utilizing hierarchical and external controls, but, despite these measures, field administration remained unresponsive to the demands of the central government.

In Germany's second experiment with democracy, the current Federal Bonn Republic, Mr. Jacob finds that at both Land and federal levels, West Germany has developed an entirely new set of controls suitable to her democratic ideology. For the first time in her history, she is encouraging local control of administrative agencies. Thus, responsive and effective administration has been promoted without sacrificing the autonomy of the *Länder* or of their local field agencies. So impressed is Mr. Jacob with this new record that he believes West Germany today provides a guide for the newly emerging nations of Asia and Africa as they seek to work out administrative systems of their own.

This book is a valuable contribution to an understanding of recent German history. Because of its interdisciplinary thinking it is a delightful surprise for the historian. Aware of the close nexus between political science and history, Mr. Jacob is not content to remain within the narrowed bounds of his own discipline with its special language and techniques.

More of this kind of work would be a boon to American scholarship.

LOUIS L. SNYDER
Professor of History
City College of New York

LATIN AMERICA

C. NEALE RONNING. *Law and Politics in Inter-American Diplomacy.* Pp. 167. New York: John Wiley & Sons, 1963. $5.95.

In this short study Professor Ronning of the Political Science Department at Tulane University surveys the impact of modern revolutionary change in Latin America on certain traditional principles of international law, specifically those affecting recognition of governments, treatment of aliens and their property, intervention, diplomatic asylum, the control of coastal waters, European colonies in the Western Hemisphere, and national claims in Antarctica. The justification for the study is that, as the author states, "more rules, once generally accepted as obligatory, are now being questioned, ignored or given totally new interpretations by more American states than ever before."

This book asks some of the questions that need to be asked about the place of law in inter-American relations and its changing role in modern times. In regard to the controversial principle of nonintervention, for example, it clearly sets forth the dilemma which perplexes the new social revolutionaries in Latin America who engage in crusades to reform their neighbors, particularly to oust dictatorial regimes, and still prate about the principle of nonintervention. They guard the principle zealously, even going so far as to oppose collective intervention, but, in fact, repeatedly breach it in practice. Interventions undertaken for allegedly humanitarian purposes are, in fact, no longer even considered to be interventions, on the theory, apparently, that principles can be waived if the ends that are sought are good.

Accordingly, says the author, "in the past two decades Central America and the

Caribbean have probably seen more cases of intervention than any other area of the world outside the Soviet sphere." The United States is finding that it, too, must intervene in Latin America to make the Alliance for Progress effective, and unless it does so its policy is no longer an alliance but becomes simply progress as defined by the United States. Much of the difficulty in inter-American relations, the author concludes, can be traced to the failure to treat the international politics of Latin America in a completely objective manner. Instead the subject is dealt with emotionally, morally, and therefore ineffectively.

This study tackles the large and important theme of the relationship between law and society in inter-American relations. But it fails to develop fully the implications of its theme. Omitted, regrettably, for example, is a consideration of the impact of modern social and political forces upon the procedures of peaceful settlement, the organization of the inter-American system, and problems of inter-American economic co-operation. The intimations given in the study as to the directions in which inter-American law on the controversial subjects under discussion is moving are, to say the least, cautious. The book is unfortunately marred by careless proofreading and by several errors of fact, as, for example, that "the first pronouncement on colonies in the New World was of course the Monroe Doctrine." But the author successfully fulfills his modest purpose of pointing out "the general directions for serious and more detailed study of the substance of rules" in inter-American relations.

DONALD MARQUAND DOZER
Department of History
University of California
Santa Barbara

JOHN GERASSI. *The Great Fear: The Reconquest of Latin America by Latin-Americans.* Pp. x, 457. New York: The Macmillan Company, 1963. $6.95.

This book, written by a former Latin-American correspondent of *Time* magazine, presents a devastating criticism of Latin-American governments in general and of the United States policies toward them in particular. The very first sentence of the work sets the tone: "Latin America's social and economic structure is decadent, corrupt, immoral, and generally unsalvageable." The author predicts that revolutions will come about, whether political or military, and will be led either from the ranks of the extreme left or the equally uncomfortable extreme nationalists. He asserts that no positive change can come from what we in the United States are erroneously in the habit of calling the "democratic forces," but which in reality are led by "political crooks, phony reformists and 'enlightened' oligarchs."

The author feels that, whether led by leftists or nationalists, the new revolutionists will be "inexcusably stamped with the same Red label by both our State Department and our press," even though the two are in fact diametrically opposed. The leftists are self-assertive internationalists who tend to view their own country merely as an instrument for the attainment of a universal goal. The nationalists are local patriots whose allegiance is to their own country and to no one else. He points out that while the former are our enemies, the latter are not our allies.

The author is of the opinion that "once in power, the Nationalists will nationalize American corporations—because it will be in their country's interest to do so. They will trade with the Communist bloc—because it will be in their country's interest to do so. And they will even vote, on occasion, against the United States in the United Nations—because it will be in their country's interest to do so. But they will not be our enemies. Nor will they desert 'Western society'—because such desertion will not be in their country's interest." His plea throughout is for the United States to encourage Latin-Americans to work out their future policy in terms of their own interests rather than ours. He concludes that "unless we change our current Latin-American policy, unless we reevaluate the Alliance for Progress, unless we realize and accept the choice that faces us, we shall not only see the Communists —despite themselves—win out; we shall also accelerate their victory."

The author reviews American policies toward Latin America from the Monroe Doctrine to the present time and concludes that the United States bears considerable responsibility for the present situation because of our policies of supporting those most likely to maintain the *status quo* in our favor and branding as Communists those who would introduce basic reforms. The last chapter contains a number of recommendations for improving United States policy. One of these is to withdraw from the Organization of American States and permit Latin-American countries to set up their own regional organization. Although the work is supercritical, it is stimulating and deserves careful reading by all concerned with inter-American relations.

N. L. WHETTEN

Dean
Graduate School
University of Connecticut

CAROLINA MARIA DE JESUS. *Child of the Dark: The Diary of Carolina Maria de Jesus.* Translated from the Portuguese by David St. Clair. Pp. 190. New York: E. P. Dutton, 1962. $4.50.

This is the translation of a diary kept by a São Paulo slum-dweller which is said to have "sold more than any other Brazilian book in history." The author is a Negress born in 1913. She came to the industrial metropolis as a young woman and eventually built herself a shack of boards, tin cans, and cardboard in a shanty town, or *favela*. Never married, she lived by foraging in streets and garbage cans for rags and food and for discarded paper to sell. In this way she supported the three children she had borne to as many men. With no schooling beyond second grade, she not only kept this diary but also spun a dream world of chandeliers, satin, and diamonds in her poems and stories. When a reporter discovered, edited, and published the diary, she was at last able to move into her longed-for house of brick.

Although the diary lacks the subtleties that an Oscar Lewis might have evoked in depth interviews, this powerful and well-nigh unique document has its own sig-

nificance as a raw, spontaneous cry from the normally inarticulate subproletariat of Latin America. Throughout her chronicle the author retains her pride, her determination, and her scorn for her slovenly, quarrelsome slum-mates and for the promises of the politicians. In Carolina's *favela*, the sociologist will find little trace of the well-knit, neighborly small group. The slum is a filthy pesthole, the city's "backyard where they throw the garbage." Its inhabitants are obscene, vindictive, conniving, and promiscuous; they "live by robbing from one another." Men and women eternally wrangle and fight. Bums throw rocks at the shack in which a prayer meeting is being held. The well-to-do try to break up the *favelas;* the politicians forget them after elections; the bureaucracy is misguided and unresponsive; only the brothers of St. Vincent show continuing concern.

The counterpoint between the routine misery of the *favela* and the frivolous pretensions of the metropolis is nowhere more dramatic than in the entry for June 18, 1958: "Today it dawned raining. Yesterday Vera spit two worms out of her mouth. She has a fever. There is no school today in honor of the Prince of Japan."

RICHARD M. MORSE

Professor of History
Yale University

STEFAN H. ROBOCK. *Brazil's Developing Northeast: A Study of Regional Planning and Foreign Aid.* Pp. xv, 213. Washington, D. C.: Brookings Institution, 1963. $3.50 clothbound; $2.00 paper-bound.

Resolution is sicklied with conventional thought. Foreign enterprises of great moment, their currents turn awry. And thus are sicklied aid programs. A temporary United Nations economist vainly seeks a transferable therapy in Brazil's bulge, where the 1960 population of 22.4 millions was 4.5 millions more than in 1950 and $140 of per capita income in 1960, half the country's average, helped it to keep its fame as a national poorhouse (pp. 34–47). As Robock has worked in four Hispanic American and six other nations, his expertise is superior. A social-science library will be more adequate if it has his book.

A drought left 500,000 dead in Ceará (p. 74), one-tenth of the total area. In this tumor, a bulge of 600,000 square miles, the *sêcas* must have killed millions of *Nordestinos* in the last 200 years. Robock gives no estimate. Competent in Portuguese, he fails to make clear whether it was only in 1877 that Ceará had no rain in setting its funeral record.

Often repetitious and needlessly imprecise, Robock says a foreign-service officer was "dispatched" to Brazil (p. 6). Why not *sent*? Not until more than halfway through the study does it become nondebatable that Merwin L. Bohan made the trip in 1961. (Robock incorrectly uses a *y* in Merwin.) What quantity of inexactitudes about data susceptible to more explicitness is permissible in a scholarly work? If 15 per cent is an elite norm, Robock is *de rigueur*.

The bulge "can benefit greatly from" the Puerto Rican achievement (p. 162). Most Latin-American reformers would disagree, for Operation Bootstrap has been chiefly Mainland-financed, as is emphasized in Ingram's *Regional Payments Mechanisms: The Case of Puerto Rico* (1962) and my doctoral dissertation (1959). "To interpret Brazilian political events" by our "standards . . . will result both in ineffective guidance for foreign aid actions," Robock accurately says, "and in erroneous evaluations of the results" (p. 185). We may be doing this, for Celso Furtado, Northeast Development Director, envisions a major Brazilian goal "is to 'bring back within the country, its centers of decision'" (p. 182). Are the centers now in the United States? Ignoring Ónody's *A inflação brasileira (1820–1958)*, Robock dismisses inflation in 220 words. For his index to omit Prebisch is like an economics encyclopedia not mentioning Adam Smith.

A perpetual flame burns for John F. Kennedy, whose dreams evoked the Alliance for Progress. A *Nordestino*, Josue de Castro, wrote *The Geography of Hunger* (p. 8). If we start a fruitful dialogue with Fidel Castro, would we again become unconcerned about Northeast Brazil? Will

some future Frost write a soliloquizing Alliance memorial, disinterring the Grace Report as a frame of reference?

BYRON WHITE
Professor of Economics
East Carolina College

ECONOMICS AND LABOR

GUNNAR MYRDAL. *Challenge To Affluence.* Pp. 172. New York: Random House, 1963. $3.95.

In 1944, Gunnar Myrdal, now Professor of International Economics at Stockholm University, wrote a summary of the results of a Carnegie Foundation two-year study of the American Negro. He called it *An American Dilemma*. The book created a real stir, as he pointed out the dire threat of a growing chasm between the American creed of liberty and equality of opportunity and the practice of that creed. Now, a generation later, in a 159-page "Challenge to Affluence," he assays, in an entirely frank and friendly fashion, the resulting national maladjustments more-or-less directly traceable to the persistence of the dilemma.

America, the recognized leader of the free world, shows a deplorably stagnant growth-rate and a threateningly weakening economy, with a concomitant high rate of "underemployment," an unfavorable trade balance, and a depleted bargaining position: all of which constitute a threat to America's world leadership. These ills can only be alleviated or wiped out by the rapid and sustained growth of the American economy, but, Myrdal insists, "it will not prove possible to change over the American economy to rapid and steady growth and full employment without taking vigorous measures within the nation to induce greater equality of opportunity and standards of living."

The impediment to America's prosperity, to this economist, is its "underclass" made up, primarily, of the old, the young, and the racial minorities—Negroes, Puerto Ricans, and Mexicans. Measuring the United States against other rich and enlightened countries, Myrdal sees it as "the most niggardly toward its elderly of any of the prosperous, contemporary Christian nations." He sees the bulk of America's young unemployables as quite without the training to make them employable. As for the politically inarticulate racial minorities, he finds them scarcely touched by the wide-ranging ameliorative programs of government. This, says Myrdal, has become not alone America's problem but, through America's assumption of international responsibility, the problem of the entire free world. "That America shall succeed in getting out of the rut of slow economic progress, while unemployment is high and rising, is therefore in the interest of the world, and not only of America. Indeed, as I see it, it is the most important problem in the world today."

Whether or not one agrees with the Myrdal thesis and its implications, this lucid little book is timely, penetrating, and stimulating reading.

CHARLES W. COULTER
Emeritus Professor
University of New Hampshire

WILL E. MASON. *Clarification of the Monetary Standard: The Concept and Its Relation to Monetary Policies and Objectives.* Pp. viii, 253. University Park: Pennsylvania State University Press, 1963. $7.50.

Dr. Mason is interested in clarifying the concept of a monetary standard. He starts out by arguing that neither the "preclassical view of the standard as the material constituting standard money" nor the "classical interpretation of the monetary standard as the material comprising the standard of value" are "presently useful" (p. 11). The "classical concept of a monetary standard was rendered obsolete by: (1) a gradual broadening of 'money' to embrace all forms of credit media of exchange, including bank deposits, and (2) a modification of value theory, eliminating the notion of intrinsic value on which the classical concept of a 'standard measure of value' was based" (p. 12). But the classical concept was retained because of "the neoclassical dichotomization of eco-

nomic theory, which appeared to render developments in value theory irrelevant to monetary theory" (p. 12). This "continued use of obsolete concepts of a monetary standard" is responsible for "the confusion of monetary objectives, policies, and standards" and "a basic cause of the communication breakdown in the area of money" (p. 12). Rejecting as unworkable the "suggested concept of a monetary standard as the principle limiting the money supply," Dr. Mason offers as both workable and widely used implicitly "the concept of a monetary standard as the criterion (referent) of monetary policy" (pp. 12, 106).

Developing the implications of this definition, Dr. Mason suggests that the United States is not on a gold standard, because under a gold standard "policies would be followed which would cause the money supply to vary directly with the national gold reserve" (p. 106). Rather, at the present time the "United States has no ascertainable monetary standard," as "the policy referent at any particular time has become utterly unidentifiable" (p. 108). In fact, Dr. Mason doubts whether the United States is "presently prepared to adopt a standard," as the "conceptual and institutional framework is not sufficiently developed to permit a choice among the alternatives" (p. 109). In his judgment feasible alternatives "fall into two categories: (1) standards based on the assumed primacy of *internal* stability and (2) standards based on the assumed primacy of *external* stability," with the first group including "the commodity-reserve standards, goods standard, and employment standard" and the second "the international commodity-reserve standard and the balance-of-payments standard" (pp. 115, 116). Among standards stressing internal stability, Dr. Mason prefers "a combination of the goods and employment standards à la Hart's 'gong and whistle'"; among those stressing external stability, he favors the balance-of-payments standard. In his judgment the final choice depends on "whether one prefers the national or international approach to such economic stability as is attainable by monetary means," with one's preference inevitably "colored to some extent by non-economic considerations which transcend the boundaries of this study" (p. 116).

I assume Dr. Mason would reject an "economic welfare standard" as not specific enough. But the only reason I can find for his wanting a highly specific standard is that it would minimize "uncertainty." Uncertainty at the level of the recent past, however, seems to me less dangerous than the possibility that acceptance of an inappropriate standard would lead to actions which, even if certain, would turn out to be undesirable. Hence, as I agree with Dr. Mason that each standard "has its advantages, as well as its disadvantages," I find myself unprepared to choose among them, believing that, for the foreseeable future, "expediency will remain the best basis for policy decisions" (pp. 115, 119)!

HENRY H. VILLARD
City College of New York

HAROLD LUBELL. *Middle East Oil Crises and Western Europe's Energy Supplies.* Pp. xx, 233. Baltimore, Md.: Johns Hopkins Press, 1963. $8.75.

Mr. Lubell's work is a published part of a research program conducted for the United States Air Force by the Rand Corporation. A slender book, consisting of three major divisions, it is but six chapters in length. In addition, there are fifty-two pages of tables, and statistical—or quantitative—analysis within three appendices. The basic premise of this book rests upon the fact that western Europe is increasingly dependent upon the Middle East's petroleum, and that twice within the past decade or so, the flow of this oil has been halted. Therefore, the author speculates as to the causes of a potential, and similar, halt in the 1960's, and the possible means by which such a crisis might be met. Chapter One, "Prologue," discusses the political and economic events accompanying the Iranian (1951) and Suez Canal (1956) oil stoppages and their ramifications. The first and second chapters deal with causes of potential crises and the implications for western Europe. Chapters Four and Five study the effect of prospective crises upon the petroleum

production of the Western Hemisphere, and concomitant price increments, and the sixth chapter contemplates the manner in which western Europe should protect herself against the loss of Middle East oil within the future.

The author indicates several potential causes for a future Middle East oil crisis—conflicts between the producing country's government and oil companies, with Western governments, with other Middle Eastern governments, internal conflict, Soviet involvement, or just plain accident. In the eventuality of such an emergency, the Western Hemisphere, by modification of policies and techniques, could meet the need. Oil costs would, of course, rise, but not prohibitively. Western Europe should prepare for such an emergency, Mr. Lubell feels, but she must maintain flexibility in source-area procurement; a surplus of supertankers must be available for emergency transport; oil must be stock-piled, and coal, which western Europe does produce, must be abundantly available, above ground, so as "to serve as a cushion of total energy consumption." Hydroelectric power is being gradually expanded; nuclear energy is for the distant future. Ending upon a somewhat enigmatic note, the author concludes that "countenancing its ever-growing dependence on imported oil from undependable sources, without ensuring itself against their loss, involves Western Europe in greater political risks than it needs to take."

GEORGE T. RENNER
Associate Professor of Geography
Arizona State University

MARSHALL I. GOLDMAN. *Soviet Marketing: Distribution in a Controlled Economy.* Pp. 229. New York: Free Press of Glencoe, 1963. $5.95.

Among the fruitful by-products of Soviet-American exchanges and visits devoted to special areas of interest are the subsequent publications related to these trips. It was the fashion in the 1930's to visit many places in the Soviet Union for a week or two. These excursions were subsequently followed, after a rather brief interval, by journalistic accounts on the economic, political, sociological, and cultural conditions in the Soviet Union. In the post-World War II era the mode has changed. Today the tours are usually for one or two months and are even repeated. Further, the area of observation and interest is highly specialized. Subsequent studies, appearing a year or so after these visits, are often thoughtful, penetrating, and accurate. Dr. Goldman's work belongs in this category. His study is one of the better results of a research procedure that seeks to combine theoretical investigation with empirical observation.

The last comprehensive examination of Soviet marketing in English was *Soviet Trade and Distribution* by Leonard E. Hubbard, published in 1938. Dr. Goldman covers the developments in Soviet marketing since World War II, with primary emphasis on the period since the death of Stalin. His study is not only up-to-date and authentic, but bears the authoritative stamp of perceptive on-the-spot observation and reporting. Dr. Goldman has carefully analyzed contemporary marketing, pricing, and distribution of consumer goods in the Soviet Union. He has singled out the problem areas that arise because of peculiarities in the Soviet price system and because of state controls related to economic planning. His work is particularly valuable because he compares Soviet marketing operations with comparable activities in the United States and with the theories of consumer distribution held by Marx. He observes that as the standard of living rises in the Soviet Union, many American marketing activities, such as price reductions, advertising, and installment purchasing, are utilized by the Soviets to sell and move consumer goods. These new Soviet developments of adapting United States marketing techniques have occurred despite their apparent conflict with the harsh and disapproving views of Marx on the activities of the middleman in economic processes.

In various areas Goldman indicates that Soviet consumer sovereignty is coming to the fore, although there are still some shortages, and queuing is not entirely a thing of the past in the Soviet Union. Of considerable interest is his discussion on the use of turnover taxes to regulate, at least partially, consumer demand in a planned and controlled economic system. Dr. Goldman points out that Soviet planning is taking consumer demand more into account than heretofore. At the same time, he notes that consumer unpredictability is becoming greater because of increases in real wage and because the Soviet consumer wants more, as he gets more, not only in quantity but in the quality and variety of the goods he seeks and is able to purchase.

The statistical tables and the diagrams of *Soviet Marketing* constitute an important and useful part of this interesting work. The author provides the Russian technical terms used in Soviet marketing and their meanings. In addition, there is a bibliography including Soviet and other sources. Dr. Goldman's book is not only well-written and provocative; it also provides valuable insights about Soviet society today.

ERNEST RUBIN

Director
Sino-Soviet Division
Office of International
    Regional Economics
United States Department
    of Commerce

JOHN O. COPPOCK. *North Atlantic Policy: The Agricultural Gap.* Pp. xv, 270. New York: Twentieth Century Fund, 1963. $4.00.

This book is intended to support European unity and greater Atlantic integration. The main burden of its author's contention is that it would be wise for the foreign suppliers of cereals—both food grains and feed grains—to come to the conference tables, as soon as the United Kingdom joins the European Economic Community, with firm assurances that they can furnish Europe with such cereals at relatively low prices within a few years. Inability to offer such assurance would prevent Europe from adopting any more liberal policy objective than that which it now seems to be contemplating. In this connection, Mr. Coppock declares (p. 222): "The voices of those in Europe—not few in number—

who have an interest in a reasonably low price structure for food and whose interest in this circumstance coincides with foreign suppliers of cereals to Europe will be substantially muted unless they can say that Europe will be foregoing an important competitive advantage if it refuses low-cost cereals from abroad—and say it without raising the cry of 'subsidies' and 'dumping' from the supporters of high prices for European farmers."

These assurances on the part of overseas suppliers will have to rest upon a resolute determination promptly to rationalize farm production in the United States, Canada, Argentina, and Australia. Efficient allocation of economic resources demands it. In these countries, as well as in those of Europe, men in the factories are often worth far more than farmers in the grainfields. Moreover, Mr. Coppock feels sure that the dumping of food and feed in the underdeveloped countries, either as gifts or at reduced subsidized prices, will in the long run do more harm than good to both the exporting and the recipient nations.

The volume concludes (pp. 223–224) with a denunciation of the spread of the "pernicious politics" of special favors: "It is probably fair to say that agriculture is the 'rotten borough' of modern politico-economic democracy in industrialized countries. . . . The economic waste involved . . . can be seen to be considerable. But it is the low-grade political infection carried by farm politics which should be of real concern to Western democracies. There are few legislative bodies in which the blatant vote-trading engaged in by farmers' representatives can be matched by spokesmen of other organized groups."

Whether the reader agrees with these contentions or is provoked by them, he can surely examine with interest and profit the first ten chapters of this twelve-chapter volume, for it would be difficult to find elsewhere in so brief a space such a clear description of the agricultural problems confronted and policies adopted in Europe and North America during the four decades starting with 1920. Both the author and the Twentieth Century Fund merit congratulation for the produc-

tion of this timely monograph—for most, if not all, of it!

J. FRED RIPPY
Professor Emeritus of History
University of Chicago

E. E. PAPANICOLAOU. *Coopération Internationale et Développement Economique.* Pp. 356. Geneva: Librairie Droz, 1963. No price.

So many accounts of international aid, co-operation, and development programs—and the role of the steadily proliferating international organizations therein—are dreary tales, and tables, of how many peanuts nation A shipped to nation B in return for how many tons of barrel staves. Or they are equally dreary series of charts, tables, and graphs virtually incomprehensible to layman and expert alike. It is indeed refreshing to have at least some aspects of the subject of international aid and the role of international economic organizations treated from a theoretical and practical—and readable—point of view.

Dr. Papanicolaou, after serving in Greece's Ministry of Industry, moved into work with various international economic organizations. As with his first book on the theory and practice of economic development, the present—and better—work is saturated with theoretical and practical proposals developed after considerable experience with international economic problems. It is not a book for a cozy session with a winter fire and will not have a wide popular circulation, but it is one that can benefit all those concerned with international relations. It should be especially useful, perhaps almost required reading, for those officials of "emerging" nations whose governments are so vitally concerned with the theory and problem of international economic aid and regional integration.

Although the book is not too well balanced in treating comprehensively the many problems associated with international economic co-operation, it nevertheless is exceptionally good in two respects. First, it has as its thesis that international aid must extend beyond mere money and technical assistance, and the author propounds a number of viable ways in which this can be done. And second, it has a lengthy section—about one-third of the book—on regional integration, with perhaps overheavy emphasis on Europe. On the other hand, the reader should, perhaps, question whether or not Dr. Papanicolaou places too much hope in the eventual achievement of a rational international economic order.

R. T. TURNER
Professor of History
Montana State University

E. WIGHT BAKKE. *A Positive Labor Market Policy: Policy Premises for the Development, Operation, and Integration of the Employment and Manpower Services.* Columbus: Charles E. Merrill, 1963. No price.

Since 1950, the average annual rate of unemployment has risen from 4 per cent to approximately 6 per cent. But even more disturbing than this increase in itself is the fact that there is a high concentration of unemployment among nonwhites, young unskilled workers, and recent entrants into the labor market. For example, the unemployment rate for nonwhites as a per cent of the nation's total work force is almost three times as high as it is for whites. And in the total age group of eighteen to twenty, actively seeking work, one out of every five has been unable to find a job.

In view of this alarming situation, what should be the central mission of such a strategic agency as the United States Employment Service? Is its major purpose to ameliorate the effects of unemployment or should the agency concern itself with the prevention of unemployment, including such special problem as underemployment of individuals with special skills? Or, with even broader social objectives in view, should the combined Employment and Manpower Services—the latter referring to the total range of employment-related manpower and labor-market activities—be centrally directed to meet the over-all requirements of a strong, stable, and growing national economy? Is this country politically ready and able to federalize such services by following the Swedish example of

setting up a Labor Market Board as an independent agency? Or would we be better advised to continue our present policy of dispersed activity through many separate agencies, each having only indirect authority to influence and co-ordinate the relevant activities of state and local agencies as well as private endeavors?

Professor Bakke and twenty-five conferees—representatives from the Senate and the House of Representatives, top employment and manpower officials in the Department of Labor, administrators of state employment-security offices and other leaders in labor, in business, and in academic circles—held a series of biweekly conferences at the Brookings Institution during January and February of 1963, to consider such questions. They found that there exists at present no clear consensus among those involved about the central mission and role of the Employment and Manpower Services. However, by talking about the underlying assumptions and policy implications of possible courses of action they performed a signal service in defining the nature of the problem.

What are some fundamental premises and assumptions that affect the attitudes and strategies of professional employees in the Employment and Manpower Services? Whenever the nation was at war, emphasis has been on the economic health of the country. However, "in the absence of the obvious need for marshalling every ounce of our human resources to provide the economic strength required for war, the dominant conception of the Employment and Manpower Services as parts of a social work and relief agency has continually reasserted itself" (p. 20).

According to Professor Bakke, the case for federalization rests basically on the belief that "(1) *uniformity* in the excellence of performance and in end results is difficult to achieve under a federal-state system; (2) the *objectives and standards* believed to be consistent with the nation's needs and essential to those end results will not be adopted and acted upon expeditiously if central authority is weak; (3) whatever may be true of particular local situations, the *initiative and leader-*

ship required to meet the nation's needs and to promote over-all and well-coordinated progress cannot come from diffused centers of initiation and responsibility; and (4) it would be easier under such a federalized arrangement to promote the kind of developments in the services the advocates of federalization and reform believe desirable" (p. 194).

However, equally cogent arguments are advanced for strong Employment and Manpower Services geared to local needs. "The vast majority of employment relations are established within the conditions characteristic of local labor market operations and the facts of labor supply and demand existing there. The initiative and effort of local people created these services in the first place, and their continued initiative and effort are required for the continuous development of those services. The big volume of business for all the services is going to continue to involve circumstances and transactions at the grass roots. The administrators who eventually bring policy and plans into life are the local managers, and their success in each case requires cooperation with thousands of people whose horizon is the local labor market. Labor market operations are the only one of the processes of community life affecting, but also affected by, the totality of those processes. The specific requirements for their integration to provide an effective working whole community in thousands of different unique local situations can never be understood and acted wisely upon solely by central directors of services removed from daily and intimate contact with those situations" (p. 107).

The conferees did not come up with specific proposals. However, they succeeded in clearly defining the issue that must be faced, an essential step before further progress can be made. Rather than debating the advantages or disadvantages of central direction or local initiative, or some form of integration, it is essential to find clear-cut answers to the key questions: "Integration and federalization of *what*, for the achievement of *what central mission*, within what *operational field?*" (p. 196). The excel-

lence of the work done so far spurs the hope that Professor Bakke and the conferees will continue their efforts to find a realistic answer to these vital questions.

PAUL PIGORS
Professor of Industrial Relations
Massachusetts Institute of Technology

KENNETH C. McGUINESS. *The New Frontier: NLRB.* Pp. xii, 268. Washington, D. C.: Labor Policy Association, 1963. $6.00.

This book is a review of the decisions of the National Labor Relations Board (NLRB)—issued after the inauguration of President Kennedy—in which there was a split in Board members' views. Despite some half-hearted disclaimers which the author himself does not appear to take seriously, there is no attempt at fairness or scholarly detachment. The result is a volume which is seriously misleading, irresponsible in tone, casuistic in argument, and deplorably inaccurate in many respects. It is also comprehensive, knowledgeable, and reliable in its recital of the facts of the cases under discussion. In short, it is a campaign tract written by a highly skilled professional which, though disfigured by bias, is not without value.

The archvillain of the piece, "the Kennedy Board," is a misnomer; for the period of time under review, a majority of the Board was composed of members appointed by President Eisenhower. The "Kennedy Board" as used by Mr. McGuiness is a pejorative term of art which encompasses all Board decisions which are considered distasteful or undesirable. The Board is castigated for adverting in its decisions to the statement of policy set forth in the Taft-Hartley Act of "encouraging the practice and procedure of collective bargaining." Despite this language, McGuiness holds that it is "inaccurate to state the policy of the present law in terms of the encouragement of collective bargaining." How is this conclusion reached? Simply by asserting that nowhere "did Congress express any concern over the protection of labor organizations as such." Accordingly, "protection of unions is a Board-imposed policy" which has no statutory basis. This is nonsense. The duty to bargain specifically makes it an unfair labor practice for an employer to refuse to bargain with a majority union. Mr. McGuiness must be reminded that the Taft-Hartley Act, by specific congressional intent, essentially incorporates all of the protective features accorded unions by the Wagner Act.

In the secondary boycott area, the author goes beyond attacking the present Board and assaults the Eisenhower Boards for making the Landrum-Griffin amendments necessary by developing loopholes in the law. Mr. McGuiness disagrees with the Board interpretations in this and other areas; therein lies the value of this book. It is useful and desirable to have a systematic criticism of Board decisions, particularly where these criticisms are representative of management's point of view. Professional students are indebted to Mr. McGuiness for his industry in assembling the cases and for the sharp commentary which frequently lights up his analysis. It is indeed unfortunate that the author felt it necessary to vitiate the genuine merits of this book with an excessive indulgence in partisanship.

PHILIP ROSS
Graduate School of Business
University of Pittsburgh

PATRICK M. BOARMAN. *Union Monopolies and Antitrust Restraints*. Pp. x, 203. Washington, D. C.: Labor Policy Association, 1963. No price.

In this volume, Professor Boarman, who is Associate Professor of Economics at Bucknell, has given us yet another monograph in the alarmist tradition of labor economics. Like his predecessors, Boarman examines the power of labor unions in the United States and finds it "awesome," "noxious," and "overweening." In his view, "the economic power of even the largest business organizations . . . is as nothing compared to the power of the great international unions" (p. 10). Yet somehow, inexplicably, despite the fact that it must deal with just such a great international union as Boarman describes —the United Auto Workers—General Motors was able to report net profits for 1963 of $1,592,000,000—the largest profit ever earned by an American corporation! In successive chapters, Boarman finds unions to be the prime cause of the misuse of labor resources, the decline of competition, unemployment, inflation, and the balance-of-payments problems—although he *does* concede that monetary and fiscal policy has *something* to do with the latter point. Considering the extent of the damage which unbridled union power is supposed to cause, the remedy Boarman proposes—simply "to repeal labor's exempt status under the anti-trust laws"—seems a weak reed to lean on. Indeed, Boarman runs into the dilemma of trying to limit union power without destroying unions altogether, and ends up lamely leaving to the courts the critical decision as to how this is to be done.

Before he accepts Boarman's analysis unquestioningly, however, the reader should be cautioned that labor's present immunity from the antitrust laws—except in cases of collusion—is not primarily the result of legislation, but of the decisions of the very courts to which Boarman would now hand the problem! For the Sherman Act really said nothing about unions; it was the court decision in the Danbury Hatters case in 1908 which brought unions under that law. And in 1940 it was a court decision in the Apex case which began the process of removing unions from antitrust controls!

Here, as in many other places in his book, Professor Boarman's apparent ignorance of the facts undermines his analysis.

MARTEN S. ESTEY
Associate Professor of Industry
Wharton School of Finance
  and Commerce
University of Pennsylvania

SOCIOLOGY AND SOCIAL WORK

RICHARD HOFSTADTER. *Anti-Intellectualism in American Life*. Pp. ix, 434, xiii. New York: Alfred A. Knopf, 1963. $6.95.

Despite its number of pages, this is a most readable, even suddenly a short book, enjoyably written, with many memorable phrases, well organized, beginning with two chapters on contemporary anti-intellectualism and on the unpopularity of intellect, then analyzing, in a successful application of a sociological approach to historical materials, anti-intellectualism in religion, politics, business, and education, and concluding with an essay on the intellectual.

"Anti-intellectualism" is not one proposition but a complex of propositions, not a pure but an ambivalent attitude, not a consistent but a fluctuating historical thread, and Hofstadter is interested in the complex, "the milieu, the atmosphere, in which American thinking has taken place" (p. 7). He achieves definition only indirectly, by substantive analysis, leaving induction to the reader—though not so much, I fear, for the reason he states in the beginning: "I can see little advantage in a logically defensible but historically arbitrary act of definition, which would demand singling out one trait among a complex of traits"—as because of his own frustration, no matter how deeply it is that of how many of us. He could have let it go at analysis, but the problem was too close, and in the last chapter, therefore, he is struggling for a stand, starting with the 1952 *Partisan Review* symposium on "Our Country and Our Culture," of which, and of the situation today, he presents an enlightening analysis. But in his wish for commitment, he does not go beyond formulating the intellectual's "personal choice" of joining or avoiding power, of making his "ideas effective" or maintaining his "purity" (p. 429). This means that he accepts contemporary alternatives, even though he recognizes that British and French intellectuals "usually take for granted the worth of what they are doing and the legitimacy of their claims on the community" (p. 417), while for Americans, whose society is their arbiter, there is only what they feel as the dilemma between conformity and alienation.

Here, more sociological analysis might have helped: Is our society still the proper arbiter? Is it still adequate as a yardstick? And is it indeed a liberal one in which "a variety of styles of intellectual life" is possible, although "the avenues of choice" may become closed? In view of this, can one say no more than Hofstadter does—in the last sentence of his book—that "in so far as the weight of one's will is thrown onto the scales of history, one lives in the belief that this is not to be so" (p. 432)?

KURT H. WOLFF
Professor of Sociology
Brandeis University

PITIRIM A. SOROKIN. *A Long Journey: The Autobiography of Pitirim A. Sorokin.* Pp. 327. New Haven, Conn.: College and University Press, 1963. $5.00.

Twice in the course of his autobiography, Sorokin himself refers to it as a light work. The reader will agree, in the sense that he peruses it with fascination, but not if "light" is equated with unimportant, nor, one suspects, would Sorokin, who has always been a prodigiously hard worker and a man with a mission.

Few stories of academic careers, certainly, can match this one in interest, in variety of social setting, in vital reactions to the vicissitudes of life-experience. From the peasant hut that is Sorokin's first memory to professor emeritus of Harvard is truly "a long journey." To correct any tendency to obeisance in the direction of the Yard, we should remember that the author is one hundred per cent happy that his life began in an elemental realm of nature, and that he occasionally has his doubts about Cambridge. What enabled the boy who walked out of his father's house at the age of eleven, never to see his parent again, to reach high position in two societies and world-wide fame remains almost a miracle of intelligence and application. There was not even an opportunity to graduate from elementary school; voracious reading, talks, and discussions with many types of people, an itinerant artisan's life, rich in "direct experience in challenging life situations" more than made up for this lack. Looking back, Sorokin can say that the integrated culture of his people and the religious climate in which he lived "played an important part in the formation of my personality, the integration of my system of values, the crystallization of my early philosophy." A remarkably satisfying and permanently unquestioned idealistic world-view seems to have been his throughout life, with the exception of a brief revolutionary period.

An entrance examination for the advanced grammar school at Gam, taken on a chance and passed brilliantly, followed by graduation at fourteen, when his record and teachers' recommendations secured him a modest scholarship at a teachers' seminary were the early stepping stones in his career. That the career early turned into that of a boy-orator acting as "itinerant missionary of the revolution" requires more empathetic effort on our part, but this may have been no more strange than the quite different enthusiasms of our teen-agers. This led to flight, arrest, imprisonment. World war and the Russian Revolution—which Sorokin was soon to discover was not a type to his liking—came to interrupt the young man's preparation for a professorship. The story is retold, with exciting detail, by liberal quotations from the earlier "Leaves from a Russian Diary." Students of sociology eager to dignify small insights into sociological laws may be forgiven for finding considerable interest in Sorokin's fine-print opinion that the requirements for the master's degree in the Russian universities were notably higher than for the Ph.D. degree in American universities, and his insistence that freedom for endless reading and independent work is much superior to the accumulation of course credits. Forty years of separation from his native country have not changed his conviction.

Parts Four and Five record the forty years of Sorokin's experience as a sociologist in America, briefly at Vassar, Illinois, Wisconsin, longer at Minnesota, and especially at Harvard, with occasional lectures and summer schools elsewhere, attendance at congresses, and always the writing of books—even in 1923 he had arrived with two suitcases filled "mainly with manuscripts and books." Among specialists, the oldsters will read this to uncover his opinions of his contemporaries, the younger generation, for whom it should be required reading, with mingled encouragement and dismay, and everyone with curiosity to see what sociology has meant to one of its most celebrated practitioners. Incidentally, they will all find that the book is an almost perfect answer to the question of what an experiment in autobiography should be like if it is to be of maximum use to the social scientist.

W. REX CRAWFORD
Fulbright Lecturer in Portugal

PHILIP J. ALLEN (Ed.). *Pitirim A. Sorokin in Review*. Pp. xxii, 537. Durham, N. C.: Duke University Press, 1963. $10.00.

Few sociologists in the world today could stand up to the critical examination of an international forum of philosophers, social scientists, and historians as has Pitirim Sorokin in Professor Allen's distinguished volume. The volume opens with a brief personal autobiography by Sorokin. Thereafter, Othmer F. Anderle (Austria), Bernard Barber, Gösta Carlsson (Sweden), F. Richard Cowell (England), Joseph B. Ford, Corrado Gini (Italy), Alex Inkeles, David R. Mace, Lucio Mendeita y Núñez (Mexico), Robert K. Merton, Mary E. Moore, Kanailal M. Munshi (India), Matilda White Riley, T. Lynn Smith, Nicholas S. Timasheff, Arnold J. Toynbee (England), and Alexandre Vexliard (Turkey) subject various of Sorokin's theories and researches to critical evaluation. Since Sorokin's writings extend over fifty years—1913 to the present—and comprise three dozen books —with forty-two translations—and ninety articles, there is much for his critics to work on. In a final chapter, Sorokin replies to his critics.

Many of Sorokin's books have already achieved the status of classics: *Social Mobility, The Principles of Rural-Urban Sociology, Contemporary Sociological Theories,* and *Social and Cultural Dynamics.* The very properties which turned them into classics placed them so firmly astride the trends as to assure that they will eventually be surpassed—such is the fate of all classics. But despite the frequently reiterated criticism of inconsistencies, questionable methods, and the substitution of moral evaluation for objective analysis, all critics are forced to admit that Sorokin is always brilliantly innovative, daringly adventurous and often penetratingly insightful.

As intriguing as any of the issues he discusses is the sociological phenomenon of Sorokin himself. This motherless son of an itinerant alcoholic workman from the nineteenth-century Russian frontier was destined to become the foremost sociologist of our day. What gave him the elemental energy and bravado of a Merovingian strayed into the intellectual forums of the twentieth century? What part did the ferment of the two Russian revolutions play in supplying him with the battle equipment for an assault upon the problems of the social sciences? How significant in his over-all development was exile from Russia at the very moment that he was coming to the fulness of his powers and the immersion at this time in the empirical traditions of the American Midwest? Or did all these experiences play a part in the formation of this wayfarer—as he described himself; this pioneer—as Toynbee described him; this self-made man with a self-made man's virtues and faults—as he is described by Gini.

With a fine disregard for ordinary usage Sorokin describes himself as a "conservative Christian anarchist" and as a philosophical and sociological "Integralist." These are euphemisms for "individualist" or "lone wolf" and for "Philosophical Idealist." But Sorokin is more than this. He is a soldier of fortune never far from the conceptual battlefields. He is a superb opportunist capable of transforming any situation he is in into sociological form. He is an intellectual warrior berserker, most fully himself when suffused with the ecstasy of battle.

DON MARTINDALE
Professor of Sociology
University of Minnesota

W. LLOYD WARNER, PAUL P. VAN RIPER, NORMAN H. MARTIN, and ORVIS F. COLLINS. *The American Federal Executive: A Study of the Social and Personal Characteristics of the Civilian and Military Leaders of the United States*

Federal Government. Pp. xvi, 405. New Haven: Yale University Press, 1963. $7.50.

The research upon which this book is based had as its "primary purposes" the determination of (1) the sorts of men and women who achieve the highest civilian and military positions in the federal government and their family and other group backgrounds, (2) the steps in their careers which led to their present positions, and (3) how they compare in these respects with the American big business leaders previously studied by Warner and James Abegglen. Beyond these primary goals, the authors sought to reach "broad generalizations about the representative character of the American federal bureaucracy and, in turn, about the nature of occupational mobility and succession in American society as a whole."

To attempt to reach their goals, the investigators gathered material on 12,929 careers, a 69-per cent return from those who received schedules. The resulting chapters and appendixes, each signed by one or two of the authors, deal with the federal elites' social origins, their family-occupational, ecological, and ethnic backgrounds; the influence of their family ties upon their opportunities; their education; their career lines; their public and private worlds. The last two-fifths of the book contain an appendix on theory and method and another of supplementary tables.

The investigators have made a competent survey within the limitations of their methods and working conditions. Their interesting statistics can scarcely be summarized or adequately characterized here. The chapters that appear to give the most useful conception of their subjects are the least statistical ones. These are the three final chapters: "Personalities of Federal Executives," "Professional Pride and the Value of Service," and "The World of the Civilian Executive." The first of these is based upon 257 intensive interviews with civilian federal executives; these include Thematic Apperception Test protocols. The second analyzes ideals and other ideas, including self- and other images, drawn from these 257 interviews. The third is a concluding "think piece."

After reading the book, I had these feelings: Vignettes of three selected personality types in Chapter Twelve suggest both how much more the investigators might have learned from the study of more detailed life histories and the limitations of their own data. Unfortunately, the authors apparently felt it necessary to mix their forthright survey project with efforts to contribute to social science on the one hand and with efforts to be polite and discreetly "constructive" on the other. This sort of thing is "high fashion" today, but this mixture of purposes can only contribute to the "social science" of organization men, and not to the more basic formulations of social scientists. Fortunately their data, to the extent that they are made available in this book and otherwise, can be useful to scientists with less mixed purposes.

ALFRED MCCLUNG LEE
Professor of Sociology and
  Anthropology
Brooklyn College
City University of New York

ORVILLE G. BRIM, JR., DAVID C. GLASS, DAVID E. LAVIN, and NORMAN GOODMAN. *Personality and Decision Processes: Studies in the Social Psychology of Thinking.* Pp. ix, 336. Stanford, Calif.: Stanford University Press, 1962. $8.00.

This volume illustrates some of the major strengths of current thought on social psychological processes *and* the unique difficulties confronting behavioral scientists which place serious limitations on their ability to capitalize fully on exciting ideas. The authors wished to investigate the extent to which, and the methods by which, characteristics of the personalities of individuals participating in decision-making affect decision-making activity. To carry out their investigation they were limited in two familiar respects. First, they were obliged to limit their inquiry to decision-making in a hypothetical situation. Teams of subjects discussed and reached conclusions as to how the parents of a son should handle each of four problems which might arise in a home situation, namely, a problem involving masturbation, one involving irregular study habits, one involving obedience, and one involving stealing. While this procedure established homogeneity of the problem over the various teams, a circumstance difficult to achieve if decision-making processes are examined as they occur, for example, in the development of a problem in a case-work agency, at the same time it entailed the sacrifice of much that is uniquely characteristic of the process. Second, they were faced with, and suffered in some degree from, the problem of subject-recruitment. Original plans as to the number of subjects were revised downward; the revision being due to the understandable unwillingness of parents to devote their time, and perhaps expose themselves and their thinking to, quasi-public scrutiny.

The problem created by the reduction of the number of subjects is especially troubling to the authors because of the techniques to be used in establishing relationships between the decision-making process and the personalities. In general, the techniques were psychometric techniques, involving the construction of psychological tests or their adaptation to the needs of both decision-making and personality analysis. The results of the psychometric work ultimately were fed into a large-scale correlational analysis, and this, in turn, provided the foundation for factor analytic work from which evidence was drawn by which relationships between the personality variables and the decision-process variables were identified. The magnitude of statistical operations may be appreciated by considering that the authors require 108 tables for the exhibition of the outcomes, some of the tables containing as many as 400 entries.

Ten characteristics of the decision process constituted the specific dependent variables of the studies. Of these ten, seven related to the evaluative phase of the decision-making process, and three to that phase in which a selection was made as between alternative strategies. As to the personality variables, these were evaluated by standardized tests of ability, tests of affect, including drive level, satisfaction with interpersonal relationships, and parental concern with child-rearing, a test of desire for certainty, a conventional test of general personality traits, certain tests of epistemological and instrumental beliefs, and a test of independence of judgment. All tests were taken by all subjects. A variety of other elements of information was elicited from the subjects by a questionnaire directed to social and demographic characteristics of the three samples. Two of the samples numbered twenty-four couples and one numbered forty-eight couples.

The work is apt to suffer in the estimation of a too-critical reader because of the absence of any guiding theoretical conceptions as to the relationship between decision-making and personality characteristics. It is frankly an exploratory investigation, and while sophisticated in statistical analysis, naturalistic in inspiration. It will probably be remembered more for what it may lead to than for substantive accomplishment. Among the gains which give promise for the future is a useful analysis of the decision process, equally applicable to the study of hypothetical decision-making and "real" decision-making, the development of an instrument for quantifying reports on the ten characteristics of the decision process, and the raising of important questions about expected utility in the context of decision-making. Substantive outcomes are less clearly identifiable. Among them is evidence suggesting the existence of differences in the process which are associated with sex and social-class membership and the identification of a factor in the battery of personality tests to which the name autonomy-dependency is given, which is found in all six subclasses of the main sample, and in five subclasses of the sample appears to be correlated in the same direction with the way in which subjects evaluate the desirability of the various possible outcomes in a decision-process situation.

MALCOLM G. PRESTON
Professor of Psychology
University of Pennsylvania

ROLAND L. WARREN. *Social Research Consultation: An Experiment in Health*

and Welfare Planning. Pp. 163. New York: Russell Sage Foundation, 1963. $3.00.

There are some books which one enjoys reading, some books one profits by reading, and perhaps other books which one wishes other people would read. No social-research worker will read this book without finding many echoes of his own problems in dealing with research-planning in an administrative or social-work setting and wishing that "they" would read it.

"Practitioners (including administrators) want easy formulas for quick action, and are not interested in furthering knowledge. They are interested only in favorable findings. They prefer dogma to research, being essentially 'antiscientific.' They are deficient in knowledge of research methodology." This is a good picture of "them." But what of the "them" when they are we? "Research investigators usually ignore the questions posed by practitioners and go off on methodological tangents. Their reports contain too much technical jargon. They lack sufficient knowledge of social work practice and needs. They do not involve practitioners sufficiently in the planning and recommendation stages of the research."

This is an excellent statement of the problem, but does the book deal with the problem? Although there are many first-class insights and penetrating statements in this book, your reviewer was disappointed. Perhaps the title, and particularly the subtitle, led to expectations which the author never intended to meet. What is an "experiment"? Many social scientists will define the term more rigorously than the author, and it is regretted that a research worker should use this term loosely. The book describes a "demonstration project" and is, in the main, concerned with consultation regarding the planning of sample surveys. Sample surveys are a legitimate part of social research, but social research, and presumably social-research consultation, ranges wider than this.

The role described is one where the research consultant has assumed a relationship with the client organization very similar to that of the social caseworker with his client. This is illustrated by the concerns expressed (p. 27): "Will I be able to function adequately in this new kind of activity? Will the research possibility uncover defects or inadequacies in our own functioning? If so, are these a threat to me? Can I really trust this behavioral scientist? Or will he let me down?" Appropriate questions, but is the role described the only available role? There are doubtless forms of social research where the role of the consultant as here described results in sound work, but is this role suitable for all forms of social-research consultation? If the book had been titled differently, perhaps we should not have expected these issues to be tackled.

Good as this work is, it seems that it misses something. Would it have been better if the record had been told as a compelling story, or better as a more systematic account? It is difficult to decide, but the author loses his reader from time to time as he moves from one style to another.

More books dealing with problems of research organization, dealing with the sociology of social action, social administration, and social research are needed. It is hoped that this work heralds a growing interest in the science of science, the behavior of the behavioral scientist, and the sociology of sociological research.

LESLIE T. WILKINS
Home Office Research Unit
Whitehall
London

KETTIL BRUUN and RAGNAR HAUGE, in collaboration with NILS CHRISTIE, CARL-GUNNAR JANSON, ERLAND JONSSON, and SVEND SKYUM-NIELSON. *Drinking Habits Among Northern Youth*. (Publication Number 12 of the Finnish Foundation for Alcohol Studies, Helsinki.) Translated from the Swedish and Norwegian by Fred A. Fewster. Pp. 97. New Brunswick, N. J.: Rutgers Center of Alcohol Studies, 1963. $4.00.

This slender volume reports on alcohol-use among boys in the four Scandinavian capitals and on the relevant impact of the four governmental control systems. It well

exemplifies the sort of information and research so frequently lacking in America. Legislative committees, Parent-Teachers Associations, state liquor authorities, churches, professional educators, law-enforcement organizations, and those in public health are frequently urged to view with alarm and do something more ‘or something different about youth and drinking. Complaints or proposed reforms may concern such specific items as age-restrictions, advertising, automobile accidents, the alcoholisms, and licensing of purchasers or such general matters as uniform state legislation, educational philosophy, the breakdown of parental or youthful morality, crime, or even replays of the old Prohibition battle. The outstanding weakness of these recurrent, nationwide attempts "to do something" is the clear absence of relevant, representative, validated, and organized information about youthful drinking. Without this, the achievement of increasingly rational controls is most unlikely.

Hauge and Bruun imply existence of a similar lack of information in a somewhat similar social setting: "Statements on the wild drinking habits of youngsters have been made in many countries, including Denmark, Finland, Norway, and Sweden. The present report provides empirical data which will facilitate judgment of whether these statements are given support by the actual circumstances." The authors also note that the pessimists, often with moral indignation, have dominated discussion on many types of youthful behavior and have so heavily emphasized reports of deviant extremes that these characteristics tend to be generalized to youth as a whole.

The book does not pretend to explain the functions of alcohol-use in society or to explain individual drinking differences. It is concerned with data of the simplest sort relevant to drinking practices and attitudes manifested by fourteen-, sixteen-, and eighteen-year-old boys who have lived two or more years in a family setting in each of the four cities: What do they drink, how much, how often, where, and with whom? Do they think their parents approve? Do they think their age mates drink more, the same, or less than they do? What is their information about legal restraints on purchase?

The data are presented to show the similarities and differences between use of distilled spirits, wines, and beers, between fourteen-, sixteen-, and eighteen-year-olders, and between the boys residing in the four different cities. The other data are related to these comparisons. The authors not only are sophisticated social-science researchers but have also presented their methodological problems and steps in fairly simple language. They have kept a clear and common-sense viewpoint about the field of drinking behavior. For students of the phenomena of alcohol use or for those with relevant responsibilities the book may be considered on the level of required reading.

SELDEN D. BACON

Director
Center of Alcohol Studies
Rutgers—The State University

RUTH GILPIN. *Theory and Practice as a Single Reality: An Essay in Social Work Education.* Pp. vi, 139. Chapel Hill: University of North Carolina Press, 1963. $4.50.

Small in size but considerable in value, this book is a professional essay on teaching and learning in social-work education. It is an informative analysis of the theory and practice of agency-school co-operation in its historic as well as present dimensions. Specifically and centrally, however, this essay presents the author's theory of concurrence as it is achieved in actual process at North Carolina University School of Social Work, a process through which school and agency attempt to fuse into a single reality the learning experience of the students.

The essay is an unusual medium for professional expression. A legitimate literary form, the essay has for Dr. Gilpin "the necessary ingredients for seeing and saying what formal research and analytic exposition cannot." She follows the basic essay form as outlined by Herbert Read in *English Prose Style:* (1) a beginning on familiar ground; (2) announcement of a paradoxical theme which is to be the subject of the essay; (3) development of the theme by appeal to common experience; (4) illustration of the theme by anecdote; (5) deduction from the illustration; (6) summary. She uses the form effectively, and it is suitable for her topic. The paradoxical theme is the split in the learning structure in social-work education—between theory and practice, school and agency, separate and unrelated courses, teachers with many doctrines and approaches. Dr. Gilpin points out that the "learning structure is not just split in two but into fragments." Consequently, a most urgent need for social-work education is to find a way to offer a student a fusion "of school and agency as the single reality he needs for choice" if he is to learn how to become a social worker.

The field-work adviser of the professional school, according to the theory of concurrence here developed, carries in himself the teaching function and responsibility, the authority and helping skill, which, when *used* as a single reality at appropriate times in the learning process, enables the student to fuse academic theory and field practice if he so chooses. As the author fully acknowledges, "the age-old puzzle about knowledge and experience, practice and theory, analytic and synthetic has not been solved in this volume" on social-work education. But it contributes substantially to a theory which can bring about elimination of the fragmenting duality which now exists across the land in professional schools.

What is the heart of that theory? It is found in these words which bespeak a conviction growing out of years of experience in the field of practice, her doctoral studies at the University of Pennsylvania School of Social Work, and years of teaching at the University of North Carolina School of Social Work; outer can become inner, theory become experience in that moment and in that relationship "when an individual in his inner being feels as truth, and takes as his own, the other's offering." That is the moment of learning. This reviewer is full of admiration for the care and devotion which is poured into a teacher's account of a school's effort to fuse into a single reality the learning experience of its students. Does it work? Imperfectly, but better than anything else. Why? Let Robert Browning supply a piece of the answer: "Ah but a man's reach should exceed his grasp, or what's a heaven for?"

EDMUND G. BURBANK
Assistant Director
Sheltering Arms Children's Service
New York City

HERTHA RIESE. *Heal the Hurt Child: Educational Therapy with Special Reference to the Extremely Deprived Negro Child.* Pp. xxviii, 615. Chicago: University of Chicago Press, 1962. $10.00.

The author of this book has a long history in the theory and practice of socially minded medicine—not necessarily socialized medicine—and psychiatry. Exemplary is her contribution in 1929 to *Accident Neurosis: A Problem of Contemporary Medicine,* edited by Walther Riese. Hertha Riese's paper was on "Traumatic Neuroses Seen as Related to Changes in the Population."

In her present book, which may be considered as her magnum opus, she deals with psychotherapeutic endeavors for educationally underprivileged, ill-sheltered, rejected children and adolescents, living with their virtually migratory, poor, Negro parents. These families belong to the hard core of poverty in America, which was recently discussed, in its outward aspects, by Kenneth Galbraith, Gunnar Myrdal, Michael Harrington, and others. Hertha Riese gives us, in detail, the psychological insight into what the economists approach from the socioeconomic angle only. She describes the orientations and motivations of children who live in one room with ten or more other persons of different age groups: grandmother, mother's companion, her lover, assorted aunts and fathers, nonrelated men and girls, related and nonrelated other children.

The Educational Therapy Center in Richmond, Virginia, which owes its existence and functioning to the author, has developed specific psychiatrically and educationally oriented therapies, destined to help this group of children. The detail of the intake, the psychological testing, the choice by the child of the therapist, and the treatment must be read in the book. An important treatment method, the day care, has the purpose of taking the hurt child out of his environment, away from his often hostile, inept, frequently unfit mother and all the other unemployed "inmates" of that one-room "home." The cases reported by the author are impressive. She, incidentally, does not forget to mention those who on intake were considered not amenable to any treatment and were therefore not admitted.

The reviewer must express his admiration for the courage and persistence Hertha Riese has shown in her attempts to bring psychotherapy to these children. He can imagine that the author must often have had the feeling she can contribute only drops where bucketfuls are needed. The book is full of excellent interpretations, based on psychoanalysis, of interfamily and human, often all-too-human, relations as they develop in the one-room milieu. Last but not least, the chapter on the problem of language (p. 312 ff.) is recommended for careful reading. It deals with speech as "barrier and weapon." "These children have known language not as a bridge but a moat in a shooting war. Either the drawbridge is raised completely or it is lowered in order to send across a steady stream of words to attack the opposing forces." On the following twelve pages, the vocabulary, the syntax, the use and abuse of names, the silence and the verbalism emerging from treatment are described—a precious contribution that should interest those trying to span the gap between the speech and the social-psychological orientations of the speaker.

W. G. ELIASBERG
New York City

M. ELAINE BURGESS and DANIEL O. PRICE. *An American Dependency Challenge.* Pp. xxiii, 285. Chicago: American Public Welfare Association, 1963. $3.00.

About one million American families with almost three million children are receiving help through the Aid to Dependent Children (ADC) program—now renamed and somewhat modified as Aid to Families with Dependent Children.

What are the effects on such families of the receipt of public financial assistance and related services? Does the program, as intended, succeed in keeping children and their parent(s) living together when they are financially in need? Do the children then grow and develop as well as other children in America? Under what circumstances do the families or their children give promise of breaking out of their cycles of poverty, inadequate education, lack of occupational skills, and ill health? To what extent do family conditions of parental conflict and physical and psychological incapacity change during the periods families are on ADC—conditions which bring them into the program? Or does ADC itself encourage, for example, paternal desertion, illegitimacy, and generation after generation of economic dependency? These are questions of widespread public concern.

They are the kinds of questions that Burgess and Price set out to answer in their survey of a sample of over 5,000 "assisted" or closed-case families. Their answers are necessarily qualified ones, and they carefully report the limitations in their final sample and the procedures by which their data were collected. As a replication of Blackwell and Gould's now decade-old *Future Citizens All,* this study limited itself also to cases which had been closed—during the first three months of 1961. Thus there are probably proportionately fewer cases which remain active over long periods of time in their sample than would appear in a random sample of active cases. Moreover, the data were collected by public-welfare workers in forty-two of the fifty states and the District of Columbia; California, with the largest ADC caseload and the highest average payments, was among the eight nonparticipating states. Probably, too, there is an underrepresentation of Negro families in the sample, if Negro family proportions in active caseloads are considered as a baseline.

No matter how one evaluates these and other limitations in this study, however, its. findings can give no public-spirited reader cause for comfort. The vast majority of these families had annual incomes of less than $2,000, with a median of 4.2 persons per family. And though in about 90 per cent of families children were living with one—or both—parents, assessments of the children's development revealed only a "mixed picture." For example, for the older children, compared with national norms, there were less delinquency and criminality but more school retardation and drop-outs. There was little evidence that many of these families appreciably improved their lots during their periods on ADC. Many lived on, with their own inadequate educational and vocational training backgrounds, in substandard housing. Many of their children had inadequate health care. In about a third of the cases, parents had grown up in families that had at some time received public assistance. About a third of the families had previously had their cases closed and re-opened at least once—and may by now be back on ADC again. And about a third of the cases were closed while the families were still in financial need.

The findings of this study are most illuminating—and shocking—on a descriptive level. Causes and effects are difficult to disentangle. What emerges is further documentation of extreme poverty and its manifold accompanying deprivations in affluent America. To modify this shameful state of affairs requires efforts far greater than simply those of understaffed county welfare departments. Community mobilization of health, educational, vocational training, and other resources seems essential, working in close relationship with welfare agencies and in innovative and knowledgeable ways. Smaller and more intensive studies of ADC families in their neighborhood contexts and experimental demonstration projects may throw additional light on the most fruitful points of entry, for concerted community programs, in efforts to help these disadvantaged families.

HENRY S. MAAS
Professor of Social Welfare
University of California
Berkeley

BIOGRAPHY AND HISTORY

FRANK E. MANUEL. *Isaac Newton, Historian.* Pp. viii, 328. Cambridge, Mass.: Belknap Press of Harvard University Press, 1963. $7.50.

A more apt title for this book would have been something like "Newton's Astronomical Chronology," for indeed its bulk is concerned with Sir Isaac's correct insight into at least one scientifically plausible way of determining the relative dates of past occurrences. The other methods, archaeological, geologic, and chemical, were yet to be developed. Only astronomy, as conceived by Newton, who is seen in this context to be as "deductivist" in his conception of science as Laplace, could serve the purpose of firmly fixing dates in the pre-Olympiadic period.

Newton's theory, simple to the point of austerity, was (1) since the precession of the equinoxes proceeds at approximately 50″ per year, and (2) since we can predict how the heavens will appear from any terrestrial observation point for any specifiable time, and (3) since we can as well retrodict such observations, and (4) since we have some eye-witness astronomical equinoctial observation reports, (5) it follows that we can fix with an heretofore unprecedented degree of accuracy the date of the observations, that is, the fluoriate of the observer and the approximate date of other events reported by him. With (5) established—very early in Newton's life—he then went on—for the better part of his life—to construct a chronology of the Ancient Kingdoms of mankind.

But for the omission of the above analytic, Professor Manuel's book is to be highly commended, especially to those of us who thrive on the history of intellectual controversy, particularly of the sort practiced in England in the seventeenth and eighteenth centuries, for example, the deistical, free-will, and origin-of-morals controversies. Here the controversy mapped by Professor Manuel is over the dating given by Newton for events and rulers in the pre-Olympiadic period.

The merits of this volume are many. We are presented with a penetrating portrait of the domain of chronological scholarship in Newton's time and Newton's life-long devotion to it and related theological matters. We are disabused—at last—of the view that Newton occupied himself with such matters due to infirmity or senility. Professor Manuel moves in the world of Newtonian scholarship with facility and exactitude, and has produced a very welcome addition to the literature. He includes two hitherto unpublished specimen pieces as appendixes; the first is a short summary of Newton's "New Systems of Chronology," and the second is Lord Keynes' manuscript of Newton's "The Original of Monarchies." The Bibliography is excellent and Professor Manuel's notes contain many riches for the slow reader who can cope with the atrocious custom twentieth-century publishers have of putting the *foot*notes at the end of otherwise readable books.

BERNARD H. BAUMRIN
Assistant Professor of Philosophy
University of Delaware

OTTO WOLFF. *Ouvrard: Speculator of Genius, 1770–1846.* Translated by Stewart Thompson. Pp. xiv, 239. New York: David McKay, 1963. $5.95.

"I was born with a passion for big business. . . . It gives me a kind of gambler's excitement which neither experience nor reason can overcome." Thus wrote Julien Ouvrard, speculator, war contractor, and financier who rather better than survived a half-dozen regimes beginning with the Constituent Assembly in 1789 and ending with the Bourgeois Monarchy of Louis Philippe. Otto Wolff, a German businessman of the 1920's, tells his story with obvious sympathy for the Frenchman's talents. His hero is a man "unaffected by new ideas, his vision undimmed by the fog of emotional verbiage" (p. 9). Ouvrard could wait for the "exalted ideas" of the French Revolution to "lose their potency" so, that "he could have his share of the power which must take over when the rule of ideas came to an end: the power of money" (p. 23).

Ouvrard made his first fortune by shrewdly guessing that the revolution would lead to freedom of the press and to an increased demand for paper. He promptly cornered the paper market by buying the entire production of the mills of Poitou and Angoumois for two years. When the large printing firms eventually had to come to him, Ouvrard realized a profit of 300,000 livres. This was only the beginning. He invested this first fortune in colonial produce at Nantes and Bordeaux, making another half-million from increasingly scarce edibles. Narrowly escaping the Jacobin campaign against hoarders, Ouvrard eventually ingratiated himself with Barras to become one of the most favored of war contractors. In 1797 he was General Victualing Master of the Navy, making some 20 millions supplying the Spanish fleet alone. In 1799 he profited from deflated prices of *émigré* property to invest heavily in land and urban real estate. Not given to ascetic living, the one-time grocer of Nantes played the *grand seigneur* at his château of Raincy, entertaining the cream of Parisian society.

Then came Bonaparte with his deep suspicion of merchants and army contractors. Eventually, even Ouvrard's elaborate network of influential friends—Josephine, Cambacérès, Berthier, Fouché, Talleyrand—could not save him from Napoleon's refusal to pay in full. The crisis came in 1805 when Ouvrard failed to execute a complex scheme to activate the Spanish treasure hoard in Mexico. Apparently near bankruptcy in 1807, Ouvrard was, nonetheless, Contractor-in-Chief during the Hundred Days. In 1818 he conceived and executed a bold plan of paying Allied reparations by borrowing from the Allies themselves. In 1823 Ouvrard was army-contractor for the French campaign in Spain, and in 1830 he was selling French government bonds short, anticipating the fall of the Bourbons.

Otto Wolff's book is thin on economic analysis and yet assumes the reader's familiarity with high finance. Political digressions are inadequate for the general reader and oversimplified for the specialist. More disturbing is Wolff's refusal to abandon chronology long enough to place Ouvrard in the context of the development of European banking. No doubt Ouvrard grasped the role of popular psychology at the root of credit, and his proposals for a national debt on the English pattern were well in advance of his conservative French contemporaries. But this question is only casually treated. By failing to depart from his exciting narrative, Wolff's "speculator of genius" emerges as a charming rogue.

ROBERT FORSTER
Associate Professor of History
Dartmouth College

FORREST C. POGUE. *George C. Marshall: Education of a General, 1880–1939.* Pp. xvii, 421. New York: Viking Press, 1963. $7.50.

This survey of the career that preceded George C. Marshall's high responsibilities during and after World War II concludes that Marshall's "education" offered not so much direct, specific preparation for his gigantic tasks as a strengthening of the best elements in his character, and that much of his subsequent achievement rested upon character.

The very background of the book is significant of Marshall's character. Marshall determined not to become involved in the recriminations characteristic of military memoirs, and he refused to write them. But, possessing a sense of history, he accepted President Truman's suggestion that he deposit his papers at Lexington, Virginia. There the George C. Marshall Research Foundation, aided by private grants, is sponsoring the preparation of Marshall's biography. Pogue has employed the support and collections of the foundation, interviews with Marshall himself and numerous persons who knew him, records made available by the presidents from Truman onward, the work of an industrious research staff to examine these and other materials, and the assistance of Gordon Harrison, who co-operated in a thorough revision of the first draft. Under the weight of detail gathered by this somewhat ponderous research apparatus, Marshall the human being proves to be too often concealed. But Marshall's own reticence has to share the blame for that, and Pogue's book offers many compensations. Especially, it is a provocative history of the Army during the years of Marshall's rise.

If we can judge the quality of institutions in part by the individuals whom they bring to flower, the United States Army should be happy to be judged through Marshall. Not least is this true because Marshall was far from being a military conformist. Pogue points out that when he was instructing at the Infantry School at Fort Benning, his fault lay in the opposite direction: he was perhaps too quick to applaud unorthodox tactics simply for their unorthodoxy. One of the main themes of Marshall's career was his effort to free the Army of outworn customs. Yet the Army rewarded him with its highest honors, and a case could be made that the American Army has a tradition of doing so. Still, Pogue stresses the narrowness of the margin by which Marshall reached the highest ranks, and thus he implies questions about the Army's readiness to accept change even when tactfully suggested by a good officer. Marshall spent much of his career in frustration and discouragement while men of lesser ability were promoted over him. Pogue points to the defects of the seniority system through which Marshall had to rise. But the reader wonders if there were not other causes for Marshall's troubles. Is it significant that Marshall's friend John McAuley Palmer similarly failed of deserved promotion, provoking Marshall to uncommonly bitter comment, and that Palmer like Marshall advocated a citizen army in opposition to entrenched professional doctrine? Did Marshall's interest and confidence in the National Guard and citizen reserves hinder his rise? Was he too critical of tactical dogma as well?

Because this is a book rich in research and information it raises questions as well as answers them. It promises to be one of the few indispensable works on the modern American Army.

RUSSELL F. WEIGLEY
Associate Professor of History
Temple University

ALLAN NEVINS and FRANK ERNEST HILL, in association with MIRA WILKINS, GEORGE B. HELIKER and WILLIAM

GREENLEAF. *Ford: Decline and Rebirth, 1933–1962.* Pp. xviii, 508. New York: Charles Scribner's Sons, 1963. $8.95.

With the publication of *Ford: Decline and Rebirth,* Allan Nevins and Frank Hill have completed their three-volume study of Henry Ford and the Ford Motor Company. And what a significant study of one of the greatest business empires of the United States this is! In the sense that this study was initiated by the company, it is an authorized biography, but the authors have used the company's archives thoroughly and objectively. No skeletons remain in the corporation's closet. There are no sentimental attachments, no glossing over of Mr. Ford's errors, no lauding of his genius, no significant omissions. Indeed, this biography of the man, his economic empire, and his times will remain as a milepost along the highway of studies of American business.

In this volume, as in the two previous ones, the authors have written not only scientifically, but in a most readable style. This book traces the disintegration of the Ford Motor Company from 1933 until World War II, a period when the company dropped from first to third among automobile manufacturers. Among the causes of the decline were lack of effective organization, gaps in basic equipment, a dearth of university-trained engineers, Ford's frequent petty interference, his set ideas that prevented his exploiting the advances of his competitors, his failing health, and the destructive plotting of Harry Bennett, who was officially director of personnel but was actually a pistol-packing, antilabor ruffian. Bennett gained and maintained an inconceivable hold over Mr. Ford during these years. Bennett was able to fire competent, talented men and to hire mediocre stooges in their places. He even supplanted the able, humane Edsel Ford with his father. The Ford Motor Company came very near bankruptcy and disintegration.

In 1944, Henry Ford II, the founder's grandson, became president of the vast international economic empire and began a new era in its unusual history. When young Ford took over the reins of control, he was handicapped by reconversion from war to peace production, by an unbelievable lack of accurate accounts and basic planning, by the general inefficiency of Bennett's henchmen, and by a restrictive price structure imposed by the Office of Price Administration. With Henry Ford II's decisive victory in 1945 over Bennett and his reactionary lieutanants, with the hiring of young, aggressive men and the delegation to them of the power to revitalize the corporation, with the creation of the Ford Foundation that preserved family control, with the engineering and promotional successes—there was the costly failure of the Edsel, however—with the shifting of the personal corporation to a public corporation in 1956 and the sale of millions of shares of stock, the dynamic and energetic Henry Ford II became one of America's foremost business leaders.

There is no better entreé to learning about and understanding giant corporate empires than reading this excellent biography of a mechanical genius and the economic empire which he founded. The authors have done themselves, the Ford Motor Company, and American scholarship a distinct service.

GEORGE OSBORN
Professor of Social Science
University of Florida

HANNAH ARENDT. *Eichmann in Jerusalem: A Report on the Banality of Evil.* Pp. 275. New York: Viking Press, 1963. $5.50.

This book is a brilliantly written set of observations and reflections on the Jerusalem trial and the events that brought it about. Written originally for *The New Yorker*, it is in the distinguished tradition of trial reports which Rebecca West established there some twenty-five years ago. Miss Arendt's book is one of three so far to appear on the Eichmann trial; the other two are *The Trial of Adolf Eichmann* by Lord Russel of Liverpool (no relation to Bertrand) and *The Capture and Trial of Adolf Eichmann* by Moshe Pearlman, who is identified as "director of information services in Israel." In contrast to these two books, which attempted to do little

more than to present the prosecutor's case, Miss Arendt has courageously confronted also some of the complexities of the case. Not that she does not share the world's pity and horror over the Jewish catastrophe and the unmitigable guilt of its major perpetrators; she leaves no doubt about this. She also points to the continuing hold these evil men still have on some of West Germany's power positions, and she even approves, rather thoughtlessly it would seem to me, of Eichmann's execution. She is satisfied that the "long forgotten propositions of . . . vengeance and retribution" in this case "supremely justify" the verdict "that Eichmann must hang."

Nevertheless, the reaction which this book evoked from the Jewish community was—overwhelming fury: a flood of letters to the editors, reviews, articles, even a public speaker sent up all the way from Israel. A late reviewer is, therefore, greatly moved to take this reaction as a clue to the book's major significance. The reasons for the uproar would seem to lie both with Miss Arendt's book and with its Jewish audience. It is not difficult to see the reasons in the book. In essence, it is her refusal to let the enormity of the horrifying crimes blind her perception of the ambiguities of the trial. To begin with, she marks the incongruity between the vastness of the holocaust and the almost ludicrous mediocrity of the man charged there with having caused it. Secondly, as the prosecution witnesses told how the Jewish communities met the onslaught, she ponders once more on the strange bonds that tied some of the victims to their murderers, such as the Hungarian deal or the round-up of Jews by Jewish functionaries in Berlin and elsewhere. She queries whether the local Jewish leadership had always acted wisely, and concludes that it had not. And she reminds us that even the ultimate Jewish situation still contains traces of the poison: the Israel laws against intermarriage evoke uncomfortable associations.

The reasons for the violent reaction that lie with the Jewish audience would seem to be more complex. There must be, first, pain and memory still so fresh and terrible that any pointing to ambiguities is experienced as an attempt to absolve the murderers. And, if such pointing is done by as sharp and ruthless a pen as Miss Arendt's, the pain apparently becomes unbearable. There is no doubt that she should have been more gentle, more aware of the open wounds, and more charitable to those who, in retrospect, can be charged with error and guilt.

But this cannot be the whole story; the Jewish reaction, while spontaneous enough, had also, one cannot help sensing, its political undercurrents. The all too systematic annihilation of Miss Arendt is in too strange a contrast to the case of another much more severe Jewish critic of the Jews. For years now, Bruno Bettelheim has done what Miss Arendt is unfairly being accused of: he has blamed the Jewish victims quite generally for having contributed in a major way to their own disaster. That perverse accusation never evoked anything like the furor against Miss Arendt. One is, therefore, forced to conclude that it is not only her concern with the moral ambiguities that caused the tumult, but her attack on the political foundations which the Eichmann trial was to re-enforce. Political trials are always dangerous to those who arrange them even if, as in this case, the defendant's guilt was clear long before the trial began. From Hannah Arendt's report it would seem that some of these dangers have materialized.

As to the historical truth, Miss Arendt's highly impressionistic book cannot pretend to tell the whole complex story. Technically, being a report on what witnesses in a trial and other people elsewhere reported, hers is often hearsay evidence twice removed. There will be other books that will, if she erred, set the record straight. But whatever her bias was, if there was one, the Jewish reaction to the book was improper and bodes ill if it is to set a pattern for things to come. If we really want to know the whole story of that terrible decade in which humanity broke down, we shall have to listen to more than the nursery tale that it is only the Eichmanns who must bear the guilt. There will be more to listen to; and we should be prepared to listen, with patience and respect, to those who tell us of our stony hearts and our political silence. But for such rare men as the royal Christian of Denmark, we all failed, one another.

HANS ZEISEL
University of Chicago Law School

H. G. RICHARDSON and G. O. SAYLES. *The Governance of Mediaeval England from the Conquest to Magna Carta.* Pp. vii, 514. Edinburgh: Edinburgh University Press, 1963. $12.50.

A historian of the old school easily imagines a kindly, gentle, well-seasoned English clergymen—headed for a bishopric —by the name of William Stubbs turning over the old chronicles and puzzling out obscure medieval records to publish forth the epic story of England's early steps toward law, order, and democracy. His three substantial volumes established him as a kind of father-figure in the sphere of this fascinating study. But the day has long seemed gone when his pronouncements were taken as unassailable gospel. The myth of the primitive German mark as the fount and origin of democracy, for example, has for many years had only the interest attaching to a curious fossil. It comes, therefore, as a shock to find a stout and serious book devoted to belaboring our venerable friend.

But as we read we begin to wonder whether Richardson and Sayles may not have at least a little reason for charging that later historians have retained some bias from that source. Central to their version is a demonstration that preconquest English institutions continued to operate vigorously after 1066. This involves a more-or-less complete elimination of any real feudalism from the story. For the most part, the Norman kings, instead of heading feudal armies, hired their fighting men. Military tenure supplied little but a modest financial claim and a terminology which became permanent in the land law. Perhaps to some extent this is a matter of dispute over definitions, and Richardson and Sayles themselves find it inconvenient to get along without the word "feudalism," albeit in quotation marks.

William the Conqueror being thus demoted from the role of statesmanlike reformer, the great administrative changes of the twelfth century require even more emphasis than that which they usually receive. But our authors continue to lay about themselves with a will. The whole financial machinery is repictured, the Exchequer, beloved of old for its chessboard, is reduced in importance, the Chamber becomes the dominant body, and the Justiciar the key figure. After this forceful piece of remodelling, we are not greatly surprised to find that bad King John is almost rehabilitated and the "bitter, self-righteous" Archbishop Langton is given only a minor part in the story of Magna Carta, which, interestingly enough, retains the moderate significance to which several generations of research have relegated it.

On the whole, though at times we are inclined to deprecate the merciless flaying of Stubbs, our authors have given us a refreshing book.

CHESTER H. KIRBY
Professor of History
Brown University

EDMUND BURKE. *The Correspondence of Edmund Burke,* Vol. IV: *July 1778– June 1782.* Edited by John A. Woods. Pp. xxiv, 474. Chicago: University of Chicago Press, 1963. $12.00.

Scholarly interest in Edmund Burke, stimulated by the availability, since 1948, of the Burke papers in the Fitzwilliam Collection, now on deposit with the Sheffield City Libraries and with the Northamptonshire Record Office, shows no sign of abating. Anthologies of Burke's speeches and writings, biographical studies of various aspects of his life, articles without end in professional journals—to keep abreast of this flood of material one must consult regularly the Burke Newsletter, dating from 1959 and, since 1962, an independent quarterly. The latest manifestation of this renaissance is in the Burke Symposium held in December 1963 at Georgetown University.

In all this activity the central enterprise remains the preparation of the definitive edition of all extent Burke correspond-

ence. It is indeed a delight, as suggested by a reviewer of an earlier volume, to add this, the fourth of ten projected volumes, to the lengthening shelf of a handsome and impeccable work of scholarship. For the years spanned in this volume, 1778– 1782, 227 Burke letters are assembled, 125 in print for the first time. This, coupled with the fact that of the 55 letters addressed to Burke 46 are entirely new, signifies that in this volume a much greater proportion of the correspondence than in previous volumes is published for the first time.

In a brief notice one can call attention only to its general character. No one theme gives unity to these letters, for Burke, as always, was interested in a variety of issues. Correspondence with friends in his Bristol constituency is the most extensive—the total quantity of letters sharply diminishes when this connection is broken in 1780—though for the most part useful only in showing the ties between a member of Parliament and a commercial constituency, and in this case a popular constituency with an electorate of about 5,000. Limited correspondence with members of the North government includes some exchanges concerning the Gordon Riots of 1780—Burke himself confronted the rioters. The reader is also stirred by Burke's conviction in the midst of his concern for religious toleration. "Wherever [in religion] they [my detractors] choose to place me, I am sure to be found in extraordinary good Company."

The bulk of the correspondence relates to Burke's significant role in shaping the policy of the Parliamentary Opposition. So we find him restless and energetic in the county petitioning movement. His agitation for administrative reform rather than parliamentary reform came to fruition in legislation during the brief second Rockingham ministry formed in March 1782, legislation which, though modest in itself, did inaugurate a long series of reforms. On such matters the letters now so readily accessible are very useful. But as in the earlier volumes, we are merely tantalized by the brief glimpses afforded of Burke's private life and of his association with the intellectual and artistic world of his time.

ALFRED F. HAVIGHURST
Professor of History
Amherst College

NOBLE E. CUNNINGHAM, JR. *The Jeffersonian Republicans in Power: Party Operations, 1801–1809.* Pp. x, 318. Chapel Hill: University of North Carolina Press, for the Institute of Early American Culture, Williamsburg, Virginia, 1963. $7.50.

This meticulous examination of the Democratic party during Jefferson's eight years as president continues Professor Cunningham's study of the practical functioning of the party begun in his *The Jeffersonian Republicans: The Formation of the Party Organization, 1789–1801,* which was published in 1957. Jefferson's inauguration marked a transfer of political power, possibly more epoch-making than the recent one from Kennedy to Johnson, because it was the first to a different political party. Like Kennedy and other presidents, Jefferson discovered that implementing a party's program and maintaining party unity were more difficult achievements than he had anticipated. Jefferson emerges, however, from Professor Cunningham's investigations as a consummate politician capable of holding his party together nationally, at least partly by his skill at retaining the loyalty of virtually all sides in the acrimonious intraparty fights in the states.

As the author shows, Jefferson, although utilizing the power of patronage for party advantage, remembered his responsibilities in using this power. Consequently he was censured almost as severely by members of his own party for not ousting practically all Federalists from office as he was by his political opponents for making too many dismissals for partisan reasons. Jefferson appreciated, used, and contributed to the Republican-party press both as an instrument for party purposes and as a means of developing an informed public that would be a bulwark of democratic government.

Readers can learn from this volume that the Republican members of Congress supplied the national party organization of the Jeffersonian party; that the party's machinery in the middle states, in the main, displayed less centralization and more popular participation in party activities and decision than in the New England states; and that, with the exception of Virginia, the formal machinery of the Republican party was less fully developed in the South and the West than in the other sections of the country.

This book should force historians and lexicographers to write more comprehensive and precise definitions of "Quids" than is now available. From our present historical dictionaries and history textbooks no one would suspect that the Quids were, as Professor Cunningham describes in detail, an important political force in Pennsylvania, as well as in New York State, and one that did not support John Randolph.

Everyone who contributed to the publication of this book deserves to be congratulated.

CARROL H. QUENZEL
Professor of History
Mary Washington College
University of Virginia

H. WAYNE MORGAN (Ed.). *The Gilded Age: A Reappraisal.* Pp. vii, 286. Syracuse, N. Y.: Syracuse University Press, 1963. $5.50.

The Gilded Age is a term invented by Mark Twain to apply to the quarter-century of American history following the Civil War. H. Wayne Morgan, of the Department of History, University of Texas, organized this reappraisal by inviting to write essays nine scholars whose main interests, like his own, lay in this period. He contributed the first one, entitled "An Age in Need of Reassessment: *A View Beforehand.*" This symposium was not designed to attack previous interpretations, but to take advantage of the right of every generation to rewrite history. In this attempt, however, there was a certain feeling that historians, and especially textbook-writers, had, without further research, accepted clichés and interpretations which someone else had set up. The Gilded Age term has generally been accepted as one of opprobrium, but out of these ten essays there has evolved what amounts to a defense; for the editor hoped "to show where and how we feel the facts and interpretations concerning these topics specifically and the period generally have been misused or misunderstood." Although it was not intended that a complete history of this quarter-century be written, the parts taken up touch upon the more fundamental aspects of the times.

The chapter on big business, by John Tipple, is an excellent synthesis of what has been written about corporations, but with the author's own interpretations, which are more judicious and friendly. Herbert G. Gutman shows that there was much more to the labor picture than merely the activities of labor organizations and their well-publicized strikes. Ari Hoogenboom takes to task the chief civil-service reformers as having turned to reform agitation only after failures in other endeavors. Vincent P. De Santis has a good word for the Republican party during this period, for having done as well as it did, considering the fact that most of the time it had no majority in Congress. Money was visualized by those of the Gilded Age as the cure-all of their ills, according to Paolo E. Coletta. There was much more to American interest and accomplishments in foreign affairs, says Milton Plesur, than has been generally stated. Robert R. Roberts defends rather convincingly the public taste in literature, architecture, and other cultural expressions. Robert Falk develops a well-rounded discussion of the "Search for Reality," which characterized many of the best-known writers of the Gilded Age, and Paul Boller, Jr. handles, in a very readable essay, the contributions of American scientists, and especially their reaction to Darwinianism.

As a reappraisal and for the most part a defense of the Gilded Age, this volume is a distinct contribution to American history and is a credit to the bold and uninhibited thinking of ten young scholars.

E. MERTON COULTER
Regents' Professor Emeritus
of History
University of Georgia

GEORGE SANSOM. *A History of Japan, 1615–1867.* Pp. xii, 258. Stanford, Calif.: Stanford University Press, 1963. $7.50.

At last Sir George Sansom's third and final volume, completing the history of Japan from earliest times to 1867, has appeared. These three volumes represent the mature views of a distinguished historian from the vantage point of a long career in Japanese studies. Written in the elegant and lucid prose that has become for a generation of students the hallmark of Sir George's writing, all three volumes are indispensable for students of Japan.

A History of Japan, 1615–1867 presents in chronological order the course of Tokugawa rule by the shoguns who presided over the military government in Edo, beginning with Ieyasu's establishment of the *bakufu,* through the highpoint in the first half of the eighteenth century of the eighth shogun, Yoshimune, to the ultimate demise of military government after Keiki. Political history shares the field with economic and social history, emphasis being laid on the problems of taxation, money currency, speculation, land allotment, rural society, and the like. Although it was not the author's stated purpose to write a cultural history, one misses even a cursory treatment of the arts, religion, literature, and thought. However, some consideration is given to the "official" neo-Confucian system espoused by the Tokugawas. One hopes that it will be possible for Sir George to provide at some future date a comprehensive survey of the nonpolitical, noneconomic aspects of the Edo period.

One of the interesting features that come out of a reading of this history is just how the economic aspects of Tokugawa rule went hand in hand with their political handling of the country. The place of the Tokugawa family was assured, politically, by control in power over all barons, whether these latter were traditionally allegiant to the Tokugawas or not: such methods as the division into groups of inner and outer lords, demanding of alternate attendance at Edo, censorship, and the like, are well known. Perhaps less well-known to the political historian is the progressive policy of escheatment followed successively by the early shoguns. For example, the chief item of annual revenue for the *bakufu* was the rice grown in lands owned by the Tokugawa family. Rice income in 1590 was assessed at about one million *koku*— of five bushels; by 1598 it had been increased to over two and a half millions; after Sekigahara (1600) Ieyasu was able to bring it to some six millions. By the end of the seventeenth century, after continuous escheatment, Tokugawa income reached close to seventeen million *koku*, well over half of the total revenue of the whole country, which was assessed at about 26 million *koku*.

Students of Japan, especially those interested in Tokugawa history, are indebted to Sir George for a distinguished and valuable treatment of the political, social, and economic history of the Edo *bakufu*.

E. DALE SAUNDERS
University of Pennsylvania

WILLIAM L. NEUMANN. *America Encounters Japan: From Perry to MacArthur.* Pp. viii, 353. Baltimore: Johns Hopkins Press, 1963. $6.50.

The author's thesis is that, under a wise policy, the United States, without surrender of vital interests, could have avoided war with Japan and, after 1949, "the breakdown of political and economic relations with China." He does not define what interests he considers vital, nor does his scholarly review of the ideas and attitudes that influenced American policy explain how he arrived at his conclusions.

Dr. Neumann is right in his estimate of the unfortunate effect on the Japanese people of our disregard for their interests and susceptibilities in our policies following the Washington Conference of 1922. The settlements reached there had provided a foundation and an atmosphere for rearing a solid structure of peace in the Far East. One item in the settlements was the Nine Power Treaty, in which were embodied the essential principles of our historic Far Eastern policy. Japan, then under a moderate civilian cabinet, was one of the signatories. Our subsequent actions, especially our tariff raises and discriminatory immigration enactments, were a shabby reciprocation of the good will Japan had manifested. By retiring into the shell of short-sighted isolationism, we contributed to the undermining of the influence of Japan's moderate group and lost what was undoubtedly our last opportunity to contribute constructively to peace.

The Japanese militarists, spearheaded by extremists, returned to power in 1927, broke loose from the Nine Power Treaty in 1931 by occupying Manchuria, and with the progressive extension of their control in China flagrantly violated American rights there. American protests went unheeded. In 1940, Japan joined Germany and Italy in a Tripartite Alliance aimed clearly at the United States, and the partners announced their purpose of creating a "new order" in the world. In 1941, Japan insisted upon our agreeing, among other things, to stop aiding China if China failed to accept Japan's peace terms. The issue was not of American wishes as to Japan's terms but one of whether, in a negotiation free from duress, China would accept them. If we had yielded to Japan's demands we would have become a party to Japan's aggression and have shared responsibility for violation of the Nine Power Treaty. We refused, and Japan answered with Pearl Harbor. How could we have done otherwise?

In regard to the second point of Dr. Neumann's thesis, this question arises: What possible room was there for an accommodation of interests with a regime which had consistently proclaimed its purpose to destroy us?

JOSEPH W. BALLANTINE
New York University

GERALD E. WHEELER. *Prelude to Pearl Harbor: The United States Navy and the Far East, 1921–1931.* Pp. xii, 212. Columbia: University of Missouri Press, 1963. $5.95.

In the Prelude, the author states the thesis of his book: "During the years 1921 to 1931 American naval leaders . . . were convinced that the United States had a national enemy in Japan. But the United States Congress, like the public that elected it during the 1920's, were less than impressed; in fact it was positively hostile to any suggestion that America might again go to war. . . . How the United States Navy solved its problem of preparing for war in an unsympathetic climate of opinion is the story here presented." The United States Navy, both for planning for possible future conflicts and for defense of its appropriations by Congress, generally voiced an expert and considered opinion of what was needed to defend and maintain the foreign policy of the United States. For many years, this meant the defense of the Philippines and the Hawaiian Islands and the Open Door policy regarding China.

From the first chapter, "The Commitments of American Far Eastern Policy: China and the Philippine Islands" to "The State Department Takes the Helm: The London Naval Conference," the author, step-by-step, and with a wealth of reference and documentation, takes us from a point of lack of interest of Congress in a strong Navy to protect the foreign policies of the United States and provide for its defense in the Orient onward to the cruiser controversy at the London Naval Conference in 1930. Those who have wondered what was done by the Navy before Pearl Harbor in the way of war plans against its logical "enemy" Japan will find most interesting a chapter on "Fleet Reorganizations and War Planning." The excellent work of the "elders," General Board of the Navy, now abolished, is indicated by comment and reference. The prescience of certain naval officers in predicting what might take place and did take place is of interest in the light of history.

The volume summarizes a most important segment of our history prior to World War II, and, with its summation and its comprehensive bibliography, is a must for those who are writing or who plan to write on aspects of our prewar Far Eastern policy. In reality, it is the factual essence of the stormy history of how our Navy planned to "meet its hypothetical enemy in the Far East with reasonable assurance of victory at sea."

LELAND P. LOVETTE
Vice-Admiral (Retired)
United States Navy

ARTHUR A. EKIRCH, JR. *Man and Nature in America.* Pp. viii, 231. New York: Columbia University Press, 1963. $4.50.

Those who read Professor Ekirch's *Idea of Progress in America, 1815–1860* will not be surprised that his new book deals with the evolution of another of the ideas that have contributed to what modern authors have called the American mind, the American character, the American image, and even the American dream in their efforts to explain the twentieth-century American and his differences from his contemporaries in other lands. Professor Ekirch emphasizes one aspect of the development of that American in this account of the changing attitude toward the American environment.

The mid-twentieth century American has suddenly become conscious of the necessity of living in harmony and balance with his environment and of the fact that his problems in so doing are the problems of other countries as well. The American dream and the American way of life that have seemed his protection and his peculiar possession now offer no panacea, so this historical account is of value. The author begins with a comment on the revival in the eighteenth century of the Greek concept of design in nature and of the emphasis, therefore, placed by the philosophers and scientists on the laws of nature and upon the idea of God as the giver of those laws. Educated Americans of the period shared these ideas and were deeply impressed by the resources and productivity of the part of the world in which it was their happy lot to live. Their success in the Revolution and the rapid expansion of the country increased this feeling of the unique position of the United States, and the writings of the European travelers in America confirmed them in their conviction that their position in the world was one of especial advantage. Democratic institutions, abundance, and limitless opportunity became the bases for the American dream.

Never, however, were Americans single-minded in regard to the environment. Professor Ekirch shows that from the beginning the philosophic and romantic ideas about the American environment differed widely from the practical and ecomomic views. While the philosophers and poets called attention to the ideas of harmony and balance between man and nature and the artists and novelists emphasized the beauties and romantic qualities of the American environment, the practical American proceeded to exploit that environment and to appropriate the largesse of nature with little thought for either romance or posterity. Rousseau's idea of the Noble Savage had no adherents, and the violence of the frontier was shown in the relations of the frontiersmen with the Indians, and indeed with each other, and in their attitudes toward the resources of the land.

The author, having made this distinction between the concept of man living in harmony and balance with his environment and the fact of his reckless exploitation of that environment, goes on to discuss the early conservationists who realized the results of such exploitation and then takes up the ideas of those who felt that men could shape the environment to their needs. It is a far cry from Thoreau to Lester Frank Ward, but the chapter on the Transcendentalists is followed by those on conservation and on a planned society, thus indicating the rapid changes in American thought in regard to the relation between man and nature.

The latter part of this interesting historical survey is devoted to the pressing problems of the twentieth century—technology, increasing population, preservation of national resources, and recurring wars—and ends with a chapter on the dangers to civilization and even the existence of man on this planet in the new atomic age. "Plainly," Professor Ekirch says, "either a nuclear war or the maintenance of the twentieth century high rate of population growth would, in two drastically different ways, bring about the effective collapse of civilization." Therefore, "the idea of man living in balance with nature offered the most hopeful course of action for the future . . . and held out the key to a harmonious, peaceful and truly civilized world."

ALICE FELT TYLER
Professor of History (Retired)
University of Minnesota

MERLE CURTI. *American Philanthropy Abroad: A History.* Pp. xix, 651. New Brunswick, N. J.: Rutgers University Press, 1963. $12.50.

Merle Curti, Frederick Jackson Turner professor of history at the University of Wisconsin, provides in this volume the first full-scale review of the development of American philanthropy abroad. He deals with the subject not only chronologically, but also thematically, and examines briefly the "charitable impulses" that underlie America's bent to assist the world outside its borders. Appropriately, the research on which the volume was based, was sponsored by a grant from the Ford Foundation.

Dr. Curti stresses the growth not only in the size of American assistance abroad, but also in its institutionalization. Tracing American philanthropy abroad from its beginnings, through help to the Greek revolutions and to the great Irish famine, he continues through the tremendous efforts organized after World War I and World War II. These private efforts, it can be assumed, developed a certain core of experience upon which UNRRA and other governmental programs were built.

In later chapters the author confesses his perplexity that private giving, as organized and conducted by the large American foundations, has perhaps more in common with public assistance abroad, as in governmental disaster-relief programs and in the United States foreign-aid program, than it does with the individually oriented efforts of the past. He speculates only briefly, however, on the motives of American philanthropy abroad: religious duty in overseas missionary efforts, personal sympathies felt by American national groups toward the homeland, the effects of plain humanitarianism, and, in the twentieth century, a sense of guilt over the contrast between the "affluent society" and poverty elsewhere.

The author does not speculate as to the deeper motives: whether there is anything special about American philanthropy abroad, in comparison with other societies, or whether it reveals anything about the contradictory and puzzling aspects of the American character in mid-twentieth century. Why is it, for example, that Americans are satisfied to hold up one standard of performance for large-scale expenditures abroad when given through private channels, and another when given through public channels? Is "charity" sufficient for private giving when the "national interest" is the minimal requirement for public assistance? Do these yardsticks mean anything, for example, in terms of the development needs of underdeveloped societies?.

The author rightly points out that an assessment of American overseas philanthropy is difficult. Here the author found the reluctance of voluntary agencies to conduct self-evaluations, although understandable, especially regrettable. Overseas testimonials of appreciation were abundant, but not to be taken at face value; published reports of foundations were helpful, but incomplete; and the more potentially useful sources of information, for example, foundation archives, were essentially closed. No doubt some of the large foundations, those with operating programs, have a problem in this respect somewhat similar to that of the government. But with due passage of time it would appear that access to all pertinent information could be made available to qualified scholars.

Any attempt to assess the impact of overseas philanthropy, however, involves focusing on the effects of American support, as against the efforts of host nationals and host governments and other outside sources of support. This is a ticklish problem, requiring research methods not yet available, or not fully enough refined to be reliable.

The book is packed with an amount of factual information that is impressive. A certain disappointment arises over the author's reluctance to draw major evaluative conclusions, even in terms of personal judgment, of the role of private overseas philanthropy in American life. The record, so to speak, is here; the major lessons of that record are still to be drawn.

CLARENCE E. THURBER
Associate Professor of Political
Science and Public Administration
Pennsylvania State University

OWEN LATTIMORE. *Studies in Frontier History: Collected Papers, 1929–1958.* Pp. 565. New York: Oxford University Press, 1963. $12.00.

Owen Lattimore is probably the last of the "explorers" of Central Asia. In many ways, he can be compared to men like Sven Hedin, W. Filchnet, and Aurel Stein. Like them, he was not academically prepared when he began his work in innermost Asia. He was interested in some aspects of nomadic life and soon found himself captured by the nomadic style of life. Like the other explorers, he devoted his life to this field and acquired the knowledge of languages and of earlier research. And, like them, he has written not only popular books which were great successes, but also scholarly essays and books which have greatly contributed to our understanding. The essays which are republished in this collection allow us to see clearly the main fields in which Lattimore has been a pace-maker.

In my opinion, his three most important contributions to Asian studies were the following. First, Lattimore developed the concept of the frontier in its specific application to conditions in Inner Asia. He was the first one who tore down the Chinese Wall by proving that neither the Great Wall nor any other state border ever was a border in our present-day sense and that, therefore, the concept of a stable state border has to be replaced by the dynamic concept of a frontier. He finds a whole zone, largely, but not completely, defined by geographical characteristics, in which non-Chinese nomads as well as Chinese farmers can make a living and in which various types of interaction, leading to various kinds of assimilation, acculturation, even to merger, have occurred and still occur. If the history of China's north is analyzed in the light of this concept of the frontier, many of the events in earlier times become understandable. But even events of the present time, for instance, the struggle between China and Soviet Russia and the role of Russian Turks and Chinese Turks (Uigurs) in this struggle, can well be interpreted with the help of Lattimore's frontier theory.

Second, Lattimore discovered a new direction of developments in East and Central Asia. In their study of China, Western scholars have usually looked at China from the East, the coast; they tended to understand China as a nation acting or reacting against pressures coming from the sea. Lattimore was the first who pointed out that, during most of its history, China looked toward the West, toward Central Asia. Central Asia was the critical area from which cultural influences as well as military dangers came. For only in about the last two centuries did the seacoast of China become critically important. Lattimore's third major contribution concerns the study of feudalism. Only in recent times have the questions of feudalism in the Far East and of nomadic feudalism been raised. Here, Lattimore created the concept of frontier feudalism. Two earlier theories about feudalism remain important: the French theory of feudalism as a result of the breakdown of an earlier, centralized state and the German theory of feudalism as a result of super-stratification by conquest. Lattimore tried to show that along the frontiers of a bureaucratic centralized state like the Imperial Chinese state, smaller organized societies tend to appear which show feudal characteristics, but are neither the result of a breakdown of authority nor the result of super-stratification. He has thus far applied this insight only to conditions along the northern borders of China; I think it could also be applied very well to conditions along the Chinese-Burmese and Chinese-Thai borders. At the same time, by using a fairly narrow, concise definition of feudalism, Lattimore has rejected the concept of a "nomadic feudalism" based upon the granting of cattle instead of the enfeoffment with land as practiced in agricultural countries.

The essays do not represent all work done by Lattimore in the last thirty years. He has made a selection and, in my opinion, he chose his best articles. In his mainly autobiographical introduction, he indicates that the essays contain repetitions as well as stages of the development of his ideas. I do not find the repetitions are very noticeable. Even when one reads one essay after the other, each one stands out by reason of its own importance. All of them are scholarly articles; all of them are permeated with something that not many other specialists in the field can claim, namely, long, personal, and intimate experience with the Asian countries and their inhabitants. While Lattimore appears in this book as a cultural historian, he differs from other cultural historians in his constant stress of the importance of geographical factors. Yet, he cannot be called a geographical determinist.

WOLFRAM EBERHARD
Professor of Sociology
University of California
Berkeley

EDWARD CRANKSHAW. *The Fall of the House of Habsburg.* Pp. xi, 459. New York: Viking Press, 1963. $7.50.

The dissolution of the Habsburg Empire on the one hand, and the biography of Francis Joseph on the other, have been subjects of numerous books. But in no other study demanding serious attention have the two topics been so closely integrated or so conspicuously treated in terms of each other. In this lies perhaps the greatest fault of the book. Whether the "tragic hero" type of historiography has much merit or not is open to debate, but that Francis Joseph does not satisfyingly fit such a role should by now be clear to historians. To overvalue the monarch may be venial, possibly even tempting, but to give his regime credit for the rationality of the "Habsburg system" and then to imply that this system was swathed in ambiguities is a strange inconsistency.

Typical of the spirit of the book is the title of the Epilogue: *"Finis Austriae"*— as if Republican Austria had never been born! If certain overzealous Austrian Socialists today claim that Austrian history began in 1918, ultraconservatives and would-be-legitimists surely err on the other side. If 1918 was to Crankshaw an unmitigated disaster, 1848 was almost as bad. The neoabsolutism following the Revolution of 1848 receives more excuses than most historians would be willing to give it. The remainder of the Empire's life is described too much in terms of the military and the personal aspects of history, and not enough in sociological and economic terms. This is understandable in an author who overestimates the impact of the Emperor and his family on the course of history.

The book is lightweight but very readable, occasionally even enjoyable. The author should not be blamed for letting history speak out her lesson to a contemporary Europe groping for a political solution. It is only when that lesson is neither sharp enough nor rich enough that the critic must protest. The professional historian reading this book can probably take care of himself, but the layman may be thrown off the track by some of Crankshaw's turgid explanations of the decline and fall of Austria-Hungary. It may be asked, incidentally, why some British historians—Crankshaw is not alone —are so smitten with everything that is archconservative in Austrian history.

Readers of Crankshaw's very stimulating and astute works on Soviet Russia may wonder why this excursion into Habsburg territory was written.

ROBERT SCHWARZ
Associate Professor of History
Carnegie Institute of Technology

JACOB WALKIN. *The Rise of Democracy in Pre-Revolutionary Russia: Political and Social Institutions under the Last Three Czars.* Pp. viii, 320. New York: Frederick A. Praeger, 1962. $6.50.

The volume under review sets forth several ambitious aims. The more important of these seem to be (1) to present a kind of institutional history or sociological analysis of Russia since the rise of the Muscovite state; (2) to offer a "full explanation of the special features of Russian civilization . . . to Western readers without prior familiarity with the subject"; (3) to analyze in some detail Russian political and social institutions under Alexander II, Alexander III, and Nicholas II; and (4) to explain why the Bolsheviks succeeded in 1917 and why the Soviet regime is an imposed one, in no way indigenous to the Russian people. In this reviewer's opinion, Dr. Walkin succeeds mainly in the third aim.

The sociological analysis of Russian history centers in a discussion of state and society. Dr. Walkin wants to show that the Muscovite Grand Princes and Tsars unified and expanded the realm and defended Russia against numerous threatening external enemies. In performing these positive functions, the rulers found their *raison d'être* in the nation. The state became abnormally powerful, and society was as nothing in relation to the state. Only when the foreign military dangers had passed—sometime early in the nineteenth century, Dr. Walkin suggests—could society begin to generate an independent life or movement against the Tsardom. The autocracy, in turn, leaned ever more heavily upon the bureaucracy for support. Thus, as the nineteenth century progressed, the situation became one in which the immovable object and the irresistible force contended. Within this theoretical framework, the author explains the actualization of the Great Reforms of the Tsar-liberator Alexander II and, conversely, the "Liberation Movement" and Revolution of 1905 against the stubborn Nicholas II and his bureaucratic entourage.

This rather engaging schematization is, finally, too constricting. Omitted from Dr. Walkin's exposition of the development of the Muscovite state and society therein are the relationships of these elements to Russian expansion, east, north, and south: the Cossacks, the Old Believers, the great servile uprisings, the nationalities—especially the Poles—and foreign policy generally. The student is often beguiled into forgetting these omissions. What of the untutored reader to whom Dr. Walkin also wishes to offer a "full explanation of the special features of Russian civilization"?

The best parts of the book are those sections which, leaving sociological theory aside, deal with the work of the *zemstvo* institutions, the police and press laws, and their enforcement agencies. Noteworthy are the descriptive surveys of the various voluntary associations which proliferated within that marginal area of freedom which existed in late nineteenth-century Russia.

Dr. Walkin's monograph is learned and stimulating, if somewhat naive and tendentious.

DAVID HECHT

Editor-in-Chief
Ken Publishing Company
New York City

ARTHUR E. ADAMS. *Bolsheviks in the Ukraine: The Second Campaign, 1918–1919.* Pp. ix, 440. New Haven: Yale University Press, 1963. $8.75.

This is the third scholarly work in eleven years to deal exclusively with the confusing but significant interregnum in the Ukraine from 1917 to 1920. In his pioneering work *The Ukrainian Revolution, 1917–1920* (Princeton University Press, 1952), John S. Reshetar has provided a firm and lucid basis for studying the veritable maze of events. Eight years later Jurij Borys published his *The Russian Communist Party and the Sovietization of Ukraine* (Stockholm, 1960)—a very thorough and comprehensive analysis of the political forces operative in the Ukraine in those years, with an emphasis on Soviet policy. Unlike the studies by Reshetar and Borys, Arthur E. Adams' book deals with a more limited period of time, six and a half months, from November 1918, when the Bolsheviks started preparations for their second invasion of

the Ukraine, until June 1919, when they were temporarily driven out of the country by peasant uprisings, the White Volunteer Army of Denikin, and Ukrainian nationalist forces. This gives Dr. Adams, a professor of Russian history at Michigan State University, the opportunity to paint in vivid colors some details that are only sketched on the broader canvases of Reshetar and Borys. Adams' study has another important advantage: quite deliberately he focuses his attention on the popular masses, the men in the field, and their immediate leaders. The two heroes of the book are the wilful Bolshevik army commander Antonov and his "subordinate," the essentially uncommited Ukrainian partisan leader Grigorev. Lenin, General Denikin, and the Ukrainian nationalist leader Petlyura are all in the background.

Another purpose of the study is to document the political and administrative chaos in which Lenin and Vatsetis—the Bolshevik supreme commander—made their decisions. For example, one Bolshevik organization arranged for the surrender of Nikolaev to themselves, but Grigorev's nominally Bolshevik partisans seized it, nevertheless, and took all the war booty (pp. 174–185). Professor Adams' characterizations of Red, White, and Ukrainian nationalist policies, and particularly that of the half-hearted and ill-informed French intervention in Odessa, are harsh, but deserved. Ample extracts from original sources support him. Possibly, a little more space ought to have been provided to clarify the intricate setting.

In summary, this is a well-written, solidly documented, and thought-provoking book, especially recommended for readers who know the general background. Somewhere between 1917 and 1920, the desire of the Ukrainian popular masses for political freedom was born. Adams' book vividly and authoritatively portrays some of the birth pangs.

YAROSLAV BILINSKY

Assistant Professor
of Political Science
University of Delaware

OTHER BOOKS

ABSHIRE, DAVID M., and RICHARD V. ALLEN (Eds.). *National Security: Political, Military, and Economic Strategies in the Decade Ahead.* Pp. xxxii, 1,039. New York: Frederick A. Praeger, for the Hoover Institution on War, Revolution, and Peace, 1963. $10.00.

ANESAKI, MASAHARU. *Religious Life of the Japanese People.* Revised by Hideo Kishimoto. Pp. 105. Third Edition. Tokyo: Society for International Cultural Relations, 1961. No price.

ARANGO, E. RAMÓN. *Leopold III and the Belgian Royal Question.* Pp. xiii, 234. Baltimore: Johns Hopkins Press, 1963. $6.00.

ARENDT, HANNAH. *On Revolution.* Pp. 343. New York: Viking Press, 1963. $6.50.

BACKSTROM, CHARLES H., and GERALD D. HURSH. *Survey Research.* Pp. xix, 192. Evanston, Ill.: Northwestern University Press, 1963. $5.00 clothbound; $1.95 paperbound.

BARNETT, A. DOAK (Ed.). *Communist Strategies in Asia: A Comparative Analysis of Governments and Parties.* Pp. ix, 293. New York: Frederick A. Praeger, 1963. $6.50 clothbound; $2.50 paper-bound.

BARTH, HANS. *The Idea of Order: Contributions to a Philosophy of Politics.* Translated by Ernest W. Hankamer and William M. Newell. Pp. vii, 209. Dordrecht: D. Reidel, 1960. $4.25.

BATES, J. LEONARD. *The Origins of Teapot Dome: Progressives, Parties, and Petroleum, 1909–1921.* Pp. viii, 278. Urbana: University of Illinois Press, 1963. $7.50.

BERGER, MORROE (Ed.). *The New Metropolis in the Arab World.* Pp. xiv, 254. New York: Allied, 1963. *Rs.* 12.50.

BERNARD, PHILIPPE J. *Destin de la planification soviétique.* Pp. 326. Paris: Les Editions Ouvrières, 1963. F. 20, 40.

BOASSON, CH. *Approaches to the Study of International Relations.* Pp. 100. Assen: Van Gorcum, 1963. No price.

BODMAN, HERBERT L., JR. *Political Factions in Aleppo, 1760–1826.* Pp. xiii, 160. Chapel Hill: University of North Carolina Press, 1963. $2.50.

The Book of Lord Shang: A Classic of the Chinese School of Law. Translated from the Chinese by J. J. L. Duyvendak. Pp. xiv, 346. Reissue. Chicago: University of Chicago Press, 1963. $6.50.

BOULTON, JAMES T. *The Language of Politics in the Age of Wilkes and Burke.* Pp. xiii, 282. Toronto: University of Toronto Press, 1963. $6.75.

BOURNE, RANDOLPH S. *War and the Intellectuals: Essays by Randolph S. Bourne, 1915–1919.* Edited by Carl Resek. Pp. xv, 197. Paper-bound Edition. New York: Harper & Row, 1964. $1.95.

BROCK, W. R. *An American Crisis: Congress and Reconstruction, 1865–1867.* Pp. xii, 312. New York: St Martin's Press, 1963. $10.00.

BRUUN, GEOFFREY, and DWIGHT E. LEE. *The Second World War and After.* Pp. vi, 190. Boston: Houghton Mifflin, 1964. $1.95.

BUCHAN, ALASTAIR, and PHILIP WINDSOR. *Arms and Stability in Europe: A Report.* Pp. x, 236. New York: Frederick A. Praeger, for the Institute of Strategic Studies, 1963. $5.00.

BURCHETT, WILFRED G. *The Furtive War: The United States in Vietnam and Laos.* Pp. 224. New York: International, 1963. $3.95.

BUSEY, JAMES L. *Latin America: Political Institutions and Processes.* Pp. vii, 184. New York: Random House, 1964. $1.95.

BUSIA, K. A. *The Challenge of Africa.* Pp. 150. New York: Frederick A. Praeger, 1962. $4.00.

CASSIRER, ERNST. *The Individual and the Cosmos in Renaissance Philosophy.* Translated by Mario Domandi. Pp. xii, 199. Paper-bound edition. New York: Harper & Row, 1964. $1.95.

CONZE, EDWARD, in collaboration with I. B. HORNER, D. SNELLGROVE, and A. WALEY (Eds.). *Buddhist Texts Through the Ages.* Pp. 322. Paper-bound edition. New York: Harper & Row, 1964. $1.85.

CORBISHLY, THOMAS, S.J. *Roman Catholicism.* Pp. 150. Paper-bound edition. New York: Harper & Row, 1964. 95 cents.

COWLING, MAURICE. *Mill and Liberalism.* Pp. xvii, 161. New York: Cambridge University Press, 1963. $5.00.

DAHL, ROBERT A. *Congress and Foreign Policy.* Pp. x, 305. Paper-bound edition. W. W. Norton, 1964. $1.55.

DE ROMILLY, JACQUELINE. *Thucydides and Athenian Imperialism.* Translated by Philip Thody. Pp. xi, 400. New York: Barnes & Noble, 1963. $10.00.

DERRY, JOHN W. *The Regency Crisis and the Whigs, 1788–1789.* Pp. viii, 244. New York: Cambridge University Press, 1964. $5.50.

Documents and Speeches on Commonwealth Affairs, 1952–1962. Edited by Nicholas Mansergh. Pp. xxi, 775. New York: Oxford University Press, 1963. $13.45.

DREW, KATHERINE FISCHER, and FLOYD SEY-WARD LEAR (Eds.). *Perspectives in Medical History.* Chicago: University of Chicago Press, for William Marsh Rice University, 1963. $4.00.

DUROSELLE, JEAN-BAPTISTE, and JEAN MEY-RIAT. *Les nouveaux états dans les relations internationales.* Pp. 494. Paris: Librairie Armand Colin, 1962. No price.

EAST, W. GORDON. *The Soviet Union.* Pp. 136. Princeton, N. J.: D. Van Nostrand, 1963. $1.45.

EPSTEIN, LEON D. *British Politics in the Suez Crisis.* Pp. xi, 220. Urbana: University of Illinois Press, 1964. $5.00.

EYCK, ERICH. *Bismarck and the German Empire.* Pp. x, 327. Paper-bound edition. New York: W. W. Norton, 1964. $1.65.

EYSENCK, H. J. (Ed.). *Experiments with Drugs: Studies in the Relation between Personality, Learning Theory, and Drug Action.* Pp. xii, 421. New York: The Macmillan Company, 1963. No price.

Foreign Relations of the United States: Diplomatic Papers, 1941, Vol. VI: *The American Republics.* Pp. vi, 622. Washington, D. C.: United States Printing Office, 1963. $2.75.

Foreign Relations of the United States: Diplomatic Papers, 1943, Vol. III: *The British Commonwealth, Eastern Europe, and the Far East.* Pp. vii, 1,151. Washington, D. C.: United States Government Printing Office, 1963. $3.50.

FREMANTLE, ANNE (Ed.). *The Social Teaching of the Church.* Pp. x, 320. New York: New American Library, 1963. 75 cents.

FREYRE, GILBERTO. *The Masters and the Slaves: A Study in the Development of Brazilian Civilization.* Translated from the Portuguese by Samuel Putnam. Pp. 432. Paper-bound edition. New York: Alfred A. Knopf, 1964. $2.95.

GARAN, D. G. *The Paradox of Pleasure and Relativity: The Psychological Causal Law.* Pp. x, 499. New York: Philosophical Library, 1963. $6.00.

GARDINIER, DAVID E. *Cameroon: United Nations Challenge to French Policy.* Pp. x, 142. New York: Oxford University Press, under the auspices of the Institute of Race Relations, London, 1963. $2.50.

GIRONELLA, JOSÉ M. *On China and Cuba.* Translated by John F. Byrne. Notre Dame, Ind.: Fides, 1963. $3.50.

GOSLIN, DAVID A. *The Search for Ability.* Pp. 204. New York: Russell Sage Foundation, 1963. $4.00.

GOTTLIEB, DAVID, and JON REEVES. *Adolescent Behavior in Urban Areas: A Bibliographic Review and Discussion of the Literature.* Pp. 244. New York: Free Press of Glencoe, 1963. $6.50.

GOULD, THOMAS. *Platonic Love.* Pp. vii, 216. New York: Free Press of Glencoe, 1963. $5.50.

GRAY, DENIS. *Spencer Perceval: The Evangelical Prime Minister, 1762–1812.* Pp. xii, 506. Manchester, England: University of Manchester Press, 1963. $11.00.

GREENE, JACK P. *The Quest for Power: The Lower Houses of Assembly in the Southern Royal Colonies, 1689–1776.* Pp. xi, 528. Chapel Hill: University of North Carolina Press, 1963. $8.50.

GROVES, HAROLD M. *Federal Tax Treatment of the Family.* Pp. xii, 115. Washington, D. C.: Brookings Institution, 1963. No price.

The Growth of World Industry, 1938–1961: National Tables. Pp. xvi, 849. New York: Department of Economic and Social Affairs, Statistical Office of the United Nations, 1963. $10.00.

GUERRY, ÉMILE. *The Popes and World Government.* Translated by Gregory J. Roettger. Pp. xvi, 254. Baltimore: Helicon Press, 1964. $5.50.

HALL, CLAUDE H. *Abel Parker Upshur, Conservative Virginian, 1790–1844.* Pp. vi, 271. Madison: State Historical Society of Wisconsin, 1964. $5.50.

HAMBURGER, JOSEPH. *James Mill and the Art of Revolution.* Pp. xii, 289. New Haven: Yale University Press, 1963. $6.50.

HANSEN, MARCUS LEE. *The Immigrant in American History.* Pp. xi, 230. Paper-bound edition. New York: Harper & Row, 1964. $1.50.

HAVARD, WILLIAM C., RUDOLF HEBERLE, and PERRY H. HOWARD. *The Louisiana Elections of 1960.* Pp. xiii, 126. Baton Rouge: Louisiana State University Press, 1963. $2.00.

HERTZMAN, LEWIS. *DNVP: Right-Wing Opposition in the Weimar Republic, 1918–1924.* Pp. vi, 263. Lincoln: University of Nebraska Press, 1963. $5.00.

HOFFMAN, GEORGE W. *The Balkans in Transition.* Pp. 124. Princeton, N. J.: D. Van Nostrand, 1963. $1.45.

HOLMSTEDT, B., and G. LILJESTRAND, (Eds.). *Readings in Pharmacology.* Pp. x, 395. New York: The Macmillan Company, 1963. $7.50.

HOWARD, HARRY N. *The King-Crane Commission: An American Inquiry in the Middle East.* Pp. xiv, 369. Beirut: Khayats, 1963. No price.

HUTT, W. H. *Keynesianism—Retrospect and Prospect: A Critical Restatement of Basic Economic Principles.* Pp. xi, 447. Chicago: Henry Regnery, 1963. $7.50.

ISIDA, RYUZIRO. *Geography of Japan.* Pp. xi, 124. Tokyo: Society for International Cultural Relations, 1961. $3.50.

JACKSON, HARRY F. *Scholar in the Wilderness: Francis Adrian van der Kemp.* Pp. xi, 356. Syracuse, N. Y.: Syracuse University Press, 1963. $6.95.

JAY, ROBERT R. *Religion and Politics in Rural Central Java.* Pp. viii, 117. New Haven: Southeast Asia Studies, Yale University, 1963. No price.

JOHNS, RAY. *Confronting Organizational Change.* Pp. 160. New York: Association Press, 1963. $4.50.

JOHNSON, ROBERT ERWIN. *Thence Round Cape Horn: The Story of the United States Naval Forces on Pacific Station, 1818–1923.* Pp. xiii, 276. Annapolis: United States Naval Institute, 1963. $7.50.

JOHNSON, STEWART, WARREN A. LAW, JAMES W. MCKIE, D. GALE JOHNSON, JAMES GILLIES, ROBERT C. TURNER, ROSS M. ROBERTSON, and J. FRED WESTON. *Federal Credit Programs.* Pp. 614. Englewood Cliffs, N. J.: Prentice-Hall, 1963. $6.50.

JONES, J. CHRISTOPHER, and D. G. THORNLEY (Eds.). *Conference on Design Methods.* Pp. xiii, 222. New York: The Macmillan Company, 1963. $7.00.

KANT, IMMANUEL. *The Metaphysic of Morals,* Part II: *The Doctrine of Virtue.* Translated by Mary J. Gregor. Reissue. New York: Harper & Row, 1964. $1.85.

KAPP, R. WILLIAM. *Social Costs of Business Enterprise.* Pp. xviii, 311. Second (Revised) Edition. New York: Asia Publishing House, 1963. $8.75.

KARLSSON, GEORG. *Adaptability and Communication in Marriage.* Pp. 89. Second (Revised) Edition. Totowa, N. J.: Bedminster Press, 1963. $4.00.

KATZ, ROBERT L. *Empathy: Its Nature and Uses.* Pp. xii, 210. New York: Free Press of Glencoe, 1963. $4.95.

KEY, V. O., JR. *Politics, Parties, and Pressure Groups.* Pp. xiii, 738. Fifth Edition. New York: Thomas Y. Crowell, 1964. No price.

KIRBY, E. STUART (Ed.). *Contemporary China,* Vol. 5: *1961–1962.* Pp. xiii, 350, iv. New York: Oxford University Press, 1963. $6.00.

KISHORI SARAN LAL. *Twilight of the Sultanate: A Political, Social, and Cultural History of the Sultanate of Delhi from the Invasion of Timur to the Conquest of Babur, 1398–1526.* Pp. xiv, 358. New York: Asia Publishing House, 1963. $13.00.

KITZINGER, U. W. *The Politics and Economics of European Integration: Britain, Europe, and the United States.* Pp. 246. New York: Frederick A. Praeger, 1963. $5.50.

KOMATSU, ISAO. *The Japanese People: Origins of the People and the Language.* Pp. xi, 72. Tokyo: Society for International Cultural Relations, 1962. $2.50.

KOT, STANISLAW. *Conversations with the Kremlin and Dispatches from Russia.* Translated and arranged by H. C. Stevens. Pp. xxx, 285. New York: Oxford University Press, 1963. $5.60.

KULSKI, W. W. *The Soviet Regime: Communism in Practice.* Pp. xii, 444. Fourth Edition. Syracuse, N. Y.: Syracuse University Press, 1963. $8.00 clothbound; $3.95 paper-bound.

LAMB, BEATRICE PITNEY. *India: A World in Transition.* Pp. vii, 374. New York: Frederick A. Praeger, 1963. $6.50.

LARSON, ARTHUR (Ed.). *A Warless World.* Pp. xiii, 209. New York: McGraw-Hill, 1963. $4.95.

LENIN, V. I. *What Is to Be Done?* Translated by S. V. and Patricia Utechin. Edited by S. V. Utechin. Pp. viii, 213. New York: Oxford University Press, 1963. $4.00.

LEWIS, JOHN P. *Quiet Crisis in India: Economic Development and American Policy.* Pp. xiii, 350. Washington, D. C.: Brookings Institution, 1962. $5.75.

LONG, DAVID F. *The Outward View: An Illustrated History of United States Foreign Relations.* Pp. 464. Chicago: Rand, McNally, 1963. $6.95.

LONGRIGG, STEPHEN H. *The Middle East: A Social Geography.* Pp. 291. Chicago: Aldine, 1963. $6.95.

LOW, ALFRED D. *The Soviet Hungarian Republic and the Paris Peace Conference.* Pp. 91. Philadelphia: American Philosophical Society, 1963. $2.50.

LOWITT, RICHARD. *George W. Norris: The Making of a Progressive, 1861–1912.* Pp. xiv, 341. Syracuse, N. Y.: Syracuse University Press, 1963. $7.95.

LURIA, A. R. (Ed.). *The Mentally Retarded Child: Essays Based on the Peculiarities of the Higher Nervous Functioning of Child-Oligophrenics.* Translated from the Russian by W. P. Robinson. Pp. viii, 207. New York: The Macmillan Company, 1963. $7.50.

LURIA, A. R. *Restoration of Function after Brain Injury.* Translated from the Russian by Basil Haigh. Translation edited by O. L.

Zangwill. Pp. xiv, 277. New York: The Macmillan Company, 1963. $10.00.

McDONALD, STEPHEN L. *Federal Tax Treatment of Income from Oil and Gas.* Pp. xv, 163. Washington, D. C.: Brookings Institution, 1963. No price.

MACRIDIS, ROY C., and BERNARD E. BROWN. *Supplement to* The De Gaulle Republic: *Quest for Unity.* Pp. vii, 141. Homewood, Ill.: Dorsey Press, 1963. $1.75.

Madame de Stäel on Politics, Literature and National Character. Translated and edited by Morroe Berger. Pp. viii, 371. Garden City, N. Y.: Doubleday, 1964. $5.50.

MANDEL, BERNARD. *Samuel Gompers: A Biography.* Pp. xii, 566. Yellow Springs, Ohio: Antioch Press, 1963. $8.00.

MARROU, H. I. *A History of Education in Antiquity.* Translated by George Lamb. Pp. xx, 600. Paper-bound edition. New York: New American Library, 1964. 95 cents.

MELADY, THOMAS PATRICK. *Faces of Africa.* Pp. xi, 338. New York: The Macmillan Company, 1964. $7.50.

MELICHAR, EMANUEL. *State Individual Income Taxes: Impact of Alternative Provisions on Burdens, Progression, and Yields.* Pp. vii, 275. Storrs: Storrs Agricultural Experiment Station, University of Connecticut, 1963. $2.50.

MENON, K. P. S. *The Flying Troika: Extracts from a Diary by K. P. S. Menon, India's Ambassador to Russia, 1952–1961.* Pp. xv, 330. New York: Oxford University Press, 1963. $7.00.

MOOG, VIANNA. *Bandeirantes and Pioneers.* Translated from the Portuguese by L. L. Barrett. Pp. 316. New York: George Braziller, 1964. $6.95.

MUELLER, E. W., and GILES C. EKOLA (Eds.). *The Silent Struggle for Mid-America.* Pp. xi, 167. Minneapolis, Minn.: Augsberg, 1963. $3.50.

MULLER, HERBERT J. *Religion and Freedom in the Modern World.* Pp. vii, 129. Chicago: University of Chicago Press, 1963. $3.95.

The New Brahmans: Five Maharashtrian Families. Translated and edited by D. D. Karve, with the assistance of Ellen E. McDonald. Pp. 303. Berkeley and Los Angeles: University of California Press, 1963. $5.50.

NICHOLSON, NORMAN L. *Canada in the American Community.* Pp. 128. Princeton, N. J.: D. Van Nostrand, 1963. $1.45.

NIKHILANANDA, SWAMI (Ed.). *The Upanishads: Katha, Iśa, Kena, Mundaka, Sve-*

tāśvatara, Praśna, Māndukya, Aitareya, Brihadāranyaka, Taittiriya, and Chhandogya. Pp. 392. Paper-bound edition. New York: Harper & Row, 1963. $1.95.

NOCK, ARTHUR DARBY. *Early Gentile Christianity and Its Hellenistic Background.* Pp. xxi, 155. Paper-bound edition. New York: Harper & Row, 1964. $1.45.

NORRIS, JOHN. *Shelburne and Reform.* Pp. xiii, 325. New York: St Martin's Press, 1963. $12.00.

OLSON, PHILIP (Ed.). *America as a Mass Society: Changing Community and Identity.* Pp. xii, 576. New York: Free Press of Glencoe, 1963. $7.95.

PALMER, SPENCER J. (Ed.). *Korean-American Relations: Documents Pertaining to the Far Eastern Diplomacy of the United States,* Vol. II: *The Period of Growing Influence, 1887–1895.* Pp. xii, 389. Berkeley and Los Angeles: University of California Press, 1963. $7.50.

PETROV-SKITALETZ, E. *The Kronstadt Thesis for a Free Russian Government.* Translated from the Russian by John F. O'Conor. Pp. 134. New York: Robert Speller & Sons, 1964. $4.00.

PIDDINGTON, RALPH. *The Psychology of Laughter: A Study in Social Adaptation.* Pp. 224. Second Edition. New York: Gamut Press, 1963. $4.50.

PIEPER, JOSEF. *Leisure: The Basis of Culture.* Translated by Alexander Dru. Pp. ix, 127. Paper-bound edition. New York: New American Library, 1963. 60 cents.

PIKE, FREDERICK B. *The Conflict between Church and State in Latin America.* Pp. ix, 239. New York: Alfred A. Knopf, 1964. $2.50.

PINDER, JOHN. *Europe against De Gaulle.* Pp. viii, 1960. New York: Frederick A. Praeger, 1963. $4.50.

PLAMENATZ, JOHN. *Man and Society: Political and Social Theory,* Vol. I: *Machiavelli through Rousseau;* Vol. II: *Bentham through Marx.* Pp. xxviii, 927. New York: McGraw-Hill, 1963. $5.95 each.

POUNDS, NORMAN J. G., and ROBERT C. KINGSBURY. *An Atlas of European Affairs.* Pp. vii, 135. New York: Frederick A. Praeger, 1964. No price.

QUIROZ, JAVIER ROMERO. *Teotenanco y Matlatzinco (Calixtlahuaca).* Pp. 159. Toluca: Ediciones del Gobierno del Estado de Mexico, 1963. No price.

RAO, V. K. R. V., and DHARM NARAIN. *Foreign Aid and India's Economic Development.* Pp. 111. New York: Asia Publishing House, 1963. $5.25.

RAPPAPORT, ARMIN. *Henry L. Stimson and Japan, 1931–1933.* Chicago: University of Chicago Press, 1963. $6.00.

REID, T. E. H. (Ed.). *Values in Conflict.* Pp. 133. Toronto: University of Toronto Press, for the Canadian Institute of Public Affairs, 1963. $2.00.

ROTH, JULIUS A. *Timetables: Structuring the Passage of Time in Hospital Treatment and Other Careers.* Pp. xix, 124. Indianapolis: Bobbs-Merrill, 1963. $1.95.

RUSHDOONY, ROUSAS JOHN. *The Messianic Character of American Education: Studies in the History of the Philosophy of Education.* Pp. xiv, 410. Nutley, N. J.: Craig Press, 1963. $6.50.

SCALAPINO, ROBERT A. (Ed.). *North Korea Today.* Pp. 141. New York: Frederick A. Praeger, 1963. $4.00.

SHARLIN, HAROLD I. *The Making of the Electrical Age: From the Telegraph to Automation.* Pp. 248. New York: Abelard-Schuman, 1963. $5.95.

SHENOY, B. R. *Indian Planning and Economic Development.* Pp. x, 152. New York: Asia Publishing House, 1963. $6.50.

SHULMAN, MARSHALL D. *Stalin's Foreign Policy Reappraised.* Pp. vi, 320. Cambridge, Mass.: Harvard University Press, 1963. $6.50.

SILVERMAN, SANFORD L, and MARTIN G. SILVERMAN. *Theory of Relationships.* Pp. xv, 111. New York: Philosophical Library, 1963. $6.00.

SINGH, KHUSHWANT. *A History of the Sikhs,* Vol. I: *1469–1839.* Pp. xiii, 419. Princeton, N. J.: Princeton University Press, 1963. $10.00.

Soviet Russia: Strategic Survey: A Bibliography. Pp. viii, 223. Washington, D. C.: United States Department of the Army, 1963. No price.

STEWART, HARRIS B., JR. *The Global Sea.* Pp. 126. Princeton, N. J.: D. Van Nostrand, 1963. $1.45.

STEWART, JOHN B. *The Moral and Political Philosophy of David Hume.* Pp. viii, 422. New York: Columbia University Press, 1963. $7.50.

STONE, DONALD C. (Ed.). *Education in Public Administration: A Symposium on Teaching Methods and Materials.* Pp. 196. Brussels: International Institute of Administrative Sciences, 1963. $5.00.

SWERDLOW, IRVING (Ed.). *Development Administration: Concepts and Problems.* Pp. xiv, 162. Syracuse, N. Y.: Syracuse University Press, 1963. $3.95.

THOMAS, NORMAN C., and KARL A. LAMB. *Congress: Politics and Practice.* Pp. x, 143. New York: Random House, 1964. $1.95.

THOMETZ, CAROL ESTES. *The Decision-Makers: The Power Structure in Dallas.* Pp. xiii, 141. Dallas: Southern Methodist University Press, 1963. $4.00.

TON THAT THIEN. *India and Southeast Asia, 1947–1960: A Study of India's Policy toward the Southeast Asian Countries in the Period 1947–1960.* Pp. 384. Geneva: Librairie Droz, 1963. Frs. 40.—.

TOWL, A. R., and M. S. DORAISWAMI. *ASCI Case Collection: First Series.* Pp. xxiii, 324. New York: Asia Publishing House, 1963. No price.

TUCKER, ROBERT C. *The Soviet Political Mind: Studies in Stalinism and Post-Stalin Change.* Pp. xiii, 238. New York: Frederick A. Praeger, 1963. $6.00.

UHLIG, FRANK, JR. (Ed.). *Naval Review, 1964.* Pp. 393. Annapolis, Md.: United States Naval Institute, 1963. $10.00.

UNITED NATIONS. *World Economic Survey, 1963,* Vol. I: *The Developing Countries in World Trade;* Vol. II: *Current Economic Developments.* Pp. ix, 120. New York: Department of Economic and Social Affairs, United Nations, 1963. No price.

VON DER GABLENTZ, O. M. (Ed.). *Die Berlin Frage in ihrer weltpolitischen Verflechtung, 1944–1963.* Pp. 44. München: R. Oldenbourg, 1963. No price.

VUCINICH, ALEXANDER. *Science in Russian Culture: A History to 1860.* Pp. xv, 463. Stanford, Calif.: Stanford University Press, 1963. $10.00.

WALETT, FRANCIS G. *Economic History of the United States.* Pp. xiii, 280. Second Edition. New York: Barnes & Noble, 1963. $1.75.

WALTON, ANN D., and MARIANNA O. LEWIS (Eds.). *The Foundation Directory.* Pp. 1,000. Second Edition. New York: Russell Sage Foundation, for the Foundation Library Center, 1964. $10.00.

WANG YANG-MING. *Instructions for Practical Living and Other Neo-Confucian Writings.* Translated by Wing-tsit Chan. Pp. xli, 358. New York: Columbia University Press, 1963. $7.50. •

WASHBURN, SHERWOOD L. (Ed.). *Classification and Human Evolution.* Pp. viii, 371. Chicago: Aldine, 1963. $7.50.

WASHBURN, WILCOMB E. (Ed.). *The Indian and the White Man.* Pp. xxiii, 480. New York: Doubleday, 1964. $1.95.

Weaver, Leon H. (Ed.). *Industrial Personnel Security: Cases and Materials.* Pp. xvi, 636. Springfield, Ill.: Charles C Thomas, 1964. No price.

Weiker, Walter F. *The Turkish Revolution, 1960–1961: Aspects of Military Politics.* Pp. viii, 172. Washington, D. C.: Brookings Institution, 1963. No price.

Weyl, Walter E. *The New Democracy: An Essay on Certain Political and Economic Tendencies in the United States.* Pp. xix, 369. Paper-bound edition. New York: Harper & Row, 1964. $2.35.

Wilber, Donald N. *Contemporary Iran.* Pp. vi, 224. New York: Frederick A. Praeger, 1963. $6.00.

Wilcox, Francis O., and H. Field Haviland, Jr. (Eds.). *The Atlantic Community: Progress and Prospect.* Pp. viii, 294. New York: Frederick A. Praeger, 1963. $6.00.

Wolfe, Roy I. *Transportation and Politics.* Pp. 136. Princeton, N. J.: D. Van Nostrand, 1963. $1.45.

Yoshihashi, Takehiko. *Conspiracy at Mukden: The Rise of the Japanese Military.* Pp. xvi, 274. New Haven: Yale University Press, 1963. $6.50.

INDEX

Origin and Purpose. The Academy was organized December 14, 1889, to promote the progress of political and social science, especially through publications and meetings. The Academy does not take sides in controverted questions, but seeks to gather and present reliable information to assist the public in forming an intelligent and accurate judgment.

Meetings. The Academy holds an annual meeting in the spring extending over two full days.

Publications. THE ANNALS is the bimonthly publication of The Academy. Each issue contains articles on some prominent social or political problems, written at the invitation of the editors. These volumes constitute important reference works on the topics with which they deal, and they are extensively cited by authorities throughout the United States and abroad. The papers presented at the meetings of The Academy are included in THE ANNALS.

Membership. Each member of The Academy receives THE ANNALS and may attend the meetings of The Academy. Annual dues are $8.00 (for clothbound copies $12

per year). A life membership is $500. All payments are to be made in United States dollars.

Libraries and other institutions may receive THE ANNALS paperbound at a cost of $8.00 per year, or clothbound at $12.00 per year.

Single copies of THE ANNALS may be obtained by nonmembers of The Academy for $2.00 ($3.00 clothbound) and by members for $1.50 ($2.50 clothbound). A discount to members of 5 per cent is allowed on orders for 10 to 24 copies of any one issue, and of 10 per cent on orders for 25 or more copies. These discounts apply only when orders are placed directly with The Academy and not through agencies. The price to all bookstores and to all dealers is $2.00 per copy less 20 per cent, with no quantity discount. It is urged that payment be sent with each order. This will save the buyer the transportation charge and save The Academy the cost of carrying accounts and sending statements.

All correspondence concerning The Academy or THE ANNALS should be addressed to the Academy office, 3937 Chestnut Street, Philadelphia 4, Pa.